FOREIGN EXCHANGE OPTIONS

Foreign Exchange Options

AN INTERNATIONAL GUIDE TO OPTIONS TRADING AND PRACTICE

ALAN HICKS

WOODHEAD PUBLISHING LIMITED

Cambridge, England

Published by Woodhead Publishing Ltd,
Abington Hall, Abington,
Cambridge CB1 6AH, England

First published 1993, Woodhead Publishing Ltd
Reprinted 1994, 1995

British Library Cataloguing in Publication Data
A catalogue record for this book is available from the British Library.

ISBN 1 85573 113 4

Designed by Andrew Jones (text) and Chris Feely (jacket).
Typeset by Best-set Typesetter Ltd; Hong Kong.
Printed by Galliard (Printers) Ltd, Great Yarmouth, England.

Contents

15 OPTION DERIVATIVES AND THE FUTURE 129

Introduction

THE Foreign Exchange option market has experienced rapid growth in the last few years and now accounts for approximately seven percent of the daily foreign exchange turnover of one trillion US dollars. This seventy billion dollar daily turnover in currency options represents a substantial market in anybody's terms but little has been written on the subject especially with regard to the largest and most dominant sector – the over-the-counter market. What has been written on currency options tends to concentrate either on the mathematic principles of pricing and hedging or on the mechanics of options listed on the securities and futures exchanges.

This book attempts to rectify the situation by examining the over-the-counter market in detail whilst still covering the two dominant exchanges for currency options – The Philadelphia Stock Exchange (PHLX) and The Chicago Mercantile Exchange (CME). The reader is taken through the basics and jargon is clarified as and when appropriate. The benefits of using options to hedge foreign exchange risk are demonstrated by various strategies and, in addition, the trading, and hedging of foreign exchange options as practised by the major international banks is explained in depth.

There are chapters devoted to pricing, option trading risks, and OTC market practice that should be of interest to newcomers to the market, users of the product (those wishing to hedge foreign exchange risk) and traders generally. This is followed up by chapters devoted to the explanation of option risk, the control and management of such and regulatory reporting requirements that would be of interest to senior managers, treasurers and those invaluable people that run the 'back-offices' of the major financial institutions. By this method, greater understanding of the trader's role and the workings of the marketplace will be gained.

Further chapters on International Currency Options Market (ICOM) terms and conditions, counterparty credit risk and accounting of options will be of interest to management, auditors and accountants wishing to understand more fully the integrated control required to run a successful options trading unit.

The final chapter (Chapter 15) lists the more popular 'exotic' options that have arrived on the scene and describes their usefulness in hedging circumstances.

All this is a very long way from the day in December 1982 when the PHLX listed the first currency option contract in the United States – sterling against the US dollar. The PHLX is recognized as the instigator of the boom in foreign exchange options although the Chicago Mercantile Exchange followed shortly after with their option on a currency future (PHLX is on cash foreign exchange) but not all exchanges have been as successful – both the London Stock Exchange and the London International Financial Futures Exchange (LIFFE) currency option products failed.

Nevertheless, the listing of options on the two US exchanges allowed the banks to hedge the options they were providing to their customers. However, around 1984 banks started to quote each other and the interbank, or OTC market was born. The exchanges continued to lead but were overtaken by the OTC market around 1987 and since then the OTC players have dictated the prices related on the exchanges – there is very little 'arbitrage' left between the two. The pros and cons of both markets are explained in a separate chapter on the marketplace.

This book focuses on the London and New York OTC markets as this is where the majority of the participants (including brokers) reside. London in particular has been instrumental in the development of regulatory control (through the Bank of England) and OTC market terms and conditions (through the British Bankers Association's LICOM and ICOM terms). The publications issued by these authorities together with the ICOM document from the Foreign Exchange Committee in New York are reproduced in full in Appendix IV so that this book may be used as a reference for such.

It is recognized that other centres such as France, Switzerland and Japan have played significant roles in OTC market development and will continue to do so in the future; consequently the Tokyo ICOM document has also been included in Appendix IV. Indeed, some of the largest individual professional institutions are based in these countries.

For the future, it is interesting to note that the emerging 'exotics' option products listed in this book are not yet traded on an interbank basis nor are they listed on any of the exchanges, and can be compared to the fledgling markets in regular options of a decade ago. Once again the flexibility of the OTC option and its use by corporate companies for hedging will dictate the eventual success of this product.

Finally, the reader should note that this book uses the international, professional market currency codes as devised by SWIFT (Societe for Worldwide Inter-bank Funds Transfer). So, DEM is Deutsche Marks, GBP is British pounds, USD is United States dollars, etc, and, for example, DEM/USD represents Marks against dollars foreign exchange.

1

The Basics

OPTIONS are available on many traditional 'physical' products such as equities (e.g. stocks and shares), commodities (e.g. gold, silver, coffee and other agricultural products) and foreign exchange (currencies). More recently, with the advent of financial futures, options have become available on futures where delivery results in a future contract rather than cash.

In all cases, the essential requirement for an option is constant – volatility in the underlying product. After all, if there is no volatility, there is no risk of price change and consequently no need for an option. In fact, the price for such an option would be at the same level as the underlying, i.e. the option cost would be zero.

As foreign exchange (FX) markets have traditionally been very volatile, the FX option is a logical product to use to cover FX exposure.

Definition

The holder (buyer) of an option has the right, but not the obligation to exchange a fixed amount of one currency for another at a fixed rate of exchange on a date in the future. (Note: Currencies, amounts, rate and date are all predetermined).

Premium

In consideration of receiving the option right, the buyer pays to the seller (sometimes called the 'writer') a fee known as the premium.

The premium is usually paid two working days ('spot') after dealing, and represents the maximum that can be lost by the buyer and therefore also represents the maximum profit to the seller.

Call and Put

An option can either be

a 'Call' – the right to buy a specified currency

or

a 'Put' – the right to sell a specified currency.

In foreign exchange, unlike other markets, confusion arises because both components of the exchange are currencies rather than a commodity and a single currency. For example, in the stock markets, all purchases and sales are conducted in units of shares with payment in currency. 'I buy 10 000 shares at 967 (and pay GBP 96 700)' or 'I sell 5000 at 467', etc. The unit being bought or sold is always clear as the currency (GBP in this example) is never the dealing unit – it is the method of payment. In FX markets, however, it is common to deal in either of the two currencies resulting in a *purchase* of one being the *sale* of the other – there is no common commodity that stands out as the dealing unit. As a result, the rate of exchange known as spot (usually two business days delivery) or forward (future delivery) can be expressed in terms of *either* currency against the other. e.g. DEM per USD (1.50) or USD per DEM (0.6667). This is all very different from other markets, such as equities, where the rate is only ever expressed in one order, e.g. GBP per share (never shares per GBP).

What all this means for options is that a Call on one currency has to be a Put on the other within a currency pair. For example, in DEM-USD, a Call on DEM is also a Put on USD because the holder's right to buy DEM would result in them having to sell USD (in order to buy the DEM!). In view of this, the Call and Put currencies should be clearly defined when entering into option transactions. While it is perfectly acceptable to ask for a 'sterling Call against the USD', it would be better to ask for a 'Call on sterling, Put on USD'.

Exercise

The buyer of an option always has the right to take delivery of the exchange, or not. If the decision is to take delivery, the buyer must notify the seller of this decision by 'exercising' his (or her) right to delivery. Hence the exercise of an option is effectively the cancellation of the option and the creation of an FX transaction, value spot.

Options are only exercised if it is beneficial to do so. It is unlikely that someone would exercise an option where the currency could be bought or sold at a better level in the prevailing spot market. Options that are not exercised expire worthless.

Option style

Options may be described as either 'American style' allowing exercise at any time during the life of the option, or as 'European style' which may only be exercised at maturity. In both cases, delivery would be for value two working days ('spot') from exercise date for over-the-counter (OTC) options and at other (usually slightly longer) periods for exchange-listed options. OTC and exchange-listed options are described in more detail in Chapter 2.

The vast majority of options are written as European style, with the notable exception of the Philadelphia Stock Exchange where the American style option continues to be the more popular.

American style options are more expensive than European in situations where exercise would result in receipt of the currency carrying the higher interest rate.

Strike

The predetermined rate of exchange at which exercise takes place.

The strike (also known as the strike price or striking price) is usually chosen at a level close to the current FX spot or forward rate but may be at any reasonable level. The price (premium) of an option is very sensitive to the relationship of the strike to the current spot rate (see Chapter 6). Some buyers prefer to set the strike at a predetermined level of premium expenditure.

Intrinsic value

The difference, if positive, between the strike price and the underlying FX spot rate (for American style options) or FX forward rate (for European style).

Intrinsic value represents the value if exercised. For example, consider a GBP Call (USD Put) European style option with strike of 1.80 (USD per pound) with spot at 1.90 on the expiry date (maturity date) of the option. Intrinsic value is USD 0.10 (1.90–1.80) and is positive because exercise of this option produces GBP at a lower level than the current FX market. In this case the buyer would almost certainly exercise the option!

If spot was 1.75 in the above example, there would be no positive value as the holder could purchase GBP at 1.75 in the market rather than 1.80 through the option. In this case, the option would expire worthless with no intrinsic value. Conversely, a GBP Put option *would* be exercised due to its USD 0.05 intrinsic value.

The price (premium) of an option will reflect the full amount of any intrinsic value and this direct relationship is further discussed in Chapter 6.

Some jargon associated with intrinsic value:

In-the-money (ITM)	An option that has intrinsic value
Out-of-the-money (OTM)	An option that has no intrinsic value
At-the-money (ATM)	An option that sits on the borderline of ITM and OTM in that its strike is close to the underlying FX rate.

2

The Marketplace

F X options are traded in two distinct markets: Over-the-counter and Exchange listed. There follows an analysis of each.

Over-the-counter (OTC)

The largest, by far, is the OTC market which comprises banks, American security houses and corporations. 'Over-the-counter' means nothing more than 'direct between counterparties' although the phrase is never applied to the FX market which operates in a similar fashion – even the tourist gets foreign currency 'over the counter'! The term 'interbank' would be better applied to the OTC options market although it is rarely cited.

Location

There is no single marketplace or building that houses this market as all transactions are conducted over the telephone, the Reuters Dealing System (a telecommunications device used extensively in foreign exchange, principally by banks), or through OTC brokers. Telex is rarely used these days except as a form of written confirmation for deals already concluded. The market operates continuously between counterparties all over the world and is therefore open 24 hours a day. The only exception is at weekends where liquidity drops to near zero although, in theory, banks in the Middle East may provide some market support if this area develops in the future.

Trading practices

The market participants deal with each other, either directly or through an OTC broker, quoting 'volatility rates' as the dealing price rather than premiums (volatility is discussed in greater detail in Chapter 6). Banks make bid-offer prices on request, based on the details of specific options (e.g. one month, DEM Call/USD Put, strike 1.70 in USD 25 million) or non-specific (e.g. one month, DEM/USD – which market convention currently stipulates is an ATM forward strike, 'dealt as a straddle'). After dealing on a volatility quote, the actual premium is then calculated based on an agreed spot rate. The premium is normally expressed as a percentage of the traded amount (e.g. 2.5% of USD 25 million = USD 625 000) except in the case of GBP/USD where the premium is usually expressed in US cents (e.g. 2.5 cents per pound × GBP 25 million = USD 625 000). The object here is to keep the premium payment in USD, the major trading currency.

After the calculation of the premium, the buyer and seller usually exchange a spot FX deal (known as the 'delta hedge') to hedge the option transaction initially unless the original volatility quote was for a 'delta-neutral strategy' such as a straddle or strangle, where net delta is zero. Otherwise, if no delta hedge is transacted, the price quote for the option is said to be 'live' i.e. the market maker is a risk to a change in the underlying spot/forward FX rate. In this case, quotes are normally held as firm for a few seconds only before being subject to change (as in the spot FX market).

Trading practices in the OTC market are further discussed in Chapter 5 on option combinations (straddles, strangles, etc), option hedging and trading (Chapter 8) and are further detailed in a chapter dedicated to OTC market practice (Chapter 9).

Brokers

The brokers in the OTC market act to bring counterparties together but have no part in the transaction itself (similar to a real estate agent). A fee is levied on both parties by the broker for such deals, hence trades concluded directly are commission free (e.g. there are no fees when a corporate deals with its bank). This follows a similar practice in the FX market. Many brokers quote volatility prices through Reuters and Telerate (information vendors specializing in live transmission of financial data to monitor screens worldwide) for information purposes.

Regulation

Trading between the banks in the OTC market is conducted in a very professional and efficient manner, given that there is no single regulatory body covering the market. Supervision varies between central banks such as the Bank of England in the UK, Federal Reserve Bank in the USA, etc, while non-banks usually comply with the interbank market practices despite being governed by other regulatory authorities (e.g. Securities & Futures Association in the UK). Standard terms and conditions for OTC options together with trading practices guidelines are encompassed under ICOM (International Currency Options Market) terms and conditions although market participants are free to trade under their own terms, if they so wish. Regulatory controls and ICOM are discussed in Chapters 11 and 12.

Contract specifications

It can be seen from the previous paragraph that the OTC market is not governed by the rules of an exchange, and can therefore quote options in any currency pair, style, amount, date, strike, premium or rate quotation, within reason. While professional dealing is conducted in volatility terms, most banks will quote prices in any of the three ways possible: as a percentage of either currency, as the first currency in terms of the second or as the second currency in terms of the first (pricing terms are explained in detail in Chapter 6).

Transaction size and volumes

The volumes transacted daily in the OTC market are, at the time of writing, well over the equivalent of fifty billion US dollars, with individual trades averaging around USD 25–35 million. The minimum varies with most banks willing to deal small amounts of, say, USD 500 000 with their own customers but keeping quotes to other banks at minimum of USD 5–20 million, depending on the currency pair and the particular bank involved. Many of the larger, active institutions have absolute minimums of USD 20 million for the popular currency pairs.

Specialization

Apart from the size of transaction, the number of market participants is at such a level that many specialize in different segments of the market. For example, Japanese banks are very active in currencies against the yen but generally less so in, say, GBP/USD. Certain banks have reputations for quoting the more 'minor' currencies such as the Spanish peseta whilst others welcome the smaller trades of USD 5–10 million in the popular currencies. The problem is knowing who does what, as there is no guide available other than contacting an experienced trader at one of the banks active in the market. It would be pointless trying to publish a list as the market is constantly evolving, and traders tend to move between banks frequently, changing the trading emphasis of the institution with which they are employed.

Summary

The OTC, or interbank, market is for banks and other professionals only. It is restricted to institutions that have a credit standing sufficient to enable transactions to take place, i.e., each participant needs a credit line for each individual counterpart that it expects to encounter. So, for most parties, access is through a bank, usually one where a relationship already exists.

The trading practices, ethics and most of the jargon have been adopted from the FX market although the OTC options professional tends to have a more academic background than his FX counterpart.

Exchange listed

Options are traded on various exchanges around the world, and these listed options form the second of the two markets.

Location

The two principal markets are the PHLX and the CME, but there are other exchanges quoting local currencies although with very little volume. Exchanges operate on the basis of trade being conducted in one specific area (the 'pit') on the floor of the exchange building. It is in this area that traders gather to reflect customer orders taken over the telephone by colleagues in adjacent booths.

Trading practices

Customer orders are transmitted with hand signals and vocal expression to the crowd in the pit, by 'open outcry'. This form of trading has been the cornerstone of exchanges for decades and is an impressive sight when there is great activity in the pit. This form of trading is very different from the 'unseen' OTC market.

Until 1992, all prices were quoted in US cents with premiums payable in that currency, but cross-currency options have since been introduced (although there were no more than a handful at the time of writing). Premium payment in currencies other than US dollars is now permissible for the first time on US exchanges – representing a major breakthrough for the listed exchanges.

Because prices are quoted in terms of value, rather than volatility, an option's 'implied volatility' has to be calculated in order to be compared with the OTC market (implied volatility is dealt with in more detail in Chapter 6). This is a major drawback for the professional OTC traders who might otherwise make more use of the exchanges. However, 'Globex', the automated system for trading CME futures and options introduced in 1992 for trading after exchange hours, does have the facility to trade in volatility terms. Also, the PHLX intends to display implied volatility directly through information carriers, e.g. Reuters.

The PHLX lists currency options based on physical delivery of the currencies if exercise of the option takes place – as on the OTC market. The CME is somewhat different in that exercise of the currency option results in a 'currency future' on that exchange.

A currency future is similar to a foreign exchange forward contract except that the future can only traded for a specific delivery date, usually the third Wednesday of March, June, September or December (at the CME). Options are, however, traded for maturities in other months, usually the two near months plus the quarter months where the future delivers. So, on October 1st, *options* will be listed for October, November, December, March, June and September, but *futures* will only be listed for December, March, June and September. Hence, exercise of an option maturing in October will result in a December future, as will the exercise of both November and December options. Exercise of the March option would result in a March future, etc.

Unlike the OTC market, a spot FX delta hedge does not form part of the transaction, hence all pricing is 'live' i.e. the price quoted is liable to change with any movement in the underlying spot (PHLX) or future market (CME). However, in the case of the CME, a broker can be instructed to transact both the option trade and a proportional futures trade at predetermined prices to construct a 'delta-neutral' strategy.

Delta hedging is explained in Chapter 8 and delta-neutral strategies are discussed in Chapter 5.

Brokers

The brokers in exchange markets differ from those in OTC in that they play a very important role in the processing of the transaction. Payments of all kinds – margins, premiums and currencies – are paid to or from the broker. Therefore it is a requirement to have an account with a broker who has a seat on the exchange in order to use such markets. When an order is executed, the trade has to be cleared by a broker acting as a clearing member (this may, or may not, be the same broker that executes the trade).

Commissions are charged on a 'per contract' basis by the broker but there are usually other fees charged by the exchange that are collected through the broker such as exercise and assignment fees. Exchange fees are set but brokers' commissions are negotiable with strong competition amongst the members of the exchange. In effect, each exchange guarantees the performance of its members so the credit risk is normally assessed as being the exchange rather than the broker.

Regulation

All trading is under exchange rules and the rules of the relative clearing corporation. Some of the practices may seem peculiar to OTC traders but most are based on rules that stipulate that all trading must be conducted in the pit (even if a broker has a buy and sell order of equal proportions). The US exchanges are regulated by other bodies such as the Commodity and Futures Trading Commission (CFTC), for futures exchanges (e.g. CME) and the Securities and Exchanges Commission (SEC) for securities exchanges (e.g. PHLX).

Contract specifications

All contracts have fixed maturity dates, strikes, currency amounts, style, premium quotation, etc, on a limited number of currency pairs. Generally, strikes are quoted in reciprocal terms, also called 'American' terms though they have nothing to do with the style of exercise. Full details are given in Appendix I.

Margins

All exchanges use the margin system to ensure performance of the members, and the members use the same system for their clients. Customers are required to pay a percentage of the contract value to their broker (for deposit with the exchange). This payment is called the 'initial' margin and covers the party on the other side of the contact against default. Since markets move and the value of the contact can change, further amounts may be paid as 'variation' margin in order to keep the default cover in place. The system works both ways in that excess margin is paid back to the client for positions that have gained in value. The variation margin is calculated by reference to the daily closing price of the contract, sometimes referred to as 'marking to market'.

Margins on option contracts can be made in cash, treasury bills and certain other securities, but futures contracts are generally margined in cash only.

For options purchased, the premium is the margin (as that amount is the maximum loss to the contract holder) and no further payments are necessary. For option sales, full initial and variation margins are required.

See Appendix I for full details of margin requirements and calculation.

Transaction size and volume

The exchanges publish daily details of the number of contracts traded together with 'open interest' figures for each of the currencies traded. At the time of writing, daily currency option volumes are around USD 5 billion for the two exchanges, a small fraction of the estimated OTC volume.

Transaction size can, of course, be as low as one contract – about USD 80 000–100 000 depending on currency (or half that number on PHLX) – or in the thousands. The average might be around 100 contracts or USD 8 million.

Specialization

Both of the US exchanges specialize in options against the USD with liquidity concentrated in the near month maturities, usually at strikes close to spot. The small contract size and the margining system allow individuals to trade resulting, in the case of the CME, in a great deal of speculative business (the so-called 'Chicago Dentist'). Speculation is generally not deemed to be a bad thing, as it adds to the liquidity of the market.

The PHLX, on the other hand, tends to be used more for hedging purposes as indicated by the level of open interest versus trading volumes.

Globex

In June 1992, the CME introduced foreign exchange options and futures on Globex – the electronic dealing system developed jointly with Reuters. This system allows for after-hours trading in certain CME contracts such as their options on currency futures.

A particularly interesting feature of the new system is the availability to trade options in volatility terms rather than the live prices experienced on the exchange itself. As is normal in the OTC markets, a volatility trade on Globex will result in a simultaneous delta hedge through the respective currency future. Volatility trading with delta hedging should attract some of the professional OTC traders on to the system, but only time will tell.

Access to the Globex system is through terminals located in the offices of exchange member firms (e.g. brokers). Other exchanges, such as the Chicago Board of Trade (CBOT) and the Marché à Terme International de France (MATIF) have enlisted the system to trade some of their own products, and other exchanges may follow if the idea of trading off-exchange is accepted. Globex is a bold move on the part of the CME who have proliferated for years on the advantages of the 'open outcry', pit trading and the success of such ideology. The only alternative approach would be to extend the trading hours on the exchange and this is the route taken by the competing exchange for currency options – the PHLX.

Summary

The exchanges will appeal to those who are familiar with equities or futures as arenas for investing, hedging or speculating – the basis of dealing currencies has been offered in the same context as the other products. This is the reason why the exchanges always quote FX rates in USD, e.g. one IBM share costs USD 88.5; one Pork Belly Future contract costs USD 40; one DEM costs USD 0.66, etc. Closing prices are published in the financial press daily alongside the other listed 'securities'.

The exchanges are open to all, albeit through a broker, and offer very competitive, open pricing for large or small amounts giving the small player access to interbank rates. Against this feature, one has to evaluate the costs of brokers' commissions, exchange fees and margin requirements.

Comparison (OTC versus exchange)

The CME option on the currency future is deemed to be European because the result of any exercise will be the future contract which cannot be delivered until maturity. However, as the currency future is marked to market (revalued at closing price) *in cash*, the early exercise of an option often takes place if this

Table 2.1 OTC versus Exchange

	OTC	Exchange listed
Amount	Any, subject to minimum	Fixed by contract size or multiple thereof
Maturity	Overnight to 5 years	Two days per month, limited months per year, limited long date contracts
Strike	Any, within reason	Only those listed per schedule
Rate quotation	As in the FX market, although exchange-type available	Up-side-down to FX market except GBP and AUD
Currency	Any pair that has active spot and forward market	Only those listed
Margins	None, but credit line required	Yes, on sales only
Price quotation	As required, usually in percent	USD per currency
Style	American or European	American or European (PHLX) European (IMM)

results in a large positive variation margin on the resulting future contract. Full details of contract sizes, maturity dates, margin requirements, etc, can be found in Appendix I.

In the Chapter 1, it was stated that foreign exchange rates may be expressed in two ways: the first in terms of the second, or the second in terms of the first, e.g. DEM per 1 USD (1.50) or USD per 1 DEM (0.6667). The international FX market generally quotes a rate that is above par, that is, above the number 1. Hence we have 1.50 DEM per USD but 1.80 USD per GBP. Unfortunately, there are exceptions to this rule (Australian dollar, for example) where the rate was originally above par but has subsequently dropped below; the FX market does not switch quoting terms in these cases. In the exchange markets, however, *all* rates are quoted in USD per currency unit so the largest traded spot currencies such as DEM, JPY, CHF (Swiss francs) are in unfamiliar, reciprocal terms. The exceptions are GBP and AUD.

To change from one expression to the other reciprocate, e.g. 1/1.50 = 0.6667; 0.6667/1 = 1.50.

Advantages and disadvantages

The reciprocal aspect of the listed market strikes and futures quotation does not help the corporate who normally expresses the rate of exchange in the same manner as the FX market making the selection of strike, etc, less convenient.

Prices and transaction volumes from the exchanges are widely available from the various information carriers and are published daily in the financial press. This makes it very easy to compare option prices for value whereas the

OTC market does not produce such information – the customer has to ask for a price from a bank.

The margin system used by all exchanges is usually considered to be a disadvantage as it employs capital and additional – sometimes daily – variation margin calls which can be administratively time consuming. However, the system does ensure that everybody has access to the market, therefore suiting individuals and smaller companies who may not be granted the credit facilities at banks for the OTC market. A few OTC participants do offer margin facilities for OTC options to cover the credit risk.

The OTC market offers options in almost any currency pair including 'crosses' (where neither currency is the USD) whereas the exchanges are only now responding to the demand in this area. Option maturities from one day to five years or longer are available in the OTC market whereas listed options are restricted to one or two days in a particular month for a few months each year.

The fixed aspect of the exchange markets means that the liquidity tends to be concentrated in strikes at-the-money in the near months. Whilst this gives tight 'spreads' (the difference between the buying and selling price) for such contracts, the far months and other strikes tend to have low liquidity and wide spreads. The flexibility of the OTC market ensures a fair spread of liquidity through both strikes and dates.

Dealing on the exchanges involves contract fees, exchange fees and assignment fees (for options exercised), whereas there are no commissions whatsoever in OTC.

Option Characteristics

3

FX position

T HE best way to look at option characteristics is graphically (Fig. 3.1, 3.2). Note first the risk associated with a straight FX position and then compare the purchase and sale aspects of option Calls and Puts.

Long Call

The profit from holding a sterling Call (USD Put) such as in Fig. 3.2 arises from an increase in the value of sterling whereas loss is limited on a fall. The purchase of this option would suit a corporate institution wishing to protect itself against the rise in value of sterling, for example, a UK exporter with receivables in USD.

Long Put

In Fig. 3.3 the profit is realized if sterling goes down but loss is limited if the pound goes up. The purchase of a GBP Put (USD Call) would suit the corporate wishing to protect against the fall in value of sterling against USD, for example, a UK importer with payables in USD.

Example:
Figure 3.1 shows the classic FX position, in this case the purchase of sterling at 1.90 against the USD. If the value of sterling goes up, the buyer makes a profit; if sterling goes down, the buyer makes a loss. The chances of either are equal so the scenario is a 50:50 or 'even money' speculation. This is the situation that a UK importer faces when the payables are in US dollars. Being sterling based, the importer is exposed to extra cost if the pound goes down (gets less dollars per pound), but receives a reduction in costs if the pound goes up (gets more dollars per pound). To avoid this speculative element, the importer could simply buy his

3.1 Long GBP FX at 1.90 (USD per GBP).

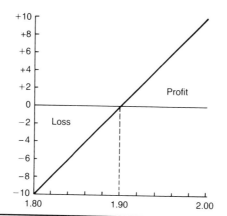

Profit and loss scenario is equal and opposite, i.e. there is 50:50 chance of profit or loss with unlimited parameters.

3.2 Bought GBP (USD Put), strike 1.90, premium .02 USD.

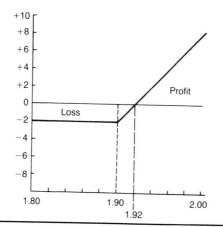

Profit potential is unlimited but loss is restricted to amount of premium paid, 2 US cents. From a speculative point of view, the breakeven is 1.92 which is the strike plus premium (1.90 + .02).

3.3 Bought GBP Put (USD Call), strike 1.90, premium .02 USD.

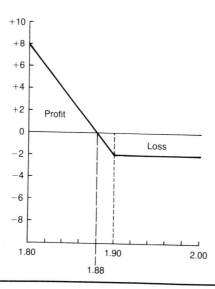

Profit potential is unlimited but loss is restricted to amount of premium paid, 2 US cents. The breakeven is 1.88 being strike minus premium (1.90 − 0.2).

or her dollars (sell sterling) forward for the date of anticipated payment. There would be no cost other than the difference between the importer's calculated rate for dollars (i.e. the rate when the goods were ordered) and that obtained on the forward deal (this could be positive). However, the FX option does offer an alternative to the forward FX deal. Figure 3.3 shows the purchase of a US dollar Call (sterling Put) at strike of 1.90 with premium of 2 US cents per pound. One can see that this option position has limited cost of 2 cents but profits from any decrease in the pound. Hence, this will offset the losses from the exporter's exposure leaving any increase in the pound as a benefit (less the premium cost of 2 cents).

To emphasize the example still further, let us assume the importer has to purchase USD 1.9 million against delivery of his or her goods. There are three possible choices:

1. Do nothing (equivalent to assuming full FX risk – Fig. 3.1).
2. Buy USD (sell GBP) forward to cover all FX risk but giving up all chance of additional profit should the exchange rate move favourably.
3. Purchase USD Call (GBP Put) option for USD .02. Premium: GBP 10526 (being GBP 1 000 000 × USD 0.02/1.90).

The three possible results are shown here in terms of *sterling cost* to purchase the USD 1.9 million:

Rate on maturity	Do Nothing	Buy Forward	Buy Option
2.10	904 762	1 000 000	915 288
2.05	926 830	1 000 000	937 356
2.00	950 000	1 000 000	960 526
1.95	974 359	1 000 000	984 885
1.90	1 000 000	1 000 000	1 010 526
1.85	1 027 027	1 000 000	1 010 526
1.80	1 055 556	1 000 000	1 010 526
1.75	1 085 714	1 000 000	1 010 526

It can be seen that the option, in the worse case possible, is never more than the cost of the premium over the forward FX scenario. The best case is never more than the premium cost over the high risk 'do nothing' scenario. The option gives the holder almost full benefit of favourable movements and protects against adverse movements for a small expense.

Call and Put together (straddle)

Having demonstrated the effects of a long Call and long Put, the next step is to put the two together to form a simple option combination (see also Chapter 5). A bought Call and bought Put with the same strike, amount and maturity is called a 'long straddle' and is represented by merging Fig. 3.2 and 3.3 to produce Fig. 3.4.

3.4 Long GBP Call and long GBP Put, strike 1.90, premium .04 USD.

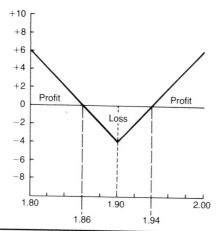

Profit potential is unlimited in either direction but loss is still limited to the total premiums paid, 4 US cents. The breakeven is either 1.86 or 1.94 being strike plus or minus total premiums.

3.5 Short GBP Call (USD Put), strike 1.90, premium 2 US cents.

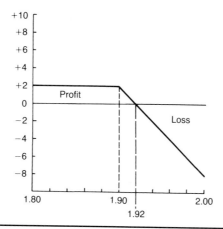

Profit potential is limited and at maximum with spot at 1.90 or below. Loss potential is unlimited. Breakeven is at 1.92.

A straddle is normally used as a speculative instrument where movement of the underlying FX rate is expected but direction of the movement is uncertain. The cost is high (two premiums) hence a strong movement in the spot rate is required to recoup the premiums expended before the profit region is encountered.

Short Options

The examples given so far have been from the perspective of the buyer, but options may be sold as well as bought. In the case of seller, the maximum return is the premium of the option even though the potential FX loss is unlimited. Note that Fig. 3.5 is the reciprocal of Fig. 3.2.

Writing (selling) options is often likened to underwriting an insurance policy in that a profit is made equal to the premium received if 'nothing happens', i.e. the option is not exercised. In Fig. 3.5 this would be with spot at or below 1.90 on maturity of the option. If, on the other hand, spot is above 1.90 the holder (buyer) will exercise the option resulting in a reduction of profit to 1.92 (the breakeven rate) and a loss above that level equal to the difference between spot and 1.92. There is no upper limit to spot so the potential loss is unlimited.

3.6 Short GBP Put (USD Call), strike 1.90, premium 2 US cents.

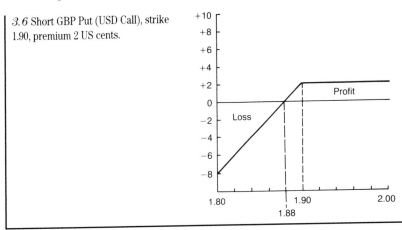

Profit potential is limited and at maximum level with spot at 1.90 or above. Loss potential is unlimited. Breakeven is at 1.88.

Most corporate users of options only sell when they are already in possession of the underlying commodity and can therefore always make delivery against any potential exercise. In this way, the premium acts as 'income enhancement'. For example, let us assume that a US company has a balance of sterling in an account earning interest valued at current spot rate of 1.90 (USD per GBP). The company will eventually convert to USD but probably not until the end of the financial year in, say, six months time. The treasurer could sell a 3 months 1.90 GBP Call (USD Put) for 3 US cents or about 1.6%. The premium received is taken up-front as income with the worst scenario being that he or she may have to sell the GBP to buy USD at 1.90 – the original rate – but only if the buyer exercises when spot is above 1.90. The negative side is that the company would give up the benefit of being able to convert to USD at a higher rate if spot is above 1.90 on maturity. If spot is below 1.90, the option would not be exercised and would expire worthless; the full negative effect of converting to USD at a lower level would be felt but offset to a limited degree by the premium received.

Note that the company sold the option for only three months rather than the six months to year end. A shorter period was chosen on the assumption that the balances might be needed unexpectedly, i.e. the reason for leaving them in the account in the first place. The treasurer could, of course, write the option for any period of his or her choosing, and in the example would probably sell the remaining three months after the first option had expired, assuming that no exercise had taken place. If it transpired that the GBP balances were needed for conversion *before* the option matured, the treasurer would simply repurchase the option and sell the GBP at spot (and therefore buy USD).

Note that in this example, the company's position is long GBP (cash) and short the GBP Call (potential sale of GBP). This position is known as a 'covered Call-write' and produces a situation that is identical to a short GBP Put known as a 'synthetic' short Put, but this is covered in more detail in Chapter 4.

Underlying position

In FX, one can be either long a currency (and therefore short the countercurrency) or short (and long the countercurrency). For example, if one is long DEM

Table 3.1 Creating FX positions through options

	Buy option	**Sell option**
Call	Long (pay premium)	Short (receive premium)
Put	Short (pay premium)	Long (receive premium)

at 1.50 (DEM per USD) against USD, one must be short of the USD otherwise there is no foreign exchange position. To avoid any confusion, the position in only one currency will be discussed knowing the opposite is true for the counter, or second currency.

Using Fig. 3.1 as an example we have bought GBP at 1.90 and are consequently long sterling and will profit if that currency appreciates. In options, we can create a long position by buying a Call on sterling (Put on USD) as the option gives us the right to buy GBP. However, we could also sell a Put on sterling (Call on USD) which would give the buyer the right to sell pounds to us (i.e. we buy sterling). Thus, there are two ways of creating a long (or short) FX position through options.

Table 3.1 shows the different ways of creating FX positions through options. The big difference is, of course, the premium cash flow and the certainty of exercise on maturity. The buyer can always take delivery, if he wishes, but the seller does not have this guarantee.

Unlike a straight long FX position (Fig. 3.1), using either of the two methods highlighted does not give the same result as be seen in the case of Fig. 3.2 – bought Call (long position) and Fig. 3.6 – sold Put (long position). Neither of the two graphs is the straight line result expected of a short FX position. However, it is possible to create a synthetic FX position by combining an option Call and Put, as explained in Chapter 4.

4

Put-Call Parity

FX options are a derivative of foreign exchange and as such there is a direct relationship between Call, Puts and the underlying FX contract known as 'Put-Call parity' (it is easier to pronounce than Call-Put parity!).

Bought Call *and* sold Put equals (long) forward FX position provided the strikes, amounts and maturity dates are the same.

Or, more simply:

Call − Put = FX (where '+' is long and '−' is short)

So, a long Call together with a short Put gives a synthetic long FX position. We can prove this by looking at the positions graphically, as shown in Fig. 4.1.

If Call − Put = FX, then it follows that:

Call − Put − FX = 0

where 0 (zero) represents no position or, in other words, a 'square' book. This scenario of long Call, short Put and short FX is often used by option traders to achieve risk free positions and to arbitrage between options and FX markets for profit. This scenario is known as a 'conversion' (or 'box' on the exchanges).

The inverse of this, short Call, long Put and long FX:

−Call + Put + FX = 0

is also used in much the same way and is known as a 'reverse conversion' although both are commonly referred to as simply 'conversions'.

Similarly, by simple algebra, one can construct synthetic options scenarios:

4.1 Long GBP Call and short GBP Put, strike 1.90, premium .02 for each option, maturity 3 months.

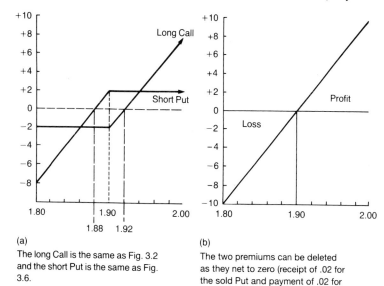

(a)
The long Call is the same as Fig. 3.2 and the short Put is the same as Fig. 3.6.

(b)
The two premiums can be deleted as they net to zero (receipt of .02 for the sold Put and payment of .02 for the bought Call) leaving the FX position of Fig. 3.1, i.e. long GBP.

4.2 Long GBP FX at 1.90 and a short GBP Call (USD Put), strike 1.90, premium .03 cents, 3 months maturity.

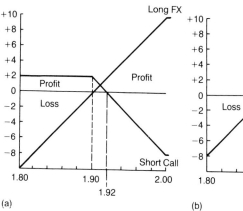
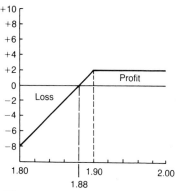

(a)
The long FX is the same as Fig. 3.1 and the short Call is the same as Fig. 3.5.

(b)
The profit and loss and elements above 1.90 cancel out, leaving the premium receipt the only reward with unlimited loss below 1.88. Therefore profit is achieved at, or above, that level, i.e. a short Put (as Fig. 3.6).

Call − FX = Put (Bought Call, sold FX equals bought Put) − Synthetic long Put

−Put − FX = −Call (Sold Put, sold FX equals sold Call) − Synthetic short Call.

We can now take another look at the example in Chapter 3 where the US company has balances in GBP and writes a Call option against those pounds to gain the premium income. The treasurer's position is long FX (GBP in account) and short the GBP Call, (written Call) which is:

$$+FX - Call = -Put \text{ (synthetic short Put), shown graphically in Fig. 4.2.}$$

The reader will recall that, in this example, the company sold a three month sterling Call against balances held in an account with non-specific maturity. In this case, the synthetic Put only holds as such if the treasurer commits the balances against the written call which, of course, he does as part of the strategy. However, a true synthetic Put would have the FX committed to mature on the potential delivery date of the option (usually by an FX swap) so that the pricing of the strategy could be determined, i.e. is the synthetic version better than the straight written Put?

5

Option Combinations

Exchange strategies

IT will have been noted that many types of option strategies can be constructed and graphic representation of a long Call and long Put together has been demonstrated, known as a 'straddle'. Using the four building blocks of long Call, short Call, long Put and short Put, one may construct a whole series of option combinations by using different strikes, amounts and maturity dates. As options have been traded on the exchanges for some time, particularly Equity options, many have been given names and these have been inherited by currency options.

There are many option combinations in existence; some use combinations of Calls and Puts with different strikes such as 'butterflies', 'condors' and 'strangles'; others use different strikes with variable amounts such as the 'ratio backspread', and others use similar strikes with different maturities, such as 'calendar spreads'.

These strategies offer some interesting scenarios for speculating on the movement, non-movement, biased movement or volatility of spot but often involve the simultaneous purchase and sale of many options which, on exchanges, could result in high transaction costs because charges are levied on a per contract basis. In fact, one or two of the listed strategies could be more accurately renamed 'broker's dream'.

The OTC market has produced its own strategies but for a different reason, that being hedging FX exposure. The option combinations still comprise Calls and Puts with different strikes and amounts, but have been invented primarily for premium reduction to reduce hedging costs. Different banks have given their own names to these products so, unfortunately, there are different names for the same strategy depending on whom one is talking to at the time.

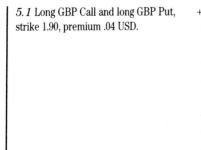

5.1 Long GBP Call and long GBP Put, strike 1.90, premium .04 USD.

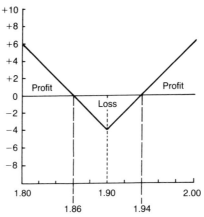

Profit potential is unlimited in either direction but loss is still limited to the total premiums paid, 4 US cents. The breakeven is either 1.86 or 1.94 being strike plus or minus total premiums.

We shall look first at the often quoted strategies from the exchanges and then at some OTC generated scenarios. The four basic building blocks of long Call, short Call, long Put and short Put are not repeated here but the straddle is included as the first example of an option combination.

The straddle

A straddle is normally used as a speculative instrument where movement of the underlying FX rate is expected but direction of the movement is uncertain. The cost is high (two premiums) hence a fairly strong movement in the spot rate is required to recoup the premiums expended before the profit region is encountered.

Figure 5.1 shows a long straddle as it is constructed using the purchase of the Call and Put options and the payment of the premiums. Of course, one could sell the two components to achieve a short straddle where the premiums received would represent the maximum profit potential (at 1.90). In this case the seller would be speculating on spot remaining *within* the 1.86 to 1.94 band; a useful strategy for quiet markets with low volatility.

Short straddles are normally expressed graphically as the inverse of Fig. 5.1 but the reader may simply change the area of 'profit' to 'loss' and vice versa.

The strangle

A strangle is normally used as a speculative instrument where movement of the underlying FX rate is expected but direction is uncertain. The cost is high (two premiums) but lower than that of a straddle due to the two strikes being out-of-the-money, but this sets the breakeven points further away (1.85 and 1.95 versus 1.86 and 1.94 for the straddle). Hence a very strong movement is required in the spot FX rate in order to enter the profit regions.

Figure 5.2 represents a long strangle but, in a similar fashion to the straddle, a strangle may be sold to achieve a short scenario where the premium income would be the maximum profit (between 1.88 and 1.92) but with unlimited loss proportions in either direction of spot FX.

Bull spread

The bull spread is a very conservative strategy used as a speculative instrument where the underlying spot rate is expected to rise but not beyond a certain level

5.2 Long GBP Call 1.92 and long GBP Put 1.88, premium 1.5 US cents for each option, total 3 cents.

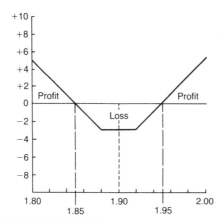

Profit potential is unlimited in either direction but loss is limited to the total premiums paid, 3 US cents.
The breakeven is either 1.85 or 1.95 being strike plus or minus the total premiums paid.

5.3 Long GBP Call 1.90, premium 2 US cents; short GBP Call 1.94, premium 0.6 US cents. Net premium 1.4 US cents.

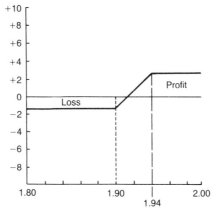

Profit potential is limited to 2.6 cents above the higher strike of 1.94, but loss is also limited to the cost of the net premium paid.
The breakeven is the lower strike plus net premium paid of 1.4 US cents, i.e. at 1.9140.

(the upper strike). The sale of the higher strike reduces the cost of the bull position making it a low cost, limited reward scenario.

The spread shown in Fig. 5.3 is constructed of Call options, one bought and one sold and can therefore be termed a 'bull Call spread' but bull spreads can also be constructed by using the equivalent Put options (a 'bull Put spread') to give exactly the same net results on maturity. This may seem odd at first so we will look at the above example again, but this time using Put options.

Long GBP Put *1.90*, premium 2 US cents, short GBP Put 1.94, premium 4.6 US cents.

The cost of the 1.90 Put is the same as the 1.90 Call as they are both at-the-money but the 1.94 Put is in-the-money by 4 US cents so cost is that amount plus the time value of 0.6 cents (Put-Call parity). This means that the bull Put spread has a net premium receipt of 2.6 US cents which becomes the maximum profit attainable at spot level of 1.94 or above – the same 'pay-off' as the Call spread. Maximum loss is at 1.90, or below where the short 1.94 Put would be exercised against the position (but protected by the long 1.90 Put that would also be exercised, if spot below 1.90); in all cases leaving a difference of 4 cents. This

5.4 Long GBP Put 1.90, premium 2 US cents; short GBP Put 1.86, premium 0.6 US cents. Net premium 1.4 US cents.

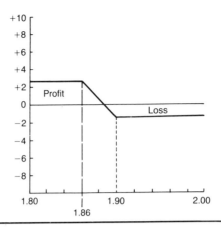

Profit potential is limited to 2.6 cents below the lower strike of 1.86, but loss is also limited to the cost of the net premium paid.
The breakeven is the higher strike less net premium paid of 1.4 US cents, i.e. at 1.886.

negative 4 cents is partially offset by the net premium receipt of 2.6 cents leaving maximum loss of 1.4 cents – the same as the Call spread.

Note that the two examples of bull spreads (one using Calls and one using Puts) shown have *exactly* the same risk rewards or pay-offs. However, the reader will notice that the Call spread has a net premium *payment* whereas the Put spread has a net premium *receipt* giving a preference to the bull Put spread as interest could be earned, rather than lost, during the period to maturity. This interest factor is taken into account in the pricing of option premiums so, in practice, the Call spread would have a slightly better payoff than the Put spread to compensate.

Bear spread

The bear spread has all the properties of the bull spread except that the spot rate is expected to fall rather than rise (see Fig. 5.4). Once again, the sale of the OTM option reduces the net cost of the spread but makes it a very conservative strategy. In the same way that a bull spread may be constructed of Puts, the bear spread can also be constructed using Calls rather than Puts – a bear Call spread – in which case a net premium *receipt* is achieved being the maximum profit attainable.

Butterfly (long)

The butterfly is another very conservative trade that can be used where spot FX rate is expected to remain within a particular range. Should the viewpoint be wrong then loss is limited by the two long options above, and below, the central 1.90 strike. Butterfly spreads are always constructed with twice the face value amount at the central strike compared with the face value amount on the 'wings'; a 1:2:1 ratio. In Fig. 5.5, this is achieved by using a short straddle in the middle at 1.90 and a long strangle with strikes at 1.86 and 1.94. This can also be viewed as a combination of a bull Call spread and a bear Put spread with the lower Call and higher Put having the same strike of 1.90. So, a short straddle and a long strangle, or a bull Call spread and a bear Put spread is equal to butterfly! (providing the strikes are similar). Either way, the butterfly in this example is made up of a combination of Puts and Calls but butterflies may also be constructed using all Calls, or all Puts in the same way as bull and bear spreads to give the same pay-offs as in the previous example.

5.5 Short GBP straddle 1.90, premium 4 US cents (2 × 2), long 1.94 Call and 1.86 Put for total premium 1.2 US cents (2 × 0.6).

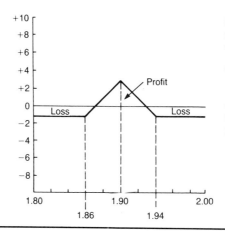

Profit potential is limited to the net premium receipt of 2.8 cents (+4 – 1.2) and is only at this level when spot is 1.90 on maturity. Loss is also limited by the long Call at 1.94 and long Put at 1.86 to 1.2 cents (1.90 – 1.86 or 1.90 – 1.94 = – 4, less net premium received of 2.8).
Breakeven is at 1.90 plus or minus net premium of 2.8 = 1.9280 or 1.8720.

5.6 Long GBP Put straddle 1.90, premium 4 US cents (2 × 2); short 1.94 and 1.86 Put for total premium 1.2 US cents (2 × 0.6).

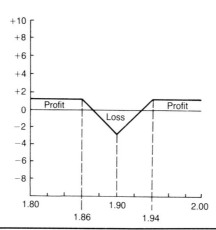

Profit potential is limited, and is at maximum of 1.2 US cents over 1.94 or under 1.86 where either of the two sold options are exercised. This is calculated as net premium cost of 2.8 US cents plus 4 cents from exercise of either the 1.90 Call or Put. Maximum loss is the net premium paid of 2.8 cents.
Breakeven is at 1.90 plus or minus net premium of 2.8 = 1.9280 or 1.8720.

Butterfly (short)

The short butterfly is a very conservative trade that benefits from a spot movement in either direction but has restricted profit potential, and so is usually applied when the spot FX rate is expected to be outside a perceived range (1.86–1.94 in Fig. 5.6). Butterflies are always constructed in a 1:2:1 ratio.

Ratio Call spread

The ratio Call spread is the bull Call spread (see page 24) with twice the amount sold (at higher strike) than that bought at the lower strike, hence a ratio of 1:2 (Bought:Sold). Consequently, the net premium paid is lower due to the extra premium receipt from the higher amount of sold Calls. This reduces the loss on GBP spot declining, increases the maximum profit potential, but has the result of unlimited losses should GBP rise too much.

The ratio Call spread is an interesting, and more adventurous, strategy that is usually initiated when current spot is close to the lower strike (similar to the bull spread) with the view that GBP will rise but not to a great extent. If the view is wrong and GBP declines, only a small loss is encountered, if GBP rises beyond the higher strike (1.94 in Fig. 5.7) profit is eroded to the point of loss, and then to unlimited loss should GBP continue to rise.

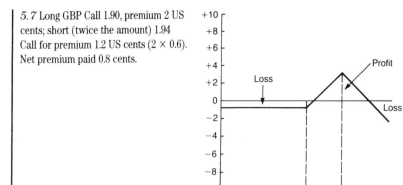

5.7 Long GBP Call 1.90, premium 2 US cents; short (twice the amount) 1.94 Call for premium 1.2 US cents (2 × 0.6). Net premium paid 0.8 cents.

Profit potential is limited and at its highest at 1.94 where the 1.90 Call is exercised for 4 cents to give a net profit of 3.2 cents (4 cents less net premium paid of 0.8 cents). Loss in one direction (down) is limited to the net premium paid (0.8 cents) but unlimited in the opposite (up) direction when the 1.94 Call is exercised for twice the amount of the 1.90 (net short GBP in single amount).
Breakeven is at 1.9080 (lower strike plus net premium paid, 1.90 + 0.08) or at 1.9720 (higher strike plus maximum profit, 1.94 + 0.032).

Note that ratio spreads are usually constructed as delta-neutral, meaning the strategy as a whole has no initial mathematical bias to spot direction i.e. the moment the strategy is constructed. This means that the actual ratio applied is determined by the delta of each option so these strategies may not always be in the 1:2 ratio – it depends on the strikes chosen. Delta is expressed as a percentage representing the mathematical likelihood of exercise at any given moment in the life of the option. In Fig. 5.7 the 1.90 strike has a delta of 50% (being at-the-money, it has a 50:50 chance of exercise on maturity) and the 1.94 strike has a delta of 25% (being OTM has less chance of exercise). So, to achieve the ratio required (to become neutral), one purchase at 50 delta must equal two sold at 25 delta (50 = 2 × 25). If a strike higher than 1.94 was chosen with a delta of, say, 20, then the ratio spread would be constructed as 1/2 or 2:5 (50 = 2.5 × 20) instead of 1:2.

Delta is explained in full in Chapter 7.

Ratio Put spread

As the ratio Call spread profits from the rise (not too far!) in the underlying FX rate so the ratio Put spread profits from the decline in this rate (but not too far!). The ratio Put spread in Fig. 5.8 can be looked upon as a bear Put spread with twice the amount sold as bought – hence a ratio of 1:2. This strategy is usually initiated when spot is close to the higher strike and can be used when a slight fall in the FX rate is expected. The fall at this point is not expected to continue otherwise the outlook is for unlimited losses. If the bearish views proves incorrect and the FX rate increases, then only a small, limited loss is encountered.

Call ratio backspread

The Call ratio backspread strategy can be seen as a cheaper form of a long straddle, the lower cost being achieved by giving up the unlimited profit profile of a lower FX rate. Another way of looking at the ratio Call backspread is that of a more expensive butterfly, due to the unlimited profit potential of a rise in the GBP FX rate. Consequently, backspreads may also be constructed using Calls and Puts rather than just Calls. In the example shown in Fig. 5.9 this could be achieved by the purchase of a 1.91 straddle and the sale of a 1.86 Put, the only

5.8 Long GBP Put 1.90, premium 2 US cents; short (twice the amount) 1.86 Put for premium 1.2 US cents (2 × 0.6). Net premium paid 0.8 cents.

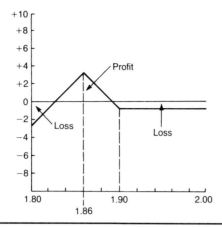

Profit is limited and at its highest at 1.86 where the 1.90 Put is exercised for 4 cents to give a net profit of 3.2 cents (4 cents less net premium paid of 0.8 cents). Loss in one direction (up) is limited to the net premium paid (0.8 cents) but unlimited in the opposite (down) direction when the 1.86 Put is exercised for twice the amount of the 1.90 (net long GBP in the single amount).
Breakeven is at 1.8920 (higher strike less net premium paid, 1.90 − 0.08) or at 1.8280 (lower strike less maximum profit, 1.86 − 0.032).

5.9 Short GBP Call 1.86, premium 4.6 US cents; long (twice the amount) 1.91 Call for premium 3.0 US cents (2 × 1.5). Net premium received 1.6 cents.

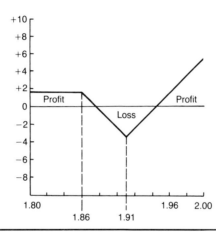

Profit potential is unlimited in upward direction of FX rate but limited on downside to net premium received of 1.6 cents from 1.86 down (where all options expire worthless). Loss is restricted in all circumstances to the exercise of the 1.86 Call, less net premium receipt, and is at maximum of 3.4 cents at the higher strike of 1.91 (1.91 − 1.86 = 5 cents less the 1.6 cents premium receipt).
Breakeven is at 1.8760 (lower strike plus net premium receipt) or at 1.9440 (higher strike plus maximum loss).

difference being that the net premium would be a payment, but the pay-off profile would be identical after allowance for the premium funding costs.

This strategy, like the straddle, can be used when the FX rate is expected to move dramatically. The ratio Call backspread, however, allows for a directional bias on the upside for lower cost (i.e. maximum possible loss).

As with the ratio spreads, backspreads are usually constructed as delta-neutral (as explained earlier). In Fig. 5.9 the 1.91 Call carries a delta of 40, being 1 cent out-of-the-money, and the 1.86 Call a delta of 80 being in-the-money by 4 cents (underlying FX rate being 1.90). Consequently, twice the amount of 1.91 Calls are bought to equate to the 80% delta of the 1.86 Call (2 × 40 = 1 × 80), a 2:1 Ratio.

Put ratio backspread

The Put ratio backspread has similar properties to the Call ratio backspread (see Fig. 5.10) except that the unlimited profit aspiration is now on the downside movement of the FX rate rather than on the upward. This strategy may also be constructed with Calls and Puts rather than just Puts, the difference being the payment of net premium rather than receipt, but pay-off profiles are the same after allowing for the premium funding costs. This strategy, like the straddle, can

5.10 Short GBP Put 1.94, premium 4.6 US cents; long (twice the amount) 1.89 Put for premium 3.0 US cents (2 × 1.5). Net premium received 1.6 cents.

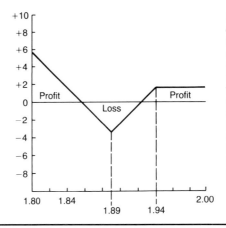

Profit potential is unlimited in downward direction of FX rate but limited on upside to net premium received of 1.6 cents from 1.94 up (where all options expire worthless). Loss is restricted in all circumstances to the exercise of the 1.94 Put, less net premium receipt, and is at maximum of 3.4 cents at the lower strike of 1.89 (1.94 − 1.89 = 5 cents less the 1.6 cents premium receipt). Breakeven is at 1.9240 (higher strike less net premium receipt) or at 1.8560 (lower strike less maximum loss).

be used when the FX rate is expected to move dramatically. The ratio Put backspread, however, allows for a directional bias on the downside for lower cost (i.e. maximum possible loss).

As with the ratio spreads, backspreads are usually constructed as delta-neutral. This principal is applied to whatever format the backspread is constructed on – all Puts or Calls and Puts.

Calendar spreads

The strategies listed above are all 'straight line', in the sense that exact profit or loss parameters can be forecast at any given level of the spot foreign exchange rate on maturity. Each strategy has the expiry date fixed as standard for all options within the scenario, the variables being the type (Call or Put), strike, amount and whether to buy or sell the option. There are other strategies that can be devised by using different maturity dates and these are usually called 'calendar spreads'.

A simple example:

BUY GBP Call (USD Put) for premium payment of US 5 cents – 3 months maturity.

SELL GBP Call (USD Put) for premium receipt of US 2 cents – 1 month maturity.
Both for same amount (face value) and strike.
Net cost: 3 US cents.

The time decay feature of FX options has the effect of pricing longer term options cheaper (pro rata) than those with shorter maturity dates (see Chapter 6 on pricing under 'time decay'). In the example, a three months option maturity has been bought for 5 US cents, and a one month option sold for 2 US cents. The next step in this strategy is:

On maturity of the sold option (i.e. after one month); sell option with same strike and for same amount for further one month for 2 US cents, and when that matures, sell the final one month for final US 2 cents.

Result:

Premium receipt of 6 US cents (3 × 2 US cents) and payment of one amount of 5 US cents. Profit of 1 US cent.

The fact that the bought option is always of longer maturity than any sold option means that there is no absolute foreign exchange risk – any exercise of a short option can be covered by the ultimate exercise of the long at the same strike. Hence this calendar spread carries limited loss of the initial net premium payment (3 US cents, in the example given).

It would appear that calendar spreads offer profit potential with no risk, but this is not the case. A further example of a calendar spread is given in Chapter 6 and this also explains the downside of such. The strategies listed in this chapter can themselves be established as calendar spreads. For example, one could take a long butterfly position for six months and sell a short butterfly for three months, etc.

Other option combinations

There are other strategies, but they are nothing more than combinations of those listed in this chapter. We know, for example, that if strike rates are arranged correctly we can construct a butterfly from a long straddle and a short strangle (or from a bull and bear spread). Similarly, by combining a long straddle (with one set of strikes) with a short straddle (with a wider set of strikes) we get what is called a 'condor'. The problem here is that we now have no less than four different strike rates and to construct these strategies on the exchanges would begin to be prohibitive in terms of dealing costs. In fact, the condor is wittily called a 'Cadillac spread' as the brokerage eminating from executing an order for such a strategy enables the broker to drive an expensive car!

The author will leave the reader with the exercise of combining some of the above to invent some new strategies – draw the resulting graph and don't forget to give it a name!

OTC strategies

While it is very easy to construct all the exchange strategies previously discussed in the OTC market, it is generally not so easy to create some of the OTC scenarios in the exchange markets. This is due to the exact nature of the option combinations – there are no restrictions on strikes, maturity dates, delivery dates or amounts. For example, the first strategy – the 'cylinder' – was invented as a zero premium hedge for FX exposure. It requires the offsetting of premiums and cannot always be constructed when the strike rates are at fixed levels (i.e. on the exchanges).

The cylinder (range forward, risk reversal, collar)

The cylinder involves the purchase of a Call and the sale of a Put (or vice versa) with different strikes, whereby the premium received from the written option offsets the cost of the purchased option, producing a zero cost strategy. We have already seen in Chapter 4 that the purchase of a Call and sale of a Put produces a synthetic FX position if the strikes are the same. The setting of different strikes produces a result similar to the FX forward position except there is a 'range' between the two strikes where there is no position on maturity. The cylinder is also called a 'range forward' or 'collar' by some institutions and a 'risk reversal' by the market generally, although strictly speaking, a risk reversal carries a simultaneous spot foreign exchange delta hedge (which would defeat the objective of using the strategy to hedge foreign exchange exposure). The cylinder is better constructed where the underlying positions of the options are long in a high interest currency and short in the lower yielding currency which has the effect of increasing the range between the strikes.

For example, consider the case of a UK company exporting to the USA who invoices for payment in US dollars. There is FX exposure in that the company will make profits from a fall in sterling and lose money from an increase, so hedging is advised. The purchase of a sterling Call (USD Put) would insure the company against a rise in the pound but at a cost of, say, 3 US cents in option premium. The company may consider this expense too high for the insurance in view of the fact that he could cover all risk (and give up the potential benefit) by selling USD in the FX market without cost.

A compromise might be the cylinder whereby the company buys a sterling Call at 1.90 to give the protection required but at the same time sells a sterling Put at a strike level that produces premium income equal to the Call premium payment. The result is a zero cost scenario with full protection above 1.90 which benefits on a declining pound to the level of the lower strike, at which point no further benefit is possible due to the ultimate exercise of the written option.

Using six months' maturity for the example with spot at 1.90, interest rates of 10% (GBP) and 4% (USD) and volatility of 10.5%, the Call option premium would be USD 3 cents for a European style option. Within the same parameters, a GBP Put with a strike of 1.80 would also cost 3 cents so the range of this cylinder would be 1.80 to 1.90. Fig. 5.11 gives a graphic representation of the cylinder.

This cylinder looks almost identical to the straight long FX position, except for the 'gap' between the strikes of 1.80 and 1.90 where neither option is exercised, leaving the company to sell USD (buy GBP) at spot rate on maturity.

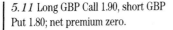

5.11 Long GBP Call 1.90, short GBP Put 1.80; net premium zero.

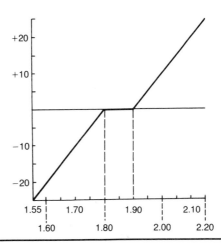

Combination of long Call and short Put but at different strikes.

Clearly, the best rate for conversion is 1.80. While this scenario looks reasonable for zero cost, there is the loss of all benefit below 1.80. Furthermore, the outright (forward) FX rate under the spot and interest rates quoted above would be about 1.8500, effectively providing a guarantee of 5 cents against the spot rate, which the company may find tempting. However, the scenario is better still at 1.80 and the cylinder would suit a company treasurer expecting the pound to decline but needing a maximum conversion rate of 1.90 – the current spot rate.

In this example, we have used the current spot rate as the starting point to obtain a zero cost cylinder, but we could use other strikes to either narrow or increase the gap between, so long as the two premiums are equal. It all depends on the risk tolerance of the user, because the higher the Call strike (more loss), the lower the Put strike (more profit), etc. Of course, if the gap is narrowed to the point of zero, we would be at the forward FX rate of about 1.8500 and would have achieved a zero cost, zero gap cylinder – a synthetic foreign exchange forward.

Profit sharing forward

The profit sharing forward is another popular OTC strategy that involves the purchase of a Call and the sale of a Put at the *same strike* but with different amounts. Like the cylinder, a profit sharing forward can be constructed with zero or reduced premium (or even premium income to a limited extent) and this is the main attraction of the strategy. In addition, it has a certain appeal in that full hedging cover is provided in one direction but, should spot move favourably, only a *proportion* of the potential profit is given up.

The following example is based on the same set of assumptions used to illustrate the cylinder strategy; a UK exporter invoicing in USD with an FX risk position equivalent to being short sterling (long USD). The company treasurer wishes to protect himself against the pound rising and purchases a six months' GBP Call (USD Put) at a strike of 1.90 (the current spot rate) for the full amount of the exposure, say GBP 1 000 000. The premium is 3 cents or USD 30 000. To offset the premium payment, the company sells a GBP Put but this time at the same strike of 1.90. We know from the cylinder example that the premium of a 1.80 Put is 3 cents, but the premium for a 1.90 Put is 8 cents, due to the fact that the forward FX rate is 1.8500. This leaves the 1.90 Put in-the-money (intrinsic value 5 cents, time value 3 cents). Thus, as the premium receipt is 8.5 cents against 3 cents, the company need only sell 3/8 of the Call amount or GBP 375 000 for the Put to net the premiums to zero. (GBP 1 000 000 × .03 = USD 30 000:GBP 375 000 × .085 = USD 30 000).

In Fig. 5.12 note that the company is fully protected above 1.90 by the Call but the loss on the Put below 1.90 is restricted to only 37.5% of the underlying FX position. Therefore, the exporter benefits by sterling depreciation to 62.5% of the unhedged position (hence 'profit sharing' forward). However, the profit sharing forward is only better than the cylinder at rates below 1.74 at which level the loss on the cylinder matches the loss on the profit sharing forward. This rate is easily calculated by reference to the face value amount sold at the lower strike on each strategy, e.g. 100% of (1.80–1.74) is equal to 37.5% of (1.90–1.74). Once again, the fixed outright rate of 1.85 is given up in preference for a maximum of 1.90, but providing 62.5% of any profits below that level.

5.12 Long GBP 1 000 000 Call 1.90; short GBP 352 941.17 Put 1.90; net premium zero.

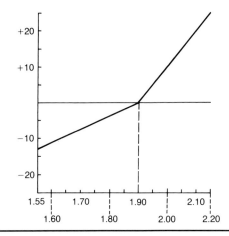

The full protection offered by the long Call at 1.90 can clearly be seen. However, the negative effect of the Put is less severe than the straight FX position outlined.

5.13 Long 1.80 GBP Put for 3 US cents; short 1/.90 GBP Put for 8 US cents; long 2.00 GBP Call for 1 US cent. Net premium receipt US 4 cents.

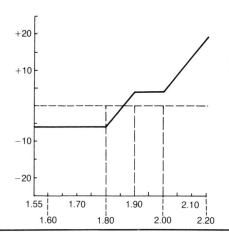

This seagull profits from an increase in GBP. Like the straight FX position, it has unlimited profit potential but differs in that loss is limited by the purchase of the 1.80 Put.

Seagull

The cylinder has two strikes; one bought option and one sold option of equal amounts. The profit sharing forward has one strike; one bought option and one sold option of unequal amounts. The seagull has *three* strikes; one bought and two sold or two bought and one sold of equal amount.

The seagull is similar to the cylinder except for the extra 'leg' (at 1.80 in Fig. 5.13) which creates a limited loss scenario against the cylinder's unlimited loss aspect. In this example, the seagull has been established to provide a premium income of some 4 US cents. However, the hedger with an underlying FX position of short GBP at 1.90 like the UK exporter in the prior examples will not have cover at that level (as in the cylinder and range forward) but rather at 2.00; although there is the premium income of 4 cents to be taken into account. On the down side, at 1.80, the seagull shows a loss of 6 cents but the hedger will have gained 10 cents from the underlying position of short GBP at 1.90. Below 1.80, the seagull provides opportunity for unlimited gains (for the hedger) through the exercise of the 1.80 Put and the underlying short GBP position at 1.90.

The seagull, like the cylinder and range forward, may be established at zero cost with full protection at 1.90 by the options shown in Fig. 5.14.

5.14 Buy GBP Call at 1.90 for 3 US cents; sell GBP Put at 1.8250 for 4 US cents; buy 1.70 GBP Put for 1 cent.

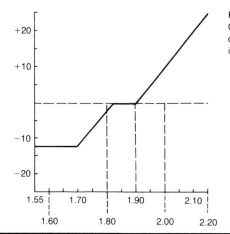

Full protection is given by the 1.90 GBP Call but the range is reduced to 7.5 US cents to pay for the 1.70 Put where loss is limited below this level.

The zero cost seagull could be used where protection is required at the 1.90 rate but where expectation is for a (much) lower rate on maturity. Unlike both the cylinder and range forward, the seagull has limited loss, in this example of 12.5 US cents, allowing the hedger to benefit from a fall in sterling. However, the viewpoint would be for a significant drop because the seagull in Fig. 5.14 would only be better than the cylinder at rates below 1.6750 and at rates below 1.5467 for the profit sharing forward.

The seagull demonstrated in Fig. 5.13, being established for a limited loss of only 6 US cents would, of course, produce a better scenario on a drop in sterling but with less protection on the upside (by the same amount of 6 US cents). One can see that it is easily possible to shift the option strikes to suit the particular circumstances of the hedger or the viewpoints of the market. One could say that using seagulls is one way of manipulating the original straight line FX risk position into one that looks like a seagull (hence the name), but inverted in this case. Astute readers will also have noticed that a seagull carries a ratio of 1:1:1 through the three strikes having the effect of 'bending' the butterfly's (ratio 1:2:1) wings!

Other OTC strategies

The majority of OTC strategies have been created to suit corporate requirements to hedge or manage FX exposure. The plain Call or Put option would be suitable for most cases except for the reluctance to pay the premium and it is for this reason that the majority of the scenarios were constructed. The fear of the premium being too expensive has also lead to other strategies that effectively 'hide' the premium until maturity when it is then paid by adjusting the ultimate FX transaction. 'Deferred premium' and 'Boston option' strategies fit into this category.

There are numerous possible combinations of Calls, Puts and the underlying FX with different strikes, amounts and maturity dates. In as much as the price of an option reflects rates from different markets such as FX, interest rates and volatility, it is possible to recreate each component synthetically by using options in conjunction with other constituent parts. We have already seen that

Put-Call parity can produce synthetic options or FX positions but it is also possible to produce synthetic interest rate positions (e.g. a loan) though options combined with spot/forward FX.

Consider the following example:

SELL: DEM Call (USD Put), strike 1.70 (DEM per USD)
              USD 10 000 000, 3 months maturity, premium received
              DEM 1 770 000
BUY: DEM Put (USD Call), strike 1.70 (DEM per USD) USD
              10 000 000, 3 months maturity, premium paid DEM 19 000
BUY: DEM (Sell USD) USD 10 000 000 forward in foreign
              exchange. Rate 1.5209.

Current market rates: Spot 1.50 (DEM per USD); 3 months DEM/USD forward
              swap +.0209 (DEM per USD).
              DEM interest rate, 9%

The position is short Call; long Put; long FX forward, which through Put-Call parity is a risk free position, i.e. − Call + Put + FX = 0. Whatever happens to the spot FX rate is irrelevant as, in three months' time, the strategy sells DEM (either through being exercised on the short Call or by exercising the long Put) and at the same time buys DEM through the FX forward contract. Note the premium cash flow:

Sold DEM Call (USD Put)	DEM 1 770 000 − CREDIT
Bought DEM Put (USD Call)	DEM 19 000 − DEBIT
NET PREMIUM RECEIPT	DEM 1 751 000

This premium is received value spot, two days after the transaction date, at the beginning of the option term.

Now look at the position on maturity, in three months time:

Option exercise at 1.70:	−DEM 17 000 000	+USD 10 000 000
Forward FX expiry at 1.5209:	+DEM 15 209 000	−USD 10 000 000
NET	−DEM 1 791 000	0

So, the premium receipt is DEM 1 751 000 value spot against net outflow after three months of DEM 1 791 000, representing a cost of DEM 40 000, or 9% per annum over three months – the original DEM interest rate for that term. The strategy is therefore a synthetic loan at that rate. This strategy was made possible by constructing the sold option as deep ITM thereby ensuring a large premium receipt. Consequently, the bought option was very inexpensive as it was far OTM and only accounted for a tiny reduction in the net premium receipt. The purchase of the DEM Put (USD Call) was necessary, however, to ensure zero FX risk after the forward purchase of the DEM (sale of USD) in the FX market.

The use of synthetic loans through options may have advantages in some countries where there are restrictions on borrowing but where options and FX are unrestricted or where accounting standards differ between the products (accrual versus mark-to-market).

It should be noted by the reader that each of the option combinations detailed in this chapter are structured for a specific result, on maturity of the scenario, whether it be for speculative reasons, in the case of the exchange strategies, or for hedging purposes in the case of the OTC scenarios. No account is made for the possible closeout or reversal of these strategies before expiry. For example, a speculator may have a change of mind, or a hedger may lose the FX risk he is covering (e.g. a customer cancels or defaults on an order) before the strategy matures. In other words, no explanation has been given to the possible ramifications of liquidating strategies before maturity.

Therefore, Chapter 6 covers the time value aspect of options, and the relevance of the strike rate versus the underlying FX rate in the calculation of such. In addition, the implication of option implied volatility is explained in detail. Without prior knowledge of these important factors, intermediate results of option combinations might be difficult to understand. However, with the knowledge of time value and volatility in hand, the reader should be able to estimate the interim results in most of the listed strategies.

The CME (Chicago Mercantile Exchange) produces a wall chart of the exchange strategies which includes a brief description of the interim characteristics. Contact numbers for the exchange are listed in Appendix I.

6 Option Pricing

EVERAL books have been written on the subject of option pricing and all tend to delve deep into the mathematics of such; the author of this book has attempted to avoid this where possible.

The acknowledged basis of modern option pricing formulae is the often quoted 'Black-Scholes' formula. Two theoreticians, Fisher Black and Myron Scholes devised a formula in the early 1970s in an attempt to produce a 'fair value' for options on equities. Of course, FX options differ because there is no dividend and both currencies of the exchange carry interest rates that can be fixed until maturity. Hence, various adaptations to the original Black-Scholes formula have been made for use in FX options pricing. The best known of these is the Garman-Kohlhagen adaptation which adequately allows for the two interest rates and the fact that a currency can trade at a premium or a discount forward depending on the structure of the interest rate differential.

American style options cause further problems in the pricing of options due to the probability of early exercise. In 1979, Cox, Ross and Rubinstein published a pricing model to take account of American style options. By using the same basics as Black-Scholes they adopted what is now known as the 'binomial' method for pricing such options. This same binomial model is now used alongside the Garman-Kohlhagen version to price FX options.

Having reached 'foreign exchange options are priced according to a formula devised by Black-Scholes and adapted by Garman-Kohlhagen with modifications by Cox-Ross-Rubinstein (for American style options)', it is time to take a look at the pricing factors and results rather than the actual mathematics.

Pricing factors

The following factors are required to price an FX option:

1. Call or Put
2. Currency pair
3. Strike rate
4. Amount
5. Style (American or European)
6. Expiration date and time

7. Spot FX rate
8. Interest rates for each currency, or one currency plus 9. below
9. FX swap rate (this can be calculated if both interest rates are available in 8)

10. Volatility of the currency pair

The reader should notice that the pricing factors have been split into three groups. Each in the first group (1 to 6) is *chosen*; each in the second (7 to 9) is *given* from the respective markets; but the third (No. 10) has only one factor – volatility – which is peculiar to options. This last factor represents the *anticipated* volatility of the currency pair over the life of the option and is the only 'unknown' factor in the options price. It is for this reason that the professional OTC market quotes in volatility rather than the actual price – the premium is easily calculated once volatility has been agreed between the counterparties.

Volatility

Volatility, expressed as the annualized percentage rate of change of a currency pair, is the key component of an option's 'time value' and so the price of the option. For example, some currency pairs traditionally have low volatility, e.g. the Canadian dollar against the US dollar (due to the very strong trade ties between Canada and the USA) and others such as the currencies within the European Monetary System (EMS), which aims to hold currencies within certain percentage movements. On the other hand, the major trading currencies such as Deutsche Marks, yen, sterling, etc. usually have somewhat higher volatilities against the US dollar.

So, high volatility equals high premium, low volatility gives low premium, but can one calculate the future volatility of a currency pair? Unfortunately, without knowing the future, historical or current perspectives are the only guide to future performance. Participants in the options market bid and offer around the perceived volatility level for any given period, with supply and demand dictating the final level. Just like any liquid market, rates (volatility) can only rise to the point where sellers become evident and only fall to where buyers enter the market.

If volatility is the key component and price can be calculated by combining the other factors using Black-Scholes, it follows that volatility can be computed if the option price is available. This is the implied volatility of the option and is frequently used in the case of exchange listed markets where options are priced in US cents or other currency. After calculating the implied volatility, comparison is made to the OTC market to seek the better value option.

The impact of volatility is further detailed elsewhere in this chapter.

Intrinsic value

Intrinsic value was defined on page 5 as:

The difference, if positive, between the strike price and the underlying FX spot rate (for American style options) or FX forward rate (for European style).

'Positive' refers to the point where exercise would result in profit against the FX rate; therefore options with zero, or negative difference, have no intrinsic value.

The intrinsic value of an option is a simple calculation but does have a significant effect on the price, especially if the option is deep in-the-money, i.e. the positive difference between strike and the FX rate is large. Intrinsic value is calculated in this way and added to the time value to give the price of the option. The Black-Scholes formula handles all aspects of intrinsic and time value and funding costs on the premium (because it is paid up-front i.e. at the start of the option).

Time value

Options which are OTM (they have no intrinsic value) are priced on their time value alone. Options in-the-money will have intrinsic value added to their time value. Through Put-Call parity, it follows that Call and Put options with the same strike and maturity will have the same time value even though one (either the Call or the Put) will be ITM (unless *both* are ATM). Hence time value represents the extra cost associated with options versus a spot or forward transaction.

The main components of time value are:

1. Days to maturity (i.e. 'time').
2. Volatility.
3. The distance of the strike from the underlying FX rate, irrespective of whether it is in- or out-of-the-money. This factor is measured mathematically as the delta of the option, but more on this in Chapter 7.
4. Interest rates (although interest rate differentials equate to the forward FX rate, i.e. it is included in 3 above).

Some very interesting points arise out of time value:

1. Time value is not linear

A three month option will cost less than three times the cost of a one month option. A one year option will cost less than twice the six months option. The reason for this is that time value decays at an accelerating rate towards maturity with little decay at the beginning of longer term options. Hence the buying of longer term options effectively gives better value for money than the purchase of shorter dates, although the premium is higher (see Fig. 6.1).

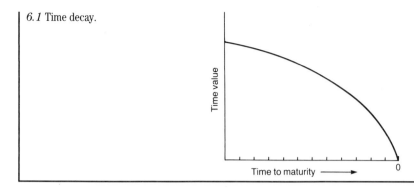

6.1 Time decay.

The calendar spread strategy (see Chapter 5) attempts to take advantage of this time factor by purchasing a long date option and selling the respective shorter dates in succession using the same strike.

Example:

Buy 6 month option for 3%, sell first 3 months for 2% and after this matures, sell remaining 3 months for further 2% to realize 1% net profit. As the sold option is always covered by the bought, the scenario has limited risk parameters.

Too easy? See below.

2. At-the-money options have the highest time value

When the option strike is at, or close to, the underlying FX rate, the chances of the option moving to ITM status is 50:50 – an 'even money' chance. Therefore, the uncertainty of eventual exercise, and so the time value and consequent option premium, is highest at this level (with relation to time value only, e.g. ignoring any intrinsic value).

In the case of an OTM option or of an ITM option, the expectations are no longer 50:50 but more certain, resulting in lower time value to the point of zero time value. At this point the option premium would be either zero, for OTM, or intrinsic value for the ITM representing the fact that, mathematically, such options have zero chance of being exercised (OTM) or not exercised (ITM).

The calendar spread scenario mentioned previously would only produce the projected profit of 1% if the second leg was sold ATM in the same way as the first leg (assuming there was no change in volatility). However, any movement of the underlying FX rate away from the strike level would reduce time value and consequently the profit expectations to the point of possible loss. In fact, this strategy depends on two major assumptions: firstly, that the underlying rate will move very little and secondly, that volatility (a major component of time value) will remain at, or higher than, the implied purchased volatility of the bought option. The problem here is that volatility is likely to go down if FX rates remain unchanged; clearly this strategy is not as simple as might be thought at first.

Shown graphically (Fig. 6.2), the ATM peak of time value shows sharp declines on either side (ITM and OTM) but there is a decelerating curve as the

6.2 Time value of options.

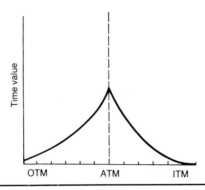

zero line is approached. Once again, curved (rather than straight) lines are evident.

3. Out-of-the-money options and in-the-money options (with same maturity) tend to have higher implied volatility

The volatility factor applied for pricing out-of-the-money options is usually higher than the volatility applied to options near-the-money. It should be noted that the mathematics of option pricing is based on the principle that movement of the FX rate is of 'random walk' nature resulting in Black-Scholes applying volatility as uniform across all strikes. However, this is not the case in market practice as foreign exchange rates tend to have a bias on occasions and also to 'jump' in one direction or the other causing the implied volatility itself to move. The result is that the market has to adjust for these inefficiencies in Black-Scholes by adjusting the volatility factor (the only 'unknown' in the options price) for there is no other in which to reflect the adjustment. Furthermore, the amount of mark-up (avoiding the word 'premium'!) of volatility will increase the further the distance from the ATM strike so in reality it is not possible to buy an option for 'nothing', even if it *is* mathematically impossible to attain in-the-money status by maturity. In other words, nobody can sell any option for nothing!

Shown graphically (Fig. 6.3), the volatility level rises on each side of the central, ATM strike point.

6.3 The curve of volatility across strikes with the same maturity.

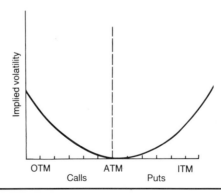

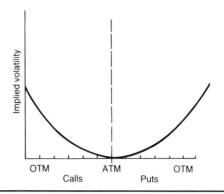

6.4 The curve of volatility across OTC strikes with the same maturity.

Figure 6.3 shows the curve of volatility for ITM and OTM options versus ATM options with the same maturity. This is known as the volatility 'smile' or curve across strikes, and is not to be confused with the volatility curve across maturities which is explained later in this chapter.

Up to this point out-of-the-money and in-the-money options with higher volatility have been discussed. The severity of the volatility mark-up is determined by the distance of the strike from the equivalent at-the-money strike, not whether the option is in or out-of-the-money. As already described, an ITM Call will have the same time value (and hence, volatility) as the OTM Put with the same strike through Put-Call parity. So the distance, or delta (see Chapter 7) is the all important factor. All things being equal the OTM Call that is, for example, 5% away from the ATM should have the same relative volatility mark-up as the equivalent OTM Put as shown in Fig. 6.4. (This is Fig. 6.3 with the X axis changed to reflect OTM Calls and Puts rather than OTM and ITM options).

4. Volatility strike curve or 'smile' is not always uniform in both directions

While Fig. 6.4 could very easily be the case for a particularly currency pair, many volatility smiles are 'skewed' in one direction or the other if there is a perceived directional bias in the underlying FX rate. For example, a currency may be under devaluation pressures with the potential for either devaluation or retaining the current level of exchange – there is very little chance of any appreciation. In cases like this, the OTM Puts would demand a premium over the OTM Calls on the currency, and this is adjusted through the volatility mark-up or smile by skewing the volatility higher in favour of the OTM Puts. The OTM Calls could even be lower than the ATM if devaluation looked probable but, normally, the Put line would stay around the ATM level as per Fig. 6.5.

Finally, the reader should note that as different currency pairs will have different volatilities, so the shape of the smile will be different which, in turn, will affect the skew. Looking at the smile factor; this could be 'flat' with very little mark-up for OTM Calls and Puts, or severe (shaped like the letter 'U') with very high OTM volatilities compared with ATM. Mathematically, the volatility of a currency pair's implied volatility (yes, the volatility of volatility!) will measure

6.5 The 'skew of the smile'.

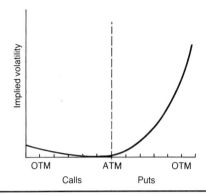

6.6 Volatility curve through maturity.

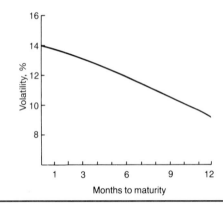

this severity factor so the more volatile the volatility, the more severe (U-shaped) the smile.

5. Volatility is not uniform across all maturities

The reader will have noted the curve, and skew of the curve, of volatility across different strikes with the same maturity. Volatility is also curved through different maturity dates, so in other words, one month volatility is unlikely to be the same as one year (although it is possible). Furthermore, the curve may be positive; the higher the volatility levels the longer the maturity, or negative with higher volatilities in shorter maturity dates. Figure 6.6 shows a typical volatility curve from 1 day to one year, sloped negatively.

Pricing terms

Having calculated the option price from the factors on page 24, the various pricing terms can be displayed in no less than four ways, i.e.:

1. Percent of first currency.
2. Percent of second currency.
3. Second currency in terms of the first.
4. First currency in terms of the second.

To obtain the actual premium amount, the price is multiplied by the relevant currency face value of the option.

Example:
DEM Call (USD Put), 3 months maturity, European style, strike 1.50 (DEM per USD) for USD 10 million (DEM 15 million).

Using spot of 1.54 (DEM per USD), interest rates of 4% (USD) and 9% (DEM) – giving FX forward rate of 1.5595 – and volatility of 10.5%, the results are as follows:

1. .71% of DEM (Premium amount is DEM 106 500)
2. .69155% of USD (Premium amount is USD 69 155)
3. .0046103 USD per DEM (Premium amount is USD 69 155)
4. .01065 DEM per USD (Premium amount is DEM 106 500)

There is no mystery in these results as the premium has to be either DEM 106 500 or USD 69 155 which implies the current spot rate of 1.54. To put this another way, it is possible to convert from one price format to the other by reference to the spot and strike price.

It is normal to quote option prices and their resultant premiums in either of the two currencies within a specified pair. In fact, there is no other method for option pricing unless one introduces a third exchange rate for conversion to another currency and this is not a feature of any option pricing formulas, such as Black-Scholes. However, some option users prefer to identify premiums in their particular accounting currency rather than that of the currency pair of the option. This can happen, for example, when a UK company hedges a FX exposure in USD against DEM but wishes to pay for the premium in sterling. This extra conversion is normally held as a separate spot transaction and not held as part of the option premium.

If a premium is paid or received in a third currency, then a further exchange risk arrives in the third currency versus the original premium currency. However, this risk is limited to that of the options premium value, not the face value of the option and is further discussed in the Chapter 7 as omega risk.

Pricing systems

Pricing of options using the models described earlier can be achieved by programming the appropriate formulas into a computer, but most option users find the purchase of a software package is a more convenient method. Software products are available ranging from simple option calculators through risk analysis models to complete pricing, risk management and accounting systems. In choosing a particular software company, the buyer should be aware of the models presently being used in the marketplace as pricing differences between systems have resulted in certain proprietary pricing systems becoming standards for the marketplace. For example, in OTC the most generally accepted model is 'FENICS' by Astrogamma Inc of New York. Other markets, such as the PHLX and CME have their own approved models for option revaluation purposes.

Option Trading Risks

7

I N the preceding chapters, the option product, its characteristics and uses, how it is priced and where it is traded have all been covered. Now risks inherent in the product itself, from the viewpoint of trading, or hedging, an option or a portfolio of options must be addressed. To put it another way, the first six chapters will have given the reader an understanding of the product and its uses to hedge against, or speculate in, FX risk. Hence, all the examples, strategies and uses have been based on the possible results on maturity of the option(s). But what about the interim results of hedged positions with varying changes in the underlying FX, interest and volatility rates? How does one hedge an option position?

The performance of an option over time and its relationship to the movement of the underlying FX rate is very important to the option writer, or buyer, who has no inherent FX exposure to cover. Many users of options are (quite rightly) unconcerned as to how the counterparty hedges, and may have only little interest in the following chapters on the trading and hedging of option portfolios. However, an understanding of the principles built around the mathematics of option risk, and the techniques of hedging these, will open the possibilities of option replication for users of options. Replication is discussed in Chapter 8.

Option risks are identified by the popular Greek letters often applied in mathematics; the first to be discussed is the delta.

Delta

Sometimes called the 'hedge ratio', the delta represents the underlying FX equivalent risk at any particular moment in time. It is usually expressed as:

The rate of change of the options value (premium) relative to a change in the underlying (foreign exchange) rate.

The delta of an option is produced as a by-product of the pricing formula discussed in the previous chapter (it is the first derivative of the model) and represents the mathematical calculation of the options likelihood of exercise on maturity. The delta of an option can have a value between 0 and 1 but is usually expressed in percentage terms.

Example:
GBP Call (USD Put), strike of 1.90 (USD per GBP), European style for 1 month maturity, premium 2.20 US cents. (Current underlying FX rate, in this case the 1 month forward, is 1.90.)

This option is ATM in that the strike price is the same as the underlying FX rate of 1.90. (Note that the option is European style so the underlying rate is the FX *forward* rate for the option maturity date i.e. one month). The probability of this option being in-the-money, and therefore warranting exercise on maturity, is 50:50 or an 'even money' chance – the underlying rate may go up or down from the current 1.90 level. The delta of this option is therefore 50 percent which means the option price will change by 50% of the change in the foreign exchange rate – if foreign exchange goes up by .01 to 1.91, premium will rise by .005 (.5 cents) to 2.70 US cents.

The delta of an option changes with any factor that influences the potential exercise probability, i.e. changes in the underlying FX rate, volatility, interest rates or even simply the passing of time. While we do not need a mathematics model to work out that the delta of ATM options is 50%, other options do require some form of calculation to be made. In the example, the effect on the option's premium of an increase in the FX rate of .01 to 1.91 was demonstrated. This would give the Call option struck at 1.90 a 1 cent intrinsic value resulting in a delta *that must exceed* 50% – there is more probability of exercise than when ATM – and in fact the delta of this option would be about 57% with one month to elapse before maturity. Hence the delta has changed from its original 50% when FX was 1.90 so the premium will now change by 57% of the FX rate. Delta is non-linear and depicts the initial rate of change only.

Note what happens if the option is extended to one day before maturity with spot at 1.95. Once again, the exercise probability is higher with one day to go than one month and even more so due to the further increase in the FX rate resulting in the delta being as high as 100%, making it mathematically certain to be exercised.

The volatility factor also plays an important part in calculating the delta of an option (except for ATM options which are always 50%) in that the probabilities of change are higher when volatility is high, compared with when it is low. This is only logical. It was mentioned earlier that a Call option with a delta of 100% with one day until maturity was certain to be exercised, but imagine that the volatility suddenly increased due to, say, a possible devaluation announcement. The increase in volatility would increase the option's time value and – in this case –

lower the delta of the Call option as it is no longer so certain to be exercised, as it was before the volatility increase. If the principle of delta is applied to the underlying FX rate we get 100% – the rate of change relative to itself. Implementing Put-Call parity, a direct relationship between the Call delta and the Put delta of any option with same strike and maturity date becomes apparent. Stated simply, this is:

(Call delta) + (Put delta) = 100%

So, if the Call delta is 50%, then the Put delta is also 50% – both are ATM and the 50:50, 'even money' synopsis above holds true. If the Call goes to 70%, then the equivalent Put option's delta will be 30% (the Call being ITM, the Put has to be OTM, with lower than 50% chance of exercise). Taking the process one step further, the 100% Call option will result in a zero Put delta – a 'no chance' mathematical calculation of exercise probability. In theory, this zero delta Put option should have no value, but try finding someone willing to sell you an option for nothing! (See Chapter 6 for details of volatility mark-up for OTM options). On maturity, an option becomes either zero delta (expiring worthless) or 100% delta (exercised into spot foreign exchange).

It should be noted that Call and Put deltas will add up to 100% on European style options only. In the case of American style there is an additional calculation made in an attempt to estimate the likelihood of early exercise which may result in the two deltas exceeding 100%.

It can now be seen that the delta gives us a mathematical probability of option exercise and represents the link (initially at least) between movement in FX rates and the option premium. It can therefore be used to hedge an option against any potential exercise by contracting a position in the underlying FX market; this is a delta hedge. A delta hedge can take the form of spot or forward; the former is simply the forward delta discounted back to spot using the relevant interest rate.

Delta hedging is discussed in greater detail in Chapter 8.

Gamma

It should now be clear that delta changes as the underlying FX rate moves, as well as with the movement of other factors such as volatility or time. Gamma measures the rate of change in delta, quite simply it is the delta of delta! As the delta is the first derivative of the pricing model, so gamma is the second.

Gamma can effectively measure the sensitivity of the delta and is a very useful tool in calculating risk within an option portfolio. It varies according to three main factors:

1.   The relationship of spot to strike (the delta qualifies this).
2.   The time to maturity.
3.   The market or implied volatility of the option.

The nearer the strike to the underlying FX rate, the higher the gamma; the nearer the option to maturity, the higher the gamma; and the lower the volatility, the higher the gamma, and vice versa. 'Higher' in this sense means a more sensitive or stronger gamma, i.e. the change in delta is larger.

We know that ATM options have 50% deltas and also have the highest time value (page 47, 41), so it follows that the nearer the option's delta is to 50%, the higher, or stronger, will be the gamma. An option's delta can be 50% with one month to maturity or one day; in both cases it is ATM but *on* maturity it has to be either zero or 100% (expire worthless or be exercised into FX). Naturally, it follows that that the delta change (gamma) has to be 'more violent' the closer the option gets to its maturity date. Finally, the volatility factor in an options price will influence the gamma, in that lower volatility will lower the probability of rate change, making the delta more severe if rates *do* move, the result of which is higher gamma.

Gamma is usually expressed as being either positive or negative depending on whether the movement of delta is good or bad from the perspective of the party concerned. Long option positions have positive gamma, short have negative; the former will gain by delta change, and the latter will lose.

Gamma is one of the major option risks taken by the professional market makers and is responsible for some of the large profits (and losses) experienced by banks and other institutions in the past. It has more relevance in hedged option portfolios and is further explained in Chapter 8.

Vega

Vega (not a Greek letter!) is sometimes called Kappa (which is) in other option markets. It represents the change in the volatility factor of an option's premium and can be expressed as:

The rate of change in an option's value (premium) relative to a change in the volatility factor.

The volatility factor in an option's price is itself subject to change depending on market perception of the future volatility in the relative spot FX rate. A change in volatility can, of course, result in a change in premium so vega represents the sensitivity of an option's price (premium) to a change in volatility and is usually measured by an increase of one percentage point.

Example:
Option with face value of USD 1 000 000 experiences a volatility increase of one percentage point (say 10% to 11%) resulting in a premium increase of USD 2500. With all other factors unchanged, this option is said to have a vega of .25% (2500 -/- 1 000 000 × 100).

Volatility is a major component of time value (page 40) and as such vega is highest when options are ATM (page 41). However, vega also increases with time so longer date options carry much higher vega than those with shorter maturities.

Vega is possibly the most popular of the option risks employed by the professional market makers (and others) for gain, due mainly to the fact that vega is endemic only to options and therefore not subject to other market influences. Outside factors will undoubtedly influence option market makers, but only the market maker can make the volatility price.

Theta

The sensitivity of an option's value (premium) to the elapse of time.

Theta is usually measured as the loss of premium value over one day, given that no other factors change. An option with theta of .025% would lose USD 250.00 over the next day for every USD 1 million of its face value.

Theta is a major component of time value (page 40) and as such is highest when options are ATM. It is also non-linear and decays very rapidly close to the expiry of the option but loses very little at the start of longer date maturities.

Theta is sometimes referred to as simply time decay or 'carry' although changes in other factors such as volatility or interest rate will change theta. It is usually referred to as either positive or negative depending on whether elapse of time accrues a profit (short option positions) or loss (long option positions) respectively. Theta risk is another frequently employed risk in options and is usually played against gamma; this is discussed in more depth in Chapter 8.

Rho

The sensitivity of an option's value (premium) to change in interest rates.

Changes in interest rates alter the FX forward rate which, of course, is the underlying instrument for the pricing of European style options. So, even if spot remains the same, the option's value will be changed. The discussion here is about the interest rate differential between the two currencies. In some circles, rho is referred to as the sensitivity of the countercurrency interest rate (usually the USD) with phi as the sensitivity of the currency interest rate. Both are reflected in the change of the FX forward rate but rho also affects the discounting of the premium. Rho and phi are usually measured by the change in the premium due to a 1% rise in the respective rate.

An active portfolio of options will always carry some residual rho risk, but it is not generally considered significant compared with other option risks. Market makers do not normally use rho as a vehicle for risk and various methods are employed to negate it where possible; this is discussed in Chapter 8.

Lambda

Lambda indicates the leverage of an option, usually measured against a 1% movement in the underlying FX rate. The premium of an option with a lambda of 30 will increase or decrease (depending on whether it is a Call or Put) in premium value by 30% for a 1% movement in the underlying rate. Lambda increases with the decrease in premium value hence OTM (low delta) and shorter date options carry the highest lambda.

Beta

Beta is the term applied to represent the risk of hedging one currency pair against another. Some currencies are closely correlated to others such as those within the European Monetary System (EMS) so, for example, French francs against the USD (FRF/USD) is likely to have similar volatility rates to that of DEM/USD. Quite often banks and other institutions will hedge less liquid option currencies with those more liquid if the correlation is close to 100%. In other cases positions are taken to derive profit for anticipated changes in correlated values, but in any event this opens beta risk – a danger of loss from negative changes.

Omega

Omega has nothing to do with the pricing formula but has been coined as a name for a risk that appears in options where neither currency within a given pair is the accounting, or profit/loss currency. Omega is the last letter of the Greek alphabet and, appropriately, should be the last option risk.

For example, in the currency pair DEM-GBP, profits may only be realized in either DEM or GBP as the original premium will have been paid in either of those currencies. Interim revaluations can only be calculated in the same manner. The problem arises because most institutions have only one currency in which to measure profit and loss so a USD based company will experience the omega effect on currency pairs that do not include the USD, as in the example.

Omega may be avoided by using a multi-currency accounting system that retains premiums in the original currency and by holding all unrealized and realized gains and losses in the same currencies, without actual conversion to the base (accounting) currency. Delta hedging of options is normally based on spot foreign exchange transactions which, by virtue of rolling forward ('Tom/Next deals') produce realized gains and losses in currencies. Although realized, these amounts must not be converted to the accounting currency while the options, to which the hedge relates, are still unrealized. Unfortunately, most institutions convert realized gains and losses to the accounting currency at set intervals, e.g. once a month, once a quarter, etc, in accordance with standard accounting practices but, in doing so, create omega risk. In other words, realized gains and losses in non-accounting currencies that have emanated from hedging options in such currencies should be held until the options mature and the premiums (in the same currencies) are realized. The net result, which is the profit or loss from the hedged options, may then be converted to the accounting currency. The problem with this method is that it is virtually impossible to operate on a mixed portfolio of options and foreign exchange. Trying to calculate what portion of realized FX belongs to what option is an impractical task. Therefore it is better to leave all balances in the original currency without actual conversion, with translation of the total realized and unrealized to provide the account profit and loss amounts at the normal accounting points (month end, quarter end, year end, etc). The only omega risk in following this method is on the net profit/loss recorded.

For institutions that do not operate multi-currency accounting, option premiums will be recorded in the base (accounting) currency which creates omega risk that needs to be hedged. Chapter 8 on hedging and trading an option portfolio details by way of example an effective method of omega hedging.

Unfortunately, omega risk is not usually evident from current option software systems and is the cause of many profit/loss differences on option portfolios in many institutions. Omega risk is only great if the portfolio is significant and/or there is a large movement in the spot rate of the currency pair.

All the risks listed above, except beta and omega, are derived from the original pricing formula. There are other risks associated with options borne out of running an active, hedged portfolio and these are dealt with in Chapter 8.

A final note of caution when discussing option 'Greeks' with others, especially those not famililar with FX options: Greek letters are often used by mathematicians in option theory and there is a danger of using different Greek letters for the same risk. The 'Greeks' listed in this chapter are, nevertheless, all standard for the OTC FX options markets.

Hedging and Trading a Portfolio of Options

8

IN the previous chapter all the option risks, or the 'Greeks' as they are sometimes called were identified. The various ways of using these to recognize risk in a portfolio of options and apply hedging techniques will now be discussed. In doing so the opportunity of trading these risks for profit is opened, and the more popular 'plays' are described in detail. One should remember, however, that these are not the strategies referred to in Chapter 5 (which are all designed for a particular result on maturity) but are truly sophisticated trading techniques developed by the market professionals over the last few years to profit from the extraordinary combination of risks found only in derivative products such as options. Generally, the profits from such techniques are generated through the interim revaluation of options and their foreign exchange hedges well before actual maturity. Hence, the trader's aim to profit from particular positions tends to be fairly short term in nature – maybe from one day to a few weeks. The principles described here are true for a single option or a portfolio of thousands. Described first is the original, and still the most popular, form of hedging – the delta-neutral concept.

Delta-neutral concept

In Chapter 7, delta was described as representing the equivalent underlying FX risk at any particular moment in time. As such delta can be used as an initial hedge to protect against adverse movements in the underlying FX rate.

Example:

A bank writes (sells) GBP 10 000 000 Call (USD Put), strike of 1.90, European style for 1 month maturity, premium USD 220 000. (Current underlying FX rate, in this case the 1 month forward, is 1.90), delta 50%.

This option is ATM in that strike and underlying are both 1.90, hence delta is 50%. As the bank has sold the GBP Call option, it is at risk of being exercised (on maturity, in one month's time) and, if so, would sell GBP 10 000 000 at 1.90 to the buyer of the option. The bank is therefore at risk if GBP should rise above the current level of 1.90. To hedge, the bank *buys* GBP 5 000 000 (being delta of 50%) at 1.90 in the FX forward market (the underlying).

If GBP immediately rises to 1.91, the options value will rise to USD 274 000 (loss of USD 54 000 to the bank) but the FX hedge of GBP 5 000 000 will show a profit of USD 50 000 (5 000 000 × (1.91 − 1.90)) leaving a small USD 4000 loss. Note that option delta is now 57% and re-hedging is required − purchase of an additional GBP 700 000 (10 000 000 × 7%) − to keep position delta-neutral and hedged against further increases in the FX rate.

If GBP immediately fell to 1.89, the option value would decrease to USD 174 000 (profit of USD 46 000 to the bank) but the FX hedge of GBP 5 000 000 would lose USD 50 000 (5 000 000 × (1.89 − 1.90)) also leaving a small loss of USD 4000. On this occasion, the option delta has fallen to 43% leaving the bank to sell GBP 700 000 to maintain hedge at correct level. In either case, the delta hedge of GBP 5 000 000 provides a good measure of protection for an initial movement in the underlying FX rate but is not an exact hedge.

Delta is not a perfect hedge because it changes as the underlying FX rate changes requiring frequent adjustments to the initial hedge. Furthermore, even if the FX rate stays the same, time, volatility and interest rates will all have an effect on delta. The rate at which delta changes, the gamma, will determine the severity of such re-hedging adjustments; the smaller the adjustment, the better delta performs as a hedge. For example, if the option maturity was one year instead of one month in the above, the FX rate change of 1 cent (up or down) would have only changed the option price by USD 51 000 instead of USD 54 000 and the delta change (gamma) would have been less than 1% in absolute terms (giving delta of 50.8%) instead of the 7% (delta of 57%) resulting in less re-hedging. Hence, the lower (or weaker) the gamma, the better delta works as an initial hedge.

Options that have been hedged (and constantly re-hedged) are said to be delta-neutral. Such hedging may be done in the underlying FX, as in the example above, and/or by using other options. Using options changes the gamma considerably and is discussed in a later section but whilst on delta, it is worth pointing out a very significant aspect of delta neutrality. The example showed a small loss (USD 4000) in hedging against an immediate movement in the FX rate. If this FX rate movement had taken place on the next day, the options value would have been lower, due to theta (time value). In fact, the theta of this option is about USD 4000 per day (with one month to expiry) on the GBP 10 000 000 face value. So, while re-hedging of the delta would still have been required (57% or

43%), there would have been no loss on the position because the seller would have received the premium, and thereby gained through time decay on the option. In other words, what the seller lost through FX rate movement would have been made up by time decay.

If the bank in this example had re-hedged the delta at 57% (by buying GBP 700 000) and the FX rate had gone back to 1.90 the following day, there would have been a loss of USD 7000 (700 000 $\times$ .01 US) on the hedge and a profit of USD 4000 through theta, leaving a net loss of USD 3000. The bank would also have to re-adjust the delta hedge back to the original GBP 5 000 000 to maintain delta neutrality. This loss on hedging and all subsequent losses through the life of the option may, on final maturity, exceed the original premium received. Alternatively, the losses may have been less than the original premium. The only certainty is that there would have been losses – the actual amount varying according to the frequency and severity of adjusting the delta which, in turn, depends on the degree of volatility experienced in the underlying FX rate over the term of the option.

The original option premium would have been calculated using all the factors listed in Chapter 5. One of these factors is, of course, volatility which introduces a basic, yet very interesting, fact of delta option theory:

> *If an option is delta hedged efficiently on each movement of the underlying (foreign exchange) rate, and the actual volatility experienced over the life of the option is the same as that used to calculate the original premium, then the delta hedge losses of the option seller will equal the original premium received (allowing for interest accrued).*

Up to this point, delta hedging from the seller's viewpoint has been observed, but the principles established equally apply for the hedging of long option positions. In this case, delta hedging always provides small interim profits but loses through theta, and the buyer would look for increased volatility in the FX rate to ensure hedging profits exceeded the original premium expenditure.

Delta hedging transfers the FX directional risk (FX rate up or down) to that of perceived volatility in pricing against actual volatility experienced over the life of the option. Those who think FX will be more volatile in the future will be more likely to buy options, and those who think it will be less volatile will be more likely to sell.

It is for this reason, volatility anticipation, that the OTC market quotes in volatility terms and transacts automatic FX delta hedges with every transaction (unless the transaction is already delta-neutral e.g. an ATM straddle). Note, however, that these delta FX hedges are usually done as spot FX deals, rather than forward FX, which leaves rho risk open. Rho is usually adjusted on a portfolio basis by transacting a foreign exchange swap; rho neutrality is dealt with in more detail elsewhere in this book.

Note the following on the frequency of delta hedging; delta neutrality theory states that options should be re-hedged on *every* change in delta based on the points of measurement for the volatility of the FX rate. For instance, if volatility is measured on an FX rate at noon every day, then delta hedging should be done once a day, at noon. If, on the other hand, volatility is measured based on a spot FX rate at every minute during the day, the delta hedge should, accordingly, be adjusted every minute.

There are, however, practical problems which arise from the above. 24 hours in the foreign exchange markets is a very long time to wait for a specified time of day, by which time the FX rate may have already made, or be making, its most significant move. Furthermore, no account of the bid-offer FX spread is taken into account, so very frequent delta hedging is not feasible. There is no ideal solution to either of these problems, but most delta hedgers tend to adjust their positions at points measured against profit/loss impact over one day forecasts (see gamma versus theta trading), or by movement in FX rates to standard deviation points.

Option replication

Instead of paying a premium to buy an option, one can replicate the performance by delta hedging. For example, to protect against a rise in the GBP, one could purchase the 1.90 GBP Call (USD Put) for USD 220 000 which would cover GBP 10 000 000 of risk for one month. To replicate this insurance, one could buy GBP 5 000 000 forward FX at 1.90 (the initial delta hedge on GBP 10 000 000), and continually re-hedge according to the 1.90 Call option's delta throughout the one month term. The result would be total purchases of GBP 10 000 000 (if spot over 1.90) or zero (if under 1.90) on the maturity date. The average rate of the purchases and sales of GBP throughout the one month period would be 1.9220 if holding 10 000 000, or a realized loss of USD 220 000 if holding zero GBP on the final day (assuming the actual FX volatility was the same as input for calculating the option delta). Assuming also that there is an underlying transaction of short GBP (i.e. the reason for the option hedge in the first place) these pounds would be finally purchased at 1.9920 (the average rate) or at a rate below 1.90 plus .022 (the realized loss equivalent in FX terms). This is exactly the same result as if the straight 1.90 GBP Call option was purchased.

The advantage of replication is that there is no initial outlay of premium and any resultant loss on maturity can be lost in the final underlying transaction (in the example, by averaging against the purchase of GBP at a rate below 1.90). The disadvantage is that the person replicating has the responsibility of continuously monitoring the option delta to ensure all movements are captured, 24 hours a day.

Naked hedging

This is not sitting at the trading desk without wearing a tie! Naked hedging is a naive method of hedging occasionally used by speculators, based on a simple principle:

An option will only be exercised if, on maturity, it is in-the-money.

Therefore no hedge is maintained when the option is OTM and 100% is hedged when ITM, all hedging being done at the strike price. This method is usually employed by writers who hope to profit by the entire premium received. Options are sold as OTM and only hedged when the underlying FX rate crosses the strike price. This method can be successful when (1) the FX rate never approaches the strike, and (2) when the FX rate goes through the strike (100% hedge transacted) and stays ITM without recrossing the strike. In the first case, the writer pockets the option premium without ever doing anything – easy money! In the second case, the writer has to put the 100% hedge on as close to the strike as possible and simply uses the hedge to deliver the currency demanded by the exercise, on maturity. Premium, again, is collected in full by the option writer.

So, what is wrong with naked hedging? Well, one can be lucky with this simple approach and one does not need a computer to work out the delta hedge at any moment in time. The problem lies in applying a 100% or zero hedge at a specific rate (the strike) over the life-span of the option. The FX rate could easily cross and re-cross the strike several times and in each case the hedge has to be put on or taken off. Each time the hedger will suffer from the bid-offer spread and may even have some sleepless nights when the FX rate just 'sits' on the strike. If unlucky, this strike/FX rate point could be crossed 20 or 30 times a day in which case the hedger would probably suffer to such an extent that he might buy the offending option back. Unfortunately, this action would not be very pleasant, as the option cost will be at its highest – an ATM option!

In the very early days of FX options, a few institutions hedged in this manner but naked hedging is no longer used by professionals. A few spot FX dealers sometimes like to play naked hedging (because they are constantly trading in the underlying) but rarely for large amounts.

Gamma neutrality

An example of delta neutrality achieved through an FX transaction has been shown. Delta neutrality may also be attained by using other options or a combination of options and FX, the big difference being the effect on the overall gamma. There is no gamma in FX as the delta is constant at 100%; therefore only options can reduce or increase the gamma within an option portfolio. Bought options have positive gamma (delta movements will result in profit) so will always assist in reducing negative gamma in a portfolio; short options will increase negative gamma, etc.

Gamma neutrality can be achieved by buying or selling delta-neutral options that have similar gamma because of strike and maturity similarities, or by increasing/decreasing the face value amounts so that the gammas look alike. The problem then is of other option risks arising such as theta and vega; the only absolute answer to permanent gamma neutrality is to buy/sell an option of identical nature, effectively offsetting the original option. This, however, is not always practicable in a large portfolio of options and most traders tend to buy or sell short date options to negate gamma. The advantages of short date options (under one month to expiry but usually under ten days) is that they carry high to very high gamma and theta but low vega (volatility risk). As many traders take vega as their main risk position, short date options will not substantially effect them.

Gamma versus theta trading

Movement of delta (gamma) is unwelcome in short option positions where losses might ensue, but it is very much hoped for in long option positions where profits should emanate. In either of these circumstances, theta tends to pull in the opposite direction; short options will accrue profit through time and long options will lose, so many option traders play the gamma versus theta scenario. Gamma and theta tend to be strong and weak at the same points; strong when ATM and close to maturity, weak when OTM with a long time to maturity. This 'natural' offset in value is usually calculated over a one day time span to give the trader a profit and loss scenario for theta versus a range of movement in spot.

Example:
Short 1.90 GBP 10 000 000 Call (USD Put), 1 month to maturity hedged by purchase of GBP 5 000 000 forward at 1.90. Sensitivity to spot movement over the next day (i.e. 1 day theta).

Fwd FX	Delta (GBP)	Gamma (GBP)	P/L (USD)
1.93	(1 800 000)	(500 000)	(28 000)
1.92	(1 300 000)	(600 000)	(11 000)
1.91	(700 000)	(700 000)	0
1.90	0		4 000
1.89	700 000	(700 000)	0
1.88	1 300 000	(600 000)	(11 000)
1.87	1 800 000	(500 000)	(28 000)

The above example shows the effect of FX rate movement on the position over a one day (the next day) time frame. If the FX rate does not move at all, then the full positive effect of theta is felt, but with any FX rate movement this profit is reduced to the point of zero at 1.91 or 1.89. The losses shown at rates above 1.91 and below 1.89 will only be recorded if no further delta hedging is done at rates between 1.90 (the start point) and those levels. Normally, the trader would try to remain delta-neutral by buying or selling sterling as the FX rate moves against the position. Many traders take the zero profit level as the indicator for re-hedging to remain delta-neutral, while others work against standard deviation points for foreign exchange movement. Whatever the method, success will depend on the volatility of the FX rate over the life span of the option, versus the rates at which the hedges were transacted.

One can also see from the example the apparent attraction of running a short option position, namely that time (theta) works in favour of the position and the general perception that one can hedge 'at the worse case' for zero profit. The problem is one of picking the right moment to re-hedge. Take the example of the trader who buys GBP 700 000 at 1.91 only to see GBP return to 1.90 over the one day time frame. The trader will lose USD 7000 (1.91 − 1.90 × GBP 700 000) on the hedge with only USD 4000 theta credit leaving net loss of USD 3000. This is known as 'whipsawing' or 'being gamma-ed'. On the other hand, the trader who set his re-hedge at a higher FX level (say, at a delta of GBP 10 00 000) would experience no gamma and would profit by the theta of USD 4000. There is no perfect solution to this problem, and the success of gamma versus theta trading ultimately depends on the volatility of the underlying FX rate versus that implied in the option's premium.

The example shows a short option position hedged in FX which will produce a short vega position. Normally, vega risk is the prime reason for such a position, not trying to profit by gamma versus theta. In other words, gamma versus theta trading is usually secondary to volatility trading (vega trading) where, in this case, the trader is expecting market volatility rates to decline by taking a short option position. If volatility rates decline by virtue of quiet FX rates, then the trader will gain by both primary (lower volatility rates) and by secondary (profitable gamma versus theta trading during the period before volatility rates drop) risk factors. It should not be forgotten that volatility rates are forecasts of future FX volatility, whereas current FX volatility is calculated from historical rates – the two (future forecast and current) volatility rates may well differ.

Volatility trading

Trading the vega risk for profit is, by far, the most popular method employed by option professionals. The OTC market quotes in volatility terms and processes transactions as delta-neutral straddles, strangles or by constructing a simultaneous foreign exchange delta hedge. In all cases each counterparty is protected against an immediate move in the FX rate and therefore assumes the major risk as vega. At the time of writing, the CME has plans to allow for volatility trading in the currency option pits, and other exchanges will, no doubt, follow.

The option trader will position his or her portfolio to take advantage of perceived moves in future volatility rates. A simple strategy to position for higher volatility would be to purchase delta-neutral options to give a long vega, positive gamma, but this would also create negative theta risk so the trader may sell delta-neutral options with shorter maturities to lower theta, though also reducing the positive gamma. It all depends on the perception of the trader as to just how volatility rates will react over time. Generally, the trader will look at his position risks on a day by day basis to coincide with daily revaluation of the portfolio. In other words, if the option portfolio is marked-to-market on a daily basis, profit and loss will accrue on the same time scale and the trader's objectives will be set accordingly.

Short date option (under one month, but more generally under 10 days to maturity) volatility rates tend to reflect the current spot FX conditions of a given currency pair. If spot is moving sharply and there is widespread uncertainty, then the option volatility rates tend to be higher and the option trader who perceived this occurrence might profit from positive gamma and through vega, both risk factors outweighing the negative theta associated with long option positions. The trader would probably take his profit at some point during the period of high volatility by selling delta-neutral options.

There are many, many aspects of volatility trading but the vega/gamma/theta scenarios are the most often encountered. Using this scenario as a base, other 'plays' will now be described.

Playing the 'smile'

Chapter 6 (Option Pricing) described a feature of volatility across strikes with same maturity – the volatility strike curve or 'smile'. The reader may find it helpful to refer to Fig. 6.4.

As OTM options carry higher volatility than those ATM, one can take advantage by selling the wings of the curve and buying the ATM. For example, a trader might sell a 30% delta Call and a 30% delta Put (a 30% delta strangle), and buy a 50% delta Call and 50% delta Put (an ATM straddle). This is, in effect, a delta-neutral butterfly and as such results in a net premium outflow, i.e. the ATM options have much greater value than the OTM. For this reason, the position would carry long vega, negative theta and positive gamma, and the trader would reduce all these risks by increasing the amount of the sold options e.g. for 130% of the face value of the ATMs. This is now no longer a butterfly, but the objectives of the position are not for profit on maturity or for profit on spot direction. They are purely for interim results. The option trader will make an instant profit through revaluation of the portfolio – unless the computer software takes the smile into account (most do not) – simply because the volatility is higher on the sold options (the trader extends the profit by selling more OTM as part of reducing the gamma/theta/vega).

Example:
Bought 1.50 DEM straddle (against USD) for USD 10 million 'per leg' (10 million of Calls and 10 million of Puts) at 12.0% vol.; sold 1.47/1.53 DEM strangle for USD 13 million per leg at 12.3 vol.; premium paid .0578 DEM per USD (DEM 578 000); premium received .0343 DEM per USD (DEM 445 900).

Revaluation at 12.0% volatility:

1.50 straddle – .0578 DEM	P/L: zero	(.0578 – .0578)
1.47/1.53 strangle – .0330 DEM	P/L: + DEM 16 900	(.0343 – .0330)

The revaluation rate used above is 12.0 as this is the ATM volatility rate. It is normal to use the ATM rate for such procedures but profit would be recorded at other rates; a higher rate would result in profit on the straddle and less on the strangle, a lower rate would give more profit on the strangle but less on the straddle, etc.

This delta-neutral strategy is initially quite low in vega, gamma and theta risk. Spot movement in either direction will cause the short options to gain value whilst the long options lose value resulting in a move towards negative gamma, positive theta and short vega. If spot stands still, then elapse of time will move towards negative theta, positive gamma and positive vega, reflecting the continuance of the long ATM options with lessening effect of the OTM short options.

Advantages in playing the volatility smile

The reason quoted for playing the volatility smile is that the position carries little initial risk and any spot movement will take the position towards the short option positions, to the point where ATM status might be achieved. If it is achieved part of the position can be reversed (buy the ATM reversing the short position, sell the OTM reversing the long position) so profiting further from the smile. However, the reality probably has more to do with taking advantage of the inadequacy of current option revaluation software systems (system arbitrage).

Disadvantages in playing the volatility smile

Sharp spot movement in either direction, depending on how close the position is to maturity, will produce strong negative gamma at a time of increasing volatility rates, both of which will work against this strategy especially as there are more sold options than bought. OTM options act as very good insurance for sharp or 'gapping' FX movements and are frequently bought to cover such contingencies, hence the higher implied volatility for low delta options in the first place. Selling these OTM options can be dangerous in cases where the spot FX rate gaps, especially if the trader is motivated to do so by a system arbitrage for profit.

Trading the volatility curve

Volatility varies according to the maturity of the option; longer date options (one year and beyond) are relatively stable, but maturities of one month are much less so. Therefore, an increase of 1% (absolute) in one month volatility may have little, or no effect, on one year volatility (for a particular currency pair) resulting in volatility curves across maturities. These curves may be positive (volatility rates increasing with time), negative (declining with longer maturities) or flat (short and long dated maturities similar) depending on the currency pair.

Table 8.1 demonstrates an example where, for the same currency pair, there can be three possibilities in terms of the volatility curve, and it is worth pointing out the circumstances that may produce such variances. All three possibilities show one year at 8.7% so longer term options will all be priced the same but in Positive, short term options are priced lower, possibly due to very quiet current spot FX rates, but anticipation that the market will not stay as such for very long. In Negative, volatility rates are higher towards the shorter term options, due possibly to the fact that current spot FX rates are volatile but not

Table 8.1 JPY/USD FX option volatilities (% p.a.)

	1 Week	1 Month	3 Months	6 Months	1 Year
(1) Positive	7.5	8.0	8.3	8.5	8.7
(2) Negative	10.0	9.5	9.3	9.0	8.7
(3) Flat	8.7	8.7	8.7	8.7	8.7

expected to remain so for long. In the case of Flat, all volatility rates are the same, indicating a perceived continuance of the current spot FX market conditions.

Volatility curves will change with market perceptions of future activity. Within the short date markets (under one month but usually under 10 days to maturity) volatility rates have peaks and troughs around economic statistic release dates; options are bought for maturity on such dates to take advantage of the gamma potential on sharp spot FX movement (should the release figures be different from those expected). Spot FX activity around such figures varies over time to the relevance of particular statistics, for example, USA Trade Data used to be the most important figure release for it is directly related to the requirement to purchase or sell US dollars. For a time, the indicators of inflation, the Retail Price Index and Industrial Price Index, were paramount but nowadays it seems 'non-farm pay-rolls' is the all-important figure to guide the markets. It all depends on the current state of the economy and what factor is being scrutinized to predict the future.

So, economic release dates tend to have higher volatilities but, on the other hand, Monday maturities have lower volatilities due to the fact that the weekend carries three days time value (Friday to Monday) with only one day of active FX markets. In other words, three days' theta for one day's risk. Again, this is only apparent in short date options but is a factor heavily traded for profit through vega, theta versus gamma, or both.

At the time of writing, short date trading accounts for something like 75% of the interbank market, hence most plays made on the volatility curve (or blips in it) are of under one month maturity. Longer date scenarios can be very profitable in that changes in vega have an increasing effect as the option maturity lengthens e.g. a 1% change for an ATM option in one month might produce .11% profit, in six months .28% and .40% in the one year. The problem is that longer date options tend to move slowly so these scenarios are usually constructed to profit over months, rather than days, or hours, in the case of short term maturities.

Trading volatility using spot direction bias

In 'Playing the smile' above a way of attaining profit from the curve of volatility across strikes with the same maturity was observed. The curve or smile in the example was uniform in the sense that 30% delta Call and Put strikes were equidistant from the ATM rate of 1.50 (DEM per USD); the USD Call at 1.53 was 0.03 DEM above, and the USD Put at 1.47 was 0.03 below. This uniformity of the curve is typical where the demand for strikes in one direction is the same as the demand for strikes in the other, so there is no real perception of the FX rate moving up or down.

However, there is often a bias in the perceived future direction of the spot FX rate which skews the smile towards the strikes in that particular direction. This feature was mentioned in Chapter 6; refer to Fig. 6.5. In this figure, low delta Puts have higher volatility than the equivalent delta Calls indicating a bias towards the FX rate moving down where the OTM Puts would gain by increasing gamma, theta and vega. While the same would apply to the Calls if the FX rate moved up, the market perception is that ATM volatility would be higher than at present in one direction (towards OTM Puts) than it would in the opposite direction (towards OTM Calls). This is somewhat difficult to understand because, in theory, an FX rate move in either direction should have the same effect on option market volatilities. The Black-Scholes option pricing formula does not make any provision for bias in FX rate direction, leaving the market to adjust the volatility factor as compensation in the same manner as for OTM options generally. The market behaves in this fashion because, in an active option portfolio, it is usually better to be long OTM options, for the benefits of gamma and vega should be underlying spot rate move towards those option strikes – this is why OTM options are marked-up in volatility terms in the first place. Now, if the underlying FX rate has a continuing trend in one direction over a period of months, the typical option portfolio will have many options outstanding with strikes in the past FX range but with few in the direction of the trend. For example, at the time of writing, the USD trend has been downward from 1.70 DEM per USD to around 1.46 in the space of around six months. As options are normally transacted with deltas in the range of 20 to 50 (strikes are likely to be around the prevailing spot FX rate) an active portfolio would consist of options dealt some months ago with strikes in the region of, say, 1.85–1.55; options dealt some weeks ago with strikes 1.60 to 1.50 and some recently traded options with strikes around 1.50 – there will be few options in the portfolio with strikes of below 1.45. Hence the 'uncharted' areas below 1.45 may carry more risk (higher volatility) for the option trader as volatility levels have not yet been experienced with spot at such levels – there are no strikes currently in the portfolio – and as such OTM USD Puts (which will have strike below 1.46) are bid higher than OTM Calls (strikes will be above 1.46).

The option trader will attempt to profit from the bias by constructing his portfolio to be long options in the direction of the spot trend, looking for higher volatilities, and short in the opposite direction where no volatility increase is anticipated, even if spot reversed trend.

The reader should understand that the option trader is not attempting to profit by directional spot movement in the sense of buying or selling a currency (he is delta-neutral) but by profiting though volatility changes (due to spot movement).

Example:

Buy   USD Put (DEM Call), strike 1.44 (DEM per USD), 2 weeks, at 12.5 volatility.

Sell   USD Call (DEM Put), strike 1.4785, 2 weeks at 12.1 volatility.

        Current FX rate: 1.4600; ATM volatility 12.0.

The two 30% delta options are neutralized against initial spot movement by buying 60% in the underlying FX at 1.46 (long 30 delta USD Put = short 30% USD in FX *and* short 30% USD Call = short 30% in FX) leaving volatility as the prime risk.

Position is currently delta-neutral, theta-neutral but carries positive gamma with increasing vega and negative theta on declining spot; negative gamma, declining vega and positive theta on increasing spot.

Assume the FX rate declines to 1.44 over two days. The long USD Puts will be ATM providing the highest time value and furthermore volatility rate have increased from 12.0 to 12.5 for ATM. The position profits from positive gamma without loss in volatility terms. If the FX rate increased to 1.4790 and there was no increase in volatility, the position would lose through gamma but would make a small volatility gain (option sold at 12.1 versus ATM unchanged at 12.0).

Buying OTM Calls/selling OTM Puts or buying OTM Puts/selling OTM Calls is a very popular OTC composite trade known as 'risk reversal'. It is quoted in volatility terms as the difference between the two volatility levels indicating whether the Call or Put is higher, and is always dealt in conjunction with a simultaneous delta hedge (the addition of the two option deltas). Without the delta hedge, the risk reversal is the same as a cylinder or range forward but for some reason the market did not pick up 'delta-neutral cylinder' as the dealing term.

Trading volatility between two currency pairs (beta play)

Each currency pair will have individual volatilities but some currencies are closely aligned with others, for example, the currencies within the narrow bands of the European Monetary System (EMS). This means that the Dutch guilder against the USD (NLG/USD) is likely to have very similar option volatility to that of the DEM/USD, the only difference being that the NLG/USD may have a slightly wider bid-offer spread to reflect the lower liquidity in that currency. Very often, banks will trade options with customers in less liquid currencies and hedge themselves in a more liquid, correlated currency – opening a beta position. The risk in such positions is that of change in the correlation between the two currencies and option traders may identify opportunities for future correlation changes and position themselves accordingly.

Delta-neutral long positions in one currency pair are initiated against short delta-neutral positions in a second currency pair. As the underlying FX rate changes, and time passes, so the two positions will accumulate individual currency deltas. Some banks do not bother to re-hedge these deltas (by transacting a cross-currency FX deal) in which case one position will carry profits and the other losses (but hopefully a net profit!). There can be problems on maturity with beta scenarios as it is possible for one option to be ITM and the other OTM even if the correlation has held over the life of the options. This is due to the variances in the forward FX rate caused by different interest rates in the two currencies. The option trader should be careful to allow for these differences at inception but, even so, interest rates can also change while the beta position is running.

There have been several instances over the last few years where beta scenarios have proven to be profitable, particularly on the EMS currencies as they move towards eventual convergence.

The OTC market is very efficient in that the participants have reduced the efforts of dealing to the one denominator peculiar to options i.e. volatility. In the same manner, volatility plays can be dealt based on quotes for such, or even combinations of plays! For example, in the beta scenario an option trader can ask for the ATM GBP/USD versus DEM/USD and receive a volatility price representing the difference between the two individuals; this avoids the negative impact of dealing across two bid-offer spreads. Examples are given in Chapter 9.

Aspects of rho

The reader will have noted that the OTC market endeavours, where it is practical, to reduce initial risk to that of volatility only, and that this is done by trading delta-neutral straddles, strangles, etc. based on the forward FX rate (the underlying rate for European style options). This avoids initial rho, or interest rate risk. However, there is a basic exception to the rule of dealing ATMF (at-the-money forward) delta-neutral straddles, and that is in the case of quoting individual options or combinations that involve buying/selling Calls and Puts against each other, such as risk reversals. These options are transacted with spot FX deals to give delta neutrality but this creates rho risk and needs to be hedged to avoid the possibly negative consequences of movement in the interest rate differential, or forward FX swap rate. In theory, rho could be negated by dealing the forward FX rate rather than spot, but market participants are reluctant to do this as it uses up counterparty credit lines for the duration of the option, whereas spot is only two days.

In addition to the above, rho will accumulate in an active portfolio of options due to anything that might change the delta of an option, i.e. FX rate movement, volatility, theta. Portfolio rho risk can be identified by reference to the options delta and hedged by a simple foreign exchange swap.

Example:
Consider this delta-neutral position:
Long USD 10 000 000 Put, 30% delta for two months; short USD 10 000 000 Call 30% delta for six months; long USD 6 000 000 FX spot.
Delta maturity position is (USD):

Spot	1 mth	2 mth	3 mth	6 mth	1 y
+6 million	0	−3 million	0	−3 million	0

To hedge rho, the trader executes the following foreign exchange swaps:

Sell USD 6 000 000 spot; buy USD 3 000 000 2 months; buy USD 3 000 000 6 months.

Rho is not considered to be a major risk but needs to be hedged if positions create large forward delta exposures. Option traders do not normally use rho as a risk to position for profit.

Proximity of expiry effects

In a delta-neutral options portfolio, gamma, vega, theta and rho are all managed on a daily basis and adjustments are made continuously. However, as individual options within the portfolio approach maturity there are dangers if the strike is close to the current spot rate. In this case, gamma and theta become more pronounced and a sharp spot FX move on the last day could produce substantial losses in the portfolio if short, or profits if long.

Sometimes, these 'last day' profits or losses are so large as to be out of context with the rationale of general volatility trading. In other words a trader may be very successful in trading volatility on an on-going basis buying low, selling high, producing unrealized profits through portfolio revaluation, only to be wiped out on maturity of one particular option due to an unlucky spot/strike convergence.

In theory, losses on such occasions should be offset by the profits from such occurrences when the portfolio is long on an option maturity rather than short. Two problems arise on this synopsis: firstly, the trader tends to react differently when short than when long, and secondly, option maturity amounts vary so the portfolio's 'lucky day' (long at spot with sharp move) may be for smaller amounts than when short; it would take a long averaging period before this effect neutralized. It would take a trader of very strong discipline and a manager with good tolerance of loss to accept this.

The usual method employed to reduce the expiry effects is to monitor the concentration of strikes at any particular level, and reduce them by buying or selling within the last week or so. In this manner, the potential danger is reduced before the proximity effects are felt. Most OTC players use some form of strike versus maturity grid to monitor, and trade against, any apparent strike concentration.

Table 8.2 shows an obvious concentration of short options in the one month between 1.46 to 1.50, but also one large maturity within one week at 1.46 – the current spot rate. Assuming that the trader is happy to assume expiry risk of a maximum of USD 20 million, he or she should reduce immediately the short 1.46 strike in the one week. A 1.44/1.46 risk reversal in 20 million will take care of

Table 8.2 Portfolio of options maturities by strike. DEM/USD (USD millions). Current spot 1.4600 (DEM per USD)

	1 Wk	2 Wk	1 Mth	2 Mth	3 Mth
1.50	10		(20)		10
1.49		50	(40)		
1.48			(35)	50	
1.47	10		(25)		15
1.46	(40)		(20)	(50)	
1.45		(10)			
1.44	20				
1.43					
1.42					
1.41					

this as the portfolio is long 20 million at 1.44. This should be done for a credit in volatility terms assuming the smile is in place as the trader will buy ATM and sell OTM. The trader may benefit further if the smile is skewed towards the lower strikes (USD Puts) which would seem to be the case due to the absence of option maturities with low strikes.

Having reduced the maturity risk in the one week ATMs to 20 million, the trader should monitor carefully the concentration in the one month 1.47–1.49 range. This can be done over the next two weeks or so when, if USD is lower (say 1.44) the trader may consider the spot move to this range unlikely and take the chance by leaving the portfolio structure as it is. If not, or if spot turns upwards, the trader may wish to reduce the concentration by buying the one month 1.48 and selling the two month 1.48 in 50 million – a calendar spread – leaving the portfolio long 15 million at 1.48 in one month. This will help reduce the dangers should spot move up over the next month, but the calendar spread will change the portfolio's vega risk structure – another factor for the trader to consider in light of his or her volatility objectives.

Omega hedging

Omega hedging will vary according to the accounting methods employed by the institution trading options. There are two basic forms of accounting: (1) using a single currency for all premiums, irrespective of the actual currency paid or received, and (2) using a multi-currency ledger holding premiums in their original currency. Unless all realized currencies are held indefinitely (see omega in Chapter 7), it becomes virtually impossible to hedge omega in the latter method without a very sophisticated system – it would be more advisable to change the accounting procedure – so omega hedging described here is in the context of the former accounting standard.

As all accounting is conducted in one currency, hedging omega is fairly straightforward, and it is only the recognition of the risk that needs explanation. Option premiums are converted to base currency on inception – when the premium is paid or received – and this is the initial omega risk that needs to be hedged (premium currency against base currency). As time moves on so the value of the option changes and the omega hedge has to be adjusted to this amount. This is fairly easy but, if the principle of portfolio delta neutrality is being observed by transacting spot and forward FX hedges, we need to allow for the realized P/L and unrealized P/L from such.

All omega hedges are conducted in the premium currency against the accounting currency so, for example, in the case of DEM/GBP options for a USD based bank, this would be either DEM/USD or GBP/USD depending on the premium currency, which has to be either DEM or GBP. (Note: It is preferable to run one option portfolio per currency pair e.g. DEM/GBP, rather than two DEM/GBP and GBP/DEM, in which case omega risk is only relevant to one-currency (GBP or DEM), resulting in GBP/USD or DEM/USD being the omega hedging pair).

The amount of omega risk in an option portfolio can be calculated as follows:

The current net *value* of all option premiums calculated in their natural currency plus net unrealized *profit/loss amounts* of any outstanding FX hedge transactions in the same currency.

The result, in currency terms, is the amount to be hedged against the base (accounting) currency.

Example:

Short DEM 28 000 000 Call (GBP Put), strike 2.80 (DEM per GBP), 3 months. Hedged by FX forward 3 months; long DEM 8 400 000 at 2.8400. Current FX forward: 2.8250.

Current option price: 0.68% of GBP 10 000 000 = − GBP 68 000.00
Unrealized FX P/L (DEM 8 400 000 / 2.84) − (DEM 8 400 000 / 2.8250) =
      + GBP 15 704.90

Net omega position is (− GBP 68 000) + (+ GBP 15 704.90) =
      − GBP 52 295.10

(Note (1): '−' = 'short')
(Note (2): Bought option = '+', sold option = '−')

In the above example, the option trader would buy GBP 52 295.10 against USD at the current *forward* rate for three months and hold same in a separate portfolio 'omega hedging'. Any negative aspects in revaluation of his DEM/GBP options portfolio against USD is now effectively hedged. However, if this exercise had been done on the day the premium was received, the trader would have bought GBP forward (three months) to the value of the original premium, say GBP 50 000, and therefore would be required to purchase the nominal amount of GBP 2295.10 only, representing the unrealized loss on the portfolio. Consequently, the original premium received is not effectively sold for USD at all, only swapped to the maturity date of the option i.e.:

Sold GBP 50 000 (buy USD) value spot (premium receipt date) to convert premium to base currency;
Bought GBP 50 000 (sell USD) value 3 months (option maturity date) as omega hedge.

Furthermore, any interim FX hedges transacted as spot (and therefore realized in GBP) should also be swapped until the maturity date of the option to which it is hedged. If these procedures are followed, then omega risk is negated entirely.

This section on omega risk is devoted to that of hedging only; explanation of the risk and the importance of recognizing that this risk exists is to be found in Chapter 7 (Option Trading Risks).

9

OTC Market Practice

THIS book would not be complete without a chapter devoted to the OTC market practices. Chapter 2 briefly outlined the major characteristics such as volatility quoting, automatic delta hedging, the broker's role, regulation and contract specifications without going into great detail. This chapter attempts to show, by way of examples, the current market practices that are considered professional (and some that are not!). It should be understood that these routines have evolved over the years and are still in the process of development. Furthermore, these practices are those employed by the market makers such as banks and other professional institutions, including many corporate companies, but are not those generally practiced by users and some non-market makers whose primary contact would normally be through the sales desk of a bank.

The easiest way to differentiate between professional and non-professional is probably by reference to the method of quote and the media of dealing. All professional institutions quote in volatility terms using the Reuters Dealer System (a form of on-screen, two-way communication with hard print copy used extensively in the foreign exchange, and other, markets) or through recognized OTC brokers. Although telephone contact is still used by some professionals in direct dealing, this is largely on the decline. Telex is normally only used for deal confirmation.

An examination of the two methods of professional OTC dealing; direct between counterparties, and using the services of a OTC broker, follows.

Volatility quoting
Direct

Markets are made in volatility terms, quoting bid and offer rates for any particular currency, term, delta, amount etc but some market makers restrict themselves to particular currencies and amounts (e.g. some are minimum of USD 20 million, others are maximum that amount). Certain banks specialize in particular currencies, for example, the Japanese banks are very active in JPY currency pairs but less so in other currencies. Other banks might specialize in low delta option, etc. It is all a question of knowing who-does-what at any particular time and this knowledge can only be gained through experience as banks adapt and change stances in the market.

Unless specific details are given, a market maker will quote a two-way price (bid-offer) on the basis of a European style, ATMF (at-the-money forward) straddle for a given period.

Example:

'Townbank' calls 'Huntsbank' (much better than Bank A, Bank B!) on the Reuters Dealer System. The conversation would go something like this:

Townbank:	'HIHÌ FRDS
	1 MONTH DEM/USD IN USD 20M A LEG?'
Huntsbank:	'HI THERE
	11.2–11.4'

In this example, Huntsbank, the market maker (read 'market maker' as the person being asked to quote a price), is willing to buy an ATMF straddle at 11.2% volatility or sell the same at 11.4%. In both cases, the principal amount would be USD 20 million for the Call option (one 'leg' of a straddle) and 20 million for the Put, (the other leg) hence '20 a leg'. It is interesting to note that the greeting 'HIHI FRDS' or 'HI FRDS' (Hello, friends) is used extensively between market participants and is very much the norm to open conversation.

After receiving the price, Townbank has three alternatives: (1) 'hit' the bid, (2) 'take' the offer, or (3) decline the quote. In any event, Townbank will answer immediately, otherwise Huntsbank cannot he held to its price; it is deemed unprofessional not to respond within about 4 seconds unless Townbank requests confirmation of the price by stating 'any change?'. Usually, the bank requesting a price (Townbank) will know at what level they wish to transact before calling another bank for a price, so immediate response is usual.

Let us assume Townbank was looking to buy the straddle at 11.4 in which case the conversation might proceed as follows:

Townbank:	'AT 11.4, I BUY' (OR '11.4' OR 'I BUY' OR 'MINE')
Huntsbank:	'AGREED (or 'DONE')
	SPOT 1.4535
	I SELL 20M A LEG STRADDLE, STRIKE 1.4597,
	15/17MAR93,
	PREM. 1.28 PC CALL, 1.28 PC PUT.
	PLEASE PAY USD 512 000 TO MY ACCOUNT
	HUNTSBANK, NEW YORK VALUE 17FEB93'
Townbank:	'ALL AGREED FRDS, TKS VM FOR THE DEAL, BIBI FN'
Huntsbank:	TKS FOR THE CALL BIBI FN'

Any one of the statements made by Townbank from 'at 11.4, I buy' is a commitment to deal and is irrevocable from this point for both parties, unless a mutual agreement is reached not to proceed (this is extremely rare). Huntsbank acknowledges this acceptance and quotes the current spot rate to be used to compute the option premiums (Townbank may challenge this rate or request another) and then proceed to confirm the details of the options transacted, including the strike rate and actual expiry (15th March 1993) and delivery date for exercise (two days after expiry or spot date on expiry i.e. 17th March 1993). Finally, Huntsbank give instructions regarding the premium payment due to them which is paid on current spot value date (17th February 1993). While Huntsbank is confirming the details, Townbank is calculating the premium amounts and strike based on the quoted spot of 1.4535, their value for the forward FX rate, and volatility of 11.4%. They confirm acceptance of Huntsbank calculations and details by stating 'all agreed' or some such similar expression. The communication is ended after exchange of thanks with another market norm – BIBI FN (goodbye, for now).

Note that Call and Put currencies were not specified – this is because the OTC market refers to the non-USD currency as the specification in currency pairs that include the USD. This is a hangover from the days when the US exchanges formed the basis of the options markets, as both the CME and PHLX quote Calls and Puts in this manner. The idea of quoting Calls and Puts on non-USD currencies is fine from the exchange's point of view because their contracts are in the same terms and dealing amounts are in DEM, CHF, GBP, AUD, JPY, FRF etc. In the OTC market, dealing amounts are usual in USD (except for GBP/USD) so, in theory, Call and Puts should be quoted on the USD – not the currency – but the habit of quoting Calls and Puts on the non-USD currency has stuck and is confirmed under LICOM (London Interbank Currency Options Market) terms and conditions that quotes are made as such. It is recommended that the currency is always quoted, to avoid any possible confusion e.g. DEM Call, or better still DEM Call (USD Put), but the market does prefer to keep narrative down to an absolute minimum.

There follows another example, but this time for a specific option rather than an ATMF forward straddle.

Example:

Townbank calls Huntsbank on Reuters Dealer System

Townbank:	'HIHI FRDS.
	ANY INTEREST TO QUOTE 1 MONTH, DEM CALL – JPY
	PUT 89.50
	FOR DEM 20MIO DELTA AROUND 19?'
Huntsbank:	'SURE, SEC PLS
	9.5–9.9'
Townbank:	'YOURS'
Huntsbank:	'OK SPOT 87.38
	I SEE .255 PC OF DEM WITH 18 DELTA USING FWD
	−7.5?'

Townbank:	'AGREED, SO I SELL DEM CALL AT 89.50 IN DEM 20MIO
	15/17MAR92
	PREM DEM 51 000 TO TOWNBANK AG, FRANKFURT
	17FEB92
	ON HEDGE I BUY DEM 3.6MIO AT 87.38 17FEB92
	TOWNBANK FF FOR ME PLS
	WHERE FOR YOUR JPY?'
Huntsbank:	'MY JPY TO RAPONGI BANK, TOKYO PLS.'
Townbank:	'OK WILL BE DONE TKS FOR DEAL BIFN'

This deal has a different tact. Firstly, Townbank is enquiring whether Huntsbank would 'be interested' in quoting the particular option. The reason for this is that this option has a very low delta and small amount – DEM 20 million is (at the time of writing) only about USD 14 million – and some banks would rather not have the bother of quoting for this, unless it suited them. The statement 'any interest' is standard in OTC for saying 'I know you are a professional market maker therefore I am sorry to bother you with this odd option – only quote if you wish.' Most banks will try.

Secondly, the quote is for a specific option so Townbank gives all the pertinent details of Call and Put currency, strike, amount, but also an indication of the delta. Providing the delta assists Huntsbank in allowing him to adjust the volatility quote (from the ATM level) quickly. In fact, if Townbank had not stated the delta, Huntsbank would have requested it. Note that it is not possible for Townbank to calculate the exact delta because the trader does not know Huntsbank's volatility, or spot reference rate used to ascertain delta. Note also that both Call and Put currencies are defined this time, due to the absence of USD in the currency pair; there is no 'automatic' reference currency. Once again no mention is made as to whether the option is European or American style as the OTC market very rarely transacts American style options – European is quoted unless specified.

Huntsbank replies 'Sure, sec pls' (one second, please) which means 'I will need a few seconds to work out the volatility price due to the unusual nature of this option, i.e. low delta'. If used in the context of normal options, 'sec pls' would probably mean 'I am very busy at the moment but please hold on'. Shortly after, the volatility price of 9.5–9.9 is set. Note that the spread is 0.4, or 4 'ticks', which is wide compared to the 2 ticks for the ATMF in the prior example. This is to allow for the illiquid nature of the specific option giving the market maker a little added protection on dealing.

Townbank responds to the quote by a simple 'yours', meaning 'this option now belongs to you' – just another short and quick way of expressing the fact that the 9.5 bid price is dealt, leaving Huntsbank the buyer, Townbank the seller. Huntsbank agrees the trade and sets current spot as 87.38 JPY per DEM (the standard way of quoting this currency pair is JPY/DEM in the FX market). Huntsbank then ask if Townbank can agree to the premium of .255% of DEM, quoting the delta and forward points used to arrive at this amount. Townbank agree, confirm the transaction and set the payment instructions for the premium.

This option requires a simultaneous FX trade to neutralize the delta and Townbank confirm this part of the transaction by buying DEM 3.6 million (18% of DEM 20 million) at the quoted spot rate of 87.38. Payment instructions for receipt of the DEM are given and a request is made as to where Huntsbank would like to receive their JPY as counterpayment. Huntsbank provide the name of their correspondent bank in Tokyo and Townbank acknowledges, thank Huntsbank for the deal and finsih with the usual 'BIFN'.

Every deal in OTC has to be 'instructed', i.e. payment instructions are exchanged between the parties at the time of the transaction. This is necessary due to the absence of a centralized clearing house (unlike the exchanges) and each OTC market participant will have its own individual arrangements for processing currency payments between countries. Instructing each deal is time consuming for the trader so a few shortcuts exist. Firstly, abbreviations are used extensively like 'FF' in the previous example, meaning Frankfurt, the usual centre for DEM payments. Secondly, payment instructions can be recorded within the Reuters Dealer System, retrieved and transmitted into the conversation by inputting a code letter for each currency payment. Finally, there are local procedures in some major centres like London and New York whereby spot FX deals between banks in the centre are verified and instructed outside the dealing room by the operations or 'back office' staff. This benefits the traders who simply state 'swap outside' on the FX portion of the option transaction. Furthermore, it also acts as verbal confirmation of the FX deal and the fact that it has been recorded in the bank's books – traders have been known to forget to write up deals!

This process of swapping instructions outside the dealing room may well extend to the OTC options markets in the future. In fact, some institutions are already doing so but it is not yet standard practice, particularly between banks in different centres.

Brokers

Most of the major FX broking houses have divisions or subsidiaries set up to cater for the OTC FX options market. In addition, there are some exclusive – FX options only – firms established with some running extended hours from one location.

Quoting is in volatility terms with transactions taking place over direct telephone lines. Where direct lines do not exist, some institutions use the Reuters Dealer System for communication. Dial-up telephone communication should be avoided due to potential problems of market making without instant access to prices.

To avoid constant answering of direct telephone lines, most dealing rooms now employ the use of 'brokers boxes' for the relay of existing prices, requests for prices and information. These are small (but loud!) speakers located in or on the dealing desks. Bank dealers respond by speaking into the direct line telephone if interested in a particular quote, or on notification that one's own price is about to be dealt on.

Brokers form a very valuable service in that they can form liquid two-way markets by combining the best offers and bids from a variety of sources. This is done by banks giving price support through various methods such as: (1) 'run downs' – some banks will regularly provide brokers with full bid and offer prices for every period from one month to one year, for a particular currency pair, (2) specific bids and offers in selected periods, and (3) bank responses to specific requests. The rest is done by the broker who in many cases is able to 'convince' bank traders to bid or offer at a broker's suggested level.

It is probably fair to say that, in normal markets, a broker's bid-ask spread should be tighter than that obtained on a direct basis which, of course, is paid for by the commission levied on the trading bank. Banks' attitudes vary to the role of the broker, and some institutions have reputations of being 'direct' or 'brokers' banks. The leading market makers may well 'have lines' (conduct broking business) with all OTC brokers, whereas other banks may restrict these to a selected few. Over time, banks may occasionally cease dealing ('line out') with specific brokers due to transaction problems or for other reasons.

A note of warning at this point. Banks pay brokers commission on every trade and this means that it is very much in the broker's interest to look after his lines, and this gives a certain amount of power to the bank trader that has to be handled on a professional basis. Many friendships are established through the broker-trader relationship, and it is incumbent on both sides that such be conducted at a very professional level. Otherwise biased pricing on the trader's part, or unreasonable requests from the broker may result which would not be in the best interests of either party, or the market as a whole. Codes of conduct are now laid down by most institutions as well as some regulatory authorities such as the Bank of England (see Chapter 11).

Returning to market practice, brokers relay prices through the boxes on a continuous basis but these are generally for specific interests or exceptional cases. Volatility rates for the regular one to twelve month periods (for the major currencies) as displayed on the Reuters Monitor System or Telerate system (information display systems – not conversational) by many brokers and a typical display is shown in Table 9.1.

The bank trader will usually have one or more of these pages on his screen and, by way of example, may hear over the broker box 'pay 11.3 in one month DEM, ATM Call, for 10 only'. This would be a middle of the market bid, yet for a small amount of USD 10 000 000. Another box may shout 'looking for a price in 6 weeks 30 delta DEM Put, up to 100 million' – here the broker is looking for a two way price for a specific option, a 30 Delta DEM Put. Assuming the bank trader has no particular interest in this option but is willing to make a market in

Table 9.1 Brokers information page

	DEM/USD	JPY/USD	GBP/USD	JPY/DEM
1 Mth	13.2–13.6	9.6–9.8	12.8–13.2	10.1–10.4
2 Mths	12.6–12.9	9.5–9.8	12.5–12.8	9.8–10.2
3 Mths	12.6–12.8	9.5–9.7	12.4–12.7	9.6–9.8
6 Mths	12.5–12.7	9.2–9.5	12.3–12.7	9.3–9.6
1 Year	12.3–12.5	9.2–9.4	12.2–12.5	9.2–9.5

it, he may respond '11.5–11.9 on 50, for starters', meaning that this price is not too aggressive (four ticks wide), and is for 50 million USD only. However, the broker will be more than pleased as this quote, 11.5–11.9 provides a base to form the market for this particular option. The broker may also get from another bank trader 'I will pay 11.7 for that one, good for your amount'. The broker now has a market 11.7–11.9, 100 million by 50 million, which is quickly reflected to the bank that asked the broker for a price in the first place. If the original request was from a bank looking to sell that option, the trader might well give the broker the following order 'I offer 100 million at 11.8'. The broker quickly goes to the bank that bid 11.7 saying 'can offer you 100 at 11.8', to which the bank responds '11.7 best' meaning that it is not interested in increasing its bid from that level. Now the broker's market is 11.7–11.8 on 100 million.

From the perspective of the bank that made the first market, 11.5–11.9, the following would have been relayed over the brokers box:

'Pay 11.7 inside you for 100'
'Original interest offers at 11.8, I am now 11.7–11.8 in 100, any interest, or shall I take you off?'

Here the broker recognizes that the original price 11.5–11.9 has no relevance, but asks the bank trader if he wishes to do anything on the new market of 11.7–11.8; otherwise he can 'take him off' i.e. cancel the price.

This is just one small example of how a broker forms his markets, after all he plays no part in the final transaction and so, in theory, is prevented from making a price. However, many brokers do give their best idea of what a price should be for a particular option, but it is up to the bank trader to actually make the price. There are many games played in the market to encourage business and the brokers are usually very experienced in most. For example, in a quiet market with no incoming orders or requests, the broker may well invent the request and ask a trader for a market in the hope of arousing interest and, hopefully, a deal. Traders are also good at this game claiming that 'customer' interest is at hand and asking other banks or brokers for prices on imaginary options.

In all of the previous examples, there has been no mention of the name of the bank behind the respective prices. Counterparty names are not exchanged or given by the broker until a firm commitment to trade has been indicated. This is very different from the exchanges where it is open knowledge who is on the bid and offer. The broker carries a professional responsibility not to pass bank names on deals except between the parties concerned, and this responsibility extends to the bank trader not to entice the broker to divulge bank names on deals other than those that bank has entered into.

Notwithstanding the above, it occasionally happens that one bank's name may not be acceptable, for credit reasons, to the other in a transaction. In this case, both banks remain committed to deal at the agreed price in which case the broker goes 'either way' on the price. For example, if the 11.8 offer was taken for 100 million (see previous example) and one bank could not accept the other's name for the transaction, the broker's market would be 11.8 either way or 11.8

'choice', meaning the market is both bid and offered at the same price but the transaction cannot be completed.

Normally, the broker will ask another bank to switch the transaction or do a Put-through in which case a third bank will step in and act as counterparty to the other two. No brokerage charge is made on the third bank for this service.

To help avoid this problem, there is an unofficial tiering of OTC participants with regard to their credit worthiness. This is not done by reference to the bank's balance sheet but by experience of the particular bank's profile in the marketplace. Hence a broker will often qualify his or her price by suggesting that there may be a problem in concluding the deal if the volatility price is agreed. For example, 'pay 11.3 for a small name' or maybe 'pay 11.3 but might be a name you cannot do'. In the later case, the broker may remember a prior case where his or her line had declined the bank on the present bid of 11.3.

Spread trading

Another popular form of trading in OTC is the spread trade practiced both direct and through brokers. There are various types including the following:

Call (Put) spreads:

Buy Call (Put) low strike, sell Call (Put) higher strike, or vice versa. Spot FX deal for difference in delta.

Risk reversal:

Buy Call (Put) with strike in one direction, sell equivalent Put (Call) delta strike in opposite direction or vice versa. Spot FX deal for total of the two deltas.

Calendar spread:

Buy options for one date, sell same strike or delta for another, or vice versa. Spot FX deal for difference in delta (if any).

Beta spread:

Buy options in one currency pair, sell in another, usually with similar deltas. Spot FX deals in both currency pairs unless spread dealt as straddles.

In addition, the market will quote for combinations of the above such as:

Buy 1 month DEM/USD 30 delta Calls, sell 2 months DEM/USD 30 delta Puts.

This is a calendar spread and risk reversal combined.

The object of quoting volatility as spreads rather than individuals is to avoid trading across two bid-offer spreads. In FX, why buy DEM (sell USD) and sell GBP (buy USD) when you can simply buy DEM and sell GBP? The same applies to options volatility trading but there are two different methods of quoting volatility spreads:

(1) By netting the two individuals and closing the spread, or

(2) By quoting one of the individuals with normal spread and quoting 'choice' price for the other.

Example:

30 Delta Calls are quoted 11.2–11.4;

30 Delta Puts are quoted 11.4–11.6.

Method (1):

Spread price based on these two individuals is 0.0–0.4 by simply netting the bid on one against the offer on the other, and vice versa. However, there would be no benefit from such a quote as it is identical to the individuals so market maker would 'narrow' or close the quote to, say, 0.1–0.3.

This means market maker would now buy Calls at 11.2 / sell Puts at 11.5 (net .3) or sell Calls at 11.4, buy Puts at 11.5 (net .1).

Method (2):

Market maker quotes the Calls 11.2–11.4 but quotes the Puts as 11.5 choice.

This is the same net result as method (1) as market maker trades on exactly the same volatility levels, however, this method is much preferred as it is more simple and has bid offer clearly defined.

Exercise procedure

OTC option flexibility means final maturity can be at any reasonable time during the day but the market has adopted two main time zones and set 3.00pm as the final point of expiry. These two 'cut-off' times are:

(1)   3.00pm London Time
(2)   3.00pm Tokyo Time.

Institutions in Australia also deal for 3.00pm Sydney time, but this is generally restricted to local transactions in the local currency.

New York have traditionally used 10.00am New York time which coincides with 3.00pm London except for a week or so each year. To avoid having two cut-off times, 3.00pm London and 10.00am New York, the market has been moving away from 3.00pm London and adopting the 10.00am New York as standard. Presumably, it is better to have traders in Europe exercising at 4.00pm London, once a year than have the confusion and possible disagreement as to what cut-off time was originally transacted. The new ICOM terms (see Chapter 12) state 10.00am New York as the Western Time Zone expiry time.

OTC options have to be exercised individually, each buyer calling the seller to notify exercise and to exchange payment instructions. As in direct volatility quoting, this is usually done on the Reuters Dealer System at a time close to the final expiry; it all depends on how close the strike is to the current spot rate. Deep ITM options are usually exercised earlier in the day.

Example:

Huntsbank is long GBP Call (USD Put) with Townbank maturing 15th February in the amount of GBP 20 000 000, strike 1.80 (USD per GBP). Current spot rate is 1.8125.

On 15th February Huntsbank will see from its portfolio that it has a bought GBP Call option maturing that day and, with spot at 1.8125, has intrinsic value of .0125 USD per GBP. Huntsbank must contact Townbank and exercise this option before 3.00pm (10.00am New York time) that day.

Huntsbank calls Townbank on the Reuters Dealer System at 2.45pm with 'XCISE' or 'EXER' as a suffix against the calling code:

Huntsbank:	'XCISE'
	'HIHI THERE I BUY GBP 20 000 000 AT 1.80 VALUE 17TH
	FEBRUARY DIRECT TO ME PLS'.
Townbank:	'AGREED, SWAP OUTSIDE'
Huntsbank:	'OK FINE BIBI FN'

Huntsbank has until 3.00pm to contact Townbank to exercise this option. The trader does so at 2.45pm when he decides that it is now very unlikely that GBP will fall below 1.80 before that time (which would make exercise unnecessary as the trader could buy GBP cheaper in the spot FX market). Contact is made in the usual fashion except for a notation that the call is to exercise an option ('XCISE') and not to request a volatility quote. Huntsbank simply gives Townbank the details of the resultant spot FX deal that emanates from exercise and adds payment instructions, in this case, direct to Huntsbank in London. Townbank agrees to the exercise but asks that details and payment instructions be 'swapped outside' – this saves a little extra time. Huntsbank agrees and ends contact.

Exercise is normally a very quick procedure, which is just as well for there may be many long option maturities on any particular day – all that are ITM will have to be exercised individually by 3.00pm. In addition, many other banks will be calling Huntsbank to exercise their options, i.e. Huntsbank's short options that are ITM. All this makes 3.00pm London time (10.00am New York time) a very busy period.

Exercise of options take place on every working day but certain dates in the calendar will be heavy maturity days in the OTC market. These are usually the IMM (International Monetary Market, the financial futures and options division of the CME) Quarter dates of March, June, September and December when the currency futures contracts of the CME settle on the third Wednesday of these months. OTC option expiries will be for the Monday before the third Wednesday in order that physical delivery can take place on the same day as the currency futures (i.e. spot delivery – 2 days). The PHLX currency options also settle for this date, although their options expire on the Saturday before the third Wednesday.

The OTC use of the IMM Quarter dates is traditional and goes back to the days when the exchanges were the dominant factors in option markets. Nowadays, most OTC dealing is done for fixed periods of one day, one week, one month, etc, without any relevance to a particular day within a month except for the dates set for important economic releases such as US employment statistics, etc.

Occasionally, a bank may not make the 3.00pm deadline or may even forget to exercise altogether. In these cases market practice is to 'forgive' the party concerned where the option is deep ITM. An example of this is given in the next section.

Other practices

The OTC market is made up of many different types of banks and other financial institutions, each with its own set of rules, practices and trader disciplines (or lack of them!). Nevertheless, the market operates on a very professional basis and, lacking any rules other than ICOM, is held together by this professionalism and the integrity of the traders.

Banks make prices to each other based on good faith and any differences are usually sorted out at the trader level by compromise. For example, when unable to agree on the premium after committing at a specific volatility level, most banks will 'meet in the middle'. Other cases of misunderstanding are usually resolved satisfactorily without recourse beyond the trading room, i.e. the courts. For example, it occasionally happens that a bank may forget to exercise a deep ITM option, or call shortly after 3.00pm in which case, all intrinsic value would legally be lost to the writer of the option. This would not happen in practice. The writer, knowing that he should be exercised has already structured his portfolio for such event and loses nothing by allowing the holder to exercise 'late'. In fact, many banks will call the buyer and remind him to exercise even though the 3.00pm deadline has passed. Note that ICOM terms (as from 30th September, 1992) allow for automatic exercise of options with intrinsic value of 1% or more, on maturity, should no notification be received. With this procedure, the writer has the choice of settling the exchange of currencies (as normal for exercise), or by cash settlement for the intrinsic value.

On the other side of the coin, it is worth mentioning the practice known as 'stuffing'. This is particularly popular with brokers (read that as 'at brokers') and comes in several forms, some are justified, others quite definitely unprofessional. Take, for example, the case whereby a broker has a market of 11.2–11.4. He relays this through the voice boxes and a bank takes the offer at 11.4. Before the broker can get back to the bank offering at that price, he hears from the potential seller (through another box) 'Off the 11.4 offer'. The broker is caught between acceptance by one line and cancellation by the other – one bank thinks he has bought at 11.4, the other thinks he has done nothing. The broker is held to finding another 11.4 offer and if this becomes impossible (due to, say, a movement up in rates), then the broker is stuffed at that price (11.4).

In the exchange markets, brokers only act on what is being quoted in the pit and this can easily change between relaying the price to the bank on the telephone and going back to the pit with a definite order. Exchange brokers do not honour their quotes and it is accepted practice that prices can change after giving the order to buy or sell. In OTC brokers *do* honour their prices as a matter of pride and professionalism (and due to a certain amount of competition).

So, having been stuffed at 11.4, the broker has a choice between asking the bank dealer to let him off the price at 11.4 – due to the circumstances this would probably be the result – or paying a difference cheque to the bank for the cost against the next offer.

Another, very unsavoury form of stuffing is where a price is quoted that is obviously wrong, and then someone insists on dealing on it. This is rare and tends to occur with non-professionals.

Next, a few words about reciprocity. The direct OTC market functions on the basis of banks making prices to each other on a reciprocal basis, i.e. if you call me for a price, that gives me the right to call you for a similar price. Market makers adopt this standard but some banks more so than others. There is nothing wrong in stating that one wishes for a non-reciprocal relationship, providing that one is asking for quotes based on customer business, and is not running positions oneself. Otherwise it would be better using the services of a broker which do not demand reciprocation.

Occasionally, banks active in the market may withdraw, temporarily, from making markets. There is usually a very good reason for doing so but sometimes excuses are made to avoid making a quote when requested by another bank. As a light hearted conclusion to this chapter, here are some of the standard 'excuses' often relayed across the Reuters Dealer System:

'Dealer at Lunch' (even though it is 10.30am!)
'Sorry, not in that market' (even though I dealt with your N.Y. last night!)
'Finished for the day/month/year' (even though it is 2.00pm/17th/October!)
'No interest at mom' (although you will get my name through a broker!)
'Computer has crashed' (but it will be working again, as soon as you ring off!)
'Staff meeting' (which finishes immediately after your call!)
'Fire drill in progress' (the deal done with you through the broker was from a
     mobile telephone!)
'Only quoting customers in that currency' (everybody, except you, is a customer!)

ICOM has a section on market practice and the reader should refer to Chapter 12 (ICOM) to complement this chapter.

10 Management Control of Active Portfolio

MOST trading portfolios have some form of restraint placed upon the amount of risk being taken at any point in time. In FX, risk is very easily identified and limits are usually placed against the amount of spot risk being taken on an overnight basis, and with intra-day limits a multiple of that amount. The limit may be in the form of USD per currency pair and/or amounts of tolerable loss on negative market movement against the position. Options, however, carry multiple risk parameters and it is imperative that the correct form of control is applied to ensure proper risk management. This chapter will give recommendations based on best current market practice.

Chapter 7 described the trading risks. Logically, most institutions build controls around these risks, so these will each be examined in turn.

Delta

Delta represents the spot FX equivalent risk of an option at any moment in time and is therefore a useful tool to spotlight any FX direction risk. If a trader applies delta neutrality to his portfolio and actively re-hedges delta then this will always show zero. Nevertheless, most traders seem to like to take some form of spot FX risk even if their main position is that of vega.

There are basically two ways of confining delta. One is to apply limits, usually set as USD or local currency amounts, on an overnight basis with intra-day limits of, say, two or three times the overnight exposure. Delta limits are defined as the net delta of all options and FX hedges within an option portfolio, *for each currency pair*, calculated on the input of one set of spot, forward, interest and volatility rates (the revaluation, or mark-to-market rates). In addition, a total delta limit is often applied to the total of all currency pairs to restrict overall exposure.

As in FX, some currency pairs are less likely to change than others. For example, the currency pairs within the EMS are confined to narrow bands resulting in low volatility and hence lower risk than other currencies outside. Recognition of the lower risk is often allowed in delta positions for such currency pairs, usually in the form of a multiple of the delta risk limit applied to a specific currency against the USD, e.g. DEM/USD. In addition, option delta positions are sometimes run against similar, correlated currencies and allowance is often made for this. For example, an option trader may be long DEM/USD in equivalent of USD 10 000 000 and short FRF/USD for the same amount. The risk here is DEM/FRF, so the position is counted once only as DEM/FRF for delta control.

This method can be extended to *all* currency pairs by netting *each individual currency*, and is the second method used to control delta exposure.

Table 10.1 Option portfolio has following delta positions (USD equivalents): (1) +DEM/ USD 10 000 000, (2) −DEM/GBD 15 000 000, (3) −GBP/JPY 10 000 000, (4) −JPY/USD 5 000 000 ('+' = long, '−' = short)

	DEM	GBP	JPY	USD
(1)	+10			−10
(2)	−15	+15		
(3)		−10	+10	
(4)			−5	+5
Total	−5	+5	+5	−5

In Table 10.1, the real risk is −DEM/GBP (5 million) and +JPY/USD (5 million) OR −DEM/JPY (5 million) and +GBP/USD (5 million). In both cases there is only a total of 10 million at risk, rather than the 40 million by addition of each currency pair. In a multi-currency portfolio of options, this method is much preferred in delta control and limits are applied to each individual currency (rather than pairs) with an overall limit representing the aggregate total of all longs or shorts, whichever is the greater.

In the United Kingdom, where the Bank of England imposes individual spot FX limits on each bank, option delta amounts are added to the spot FX amounts for each particular bank under 'Annex B' reporting and netted in a similar fashion to method two above. Limit is only applied to the total shorts (no individual currency limits).

While delta does give a good signal to directional spot FX risk, it is not as straightforward as FX risk due to the fact that delta changes with spot movement – gamma – and can therefore be misleading if compared directly to spot FX risk. For example, assume a bank has the following risks:

Options portfolio:	Net delta	Long USD 10 000 000
FX portfolio:	Spot position	Short USD 10 000 000

From a management perspective, it looks as though the bank has no risk as the two positions between the FX department and the options desk are offset. However, on any spot FX move, the delta of the option portfolio is likely to change, due to gamma, whereas the FX will not (delta of FX remains at 100%) resulting in a residual risk. Bank management should be aware of this and view the options portfolio as a single entity, separate from FX, in respect of delta.

Gamma

Gamma represents the rate of change of delta and is usually measured against a specified movement in the spot FX rate of, say, one standard deviation or a particular percentage. Standard deviation is preferred as the likely spot FX movement is automatically adjusted for any particular currency pair through the market implied volatility rate. For example, one standard deviation in DEM/USD (high volatility) might produce the equivalent of 1% of spot movement, but one standard deviation in FRF/DEM (low volatility) is likely to be something very much less than a 1% move in spot.

There are two methods commonly used to restrict gamma. One is limiting the absolute change in delta, and the other is applying risk tolerance amounts expressed as maximum loss, both for a given movement in spot FX (e.g. one standard deviation). As losses can only be achieved through negative gamma limits are only applied in these cases – there is no point in restricting potential profits!

Example of Method 1

For a given movement of one standard deviation of spot FX, assume delta changes *negatively* by USD 8 000 000 for an increase in the spot FX rate and *negatively* by USD 6 000 000 for a decrease in a particular currency pair. Gamma limit may be set at, say, USD 10 000 000 for the higher of the two delta changes, or perhaps, the average of the changes.

Example of Method 2

For a given movement of one standard deviation of spot FX, assume delta changes *negatively* resulting in a projected loss of USD 200 000 if spot FX moves in upward direction and USD 150 000 in a downward move. Gamma limit could be set as maximum loss of, say, USD 250 000 in either direction.

As in delta, gamma in one currency pair can be hedged in a correlated pair and some approval against set gamma limits can be allowed in such circumstances (trading volatility between two currency pairs, a beta scenario, will produce gammas for such a case). For example, a gamma loss of USD 250 000 for a one SD (standard deviation) in DEM/USD might he hedged by positive gamma in FRF/USD for a similar amount. As DEM and FRF are both within the constraints of the EMS, this reduces the risk of losses to the movement of the cross rate FRF/DEM. Normally, gamma limits are placed on each currency pair with an overall aggregate limit of all pairs, i.e. portfolio.

In Chapter 8, it was noted that gamma increases substantially when close to maturity, and on the last day is particularly pronounced as the final delta has to be either zero or 100% (the highest possible gamma). When setting trading limits for gamma, management should realize that the maturity proximity effects will almost certainly cause excesses against such limits, especially if the trader has been running gamma positions close to the authorized limit prior to option maturity. Strict gamma limits will force the trader to either close the offending position as maturity is approached or purchase some short date options (which have high gamma), to offset the negative effects of the offending position. This may not be the worse scenario. However, most traders will plead that the zero–100% delta on the last day is all part of option trading and as such, gamma limits should be doubled, or trebled, for the final day of an options life. The decision as to how much risk is allowed rests with the institution concerned and its appetite for such risk.

Vega

Vega is the major trading risk in options and is usually measured by the change in value of a portfolio over a 1% change in market volatilities. Limits are then placed in terms of the maximum loss that would be tolerated given the 1% move, in either direction (market volatilities up or down).

In Table 10.2, a vega limit of, say, USD 150 000 might be applied by management as the maximum tolerable loss for a 1% change in market volatility.

Despite the fact that most banks and other institutions apply vega limits based on the above structure of a straight 1% move, it has a big flaw i.e. market volatilities do not move in unison across the different maturities. An increase in one month market volatilities of 1% would not mean that the one year maturities would move by the same amount; in fact the one year would probably not move at all. This makes vega risk more difficult to control because a trader with a large vega position in say, one month, counld hide the exposure by transacting a small amount of one year options. The one month vega risk is high as the shorter end of the volatility curve is, itself, more volatile whereas the longer end is very much less so. To put this another way, we have to look at the volatility of the different periods of market volatility (yes, volatility of volatility!) and weight these periods accordingly to more accurately reflect vega risk, and control it.

This can be done by establishing the various 'shifts' for each period with reference to a known standard e.g. the one month. So, if one month moves by one percentage point, then we can fix two months to move by 0.8 of the one month,

Table 10.2 Portfolio of options and FX hedges is currently valued at the following market volatilities

	1 Week	1 Month	3 Months	6 Months	1 Year
	7.5	8.0	8.3	8.5	8.7
(1) Plus 1%	8.5	9.0	9.3	9.5	9.7
(2) Minus 1%	6.5	7.0	7.3	7.5	7.7

Result of (1) is portfolio increases in value by USD 135 000.
Result of (2) is portfolio decreases in value by USD 140 000.

Table 10.3

	1 Week	1 Month	3 Months	6 Months	1 Year
	7.5	8.0	8.3	8.5	8.7
Shift	1.4	1.0	0.6	0.3	0.1
(1) Plus	8.9	9.0	8.9	8.8	8.8
(2) Minus	6.1	7.0	7.7	8.2	8.6

Result of (1) is portfolio increases in value by USD 85 000.
Result of (2) is portfolio decreases in value by USD 86 000.

three months 0.6 of the one month, etc. These shifts are calculated by reference to historical volatility of the relevant period market volatility. A quicker way is to simply talk to a broker, another bank or some other outside source and gather information as to the perception of such changes. All traders have this information in their heads as it is one of the most important facets of volatility trading. Table 10.3 shows the appropriate shifts applied rather than the straight 1% move.

A completely different picture emerges in Table 10.3, showing much smaller profit and loss parameters perhaps due, in this example, to longer date maturities having less impact on the overall vega risk because change is now smaller than the original one percentage point. This method is a far more accurate measure for portfolio vega as it is closer to what would happen in reality and control limits should be fixed against maximum loss tolerance. Note that vega, by definition, is measured on a one percentage point move in market (implied) volatility and this is fine for an individual option but not for a portfolio.

Another method of controlling vega is by limiting the actual maturities by reference to the vega of each period per one percentage point move. This requires the portfolio to be broken down by maturity, the so called 'ladder'.

In the example shown in Table 10.4, limits have been placed on each of the maturity 'legs' but an overall limit of USD 150 000 is still maintained. This allows the trader to take positions across different maturities, but not all in the same direction; the trader can only go up to each individual leg limit as long as the net total is not exceeded. Management have realized that longer date market volatilities do not change as much as the shorter end (they are less volatile) and are therefore content to have larger limits in these areas. Please note that the limit structure here is for example only and is not calculated using the shifts indicated in Table 10.3.

Ladders are used by the traders to identify the extent of vega positions when trading the volatility curve (see Chapter 8).

Table 10.4 An example of the 'ladder', showing change in P/L (USD) per one percentage point move in market volatility

	1 Week	1 Month	3 Months	6 Months	1 Year	Total
Plus	20 000	40 000	(25 000)	75 000	25 000	135 000
Minus	(20 000)	(40 000)	23 000	(78 000)	(25 000)	(140 000)
Limit	50 000	75 000	85 000	100 000	125 000	150 000

Up to this point, vega control has been discussed with respect to any particular currency pair and it has been suggested that limits be placed to control the potential losses. This is true for each currency pair and furthermore a limit should also be placed on the aggregate total of such pairs. However, some currency pairs have much lower volatilities than others – it will have been noted from previous chapters that DEM/GBP is less volatile than DEM/USD – in which case vega limits should be higher for those currency pairs. An alternative would be to keep the same vega limits as other, more volatile pairs, but measure the change on a lower percentage basis. For example, if a one percentage point (shifted or otherwise) measure is used for DEM/USD where market volatility is, say 12%, then a half percentage point measure could be used for DEM/GBP where market volatility would be lower, around 5%.

Just as in delta and gamma, vega risk in one currency pair may be hedged in another of close correlation such as DEM/USD and GBP/USD where both DEM and GBP are within the constraints of the EMS. It is unlikely that DEM/USD market option volatility will differ too much from that of GBP/USD and beta positions (see Chapter 8) are often taken if market volatilities move out of line with the correlation expectations. Management should recognize such hedged positions when placing vega limits on an active option portfolio.

The whole objective here is to get closer to actual risk being undertaken in order to make the decision as to how much loss can be tolerated in order to set trading limits.

Note one final point on vega. All measurement of potential profit and loss relies on accurate input of market volatility rates in order to compute the portfolio values. Volatility is the one factor in an options price that is not available from another market source, unlike spot FX, forward FX and interest rates. Consequently, management should ensure the availability of independent rates for volatility, such as those from a broker, and never rely on any input from the institution's own traders as these could be manipulated like the objective away from remaining within set management limits.

Theta

Theta risk, the potential of losses through time decay, is not normally considered to be a high risk and many institutions do not bother to place limits on it. To have theta risk would mean being long options and therefore having the potential to gain through gamma. We have seen that gamma and theta are at their strongest at the same points, i.e. when ATM and close to maturity, but pull in opposite directions (see Chapter 8 on gamma versus theta trading). Theta is usually measured over a one day time lapse except at weekends, where one day's trading risk is decayed over three days and, in this scenario, theta can be considerable.

Limits are placed in terms of maximum allowable loss over a one day period, but are normally established on the entire portfolio rather than by currency pair.

Gamma, vega and theta controlled together

Gamma, vega and theta have been discussed individually, but are best controlled as one by combining the movements of spot FX with market volatility movement over a one day time frame, based on the maximum loss tolerable on all three. In this way, the positive (negative) effects of theta are automatically offset against the negative (positive) effects of gamma. Vega can then be added as another dimension giving the trader a 'grid' of risk versus reward, over a one day time frame.

Example:

Portfolio of options showing change in total net value over a one day time decay for given movements in spot FX (gamma) and volatility (vega). Currency pair GBP/USD; current spot, 1.90 (USD per GBP); volatility (1 month), 12.0%. Figures are USD 000's

		Volatility		
Spot		**11.0**	**12.0** (current)	**13.0**
1.94		(11.5)	(59.5)	(88.0)
1.92		46.5	(3.5)	(38.5)
1.90	(current)	50.5	8.5	(33.5)
1.88		3.0	(34.5)	(73.0)
1.86		(92.5)	(123.0)	(155.0)

Delta of above in GBP millions:

		Volatility		
Spot		**11.0**	**12.0** (current)	**13.0**
1.94		(4.0)	(3.8)	(3.5)
1.92		(1.6)	(1.5)	(1.4)
1.90	(current)	1.1	1.0	0.9
1.88		3.6	3.3	3.1
1.86		5.8	5.4	5.1

The first matrix shows the profit and loss aspects of both spot movement and volatility whilst the second matrix shows the delta positions. Control limits would be set on the first matrix for maximum tolerable loss at any point which gives a very effective method of controlling gamma, vega and theta. This technique is, in effect, a worst case scenario as some of the movements are somewhat unlikely. For example, if spot moved from 1.90 to 1.86 or 1.94 (over 2%) in one day, the chances of market volatility falling would seem remote.

The delta matrix is included here for clarity in order that the profit and loss aspects can be explained. For example, the reason why losses are more if spot declines is due to the fact that the position is carrying long GBP 1 million delta at the neutral point of 1.90 (spot) and 12.0 (volatility). Furthermore it illustrates the changes in delta due to spot movement (i.e. gamma) and also volatility (no Greek for this one, yet!). It can be seen that volatility change has only a minor effect on delta.

The following information can all be gleaned from the two matrices:

Position has negative gamma (losses, if spot moves with volatility static).
Position has positive theta (profit, if spot and volatility are static).
Position is short vega (profits from fall in volatility).

Some institutions will combine the two matrices to show delta alongside the profit/loss figures.

Rho control

Option traders do not normally aim to profit from movement in interest rates but sometimes sizable rho risk may build up in an active portfolio of options. Rho can be reduced easily by transacting FX swaps but sometimes traders are a little reluctant to do so due to the cost of dealing on the bid-offer spread which results in the build-up of rho.

Because rho is not normally taken as an intentional position risk, many institutions do not place formal limits on it, leaving it to the trader's discretion. However, controlling rho is relatively simple in that limits can be applied to either delta amounts in periods through the portfolio, or by reference to expected losses on movement of a currency interest rate.

Example:
A portfolio of options (and FX delta hedges) has the following delta profile across the various maturities (USD, millions):

Spot	1 mth	2 mth	3 mth	6 mth	1 y
−16	−80	+70	+6	+10	+10
Cum.	−96	−26	−20	−10	0
Limit	125	65	50	30	20

Here limits are applied to the cumulative totals of the delta amounts in each period. Higher limits are given for the shorter terms because of the lower impact of interest rate risk compared with similar movement in longer dates. The cumulative totals method is that traditionally applied to control interest rate risk in other markets, such as the Eurodollar market. Alternatively, limits can be applied to the maximum tolerated loss should interest rates move by a fixed amount, usually 1%.

Example:

	Spot	1 mth	2 mth	3 mth	6 mth	1 y
	−16	−80	+70	+6	+10	+10
P/L	0	64	(105)	(12)	(30)	(20)
Total P/L = (103)						
Limit	(100)					

Here we can see the effect of a 1% move in interest rates against the position, resulting in a small excess of the limit of USD 100 000 applied to the rho risk.

Maturity concentration control

The effect of a single option within a delta-neutral portfolio is not evident (unless it is very large compared with average option size) until maturity when, if the strike is close to the spot rate, it may have a strong impact on delta, gamma and theta. Proximity of expiry effects was discussed in Chpater 8.

Given the dangers of negative gamma on short options and negative theta on long positions, many institutions attempt to limit these maturity effects by placing 'concentration limits' on option maturity size (face amount) against strike and date.

Example:
Portfolio of options maturities by strike. DEM/USD (USD millions)
Current spot: 1.4600 (DEM per USD)

	1 wk	2 wk	1 mth	2 mth	3 mth
1.50	10		(20)		10
1.49		50	(40)		
1.48			(35)	50	
1.47	10		(25)		15
1.46	(40)		(20)	(50)	
1.45		(10)			
1.44	20				
1.43					
1.42					

In this portfolio, the options maturing with the next seven days will start to have a strong influence on the overall position in terms of delta, gamma and theta. With spot at 1.46, the 40 million short maturity of same strike could be particularly dangerous. Management could curtail the negative influences by limiting the size of options maturing that have strikes close to the current spot rate. For example, if a limit of 20 million was placed on maturities within seven days, the trader would simply buy the 1.46 in 20 million and sell the 1.44 strike for a similar amount – a risk reversal – to reduce to within the limit.

Other option maturities in the one month and beyond are not affected by the limit, but the option trader will know that he will have to reduce to the 20 million level at some point as those strikes approach the seven day area. This encourages traders to manage any impending concentrations that may build up in a portfolio through volatility trading.

Total book size

Some institutions limit the size of the options portfolio as a method of containing the overall risk. This is a weak measure as many options within a portfolio may be offset exactly, i.e. a sale to one institution is repurchased from another leaving no trading risks whatsoever. If the overall book size, sometimes referred to as sigma, is to be limited, it is preferable to exempt zero risk transactions such as matched options and conversions. This is easily achieved by separating the zero risk items from the trading portfolio and placing them in separate sections e.g. matched trades, conversions etc.

If zero risk transactions are separated as recommended above, management should occasionally run the normal risk control functions (delta, gamma and vega) on such portfolios to ensure that all the Greeks are reported as zero. In this manner, management can feel confident that no rogue options (i.e. not truly risk free) are present.

While on the subject on book size, it is worth mentioning an important factor evident in large portfolios, matched or otherwise, and that is exercise procedure on expiry day. A large number of transactions maturing on the same day, with many exercises taking place, will stretch the resources of both traders and operations staff to the point where exercise may be missed. Even matched trades, which carry no trading risks, still have to be exercised if ITM on maturity day. Take, for example, the case where an institution is long one option with one counterparty and short an identical option with another. If strike is close to spot on the last day, the institution will not want to exercise the long until they have been called upon to exercise the short. But the counterparty on the short side will not call the institution until very close to the cut off time of 3.00pm leaving a last second panic to exercise the long option. This situation can be extended to cover many different counterparties; imagine that a bank sold 100 million 1.90 GBP Calls a year ago and has covered by repurchasing throughout the year in 10 million tranches. The bank will have one short of 100 million and ten longs of 10 million. If spot is close to strike at 3.00pm on expiry day, the bank will be waiting for one call from the purchaser, but has to make ten independent calls to exercise the longs. In this sort of situation, mistakes are easily made, for example one of the longs is not exercised, leaving the bank to cover in the spot market at whatever rate is available when the error is detected (this could be either good or bad).

Premium payment control

It has been known for some corporate institutions to raise capital by selling very deep ITM options, covering the FX risk by forward purchase of the deliverable currency and purchase of the appropriate OTM option i.e. a conversion (see Chapter 4). The deep ITM option sold carries a large premium which, of course, is paid up-front (value spot) making the whole scenario a synthetic loan. The difference between the net premium received spot and the fixed loss on maturity through exercise will equal the appropriate interest rate for the term of the option. So why not just borrow the funds in the first place?

Banks and other financial institutions grant credit facilities to corporate clients according to the perceived risk of the particular product. Unsecured loans are high risk and carry big spreads over the market rates but FX, being nothing more than a swap of currencies, is usually viewed as a much lower risk so there will be cases where loan facilities to a particular institution may not be forthcoming, but FX facilities may be granted. Banks normally apply FX limits to sold options (see Chapter 13) so an institution can thereby construct synthetic loans though options (very cheaply as there is no mark up), unless there is another limit, the premium payment limit. A limit is set on the amount of premium paid to certain clients, or options are restricted to sales only. Some banks have a set limit for all institutions just to highlight any unusual behaviour.

Note that beside credit considerations, borrowing funds synthetically through options does not appear as a loan on the balance sheet, the premium being held as a 'suspense item' under current accounting procedures. This may also circumvent other borrowing restrictions, such as regulatory or central bank rules.

Intra-day control

All the limits and controls suggested in this chapter are based upon the daily reporting of option portfolio position risks, usually done at the end of each day. Reporting at one point in the day is fine for accounting purposes, but option traders may be taking much higher risks during the day only to reduce to within limit towards the close. So how does management control these risks?

Firstly, it should be recognized that there will always be a gap between dealing on a price and covering it in the marketplace. This is dealing, not broking. Secondly, it is difficult to ascertain just what risks are being run at any given point because the trader always has control of the deal input. In other words even the most up-to-date computer cannot show what has not been entered. Intra-day limits are therefore somewhat tenuous and are best constructed as multiples of the overnight limits and given to the chief trader as his responsibility to implement.

The only other alternative is to have set points during the day ('rule off' points) where risks are calculated and checked against set limits. However, even if this is done, there are still the periods between those points where traders can deal above limits.

Omega control

Omega is included in this chapter for the simple reason that many institutions do not realize that this risk exists. It is not apparent from most of the software systems available in the market and varies considerably according to the accounting method adopted by the institution concerned. Furthermore, as omega is only evident in currency pairs that do not include the accounting (profit and loss) currency, it will not be of concern if one only trades pairs that include the accounting currency e.g. a US dollar-based bank trading in currencies against the USD.

Management should satisfy themselves that omega is not of any consequence. If it is, then omega can be treated as straight FX risk (which it is), by including it in the relevant currency portfolio. For example, a US dollar-based bank trading DEM/GBP should include any omega risk as either DEM/USD or GBP/USD, depending on the currency of the premium and the set up of that particular currency pair (whether DEM/GBP or GBP/DEM). There is no point in placing control limits on omega.

Chapter 7 describes omega risk and Chapter 8 gives a hedging example. There has been discussion in this chapter of the risks arising from running an active portfolio of options and FX delta hedges. Further considerations or risks are covered in the following chapters on regulatory controls (Chapter 11), bank commitments under ICOM (Chapter 12), counterparty credit (Chapter 13), and accounting (Chapter 14).

11 | Regulatory Controls

THERE are two distinct markets for foreign exchange options: the listed exchanges in the United States (PHLX and CME) and the world wide OTC market.

The listed markets in the USA each set rules and regulations for the members of the exchange, and the exchange itself is governed by either the Securities and Exchange Commission (PHLX) or the Commodity Futures Trading Commission (CME). Access to trading on the exchanges is only through a registered member, therefore an institution can feel reasonably comfortable that its interests are being protected. In fact, the exchange effectively guarantees the performance of its members and hence all the transactions that take place. Exchange rules, regulations and market practices as generally issued are reproduced in Appendix I and further information can be obtained through a registered member, or the exchange itself. Full details are given in the appendix.

The OTC, or interbank market operates internationally with each transaction being a separate contract between each party. These contracts are governed either by the old LICOM terms, the new ICOM terms (see Chapter 12), local terms if available (e.g. Association de Banque Francais – ABF terms in France), or each institution's own terms and conditions depending on the counterparty concerned. Regulatory controls on the institutions vary according to each country and the classification of the party concerned. For example, a bank will be treated differently from a manufacturing company because one has financial risk as its main business, the other does not. Banks generally, by nature of their business, are governed by more regulations than other companies.

The OTC market developed very rapidly in the United Kingdom during the period 1983–1988 and is characterized by certain landmarks of that period. The first was the recognition of currency option risk by the Bank of England in April 1984 when it issued guidelines for risk reporting for banks in the UK (Annex A and B); the second was in August 1985 with the publication of LICOM terms and conditions and the third was the publication of *The London Code of Conduct* ('The Grey Book') by the Bank of England following the Financial Services Act of 1986. OTC broking started in London around the beginning of the period. All this meant that London became the centre of OTC trading and its market practice and regulation, the norm for banks trading in other countries. LICOM had become widely accepted, generally in the absence of any other guidelines. To this day, many countries have still not defined the rules governing FX options.

The United Kingdom has led the development of the OTC market in terms of participating banks, terms and conditions and regulatory control. Banks in the UK are governed by the central bank the Bank of England, with Self Regulatory Organisations (SROs) covering other institutions. SROs were empowered by the Financial Services Act in 1988.

The Bank of England's guidelines issued in 1984 are still in force at the time of writing and are reproduced here to give the reader a clear perspective of regulation.

Bank of England Reporting Guidelines, April 1984 (these are sometimes referred to as the Annex B reporting guidelines)

'A number of banks have shown considerable interest in writing currency options for customers or for other banks, or in dealing in contracts on option exchanges.[(i)] The Bank's paper 'Foreign Currency Exposure' published in April 1981 does not cover this topic. The purpose of this paper is to explain how the Bank of England will treat banks' option business, particularly in relation to the guidelines agreed individually with banks for monitoring their foreign exchange exposure.'[(ii)]

(i) In the early days, PHLX (and, later, the CME) listed market dominated the OTC market and many banks hedged themselves in the closest contract on the exchange.

(ii) In the UK, each bank has an individual FX limit agreed with the Bank of England, for risk reporting purposes.

'The Nature of the Risk
An option contract allows the holder to exchange (or equally choose not to exchange) a specific amount of one currency for another at a predetermined rate (the "exercise price") during some period in the future. In exchange for this right, the holder pays a premium to the person granting the option. The premium is charged to cover the risk borne by the bank or other institution writing the contract; some of this is absorbed by the transaction costs of the bank in covering the risk.

The main risk, therefore, rests with the institution writing the option. Its exposure to movements in the exchange rate between the two currencies involved may be as great as having the open position of the same size as the value of the contract written; it may of course be less to the extent that options are not exercised. An institution which holds an option has no exposure *to loss, only the possible opportunity for gain (unless it is treating its expenditure on the premium payment as an investment rather than writing it off. If it treats it as an investment it is exposed to the extent of the book value given to the asset.)*

A bank which writes currency options for its customers may protect its position to the extent that it is able to purchase a corresponding contract either on an exchange or from another bank; but its position is only fully protected if the terms of the contract purchased are at least as favourable as those of the option written. As the organised options exchanges work to specific delivery dates they can never be used as perfect cover against a contract which is exercisable over a period beyond the delivery date of the exchange contract.'[iii]

(iii)   Bank customers were demanding options that fitted their particular circumstances; strike, date, amount and quoting convention (reciprocal rates on exchanges) were rarely comparable.

'As an alternative to taking cover on the option exchanges, a bank might hedge its position on the cash market. If the bank can find a suitable formula for doing this – see below –, it is then able to write options for customers for non-standard periods, and in any freely traded currency, thereby offering a tailor-made product for its customer needs. It should be noted that because the risk needs to be monitored continuously the use of cash markets to hedge options is restricted for banks which lack the ability to deal in all time zones.[iv]

In assuming the risk which a bank bears in writing currency options it is necessary to assume that its counterparties behave in a rational manner. A customer would not exercise his option to buy a currency from the bank if he could purchase it more cheaply on the spot market; similarly he would not opt to sell a currency to a bank at a rate less favourable than obtainable on the spot market.

At first sight it would appear that all a bank need do to protect its position is to cover fully those options which currently it would be in the customer's interests to exercise ("in the money" options), and leave uncovered those which it would not ("out the money" options). This method however fails to account for a bank being at risk not only from the current spot rate in relation to the exercise, but also to future changes in the spot rate until the expiry of the option. Such changes might alter the banks position from being exposed to a loss – when the rate favoured the customer's exercising the option – to being exposed to no loss – when it would be to the customer's disadvantage to exercise the option. If the spot rate fluctuated around the exercise price the bank would be involved in considerable costs fully covering and then fully uncovering its position, whilst the option holder delayed exercising his option in the hope of the spot rate moving (further) into the money, so enabling him to make a (larger) profit.'[v]

(iv)   The FX market is open 24 hours a day and banks hedging in FX must be able to adjust hedges continuously.

(v) This is naked hedging (see Chapter 8) – an early, simple form of option hedging that caused many losses. Not used by professional option traders but often used by smaller institutions and individuals.

'Several banks have developed techniques based on mathematical formulae to determine the premium which should be charged for writing an option contract, and the position which should be taken in the cash market to hedge its option contracts.[vi]
The variables on which the formulae depend include: the current spot rate and its relation to the exercise rate; the remaining period of the contract; the volatility of the exchange rate; and interest rates in the two currencies concerned. Thus a contract which is a long way "out of the money" and which only has a short time to run requires virtually no cash cover; one which still has some time to run, other things being equal, will require more cover, particularly if the exchange rate is volatile. Such formulae have become widely accepted as the basis for both hedging and pricing contracts, although individual banks are developing various refinements which they hope will enhance their hedging techniques. [vii]
For accounting purposes banks which are active in the market are proposing to value their option contracts by marking them to market (e.g. options written are valued to the price which would have to be paid to buy back the rights which have been extended to the option holder)'.[viii]

(vi) Delta hedging.

(vii) Gamma and vega hedging (using other options, as well as cash).

(viii) Mark-to-market or revaluation of option portfolios rather than amortising of premium.

'Foreign Exchange Guidelines
For the purposes of monitoring a bank's risk the Bank (of England) will expect any exposures arising out of option business to be contained within existing guidelines rather than additional to them.[ix] *The Bank (of England) will need to have reported to it the extent of banks' exposures; reporting will take one of two forms. Unless a bank is able to satisfy the Bank (of England) that its hedging techniques are sufficiently developed, the Bank (of England) will take a "worse view" approach. The approach will take account of the potential effect of the exercise of option rights held by the bank's customers on its open position in individual currencies, including the possibility that the bank's position in a particular currency may be transformed from a long position to a short (or vice versa). It is recognized that this system fails to take any account of the exercise price relative to the current spot rate (and therefore the likelihood of the option being exercised), nor is any credit given for options taken – on the grounds that without knowing the full details of the period and exercise rates of options written and options held there is no way of knowing whether options held are of any value in hedging the risks on options which the bank has written. An example of the reporting form (an annex to the existing S3 form and instructions) is given as Annex A.'*[x]

(ix) The Bank of England wanted the new options market to be contained within existing individual risk guidelines rather than as an excuse for increasing them.

(x) 'S3' form is a monthly return to the Bank of England required from each bank in the UK that has outstanding contracts in FX. It shows the net exposures by currency reported in GBP equivalents, with a limit placed on the total net aggregate shorts (i.e. total currencies 'short').

Annex A only applies to options sold and requires reporting the face value of the option currencies with the same effect as though it were a FX transaction, even if the option delta was zero.

> *'Where a bank has considered the mathematics of options in some detail, the Bank (of England) will allow it to use its own formula for measuring the extent of its exposure on currency options, which will be assessed with that on cash markets to determine the overall open position for the purposes of monitoring a bank's foreign exchange exposure against the agreed guidelines.*[xi]
>
> *Before a bank will be allowed to use its own formula for calculating its exposure for guideline purposes, the Bank will need to be satisfied not only with the mathematical basis of the formula and procedures for monitoring its continued validity, but also that the operating systems for conducting the business with these banks on a frequent and regular basis. An example of the reporting form for these banks is given in Annex B.'*[xii]

(xi) Option exposures assessed with that on cash markets – reporting option transactions by their spot equivalent, i.e. delta.

(xii) Operating systems for conducting the business – in the early days there were only a few systems available on the marketplace (e.g. Devon Systems and COTS Currency Options Trading System) that could handle OTC options and some in-house systems developed by banks were very limiting in reporting risk.

> *'The arrangements outlined in this note will form the basis on which the Bank (of England) assesses banks' foreign currency options for prudential purposes. However the case for separate guidelines for options business will be reviewed by the Bank in the light of market developments and discussions with individual banks.'*[xiii]

(xiii) The Bank of England was usually accommodating to banks wishing to offset options bought with options sold where the details were exactly the same. This allowed many banks who had customer demand for options to simply act as 'middlemen' without taking any risk other than the counterparty credit. Without this concession, reporting of banks under Annex A would show only one side of the transaction, the short, thus impacting a bank's FX exposure inaccurately.

The Bank of England's paper on Currency Options (April 1984), the S3 FX reporting form, Annex A and B, and completion notes are reproduced in full in Appendix II, with the kind permission of the Bank of England.

The London Code of Conduct

This code is issued by the Bank of England and applies to trading in the 'wholesale' markets centred in London. OTC options with a minimum face value of GBP 500 000 (or currency equivalent) fall within the scope of the code and all transactions are covered even if one of the parties to the transaction is operating from overseas. Its main aim is to set out in a clear manner the principles and standards which market participants and their employees are expected to observe. Wholesale transactions are those (for OTC options) that are for GBP 500 000 or over (or currency equivalent), while smaller amounts are covered by the Financial Services Act of 1986.

The code lays out the following:

General Standards
- Responsibilities of principal/broker and of the employee.
- Clarity of role of principals and brokers.
- Complaints procedure.
- Money laundering.
- Confidentiality.
- Taping (of telephone conversations, deals and confirmations).
- Deals at non-current rates (including after hours dealing, stop loss orders and dealing for personal account).
- Conflicts of interest.
- Marketing.
- Entertainment, gifts and gambling.
- Abused substances (including drugs and alcohol).

Dealing Principles and Procedure – A Statement of Best Practice.
- Scope.
- Overseas market conventions.
- Know your customer.
- Procedures.
- Settlement of differences.
- Arbitration procedure.
- Commission/brokerage.
- Taking of security and repos.
- Market terminology and conventions.

Market Terminology and Definitions
- Sterling deposit market.
- Foreign Exchange and currency deposit market.
- Currency assets markets.

Market Conventions

Guidelines for exchanging Standard Settlement Instructions (SSIs)

The code covers all wholesale markets in London of which OTC FX options is but one. All the guidelines given are to be applied to options but the schedule for 'Market Terminology and Definitions' does not specifically have a section for FX options. The FX portion certainly applies but there is other terminology exclusive to the option market missing e.g. volatility. However, the code does refer to ICOM terms (see Chapter 12 where FX options are covered in full).

The London financial markets have a long-established reputation for professionalism and the maintenance of a high standard of business conduct. The development of the London markets in terms of regulation and control is well advanced compared with other international centres.

The London Code of Conduct is reproduced in Appendix III with the kind permission of the Bank of England.

Other countries

The regulatory control of OTC FX options in the United Kingdom is generally more advanced than in other countries, but a very brief comparison with the other major centres is interesting. In the United States, OTC FX options are reported as 'contingent items' on a return to the Federal Reserve for FX outstanding. Beside this requirement, there are no other controls. In Japan, there are no specific reporting requirements for banks.

The International Currency Options Market (ICOM) Terms and Conditions

12

THE reader will have observed in previous chapters that OTC market development was centred on London from the early 1980s. The PHLX certainly provided the impetus in December 1982 when they listed the first currency option contract (GBP/USD, American style) but the OTC market grew out of the commitment of certain banks in London to quote each other two way prices (bid and offer) in 1984. In the same year, the Bank of England announced the reporting requirements for FX options (see Chapter 11), and OTC brokers were set up to service the fledgling market. One thing was still missing; a set of rules to reflect proper market practice with written terms and conditions to cover the legal aspects of OTC transactions. The British Bankers' Association (BBA) formed, in 1984, a Working Party to draw up the terms which resulted in the publication of LICOM Terms and Conditions in August 1985. Although intended to cover only the London market practices, LICOM soon became the standard for nearly all OTC contracts. In the USA, LICOM was more or less duplicated and published, in 1986, as NYICOM (New York Interbank Currency Options Market) which was later retitled USICOM.

By 1989, it had become apparent that the original terms did not adequately reflect market practice, which had developed into quoting in volatility terms with FX delta hedges. Furthermore, the number and diversity of market participants had increased substantially and was truly international. In May 1989, the BBA re-established a Working Party to liaise with market interests, with a view to updating the 1985 terms and to provide guidance for market practice. In addition, emphasis was placed on the international acceptance of the revised terms hence the new title of ICOM. As with the LICOM Working Party, the Bank of England was represented as an observer on the ICOM Working Party.

At about the same time as ICOM was being addressed, a similar effort was underway in the United States to redraft USICOM terms. In 1990, representatives of the BBA Working Party for ICOM and the New York Foreign Exchange Committee for USICOM met to resolve the differences between the two sets of terms, and to develop a single document for use in the international OTC FX options market. One aspect of the work done in New York was to address the increasingly important issue of counterparty credit risk and, in particular, the rights and obligations of the parties upon non-performance, insolvency and *force majeure*. The new ICOM terms now provide a method for closing out and liquidating options upon the occurrence of one of these events. Furthermore, the document has been drafted in the form of a 'master agreement' which reflects market practice with respect to the formation, exercise and settlement of options (including matters such as net cash settlement and automatic exercise) as well as setting forth the legal rights and obligations of the parties.

The New York committee comprised representatives from the legal departments of banks in the United States while the BBA Working Party was made up from senior trading managers of banks in London. This proved to be a very complimentary fit. In addition, the BBA Party embraced representatives of other countries, such as Japan, and appointed a member to look after brokers' interests.

In Japan, the Tokyo Foreign Exchange Market Practices Committee published ICOM terms in March 1993, in a similar manner to the New York Foreign Exchange Committee. The BBA has maintained full liaison with both.

ICOM should form the base for further expansion of the OTC markets once the individual banks and other institutions have digested the impact of having a legally binding document supporting transactions with the provision of reduced credit risk through the netting of contracts in cases of default.

ICOM is confined to practices in the interbank and professional markets and is not directly concerned with the terms and conditions upon which individual institutions may choose to deal with their clients, although ICOM could be used for such circumstances. Banks and other professional market participants are free to use other terms or agreements if they so wish, but should consider themselves under an obligation to make clear to each other in what way their terms differ from ICOM. In this way, ICOM will always form the basis of the market and be considered the norm for OTC FX option transactions.

ICOM is in two parts. The first is a Guide to the Master Agreement which has sections on market practice and master agreement provisions. The second is the master agreement itself. The master agreement stands on its own as a legal document and some banks may wish to record their entry into a master agreement on ICOM terms in hard copy by signing with each, or some, of its counterparties.

The market practice section of the Guide is reproduced here (except for the introduction) for comment and to complement Chapter 9 (Market Practice).

Market practice

Price quotation

'There are two generally accepted methods of price quotation – Premium and Volatility. In each case, the counterparties shall agree upon:

Option Style (American or European),
Call Currency,
Put Currency and Amount,
Expiration Date,
Expiration Time,
Premium Payment Date,
Settlement date, and
Strike Price.

Counterparties should also agree upon whether they are entering into a contemporaneous foreign exchange transaction (commonly known as a Delta hedge), although such a transaction would not be subject to the Master Agreement.'

In practice, traders very rarely state the option style, as American is not generally used in the interbank market, leaving European style as the default. Premium payment date is not specified before the quote is made, but is included if a deal is concluded along with payment instructions etc (see example, Chapter 9). Delta hedge is taken as automatically included on volatility quotes unless specified (rare) or quote is for a delta-neutral combination of options (straddle or strangle).

'Price quotation should be in the form of either:

(a) a Premium, where the counterparties agree upon the above terms and on how the premium price should be expressed, e.g. as a percentage of either currency or as one currency in terms of the other (it is also necessary to agree upon a spot rate in the case of a Premium quotation where a Delta hedge forms part of the trade); or

(b) Volatility, where the counterparties agree upon the above terms and that the Volatility be expressed as a percentage per annum. It is this factor which, when combined with the Spot Rate, interest factors of the Currency Pair concerned, the days to expiry of the Option and the Strike Price, is used to compute the Premium.'

If premium price quotation is requested, it is normally on a 'live' basis – without a delta hedge – and expressed as a percentage of the underlying, except for the currency pair GBP/USD where US cents per GBP is the normal method. For example, in DEM/USD, price would be expressed as a percentage of USD; in DEM/GBP, as a percentage of GBP but in GBP/USD as US cents per GBP. Exceptions occur in countries that do not use USD as their base currency, in which case currency units per USD is the normal method e.g. DEM/USD would be quoted in DEM per USD. Premium quotation is not the norm among market professionals but is still used by some smaller banks that have not yet invested in option pricing systems (if a bank has a foreign exchange department, it is better to deal volatility with delta hedge thereby gaining the foreign exchange element of the transaction).

'An option is not a legally binding contract until, among other things, the Premium has been agreed. Therefore, to ensure the ongoing viability of the Volatility method of dealing, it is incumbent on the counterparties to agree on the Premium Price as soon as possible, and it is imperative that the calculation of the Premium accurately reflect the agreed Volatility and market conditions at the time Volatility was agreed. In the event of a dispute that cannot be resolved between the counterparties through good faith negotiation (or, in the first instance, by reference to recordings of conversations between the Parties during which pricing was discussed), prompt reference to mutually acceptable third-party arbitration is suggested. Market participants should note that, as Premium calculation differences are more likely to occur in transactions involving American Style Options, due care should be exercised in entering into such Options.'

Volatility quoting in very busy markets sometimes takes the form of banks agreeing on the volatility price and spot reference for the delta but agreeing premium at a later time when markets are quiet, hence the statement regarding the legality of this.

Disputes over premium differences are rare as most market professionals simply 'meet in the middle'. As spot and volatility rates are preset, disputes can only arise from the other factors in an options price: the forward FX rate, and interest rates. If these are also agreed, then differences are down to the option pricing model. It should be noted that, at the time of writing, Astrogamma Inc.'s FENICS option pricing system is the current standard of the marketplace, and a bank not agreeing premium from a volatility quote should refer to this system through a third party, such as a broker, as a basis to resolve disputes. It should be further noted that FENICS has a facility to price options according to the time of day – a clock – which if 'switched on' may produce a different premium for the same volatility rate than if 'switched off' (the pricing model splits time into days and fractions of days instead of just days). Market standard is to calculate premiums with FENICS clock switched off; any adjustment required due to the length of day remaining should be made to the volatility quote in the first place.

Pricing American style options produces many differences across different systems, largely explaining the decline in the popularity of this style. Differences tend to occur when the two currency interest rates are similar.

'In addition, when trading Volatility, it is necessary that a spot rate be agreed upon by the counterparties immediately upon entering into the Option. This forms the basis of the underlying foreign exchange transaction (Delta hedge), if any.'

This is normal market practice for volatility quoting and it is very rare to trade from a volatility quote without the delta hedge (unless it is a delta-neutral composite transaction such as a straddle or strangle, in which case delta is zero).

Quotation of expiration dates

'Generally, there are two methods for quotation of Expiration Dates – quotation of straight Expiration Dates and quotation of Expiration Dates by calendar month.'

Straight expiration dates

> *'An Option quoted for straight periods (such as 1 month, 2 months etc.) has its final Expiration Date the date preceding the equivalent forward date (as dealt in the interdealer foreign exchange market) that will result in settlement on the forward date, if it is exercised on the Expiration Date. If there is more than one solution, the furthest date from the Trade Date will be the Expiration Date.*
>
> *Example:*
> *Today's date: 4 March – Spot date: 6 March*
> *1 month FX date   – 6 April*
>
> *The Expiration Date for a one-month Option quoted on 4 March will be that date which will result in a Settlement Date of 6 April, i.e. 4 April, (assuming no weekends or holidays between). To avoid misunderstanding, in the case of periods under one month, it is recommended that the parties refer to an actual date.'*

This is relatively straightforward, though there are occasions when it is difficult to calculate the option expiration date when there are holidays present. If, having agreed expiration date, it subsequently transpires to be a holiday, the contract stands on those agreed dates unless both parties agree to amend (usually by changing original premium value). Periods of under one month should be specified by actual date, not one week, ten days, etc, because it is possible for the forward FX market to be quoting the period of say one week as eight days due to holiday. Despite this recommendation, option market practice is still to call the short periods of under one month as 'days to maturity from today' e.g. 'what is one week DEM/USD volatility?' meaning 'option to mature this time next week', whereas the rule above might produce a period of eight days i.e. spot one week is eight days resulting in option expiration of same period. Care should be taken at all times.

Expiration dates by calendar month

> *'Currently, it is market practice to quote for expiration in a particular month without reference to the actual date. In these circumstances, it is generally understood that the Expiration Date of the Option is the Monday before the third Wednesday of that particular month.'*

FX options, in common with those of other markets, sometimes trade expiry dates that coincide with the futures delivery dates of the International Monetary Market (IMM) contracts on the CME. IMM delivery is on the third Wednesday of March, June, September and December hence OTC option expiry is for the Monday before the Wednesday in order that any exercise of the OTC option would result in delivery on the Wednesday (spot delivery – two days). The PHLX currency option contracts also trade for other months that deliver on the third Wednesday hence the OTC practice extends to cover all months of the year.

Notwithstanding the above practice, the majority of OTC transactions are for fixed periods to maturity – one month, one week, one day, etc – rather than for specific dates in the future.

Expiration on non-business days

'Although the Master Agreement does not provide that the Expiration Date must be a Business Day (i.e. a Local Banking Day for the office of the Seller that has written the Option), this will customarily be the case. However, some dealers regularly sell Options with Expiration Dates that are not Local Banking Days for their applicable Designated Office. (Similarly, some dealers will accept Notice of Exercise on a non-Business Day.) If the Expiration Date is not a Local Banking Day for the Seller's Designated Office (or if the Seller is not willing to accept Notice of Exercise at its Designated Office on a non-Business Day), it is incumbent upon the Seller to make other arrangements (such as designating a different office or an agent for receipt) to enable the buyer to exercise its Option. In these circumstances, the Seller should notify the Buyer of such arrangements as soon as possible and reconfirm them to the Buyer prior to the Expiration Date.'

Options are frequently traded for expiry on dates that are local bank holidays. The most important holidays that restrict trading are generally those of the USA, and to a lesser extent, those of the UK, Germany and Japan. Many of the international banks have traders working on local bank holidays so exercise of options maturing is no problem. Even those banks that do not work on local bank holidays can easily arrange for exercise through overseas branches.

Confirmations

'The significant terms of an Option should always be established by the Parties at the time the Option is entered into. The agreement of the Parties on those terms will be set forth in the Confirmation. However, there may be matters relating to an Option that are not required to be set forth in the confirmation. Market participants are encouraged to include information as to such matters in the 'Other terms and conditions' section of the Confirmation. In addition, market participants should indicate at the beginning of negotiations, and prior to entering into an Option, in which way their dealings and the formation, exercise or settlement of the relevant Option will differ from established market practice. Similarly, brokers should be mindful of, and adhere to, market practice with respect to the formation of Options and their dealings with Option counterparties (including the issuance of Confirmations in the recommended form).'

Confirmations play a very important role in the OTC market as there is no central clearing house (as on the exchanges) to match each bought and sold contract. This first paragraph in ICOM is simply stating that traders and brokers should be mindful that their dealings should always be according to market practice and anything 'unusual' should be stated when starting to obtain quotes, etc, and, if trade is concluded, then the pertinent details should be added to the regular confirmation.

'As in the cash spot and forward currency markets, the prompt exchange of Confirmations (preferably electronically) and their immediate and thorough checking upon receipt (and querying where necessary) is vital to the orderly functioning of the market-

place, as well as providing a principal defence against many types of fraud. However, the Option markets are more complex than the cash markets because of the greater number of parameters that need to be specified for each transaction and the different types of Options that might be transacted. This additional complexity reinforces the requirement for Confirmations to be issued promptly by each of the Parties. If there has been a misunderstanding between the Parties as to the Option terms, this will usually be discovered upon review of the Confirmation. The non-receipt of expected Confirmations or any inconsistencies or inaccuracies should be queried or objected to within the time period recognised by local market practice or, at most, within three Business Days of the date of the trade. It is suggested that brokers, as well as the Parties to an Option, send Confirmations of any Options which they arrange to the counterparties.'

Confirmation issue, the checking of those received and follow-up of those not received is paramount to the reduction in misunderstanding which occur in OTC options. ICOM has attempted to address the problem of misunderstandings by reiterating the importance of 'immediate and thorough checking upon receipt', and by recommending electronic exchange of confirmations (rather than the mailed version). In addition, a three day (maximum) time limit for queries or non-receipt has been introduced.

To this day, the most persistent error that occurs is the recording of a Call instead of a Put (and vice versa) which, if missed at the confirmation checking stage, will only come to light on the expiration date when one party will expect exercise to take place whilst the other party will believe the option is OTM. This type of misunderstanding is sometimes missed at the confirmation checking stage because one party is referring to a Call on one currency in a pair, whilst the other party is referring to a Call on the countercurrency.

'A recommended form of Confirmation is included as Exhibit I to the Master Agreement. Market participants (including brokers) are encouraged to follow the format and terminology suggested in order to reduce the risk of misunderstandings.'

If all OTC market participants were to adopt the recommended format for confirmations, then checking would be made very much easier and the kind of misunderstanding mentioned above (Call instead of Put) would have a better chance of being spotted.

'Market participants frequently enter into a contemporaneous Delta hedge at the time they enter into an Option (either with the Option counterparty or a third party). It is market practice (and market participants are encouraged) to separately confirm such transactions. In addition, it is suggested that brokers send confirmations of any Delta hedges which they arrange to the Parties involved.'

Delta hedges are usually confirmed as separate FX transactions but with a notation of 'Ref. FX Option' or similar. Brokers usually confirm the delta hedge along with the option confirmation on telex, and issue written confirmations separately.

It is worth noting that many errors are discovered by reference to the delta hedge. For example, in the Call-Put problem mentioned previously, the delta would have been constructed as a buy instead of a sell (or vice versa) resulting in incorrect payments of FX. As most hedges are done as spot, the misunderstanding is detected within two days.

The whole procedure of confirmation issue, receipt and non-receipt varies a great deal in the marketplace. Generally speaking, banks should place more emphasis on the subject and invest in bringing their systems and procedures up to date. All too often, confirmation checking is left to junior staff and is mostly done by the 'eyeball' method; the clerk visually ticks one record against the other. The success of this method is down to the individual performing the task. A better way to check confirmations and tract non-receipt etc, is by secondary input i.e. the clerk enters all details provided by the counterparty's confirmation into a computer which does a comparison check with the current database, showing any differences immediately. The computer could also then tract transactions where no comparison has yet been made to highlight non-receipts.

Confirmations should also be issued electronically (e.g. through SWIFT) rather than mailed. In addition to the written confirmation, many banks are now doing verbal deal checks over the telephone on the day of the transaction as a better (and much quicker) method of locating potential errors. This check can be done at the same time as swapping instructions for delivery of premiums, value dates, etc.

The schedule

There follows an outline of the schedule of the Master Agreement, which asks for the following:

Part I: Designated Offices.
          Details of the Party's Designated Office for the purpose of the agreement.
Part II: Notices.
          Details of the Party's address, telephone number, telex number, facsimile number and name of individual or department to whom or to which 'Notices' should be sent for the purposes of the agreement.
Part III: Payment Instructions.
          Details in relation to the Party's instructions for payment of currencies.
Part IV: Base Currency.
          Notification of the Base Currency for the purposes of the agreement.

Banks adopting ICOM terms should notify their counterparties of the details relevant to Parts I to IV of the schedule. In particular, Part IV would normally be the accounting currency of the bank concerned which may not be the local domestic currency of the branch location. For example, in London, US banks would probably designate their base currency as USD and not sterling which is the default currency under the BBA, London ICOM terms.

Other comments

The New York version took effect in April 1992, in the London version September 1992, and the Tokyo version in March 1993. Although essentially the same, the presentation differs:

New York

(1) Preface detailing names of bank attorneys who worked on ICOM.
(2) Master Agreement in form of legal document with space for signatures.
(3) Master Agreement Guide.

London

(1) Notice stating that ICOM takes effect from 30th September 1992 and that LICOM terms are no longer available. More importantly, it states that banks dealing in the London market are dealing under ICOM unless the bank states otherwise. The notice also gives advice regarding banks declaring the details required in the schedule (see above).
(2) Guide to Master Agreement.
(3) Master Agreement without any signing paragraphs.
(4) Heading Sheet and Signing Sheet for banks wishing to use (3) to form a legal document.
(5) Legal opinion.

Tokyo

(1) Preface explaining adoption of ICOM.
(2) Master Agreement in form of legal document with space for signatures.
(3) Master Agreement Guide.
(4) Legal Opinion.

In London and Tokyo, the legal opinion (from Clifford Chance and Mitsui, Yasuda, Wani & Maeda respectively) form part of the release booklet. In New York, the legal opinion (by the New York firm of Stroock & Stroock & Lavan) is not part of the release booklet.

In the London version, the Master Agreement and guide are in reverse order, but otherwise the only difference is that London have omitted the signing paragraphs from the Master Agreement and included separate signing sheets for the purpose of forming a legal document.

The Tokyo ICOM is essentially the same as that issued in London and New York except that the Schedule in the Master Agreement has, under Part V (Other Provisions), made the following sections non-applicable to the Agreement:

5.3 'In-the-money amount settlement';
6   'Dischange and termination of Options';
7   'Payment netting';
8   'Default'.

The legal opinion from Mitsui, Yasuda, Wani & Maeda gives details of the above. Furthermore, the first two paragraphs under section 12 (Law and Jurisdiction) have been amended to reflect Japanese law.

Finally, it should be emphasized that ICOM terms require banks to notify each of their counterparties of any terms that differ from those stated in the document. For example, many banks are not presently able (due to system constraints) to net premium payments as called for under 7.1 of the Master Agreement. Another example could be the relevant law applicable, which is stated as US or UK in the Agreement. At the time of writing, the following items are the most common changes being made to terms stated in the Master Agreement:

(1) 7.1 Premium Payment netting (Deleted).
(2) 7.2 Other Netting (Deleted).
(3) Legal Jurisdiction.
(4) Base Currency (Not always sterling in London).

ICOM terms, as released by The Foreign Exchange Committee in New York and the BBA in London are reproduced, in full, in Appendix IV with the kind permission of those bodies, and for record purposes, the Tokyo ICOM terms are also reproduced in this appendix.

ISDA

The international interest rate swap market operates under terms and conditions issued by the International Swap Dealers Association (ISDA). In 1992, currency options, as a product, were added to ISDA terms to allow for cross-product netting in cases of default situations, etc. The currency options addition is similar to ICOM which effectively gives institutions a choice of using either, or both, terms. Institutions active in both FX options and interest rate swaps may use ISDA or both ICOM and ISDA. In these cases, the only advantage in event of counterparty default is that there is one net payment due (i.e. across the two products) rather than two (one for FX options and one for swaps). Unlike ICOM, ISDA terms and conditions do not carry FX options market practice guidelines.

Counterparty Credit Risk (OTC)

13

ONE benefit of trading on the listed markets is that the counterparty credit risk is absorbed by the relevant exchange or clearing house. This benefit is paid for in the cost of maintaining margin payments and the administration of such, which can be very time consuming. Nevertheless, the margin system does work very well and few institutions worry over the credit aspects of dealing on the exchanges. Consequently, this chapter examines the credit issues as applied to the OTC market but, before we address option counterparty credit risk, we must first look at the system employed by the FX market for spot and forward transactions.

In April 1992, a survey was carried out by 26 central banks to ascertain the daily volume in foreign exchange. The results were published in September 1992 and show a total of over one trillion US dollars (one thousand billion dollars!) A more recent survey by the Bank for International Settlement (BIS) gives the daily volume as 880 billion USD. This volume is transacted between banks worldwide without the use of one single clearing house – it is truly 'over-the-counter'. The FX market has seen continued growth for some years with options estimated at the time of writing to form about 7% of the total, about 70 billion US dollars a day. In the absence of a clearing house, each FX market participant has to make and receive payment of principal on an individual basis and each transaction is open to counterparty credit risk. Every deal has a payment of one currency and a receipt of another, often in currencies other than a bank's own domestic currency. For example, a bank in Germany trading the USD against the JPY will have to pay and receive currencies through accounts in New York and Tokyo. As currencies are exchanged on the same day (the value date), a bank is at risk in that the purchased currency may not be received after the sold currency is paid.

This risk is recognized and banks apply 'credit lines' to each and every counterparty, including a bank's own customers.

Foreign exchange limits

Credit lines for FX vary between institutions but are generally in one or more of the following forms:

Maximum outstanding limit (credit line)

The maximum outstanding limit is applied to the total of outstanding FX contracts by face value (usually converted to a base currency, either USD or the accounting currency for the institution concerned). This limit prohibits the build up of transactions with one particular counterparty, and given the liquidity in FX, this is not usually a problem unless the limit is on a customer of the bank rather than a market counterparty.

Some institutions segregate currency purchases from sales and place a limit on the higher of the two.

Maximum daily delivery risk (MDDR)

The maximum daily delivery limit, or settlement limit is a restriction usually forming a percentage of the maximum outstanding limit, and attempts to control the accumulation of risk on any one day. For example, a bank with FX contracts outstanding for USD 100 million for delivery on one day is more at risk than the bank with similar amount but with delivery spread across different dates, because default of one payment would suspend the following payment pending receipt of the first (or inquiry into breach of contract, etc).

Revaluation, mark-to-market, or market replacement cost limit

Calculating the contract replacement cost is a very valuable aid in assessing true FX counterparty risk. Each transaction with one counterparty is assessed on the basis of the cost that would arise if the bank concerned were to replace a contract in the marketplace. The result ought to show the risk should the counterparty enter bankruptcy before the delivery date of the foreign exchange.

This form of credit control is very different from the maximum outstanding and maximum daily delivery limits, which are only concerned with the exchange of payments on delivery i.e. the full face value amount. It is not concerned with whether to do so is beneficial (profit against current spot rate) or not (debit against spot rate). The revaluation method measures the possible loss impact on non-performance by the counterparty in not delivering on maturity of the contract. The limit is thus set in terms of maximum revaluation loss amounts, not face value amounts. The loss limit is very similar in profile to that of an unsecured loan to the counterparty; the most that can be lost, in case of default, is the amount advanced (plus interest).

Example:
Outstanding FX contract – buy USD 10 000 000 at 1.50 (DEM per USD), value 6 months from now. Current 6 months forward rate: 1.60.

Delivery risk: USD 10 000 000	DEM (15 000 000)
Mark-to-market at 1.60	DEM (16 000 000)
Market replacement cost	DEM (1 000 000)

In this example, the institution is expecting to buy USD 10 million at the rate of 1.50 DEM per dollar and thereby sell DEM 15 million, six months from now. The applicable credit limit for delivery is the face value amount of USD 10 000 000 (or DEM 15 000 000). However, if the counterparty were to become bankrupt within the next six months, the delivery limit would become irrelevant but the institution would be left to replace the contract in the marketplace at the new rate of 1.60 thereby locking in a loss of DEM 1 million.

It can be seen that, in this example, the loss of DEM 1 million (USD 625 000 at 1.60) is only a small percentage (0.625%) of the contract face value of USD 10 million and represents the degree of movement in the forward rate from 1.50 to 1.60. Obviously, the movements in FX can be very much larger than this and the tenor of the contract will play a significant part in the probability of such movement; a spot transaction of two days will carry less risk than one of six months.

Of course, this method of credit control is only applied to negative consequences of FX rate movement. A positive move in FX would leave the institution in a profitable position i.e. the market replacement cost would be lower than the outstanding contract. In the example above, let us assume the DEM/USD rate declined to 1.40. The position would be:

Delivery risk: USD 10 000 000	DEM (15 000 000)
Mark-to-market at 1.40	DEM (14 000 000)
Market replacement benefit	DEM 1 000 000

Of course in practice the institution would not actually benefit from the transaction as the DEM 1 million would be claimed by the creditors of the bankrupt counterparty but nevertheless, no loss would occur.

Netting

There are two netting concepts: closeout netting and payment netting. Both reduce counterparty credit exposure but are essentially unrelated.

Closeout netting

Closeout netting is a contingent right affecting unmatured trades, whereby an institution is allowed to close out (terminate or liquidate) all the outstanding transactions with a defaulting counterparty, and to protect against 'cherry-picking' in the event of bankruptcy or liquidation of such counterparty. Closeout netting agreements for FX are usually constructed as master agreements between one institution and another on a multi-branch basis similar to the ICOM Master Agreement for FX options.

A closeout netting agreement reduces potential post-default increases in credit exposure by permitting closeout of all unmatured trades upon default. It also reduces current credit exposure by protecting against cherry-picking, thus reducing exposure to the net rather than the gross ITM value when there are both ITM and OTM transactions with the counterparty.

A closeout netting agreement will reduce an institution's internally allocated capital requirements but is not yet recognized for regulatory risk-based capital requirements.

There are potential balance sheet benefits from closeout netting agreements. For example, in the USA under FASB 105, an institution will report net (rather than gross) ITM amounts per counterparty (or zero, if net ITM is a credit – see example for revaluation limit).

Payment netting

Payment netting is a routine operational act applying to transactions as they mature. All payments with the same currency arising from trades with the same value date are paid on a net (or combined) basis. For logistical reasons, payment netting agreements are constructed on a bilateral basis rather than multi-branch.

Credit exposure is reduced through lower delivery risk (maximum daily delivery risk). A payment netting agreement should be based on novation netting, which means that all transactions with the same value date from which offsetting payments arise are deemed cancelled, and are replaced with the residual net obligations.

Payment netting has no effect on an institution's capital or balance sheet.

Many of the major participants in the FX market have arranged payment netting procedures as bilateral agreements, to make the currency payment process, more efficient. In any one day, one of the major FX banks may transact exchange contracts many times with the same counterparty. Without a netting agreement each deal would have to be settled independently involving much cost and time. Netting across common currencies and paying and receiving the net differences is very much more efficient and the FX market is attempting to move towards netting agreements as standard.

In addition to the bilateral agreements, banks can sign up to FXNET, a form of multilateral netting done electronically, operating only in London at the time of writing. It is expected to extend to the USA, Hong Kong and other countries in due course. FXNET may seem to be acting in the role of a clearing house for FX except for one obvious difference; payment and receipt of currencies, although netted, is still with individual banks and there are no margin requirements (although there are fees to join the system).

The advantages of netting extend beyond the obvious reduction in payments because it also represents a decrease in counterparty credit risk; one net payment instead of many means delivery risk is brought to a much reduced level. Option exercises, being spot FX transactions, also fall into the netting procedure to add to the efficiency of the system.

Option counterparty risk factors

The reader will have noted the FX market methods of recording counterparty credit risk and the forms of netting that take place. Exercise of an option will, of course, produce an FX transaction which will fall under all the procedures of that market. An institution can apply the risk factors for FX to options, except in the following instances:

(1)   The option may not be exercised, i.e. expire worthless with no consequent delivery of foreign exchange.

(2)   Control of the exercise (and the creation of a foreign exchange trade) is in the hands of one of the parties to the transaction, the option buyer.

The application of the FX risk factors for options would be conservative because of (1) above. Furthermore, market replacement cost to the seller of the option is always zero; the maximum profit is the premium which has already been received hence market replacement risk lies only with the buyer of the option.

Option counterparty risk is therefore more one-sided than FX. The buyer of the option has all the risks of FX (plus an additional one of premium payment) whereas the seller only has potential delivery risk (and has received a premium payment).

Option market participants have developed many types of measurements for option counterparty credit risk but generally these measures fall into one of two categories; those that use existing FX credit assumptions (i.e. include options as part of FX exposure) or those that have separate option credit limits for each counterparty.

Using existing foreign exchange credit lines

Many banks and other institutons use existing FX counterparty limits due to the administrative burden of establishing separate option facilities, and for other reasons often prefer not to segregate.

(1) State option face value as deliverable in all cases

Stating the option face value as deliverable is treating options as though they are FX contracts which is conservative but not representative of the actual credit risks. Full line and MDDR limits are applied and no allowance is made for the fact that options sold carry no risks other than (potential) delivery risk. They are very simple to implement, but are very inaccurate.

(2) State option face value as deliverable, with allowances

Stating the option face value as deliverable, with allowances, is the same as (1) except option sales are not recorded under the counterparty credit line, but only as deliverable (MDDR). Other concessions may be made to further increase the accuracy of the credit reporting. For example, in the case of option straddles where only one option, the Call or the Put, can possibly be exercised on maturity (although one *must* be exercised). Allowance is made to count straddles for the value of one leg i.e. the Call or the Put instead of both. This example can be extended to other recognized strategies such as the strangle where one, or neither, of the Call or Put will be exercised on maturity.

This method is considered to be better than (1) but the processing system must be able to recognize bought from sold (very easy as it is the same as foreign exchange), and strategies such as straddles and strangles (which is not so easy, unless indicated at input level).

(3) State option delta as the deliverable

The delta of an option can be used as an indicator as to the potential exercise on maturity. This is normally only a percentage of the face value but is more accurate than recording the full face value as in (1) and (2) – options with little chance of exercise will be reflected as such while deep in-the-money options will show something like face value.

Option purchases are recorded against both credit line and MDDR but sales only against MDDR, as in (2) except by delta amount only. No allowance need be made for option strategies such as straddles and strangles as these will automatically be adjusted through the delta calculation.

This is a much more accurate measure of options delivery risk, but reveals a big disadvantage when incorporation into FX systems is attempted; the delta value changes with spot movement and with time decay. Thus a counterparty may be within an assigned credit or delivery limit on one day, and over the limit the next day, due to delta change without any further transactions.

The examples of current market practice discussed here are but a few and are only concerned with delivery risk. Market replacement cost methods are similar for FX and for options bought, in that a limit is applied based on the acceptable amount of risk for the counterparty concerned. This method also controls any attempt to construct synthetic loans through options that would otherwise not be evident i.e. using solely delivery risk methods.

Using separate option credit lines

Specific option lines, rather than being incorporated into existing FX facilities, bring some major benefits. The options trading is not tied to the same counter-parties as in FX, which is a considerable benefit in the cases of transactions with non-professional parties who normally purchase options as hedging instruments.

(1) Delivery risk

Selling options carries just one risk – potential delivery of the currency – but this can be negated entirely (for client transactions) by application of the 'cash settlement' principle. Instead of exchanging currencies on the value date, a payment is made to the client which represents the intrinsic value of the option on the expiry date, in a similar manner to that described in the old LICOM terms and the current definition in the ICOM Master Agreement of 'In the Money Amount'.

Another way of evading delivery risk is to pay currency only upon receipt of the countercurrency. This may involve a leg of one day but interest can be paid on the due amount.

If either of these methods is used, option sales require no credit considerations other than receipt of the premium, and this can be avoided by having funds available prior to the option transaction being made i.e. on account. However, both cash settlement and delayed delivery can only be used for an institution's own clients as the interbank market does not operate on these terms.

In the case of option purchases, things are very different. While delivery risk can be avoided by cash settlement or delayed delivery – the same as for options sold – the option buyer is always at risk to the value of the option in the marketplace (market replacement cost risk). Therefore, a suitable limit based on current option valuation has to be applied.

Dedicated option credit lines may address delivery risk in any of the ways discussed earlier, but many institutions tend to use the MDDR method, adjusted for strategies etc. Although the delta method is more accurate, the variable nature of this technique has proved difficult to explain to credit risk managers who distrust any system that does not fix a maximum exposure.

Another interesting point regarding delivery risk arising on exercise of an option is that the option credit risk drops to zero, leaving FX delivery risk in the resulting spot transaction. This is normally absorbed into the FX credit line for the counterparty but, on occasions, the FX line may already be 'full', so some internal control is required to note the fact that the options line has declined at the same time leaving the net exposure the same. This effect will not occur if the options credit line includes the delivery process, but the vast majority of institutions use a different system for FX settlement than for options processing.

(2) Market replacement cost risk

Market replacement cost risk methods are similar for FX trades and options purchased (not options sold) in that both take the current market value of the transaction. In FX this is calculated as the current exchange rate minus the original trade rate, the result being either positive or negative. In option purchases the calculation is simply the current premium value of the option in the market-place, which is therefore always negative (it is impossible to buy an option for less than zero!). 'Negative' here means it is a cost (debit) to replace an existing contract with one in the marketplace on the basis that counterparty default has resulted in loss of the option rights held through the original purchase.

Option sales, on the other hand, always have a positive market replace-ment cost due to the fact that the original premium has already been received and is the maximum profit that can be gained from the transaction. To replace this contract from the market would result in another (extra) premium – a credit. Thus, option sales do not have any counterparty credit risk, other than potential delivery risk.

Both FX and options bought contracts share a common factor in market replacement cost risk i.e. the risk varies according to market movements. This makes credit assessment difficult in that the amount at risk is, technically, infinite. FX rates can rise or fall without restriction whereas other markets are, at least, held on the downside – for example, a stock or share cannot fall below zero.

This 'limitless' risk factor does cause some problems in controlling coun-terparty risk should the contract reach unacceptable potential loss levels. One method is to build a buffer on the replacement cost amount – e.g. 120% of market value – so when credit limit is reached, there is still some leeway before the actual risk limit is reached. All this does is provide breathing space in which to assess the situation and act accordingly e.g. the counterparty may warrant a higher limit or, if there are very serious doubts about the counterparty, the option writer may wish to consider a request for 'adequate assurances' under the 'Events of Default' definition in ICOM terms and conditions.

Another, less drastic way of reducing accumulated credit risk is to call for a deposit to support the outstanding position; an informal kind of margin. The problem here is knowing one's customer and whether such arrangements are informal or part of the terms of trading. Interbank uses ICOM but each institution has its own terms for customer transactions (which may also be ICOM), so contingency arrangements such as margins should be advised to potential clients before trading commences.

Margins

Margins are normally associated with exchange trading and, of course, they provide the security that enables the exchanges to guarantee the performance of each and every transaction. This methodology can also be applied to OTC contracts to reduce, or negate entirely, the market replacement risk.

Some institutions do provide 'margin accounts' for option trading with counterparties whose credit rating is insufficient for normal purposes. Margin accounts with cash settlement facilities (to negate delivery risk) are sometimes used by individuals or small companies. They benefit from avoiding exchange fees, brokers' commissions and are able to deal in any strike, currency pair, or amount in the OTC market. The banks benefit from having a captive customer who can only close out contracts with the same bank, although the administrative burden of maintaining margins can be costly.

At the time of writing, margin accounts in OTC are not very common, but are gaining in popularity as more banks begin to market the product.

International currency options market (ICOM) terms and conditions

ICOM terms and conditions were introduced in New York and London in 1992 and Tokyo in 1993. These new terms bring a very important aspect to the OTC interbank market with regard to counterparty credit risk i.e. the netting of outstanding contracts and subsequent cash settlement in cases of default. Banks and other institutions operating under ICOM terms using the Master Agreement facility with other market participants will effectively reduce counterparty credit risk by a large extent.

While it will take some time before it is generally adopted, ICOM is a big step forward in the reduction of credit risk and will eventually spurn further liquidity in the marketplace.

Other markets terms and conditions, such as the International Swap Dealers Association (ISDA) are also likely to adopt terms similar to ICOM to enable netting across products, further reducing credit risk. Perhaps, in the not too distant future, there will be just one set of terms and conditions ruling across all the professional OTC markets: foreign exchange, FX options, Eurodeposits and loans, swaps, interest rate options, bullion, etc.

Conclusion

Each institution will evolve its own system for the measurement of counterparty credit risk but the techniques outlined in this chapter are fairly common. Risk profiles differ greatly in the marketplace as some institutions are more risk conscious than others and some are more active in the markets.

The development of netting in the FX markets through agreements has already arrived in options with ICOM and this process is likely to continue. It is even conceivable that there may be the formation of 'clearing houses' for OTC trades but one thing is certain, the reduction of counterparty credit risk will continue whatever methods are available. The reasons for this are twofold. The first is the capital adequacy requirements due to be placed on banks by the central banks and the second is the vast amounts of losses accumulated by banks in the late 1980s/early 1990s through loan losses. Reduction of risk and expansion of product volume can be achieved but it will be in the form of derivative instruments, such as options and swaps.

14

Accounting for Currency Options

THIS chapter sets out an overview of the accounting aspects of OTC FX option contracts by reference to current common practices. The following describes the treatment of premiums, the accounting for an option as a hedge, accounting for options in a trading book, regulatory guidance, and risk controls. They aim to provide the reader with a general understanding of the principles involved but are by no means exhaustive. Management and accountants are advised to evaluate the appropriateness of these practices in light of their own circumstances. In addition, related funding issues are beyond the scope of this chapter.

Premiums

For individuals who have limited exposure to accounting for options, an option could hardly be an easier instrument to handle as it apparently involves just one cash inflow or outflow i.e. the settlement of the premium. A premium received or paid account is required to record the original transaction value of an option in an organization's balance sheet. In the case of a purchased option, the payment of the premium is the consideration to acquire a right that an option provides. The corresponding double entry is:

Debit: Premium paid account
Credit: Cash with the premium amount

This right lasts until the option expires, is exercised or closed out. The premium settled remains in this account until such time when the option is no longer 'live'.

Similarly, for a sale of an option, the double entry is:

Debit: Cash

Credit: Premium received account with the premium amount

With the receipt of premium, the writer of an option grants to the buyer the rights that an option gives and this liability is reflected in the balance sheet of the writer. Again, since the option premium received reflects an obligation granted, it remains in the premium account until this liability is eliminated as a result of option expiry, exercise or closeout.

Where multi-currency accounting is used, the option premium may be held in the currency in which it is cash settled. However, it should be noted that United States accounting standards require that options settled in non-US currency are to be translated into US dollars using the spot rate at the time of the transaction and that option premium received and paid are to be recorded separately. Also, in deciding the currency in which option premiums are to be recorded, one ought to consider how these option positions are to be revalued. A valuation system may price all options in terms of the accounting currency or in terms of the currency in which premiums are settled.

Some organizations also set up separate premium received accounts for the purchase of a Call and a Put. Likewise the sale of a Call and a Put may also be reflected in two balance sheet accounts. All that seems to be required is the recording of this one cash movement.

This is, however, an over-simplistic approach to option accounting as it overlooks the measurement of profit and loss and other relevant elements. By broadly categorizing option accounting into two types, we can outline some of these other areas of relevance. The types are:

(1) Accounting for an option when it is transacted for *hedging purposes* e.g. a company buys an option to safeguard its foreign currency earnings.
(2) Accounting for an option *within a trading book* e.g. a portfolio of options in a bank trading desk.

Accounting for options as hedges

In order to protect foreign currency exposure against the movement of exchange rates, currency options are now popular tools for corporate treasurers. In this case, the purchase or sale of an option is outside the ordinary business of the organization and is entered into with the primary intention of avoiding FX risk arising from assets or liabilities incurred as part of its normal business. Generally, for an option to qualify as a hedge, the following criteria should be met:

– The transaction is intended as a hedge at the outset with identifiable purposes and is being recorded as such with reference to the asset or liability being hedged. This may be specific to an asset or a liability as well as a pool of assets or liabilities.
– There is reasonable expectation that in the case of a contingent commitment (for which an option is transacted), this commitment will be fulfilled.
– The option should match the related assets and liability in terms of principal amount, maturity and exercise period. The period for which the hedge is

effective matches the exposure of the underlying assets or liabilities being hedged and the hedge is recorded as such. Also, the price movements between them are closely correlated. These will normally require the asset or liability to be sensitive to the same risk parameters as an FX option.

The accounting treatment for options that qualify as hedges should correspond to the accounting treatment of the underlying transaction being hedged. Hence, if these transactions are being revalued, the options ought to be revalued on the same basis. The objective of a hedge is that the gains (or losses) arising from the underlying asset or liability are offset by the losses (or gains) attributable to the FX option.

In addition, option premium settled is either amortized over the period that the option is hedging, or is deferred until a commitment is fulfilled. If the option is transacted to protect foreign currency remittance to be received in three months time, then the payment is written off over the three month period. Adopting the same approach, if the option is transacted to hedge exposure giving rise to the outcome of a tender which may not be known until one month later, the premium settled for this anticipatory hedge is not taken to the profit and loss account until then. However, the argument against such treatment is that it goes against the prudence concept of accounting. Indeed, the Securities and Exchange Commission (SEC) in the United States has stated against hedge accounting being applied to complex options (for example, range forwards) transacted to hedge anticipatory FX exposure, although purchased options with little or no intrinsic value are allowed.

If the event (that an FX option is hedging) ceases to exist prior to the option expiry, then until such time as the option is closed out, it may be treated as a trading option.

Generally, options that are transacted as hedges tend to be held at the original premium cost, or are only revalued when the underlying assets or liabilities are so treated, using the same revaluation basis. An issue which is worth noting is that one of the pricing factors specific to an option is volatility. If volatility suddenly jumped to a significant level, the profit or loss effect on the option would very likely exceed the loss or profit arising from FX rate movement with respect to the assets or liabilities being hedged when both are revalued.

The unrealized gains or losses arising from the revaluation may be recorded in the same premium paid/received account or in a separate option revaluation account on the balance sheet, with the offset on an unrealized profit and loss account. If a separate revaluation account is used, the unrealized gains and losses are generally recorded separately. Fees and expenses relating to the hedging transactions may be deferred under the same accounting treatment as the option itself for consistency, although if the amount is insignificant, they may also be written off when incurred.

Commitments and contingencies in the form of notional principals involved in FX options transactions should also be recorded. They normally form part of the financial accounting disclosure requirements, noting the transactions attributable to hedges and those to trading. Since an FX option is an off-balance sheet instrument which involves the potential purchase of a currency against the sale of another, the notional amounts of each of the two currencies may be recorded as memorandum entries. In a multi-currency general ledger, eight memorandum accounts and their corresponding contra accounts may be set up to record these entries. They are:

(1)   Call options sold – purchase currency (the Put currency)
(2)   Call options sold – sell currency (the Call currency)
(3)   Call options bought – purchase currency (the Call currency)
(4)   Call options bought – sell currency (the Put currency)
(5)   Put options sold – purchase currency (the Put currency)
(6)   Put options sold – sell currency (the Call currency)
(7)   Put options bought – purchase currency (the Call currency)
(8)   Put options bought – sell currency (the Put currency)

The memorandum contra accounts to (1)–(8) are set up in the format:

(9)   Contra account – Call options sold – purchase currency
(10)   Contra account – Call options sold – sell currency

and so on to produce a total of 16 memorandum accounts.

The above reflect the contingent obligations in the Call and Put currency attributable to an option position and the double entries may be summarized as follows:

Call Options Sold (sell the Call currency; buy the Put currency)

Debit:	Memorandum contra account	With the
Credit:	Call options sold – sell currency	Call currency
Debit:	Call options sold – purchase currency	With the
Credit:	Memorandum contra account	Put currency

Put Options Sold (sell the Call currency: buy the Put currency)

Debit:	Put options sold – purchase currency	With the
Credit:	Memorandum contra account	Put currency
Debit:	Memorandum contra account	With the
Credit:	Put options sold – sell currency	Call currency

Call Options Bought (buy the Call currency; sell the Put currency)

Debit:	Call options bought – purchase currency	With the
Credit:	Memorandum contra account	Call currency
Debit:	Memorandum contra account	With the
Credit:	Call options bought – sell currency	Put currency

Put Options Bought (buy the Call currency; sell the Put currency)

Debit:	Memorandum contra account	With the
Credit:	Put options bought – sell currency	Put currency
Debit:	Put options bought – purchase currency	With the
Credit:	Memorandum contra account	Call currency

All notional amounts recorded are reversed upon maturity, exercise or closeout of the relevant position.

This might seem confusing to those who are not accounting types! A couple of examples may help clarify the process:

Example (i)

A company in the United States importing wine from France is billed French Francs (FRF) 5 000 000 with payment due in three months. To hedge the risk of the FRF rising (USD falling), the company buys an FRF Call (USD Put) with three months maturity for FRF 5 000 000 struck at 5.2500 (FRF per USD).

The memorandum account entries for the option purchased are as follows:

Debit:	Call options bought – purchased currency	FRF 5 000 000
Credit:	Memorandum contra account	FRF 5 000 000
Debit:	Memorandum contra account	USD 952 380.95
Credit:	Call options bought – sell currency	USD 952 380.95

Note: FRF 5 000 000 at 5.2500 (strike price) = USD 952 380.95

Example (ii)

A GBP Put (USD Call) option, strike 1.50 is sold by a company that would benefit from a decline in the pound sterling.

Memorandum account entries as follows:

Debit:	Put options sold – purchase currency	GBP 10 000 000
Credit:	Memorandum contra account	GBP 10 000 000
Debit:	Memorandum contra account	USD 15 000 000
Credit:	Put options sold – sell currency	USD 15 000 000

Accounting for options in a trading book

Any option position transacted for reasons apart from hedging an identifiable FX risk arising from an asset or liability may arguably be considered a trading position. This covers dealers' and speculators' positions as well as short positions transacted to enhance returns from underlying liquid assets by the premium earned.

Trading positions are revalued daily using current market volatility, FX and interest rates. Given present OTC market conditions, most of the input required to price an option position is easily available, hence also the revaluation. In the Risk Controls section that follows, other factors which may affect the current value of an option are discussed.

The mark-to-market process essentially calculates the current value of open positions held as if they had been liquidated. The marked-to-market profit or loss of any period is derived by taking into account the movement of closed out value from the start of the period to the end, with regard to the settled amount.

To arrive at a realistic marked-to-market revaluation, a long position may be revalued at the bid price, and a short position at the offer price, although most banks revalue their books using mid-market prices on the basis that positions are changed constantly. Also, option positions may be revalued using a two dimensional volatility matrix based on the strike prices and maturity, instead of maturity only.

An important issue which might appear obvious but which is often overlooked is the consistency of the valuation methods and models used between the trading system and the accounting system in an organization if these systems are not integrated. There should be no discrepancies between the profit and loss conceived by the trader and that recorded in the books i.e. arising from differences in valuation approaches of two systems. Very often, however, a trader will use a software options package running on a personal computer (PC) for risk management that is different from the main processing and accounting systems used by an institution.

For simplicity, it is assumed that the only two hedging means used in trading FX options are: (1) hedging with FX transaction (whether spot or forward) and (2) other FX options. There may also be other FX positions which are related e.g. the conversion of foreign currency premiums to the profit or loss accounting currency. The profit or loss movements of all these is arrived at on a net present value basis so it reflects the cash value at the valuation date.

(1) Hedging with foreign exchange transactions

In the preceding chapters, much has already been said about delta hedging and the resultant gains or losses of these and other related FX positions. These hedging costs and credits must also be accounted for as trading profit or loss.

Until an option reaches its maturity date or an FX transaction reaches its value date, the marked-to-market profit or loss is unrealized and changes in the actual value of these positions from one day to another forms part of the daily profit or loss. The gains or losses attributable to the options and FX positions are recorded in separate accounts but the double entry for both is:

| Debit: | Revaluation gains account | In case |
| Credit: | Unrealized profit or loss account | of profit |

| Debit: | Unrealized profit or loss account | In case |
| Credit: | Revaluation losses account | of loss |

The unrealized FX profit or loss represents the net present valued difference between the dealt and the current market rate of the position. On maturity (value date), the realized profit or loss is the difference between the dealt and the value date spot rate which is crystallized by closing out the relevant position. The unrealized profit or loss to date is reversed as follows:

| Debit/credit: | Revaluation gains or losses |
| Credit/debit: | Unrealized option profit or loss |

(2) Hedging with other options

For options, the unrealized gains or losses may also be recorded in the manner described in (1), or by passing the entries through the premium paid/received accounts. The sum of the revaluation gains/losses accounts and the premium paid/received accounts should always be equal to the current market value of the options positions held.

The other part of the profit or loss account consists of the realized components. Since option premium paid or received is all that can be incurred when an option matures, is exercised or closed out, this constitutes option realized profit or loss. At this point, the premium paid for an option bought becomes a realized loss, whereas the premium received for an option sold becomes realized profit. All the unrealized profit and loss to date is reversed when an option is no longer in existence.

The double entry here (maturity, exercise or closeout) is as follows:

Debit:	Option realized profit or loss	Bought option
Credit:	Option premium paid	premiums
Debit:	Option premium received	Sold option
Credit:	Option realized profit or loss	premiums

And

Debit/credit:	Revaluation gains or losses
Credit/debit:	Unrealized option profit

(3) Hedging with equal and opposite options

It is common to find that part of a trading options matched with other options that have identical specifications other than the counterparty name. In other words, a bought option is offset (hedged exactly) by a sold option with similar amount (face value), strike rate, style (American or European), and type (Call or Put) but with a different counterparty. There are no trading risks with this, but there is the possibility of counterparty credit risk (see Chapter 13).

For a perfectly matched portfolio, an option's unrealized profit or loss should remain the same from inception to maturity. This amount will represent the difference in premiums between these options. The double entry is as described above, but as there will be no delta risks, the profit or loss of this portfolio does not consist of any foreign exchange gains or losses arising from such delta hedging.

In summary, the trading profit or loss of an option book at any point in time comprises of unrealized option and FX profit or loss. These four components are normally recorded separately but must be aggregated together to obtain a complete profit or loss figure. In most banks and organizations which also deal heavily in FX, the FX components tend to be internal deals between the FX department and the options desk. An exception to this would be the 'automatic' delta hedge FX transaction concluded with interbank option deals in the OTC market (see Chapter 9).

Fees and expenses associated with options trading are generally written off in the period in which they are incurred. All notional amounts involved in options transactions are recorded in the ways described earlier and are reversed upon maturity, exercise or closeout of the relevant positions. They form part of the financial accounting disclosure requirements, noting those transactions attributable to hedges and those to trading. With respect to a trading operation, it is common to find that these commitments and contingencies also form part of the exposure limits reported to regulators e.g. Bank of England Annex A/B (FX position return S3) reporting of options for banks in the United Kingdom (see Chapter 11).

With respect to option derivatives or 'exotic' options (see Chapter 15), the accounting principles and treatments are similar to those described in this chapter. Other options strategies, such as the range forward or participating forward, can be recorded as a combination of Calls and Puts in the manner already described, rather than treating each 'product' as independent.

Regulatory guidance

With the enhanced use of derivative products by financial institutions and continuous market developments, regulators in most countries, especially the United States and the United Kingdom, have shown increased awareness of the need to provide institutions with further supervision and regulatory guidance, both in terms of accounting and risk management. Various bodies including the US General Accounting Office, the Emerging Issues Task Force of the US Financial Accounting Standards Board, the US Securities Exchange Commission, the UK Accounting Standards Committee and the British Bankers Association have all engaged in efforts to keep pace with the market.

Some of the regulatory recommendations are also reinforced by legislative provisions, for example, in the UK Companies Acts. The author does not wish to discuss the individual works of these bodies here and a titles listing of some of the relevant regulatory releases are to be found at the end of this chapter.

The ultimate object of regulation and supervision is to ensure that the financial accounts of an institution give a true and fair view of the profit or loss of a particular period and state of affairs at the balance sheet date. Where off-balance sheet derivative instruments are involved, this should also mean the accounts provide an indication of the inherent exposure and risks.

Guidance from, and recommendations made by, regulators for the accounting of these new derivative instruments is evolved from and consistent with the fundamental accounting principles and concepts of prudence and accruals. The prudence concept states that all known or probable expenses, losses and liabilities should be provided for whilst earnings and profits are only accounted for when these are certain to be realized. To satisfy the principle of accruals, related income and expenses are accrued so that they are matched in the same accounting period. In the case of conflict, the prudence concepts should be adopted. In addition, the accounting methods and treatments applied to similar transactions and issues should be consistent from one period to the next. Materiality of the item is to be taken into account when deciding its accounting treatments.

An important consideration is that option transactions are recorded in light of their substance and not their form. This means the accounting methods adopted take into account the business objective and reflect the exposure, as well as any associated profit and loss, in a realistic manner.

Risk control

Accounting for options should not be confined to bookkeeping general ledger entries. At the outset, the correct recording of the transactions are crucial as very often a profit or loss that cannot be agreed between a trader and the accountant leads to the discovery of an error. In addition, the accounting records are a prime source of management information data that quantifies risk. The completeness and accuracy of this information has a direct impact in business decision-making and assessments. It is therefore important to ensure that the accounting systems should be able to support the business.

A thorough understanding of the business and a full appreciation of the risks associated with the option product is also essential. These qualities provide management and accountants with the ability to make objective assessments in areas diversified from the quality of counterparty credit to the effectiveness of the back office operation; from whether additional provision has to be made as a result of illiquidity of the positions, to the viability of the business and to be able to make informed decisions.

Finally, an accounting system must at least be able to record the transactions correctly and accurately. This is just as vital to an FX option operation as an effective derivative risk management system. However, without an appreciation of risks, there can be little given to the true meaning of accounting for options. It is very often the interpretation of the accounting information that gives warning signals of the risks involved. This does not only apply to banks actively trading but also corporate users. The substantial loss suffered by a UK corporate recently in FX options trading is a case in point. Therefore, it must be ensured that accounting for options, and indeed for all derivative instruments, is not treated as just another 'bean counter' job.

List of relevant regulatory releases

Set out below are some of the accounting and legislative releases which affect current accounting practices:

United Kingdom
- Statement of standard accounting practice No. 2: Disclosure of accounting policies.
- Statement of standard accounting practice No. 18: Accounting for contingencies.
- Statement of standard accounting practice No. 20: Foreign currency translation.
- Statement of recommended accounting practice on off-balance sheet commitments and contingencies.
- Exposure draft ED 49: Reflecting the substance of transactions in assets and liabilities.
- Companies Act 1985 (as amended by the Companies Act 1989) implementing the EC Company Law Directive.
- Companies Act 1985 (Bank accounts) Regulation 1991.

United States
- Statement of financial accounting standard No. 52: Foreign currency translation.

- Statement of financial accounting standard No. 80: Accounting for futures contract.
- Statement of financial accounting standard No. 105: Disclosure of information about financial instruments with off-balance sheet risk and financial instruments with concentrations of credit risk.
- Financial Accounting Standard Board interpretation No. 39: Offsetting of amounts related to certain contracts.
- Statement of financial accounting standard No. 107: Disclosures about Fair Value of Financial Statements.
- Financial Accounting Standard Board discussion memorandum on recognition and measurement of financial instruments.
- The Emerging Issues Task force Issue No. 91-4: Hedging foreign currency risks with complex options and similar transactions.

Others
- International accounting standard IAS No. 30: Disclosures in the financial statements of banks and similar institutions.
- International Accounting Standards Committee exposure draft No. 40: Financial instruments.
- Canadian Institute of Chartered Accountants exposure draft entitled Financial Instruments.

Option Derivatives and the Future

15

THIS book has been devoted to the rapidly expanding FX options market, recently cited in a BIS (Bank for International Settlements) survey as the fastest growing segment of the FX market and which now accounts for about 6–8% of the one trillion dollars a day FX market. The currency option is a derivative of the FX market but there is another market emerging – that of the option derivative, or 'exotic' options as they are sometimes called. These options have been invented by banks and other financial institutions to tailor specific client needs, either to better match the risk profile of the customer or, more commonly, to reduce premium expenditure. Exotic options are true derivatives of the ordinary or 'plain vanilla' options described in this book. They are not combinations of plain options with fancy names such as those invented on the exchanges and described in Chapter 5, so forget butterflies and enter the world of 'barriers', 'look-backs', 'compounds', 'average rates', 'digitals', 'rainbows', 'contingents', and others.

Exotic options are only traded OTC and, at the time of writing, only between bank and customer. There is no true interbank market (yet) in these products but this is likely to change once the number of institutions using these products increases.

There follows a description of the most popular options in the exotic range, but the list is not exclusive as new types appear regularly.

Compound options

The underlying instrument for a normal currency option is the exchange rate between two currencies e.g. a JPY Call, DEM Put option would allow the holder to buy JPY and sell DEM at the strike price. With a compound option, however, the underlying instrument is itself a currency option so it is an option on an option!

The buyer of a compound Call option has the right to buy the underlying option at a fixed premium on a fixed date in the future. Likewise the buyer of a compound Put option has the right to sell the underlying option for a fixed premium on a fixed date in the future. In either case, the buyer of the compound option will be required to pay a premium for this right in the same manner as for plain options. This means there are two premiums involved in the transaction, the first to buy the compound and the second, the underlying option premium which was agreed at the outset. The second is therefore the compound option's strike.

Example:

Underlying Option – JPY Call / DEM Put, strike 78.50 (JPY per DEM), 6 month expiry, DEM 10 000 000, premium JPY 2.75 per DEM.

The buyer of a one month compound Call option with strike of JPY 2.75 would have the right, but not the obligation, to purchase the underlying JPY Call (DEM Put) *in three months time* for JPY 2.75 per DEM.

The buyer would only exercise the compound Call option if the underlying JPY Call struck at 78.50 would be worth more than JPY 2.75 on expiry of the compound, after one month. If exercised, the buyer would then pay the second premium of JPY 2.75 per DEM (JPY 22.75 million, in this case).

The buyer of a compound Put option would have the right to sell the underlying option, and would therefore only exercise if the underlying option struck at 78.50 would be worth less than JPY 2.75 per DEM on expiry of the compound, after one month. If exercised, the compound buyer would receive the premium of 2.75 JPY per DEM (JPY 27.5 million).

Uses for compound options

The most common use of compound options is to be found in the cases of tender-to-contract situations. Consider an exporter in Japan tendering to supply equipment to a foreign buyer priced in DEM. The Japanese exporter is bound to hold its price firm for the period of the tender and is therefore at risk from changes in the JPY/DEM exchange rate. The company will not want to cover this risk in the forward FX market as the contract may not be won. For the same reason, a normal JPY Call (DEM Put) option will look rather expensive. A compound option could be purchased for the period of the tender which would cover this contingent risk. If the contract is won, the underlying option could be exercised (if ITM at that point, because if not, the exporter could purchase the same underlying option cheaper in the marketplace). If the contract is lost, a considerably smaller premium has been paid (for the compound) than if a normal option had been purchased. Of course, even if the tender was unsuccessful, the compound may still have intrinsic value on expiry, in which case the exporter would simply exercise the compound and sell the underlying option to gain this value, reducing the overall cost of the hedge.

As with normal options, the strike price of the compound is chosen by the buyer and this may be in, at or out-of the-money. Using the previous example, the strike price *of the compound* will depend on how much the buyer wants to pay for the underlying three months JPY Call (DEM Put) struck at 78.50. The present value of this option is 2.75 JPY per DEM therefore a compound call option with a strike of 2.75 JPY per DEM is ATM. Let us assume the compound Call option premium for this strike is 1.25 JPY per DEM.

What if the buyer were to choose a compound Call option strike of, say, JPY 3.50 JPY per DEM? Here the buyer would be willing to pay JPY 3.50 for the underlying JPY Call (DEM Put) which is more than the current value of JPY 2.75, so the compound option is OTM i.e. the underlying option is not worth exercising at 3.50 when it can be bought for 2.75. Consequently, the compound Call option premium will be less than that struck ATM.

Using the same logic, a compound Call option with a strike of JPY 2.0 per DEM will be ITM as the underlying option is currently worth 2.75 i.e. the compound is worth exercising as it has intrinsic value of JPY 0.75. The compound premium of this option is JPY 1.50.

So, the more the buyer pays for the compound option, the less he pays for the underlying, and vice versa. However, the absolute cost of the hedge, if the compound is exercised, is always the total of the two premiums – one for the compound and one for the underlying – and this total is a function of the strike price of the compound. Using the examples given, it can be seen that the cheapest is the purchase of the ITM compound (JPY 1.50 + JPY 2.00 = JPY 3.50), the most expensive is the purchase of the OTM compound at JPY 4.50 (1.00 + 3.50), with the ATM falling in the middle.

Stated simply, the more one pays for the compound, the less one pays later and the cheaper the absolute cost (assuming exercise of the compound). So the buyer's determinate of the compound strike is the likelihood of winning the tender. If a high probability, one will pay more for the compound (and less overall), while if the probability is low, one will pay less for the compound, which will be the only cost (tender unsuccessful, no need for underlying option, no exercise, no second premium).

Hedging

There is no interbank market for compound options, so the only available hedging method is that of delta neutrality. Compound options have deltas expressed as a percentage of the underlying in the same manner as ordinary options, so the compound Call (Put) option writer will need to buy (sell) the underlying option according to the compound delta and re-hedge through the life of the compound.

Example:
Bank sells 1 month compound Call option, strike JPY 2.75, on the underlying: JPY Call (DEM Put), DEM 10 000 000, strike of 78.50 (JPY per DEM), three months expiry for premium JPY 2.75.

This compound option has a strike of JPY 2.75 which is the same as the underlying option premium and is therefore ATM. Delta is 50%.

The bank trader, having sold the compound, needs to apply a delta hedge and this is done by purchasing DEM 5 000 000 of a 78.50 JPY Call (DEM Put) option for three months. The trader is now neutralized from an initial movement in the underlying option premium. Over time, the compound delta will probably change, for example to 60% in which case the trader will need to buy an additional DEM 10 000 000 of 78.50 JPY Calls (DEM Puts) for the same expiring date as the original purchase i.e. three months from origination date. The process of continually adjusting and re-adjusting the hedge according to the delta continues throughout the life of the compound i.e. one month. At the end of this period, the bank trader will either have a 100% hedge or zero, to cater for either exercise of the compound, or worthless expiry of same. This is the normal effect of delta hedging.

Average rate options

Sometimes referred to as 'Asian' options, average rate options (AVROs) are one of a series termed 'true hedging instruments'. They compare to regular FX options in that the buyer is protected against adverse movements in FX rates, while benefiting from favourable movements. The big difference is in the fact that intrinsic value on maturity of an average rate option is based on the comparison between the strike and the average FX rate over the life of the option, not the spot rate on maturity.

FX rate fixings are taken at predetermined, regular intervals from an agreed source, to produce an average rate for the period. Due to the averaging process, the volatility of such rates is much less than that of regular spot rates, thereby producing a lower premium than for normal options. This factor is the major reason for the popularity of average rate options.

Cash settlement

Another difference with average rate options is that they are cash settled i.e. the intrinsic value on maturity (if any) is paid by the writer to the buyer of the option. This is because it is not possible to gain the intrinsic value through exercise at the strike price. Normal options are exercised on maturity to produce a spot FX transaction at the strike rate; this can be easily realized into cash by reversing the spot deal in the market at the prevailing rate. To do the same for an average rate option would require the ability to trade in the spot market at the historical average rate, which clearly is not possible.

Rate fixings

Fixings can be taken daily, weekly, or monthly, but the interval between fixings should be constant. The source of such fixing has to be agreed between the counterparties, and is generally a third party reference according to the currency pair involved; examples include the daily Frankfurt fixing for the DEM, the Milan fixing for the lira or, in the absence of an official fix, the published rate on Reuters or Telerate at a specified time (e.g. 11.00am London).

Uses for average rate options

Average rate options are the perfect hedging tool for companies who have FX exposure in the form of regular cash flows in known amounts. This is especially relevant where the company uses an average rate for annual accounting or budget purposes.

Example:

A Swiss exporter has a regular cash inflow of USD 1 000 000 per month on the 15th of each month for a year. Profit for the year has been assessed using the current CHF/USD exchange rate leaving the company at risk to the decline in the value of the USD against the Swiss franc (CHF).

To hedge this position the company could:

(1) Buy regular USD Put (CHF Call) options in the amount of USD 1 million for each of the twelve one-month periods struck at the current CHF/USD rate. Total cost of premiums – USD 360 000.

OR

(2) Buy a one year average rate CHF Call (USD Put) option, struck at the current CHF/USD rate for USD 12 million. Cost of the one premium – USD 240 000.

There is a cost saving to the company of USD 120 000 between (1) and (2), but it is worth looking at what would happen in each case. Assume the current CHF/USD rate is 1.40 (CHF per USD) and this is the chosen strike rate in both cases:

(1) Each month would, in turn, involve the company selling USD 1 000 000 on the 15th either through option exercise (if the spot rate was lower than 1.40) or at the prevailing spot rate (if higher than 1.40). The net effect is a worse case scenario is selling at 1.40.

(2) With the average rate option, the company sells the USD 1 000 000 on the 15th of each month at whatever rate is prevailing in the spot market at that time. After 12 months the company will have sold 12 million USD in the spot market. These sales will take place at the same time of day as the fixing for the average rate option in order that the average, when calculated after the 12 months period (i.e. for the average rate option), is very close to that obtained by the company in the spot market.

Now assume the calculated average turns out to be 1.35 CHF per USD over the 12 months. This rate is lower than the average rate option strike of 1.40, so the company receives a cash payment as settlement of the average rate option. This amount is CHF 600 000 with average rate strike of 1.40 less calculated average of 1.35, multiplied by USD 12 000 000.

In the first case the company never sells USD below 1.40 and may sell some of the USD receipts at above 1.40. In the second case, the company sells USD at the prevailing spot rate, which may be above or below 1.40, and achieves an average of 1.35 (indicating that many of the sales were below 1.40). In this case the company is compensated to 1.40 by the payment of CHF 600 000 as cash settlement of the average rate option.

In effect, the two strategies have much the same outcome. The worst case is selling USD at 1.40 and if the average is higher than 1.40, then the company would have sold USD over the life of the option at that higher rate (but, of course, with no cash settlement from the average rate).

The main difference is in the premiums paid. In this example, the average rate is cheaper by USD 120 000 being about 33% cheaper than the twelve individual options. Average rate options will always be cheaper than a strip of individual (regular) options and a 30% saving is fairly typical.

Despite the apparent cheapness, the buyer of an AVRO does concede a potential benefit that is not always evident (and may not apply) but does warrant comment. Note again the earlier example; in (1) the company always sells USD 1 million at a minimum rate of 1.40 if the spot is lower than that level, and indeed the average (on the AVRO) was below 1.40 at 1.35. Nevertheless, it is possible to achieve an average rate of 1.35 where certain points in the averaging are above 1.40, in which case the company under (1) would benefit from the difference on USD 1 million for the amount over 1.40 (the AVRO strike) each time it occurred during the 12 month period. Obviously, this benefit has to be limited otherwise the average would not be below 1.40.

AVROs are popular not only because of the lower premium but because they fit the requirements of the budget or accounting practices adopted by many companies.

Hedging average rate options

The delta of an AVRO behaves in a different way to that of an ordinary option, in that it will always approach zero at expiry. This is due to the averaging effect on the underlying rate and the fact that the option is cash settled. For example, consider an average rate option with weekly fixings over two years (104 points to produce the average) that has one week left before expiry. Since the last 103 rates are already known, the last fixing will have very little effect on the overall average. Thus, we can see that the more fixings that are taken, the more sensitive the price is to the spot FX rate reductions, and with this process the sensitivity of the delta itself (the gamma) reduces. As a result, most of the risk in hedging an AVRO is in the early stages. This is the opposite of a normal option where the gamma increases towards maturity, assuming it not too far from ATM status.

An AVRO could be hedged with a strip of regular options (one for each of the periods) which would adequately negate the risk. The problem with this is that it would defeat the object of selling the average rate in the first place, in other words, why reduce premium cost (to the buyer) by averaging and then hedge with a strip of regular options which will cost more? A better method is to use the delta process and/or buy a regular option at the same strike as the AVRO to take care of the risks over the first few fixings, say, 30 to 40% of the AVRO's life span. This is not a perfect hedge by any means, but it does give some good protection where it is needed (in the early stages) and less when it is not (at the later stages of the AVRO's life), leaving some potential for profit.

Average rate options – variations

There are some variations to the AVRO which have been designed to meet more specific customer requirements.

Forward start average rate options

The forward start AVRO is a product which differs only slightly from a conventional AVRO in that the first reference fixing for the average will take place in the future (on a specified date). The AVRO then continues to average in the same way as a normal AVRO, and at maturity is settled in the same way i.e. cash settlement. This variation allows a company to hedge in advance, perhaps at a time when the current spot FX level is considered to be advantageous.

The cost of a forward starting AVRO is usually a little higher than that of a regular AVRO as, before the averaging period begins, the option behaves like a normal 'plain vanilla' European style option. As a general rule, the longer the forward start period and the shorter the average period, the more it behaves like a 'plain vanilla' with the accompanying higher premium cost. So, for example, a forward start AVRO with a one month forward start period and 11 month averaging will be cheaper that one with the same strike and amount for three months forward start and nine months averaging period.

Weighted average rate option

The conventional AVRO and the forward start AVRO assume that the buyer is hedging the same amount of currency on each fixing date. In practice, many companies experience irregular-size cash flows, due to seasonal factors for example, and the more irregular or violent these swings, so the less efficient the hedge provided by the regular AVRO. The weighted AVRO remedies this problem.

As long as the amounts of each cash flow can be projected, the weighted AVRO can be used. The mathematics are slightly different in order to take care of the weighting required and, at maturity, the strike price is compared to the weighted average of the fixings to calculate the cash settlement (if any). The cost of a weighted AVRO is not easy to predict as so much depends on the weighting, and how much it varies from fixing date to fixing date. Generally, if the cash flows are larger at the beginning and then decrease in size, the cost will be lower than if the reverse were true.

Summary of average rate options

It can be seen from the above descriptions of AVROs that they can provide an efficient solution to FX risk as encountered by many companies. The flexibility of the AVRO's structure allows each option to be tailored to suit individual requirements. For example, a company's budget rates could be guaranteed be using AVROs, and yet full benefit could be taken from beneficial moves in the underlying rate – the basic principle of all options purchased.

For the buyer, the AVRO is much more cost effective (lower premium) than the equivalent regular European style option, and one option can cover many cash flows thus saving in administrative expenses. For the writer, credit risk is reduced to near zero due to the cash settlement feature on maturity (no exchange of currencies), leaving premium receipt the only consideration (this can also be avoided by having the buyer's funds on account).

Finally, it should be noted that all types of AVRO collectively form just one of a series termed as 'path dependent'. These options have pay-offs that depend on the movement of the underlying (spot FX rate) during the life of the option, rather than just on maturity in the case of regular options. Thus, AVROs are path dependent, but compound options are not.

Average strike options

Another path dependent option, the average strike has fixing dates similar to the average rate option but no initial strike rate is set. Instead the spot rate fixings are averaged on maturity of the option and this average becomes the strike rate of the option. Comparison is then made to the prevailing spot rate to determine whether exercise should take place. Settlement is as per plain vanilla options, but cash settlement can also be used.

Average strike options are used more for speculative rather than hedging purposes.

Barrier options

Barrier (sometimes referred to as 'trigger') options are also in the path dependent group of exotic options and consist of two types: 'knockout' or 'knock-in'. They are regular European style options with a twist – the option can disappear with a knockout barrier option, or be created with a knock-in barrier, if the underlying spot FX rate hits a pre-set barrier or trigger point. The barrier can be set either above or below the current spot FX rate resulting in two types of knockout: 'up-and-out' and 'down-and-out'; and two types of knock-in: 'up-and-in' and 'down-and-in' – giving four kinds of barrier options. Because of these extinguishing or activating features, barrier options are cheaper than ordinary European options, and so are popular with option purchasers who are premium adverse.

Knockout – up-and-out

The knockout up-and-out option ceases to exist if the underlying spot rate rises to a predetermined level.

Example:

A United Kingdom importer has FX risk in GBP falling against the USD. To negate this risk, the importer buys a 6 month, GBP Put (USD Call), struck at 1.50 (ATM, spot) with knockout barrier of 1.60; premium USD 6.75 cents.

In this example, the importer is fully protected against GBP falling against the USD by the purchase of the GBP Put struck at 1.50, the current spot rate. However, a rise in the value of GBP would result in the option being cancelled at the 1.60 barrier point, but the importer would benefit from his underlying FX position (long GBP against USD) by purchasing USD more cheaply than if GBP was at a lower level. This knockout option provides the same benefits as a regular GBP Put option providing the spot GBP rate does not retrace (after hitting the barrier) back to, and below, 1.50 where the importer no longer has the protection of the 1.50 Put.

In the above example, a regular GBP 1.50 Put (USD Call) for six months would have cost 7.20 US cents, against the 6.75 for the barrier. This cost saving has to be weighed up against the risk of the FX rate retracing to the original level after knocking out the option at the set trigger point. Thus the up-and-out barrier option will perform the same as an ordinary European option providing that the spot rate never reaches the barrier during the life of the option i.e. spot can go down (to any degree) or up (but only to just short of the barrier level).

The pricing of a knockout barrier option reflects the probability of spot reaching the trigger point. Thus, the nearer the barrier to the current spot rate, the cheaper the option (the higher the chance of the barrier being hit); the further the barrier is set from spot, the more expensive the option (the lower the chance of the barrier being hit).

The up-and-out barrier is usually constructed with the trigger point set OTM relative to current spot (as in the earlier example with the GBP Put). An up-and-out that has the barrier set ITM relative to spot (a GBP Call in the above example) produces a seemingly odd scenario, of an option that has increasing intrinsic value that suddenly disappears at the barrier point. The price of such an option can be very low compared to the regular European option but are little used as they do not fit everyday hedging requirements.

Knockout – down-and-out

The knockout down-and-out option ceases to exist if the underlying spot rate falls to a predetermined level and, like the up-and-in, is usually constructed with the barrier set OTM.

Example:

The UK branch of an American bank has local expenses in sterling but income, and accounting, is in US dollars. The sterling expenses are open to risk in the GBP rising where each pound will translate into more USD. Budget has been set at exchange rate of 1.50 (USD per GBP).

To protect against the rise in GBP, the bank buys a GBP Call (USD Put) struck at 1.50, with a barrier of 1.40. Current spot rate is 1.50 so option is ATM.

In this example, the bank is fully protected with GBP above 1.50 by the Call but has a barrier of 1.40 at which point the option ceases to exist, should the spot rate drop to that level during the option's life span. However, at 1.40 the bank can buy GBP to cover its expenses at a lower rate and is therefore not concerned with the 1.50 Call cancellation.

As with the up-and-out barrier, the down-and-out is cheaper than the straight European option. Using the above example, for a six month, 1.50 GBP Call (USD Put) with a barrier at 1.40, the cost is 2.85 US cents per GBP compared with 3.07 US cents for the ordinary European GBP Call (USD Put). The pay-off is the same providing that the spot GBP FX rate does not drop to 1.40 where the option would cease to exist (hence 'down-and-out'). The risk versus the straight European 1.50 GBP Call is that it is possible for the spot rate to return to the 1.50 area, or above, after triggering the option cancellation at 1.40, leaving the bank with no protection (and having already paid a premium).

The barrier of 1.40 has been set OTM with regard to the spot rate of 1.50, which is normal for this type of barrier option.

Knock-in – up-and-in

The two knockout barrier options each had a feature whereby the option was cancelled when spot reached a trigger point (the barrier). The two knock-ins each have an option creation feature when spot reaches the barrier point. The first of these is the up-and-in barrier option where no option exists until spot climbs to the trigger point.

Example:

A speculator believes that a forthcoming United Kingdom general election will be won by the existing government. In this case, the GBP/USD rate (currently 1.50 USD per GBP) is likely to go up on such a result. However, the speculator also believes that such increase in sterling with be short-lived and ultimately GBP will devalue against the USD, which itself is considered undervalued.

The speculator buys an up-and-in barrier option, a 6 month, GBP Put (USD Call) struck at 1.50 (ATM spot) with trigger point at 1.60. Premium is very small – just 0.42 US cents per pound.

In this example, no option exists unless the spot GBP/USD exchange rate increases to the trigger, or barrier, of 1.60. At this point, the 1.50 GBP Put (USD Call) is created to mature on the original maturity date. If this event occurs, the option buyer will be looking for the GBP/USD rate to reverse and decline to below 1.50 where the option will have intrinsic value. Hence, an up-and-in will only suit a buyer who expects the reversal of the exchange rate, such as the speculator in the example.

The price of this knock-in, 0.42 US cents, compares very favourably with the ordinary 1.50 GBP Put (USD Call) at 7.20 US cents. However, imagine what would happen if the buyer was to wait until spot reached 1.60 before buying an ordinary 1.50 GBP Put (USD Call). The cost of this would, at the most, be 2.78 cents if this was done on the same day (although this is unlikely, given spot would have to rise by 10 US cents!). After one month, the cost of a five month GBP Put (USD Call), with spot at 1.60, would still be 2.20 US cents. Even after four months, the cost (of a two month option) would still be 0.48 US cents. Therefore, the up-and-in barrier is a very inexpensive way of buying an option, and the buyer needs more than one event to occur to benefit from the transaction – spot GBP/USD rate must first move up to the barrier during the period selected, reverse direction, then regain all the 'lost ground' back to the strike rate before the option expires. This is a lot to ask for!

The pricing of a knock-in barrier option reflects the probability of spot reaching the trigger point. Thus, the nearer the barrier to the current spot rate, the more expensive the option (the higher the chance of the barrier being hit); the further the barrier is set from spot, the cheaper the option (the lower the chance of the barrier being hit).

Up-and-in barriers are usually constructed using trigger points that are OTM relative to spot, as in the above example.

Knock-in – down-and-in

The down-and-in option is created only when the spot FX rate declines to a specified barrier, or trigger, point. Like the up-and-in, its use seems to be speculative, and can be applied to cases where the spot FX rate is expected to go down to a certain level, the barrier point, and then reverse to climb back up to, and beyond, the strike rate.

Example:

A speculator feels that the GBP/USD exchange rate will fall sharply when unexpected interest rate cuts are announced, but will recover steadily from the lows as the stock market and government bonds markets pick up through overseas investments.

The speculator buys a GBP Call (USD Put) struck at 1.50 (USD per GBP) with down-and-in barrier set at 1.40. Current spot rate is 1.50 and premium for the six month option is just 0.22 US cents per GBP.

The tiny premium of 0.22 US cents compares to 3.07 cents for a regular European 1.50 GBP Call (USD Put) for six months but, of course, the GBP/USD rate has to decline 10 cents from the current spot rate of 1.50 before the option is created. If this event does occur, then the buyer has to evidence the rise in GBP/USD to beyond 1.50 by the maturity date. These circumstances are mathematically 'long odds', and the very small premium reflects the probability of the events occurring. Nevertheless, there is very little to lose and such 'bounces' in exchange rates do occur frequently in the marketplace. The timing of this, and the setting of the trigger point, is where one needs a bit of luck.

Down-and-in barriers are usually constructed using trigger points that are OTM relative to spot, as in the above example.

Summary

Like a lot of things in options, barriers are less complicated than they might at first appear. With regular European options, there is really only one derivative – the option – and whether it is a Call or Put is irrelevant, because we can convert one to the other through the underlying FX (Put-Call Parity). It is the same with barriers. There is only one derivative – the barrier – but in this case it is split into two by the direction of the trigger, otherwise we could not convert one into the other through the underlying regular European option.

For example, consider the case of buying an up-and-out and an up-and-in with the same strike, barrier, amount and maturity. The buyer would have one option that would be cancelled and one option that would be created, when spot rises to the common trigger point. In all cases the buyer always has the option, whatever happens, which is the same as buying a regular European option in the first place. Note this very simple rule:

Knockout option + Knock-in option = Ordinary European option
(providing strike, trigger, amount, and date are the same)

This very simple formula can be used to calculate the price of one type of option, assuming the other two are known. It can now seen from the examples that the regular GBP Put (USD Call) European option with premium at 7.20 US cents less the up-and-out premium of 6.78 US cents gives the price of the up-and-in with premium of 0.42 US cents. Similarly, the GBP Call (USD Put) European option equates to the down-and-out and down-and-in barrier options.

Up-and-out, up-and-in, down-and-out, down-and-in are nothing more than convenient terms to describe the direction of spot for trigger and the option type. After all, an up-and-out GBP Put (USD Call) is fine in terms of GBP – 'up' is spot increasing – but in terms of USD is not accurate. Up is a decreasing value for the dollar (the higher the number, the lower the dollar!) – so is this a *down*-and-out USD Call (GBP Put), or is it still considered to be up-and-out because the number increases? Whatever method is used for spot quotation, it is only the direction of the trigger that is important.

Rebates

Occasionally, barrier options are constructed with rebates. These fixed payments are made under the following circumstances:

Knockouts –   A rebate is paid if and when the trigger point is hit, cancelling the option.

Knock-Ins –   A rebate is paid on maturity providing the trigger has not been hit during the option's life.

Barrier options with the rebate feature are more expensive in premium terms than those without, because of the potential rebate.

Determination of spot touching barrier

The spot FX market is a true 24 hour market and as such, one may need to know if spot traded at the barrier point in some far off land at a particular time. Most banks offering barrier options state that this factor is at their (the bank's) determination, and will usually qualify a spot trading level by reference to an information vendor such as Reuters or Telerate. In other cases, the bank will justify the trigger rate with evidence that the bank itself dealt at such a rate; this is very feasible as the bank will have to adjust its delta at a trigger point.

Some institutions have offered barriers tied to a particular daily fixing e.g. the Bundesbank fixing for the DEM in Frankfurt. Such fixings are published in the financial press.

Variations

There are many variations to the basic barrier options detailed above. For example, they may be constructed with specifications that only allow the option to knock out or in on a particular day, week or month. In these cases the knockouts become more expensive and knock-ins become cheaper, due to the restriction.

All the examples under barrier options are constructed with the trigger point set as OTM relative to spot, which is normally the case. Barrier points can also be set against the forward FX rate, rather than spot; these options are known as forward knockouts or knock-ins or forward barriers.

Furthermore, the examples are shown from the buyer's perspective only, whereas many institutions sell barriers as a lower risk form of selling regular European options.

The barrier option is certainly here to stay, and this product is likely to be the first of the exotics to be traded interbank, rather than just between bank and client.

Compound, average rate and barrier options are the most popular of the exotics currently being offered by the banks. The following section gives a brief description of some of the others.

Lookback options

Another option of the path-dependent type, the lookback Call option, gives the purchaser the opportunity to buy at the lowest spot rate that existed during the life of the option. Likewise, a lookback Put gives the opportunity to sell at the highest spot rate. This is done by setting the strike on maturity against the lowest spot rate (for a Call) or the highest (for a Put). In theory, there are great benefits in using lookback options as, for example, a company could guarantee to deal at the best rate that existed, and keeping the shareholders quiet! The problem is cost; a lookback option can be 100% more expensive than standard European options, depending on the volatility and maturity of the lookback, so buyers should be convinced that market volatility will be high enough to justify the cost.

A lookback straddle gives the buyer a 'hi-low' option enabling the purchase of a currency at the lowest rate and the sale at the highest; the payout being the difference between the two strikes. The buyer of a hi-low option is betting on the future volatility of the market being greater than the implied volatility of the lookback straddle.

The lookback option receives many enquiries due to its 'perfect' hedging qualities, but very few transactions actually take place due to the cost of the premium. Most corporate treasurers have premium reduction in mind, (if granting some concession in the protection offered by the option e.g. barrier options) than by premium increase for protection enhancement.

Chooser options

A chooser option ('you choose option') allows the buyer the choice between a regular Call and Put option, after a predetermined period. For example, a nine month chooser option struck at 1.60 (DEM per USD) with a three month 'choice date' would allow the buyer to choose between a six month 1.60 DEM Call (USD Put) or a six month 1.60 DEM Put (USD Call) after three months have elapsed.

The chooser is similar to the ordinary straddle except for the fact that the buyer has to make the choice before final maturity. The chooser is therefore cheaper than a straddle and can be used for similar purposes e.g. where (sharp) spot movement is expected but direction is uncertain.

This option is not really in the 'exotic' class as it can be near-replicated by using ordinary European options. All that is required is the following:

> Using earlier example of nine month 1.60 DEM/USD chooser with three month choice date;
> (1) Purchase of nine month DEM Call (USD Put), strike of 1.60
> (2) Purchase of three month DEM Put (USD Call), strike of 1.60

After three months, the choice has to be made (by the buyer) as to whether a DEM Call (USD Put) or DEM Put (USD Call) is to be held for the remaining six months. If the choice is a DEM Call, then the buyer will let (2) expire leaving six months remaining of the DEM Call. If DEM Put is chosen, the buyer should exercise (2), resulting in a sale of DEM (purchase of USD) at 1.60. This leaves (1), a long DEM Call; the buyer now holds a synthetic DEM Put through Put-Call parity (long Call, short FX = long Put).

There is one snag with this process; the underlying FX at 1.60 is delivered after exercise at the three month period, whereas the straight chooser will deliver at the nine months term. While the three month FX can be swapped to nine months (by executing a six month forward swap), this will involve a debit or credit to reflect the interest rate differential between the two currencies (short DEM, long USD would be a debit at time of writing as DEM interest rates are higher than USD). The situation can be rectified by buying the three month DEM Put (USD Call) as deliverable six months after option maturity, rather than spot. Although this type of option (delayed or extended delivery) is not normal, many banks will provide prices in this way.

Contingent options

Contingent, or pay later, option premiums are only paid on exercise of the option. There is no initial payment and zero payment if the option is OTM on maturity. Does this look too good to be true? The drawback is that the buyer has an obligation to exercise if the option is ITM on maturity, regardless of whether there is sufficient intrinsic value to cover the premium.

Contingent options are priced at the outset so the pay-later premium is known in advance, should the option be exercised. An ATM pay-later option is likely to cost more than double the equivalent ordinary European option, depending on maturity and volatility. This difference in pricing implies expectation of a large one way movement in the underlying FX rate for the buyer of a pay-later option. Nevertheless, many companies seeking protection against an adverse movement in the FX rate will feel comfortable that no premium is paid up-front and there is no cost at all should the option expire OTM. If this was the result, all the benefits from a favourable movement would be available, at no cost.

This does seem one-sided. If the FX rate moves favourably, a company benefits from no premium payment and by converting currency at a more advantageous rate. On the other hand, if the rate moves against a company, it pays a large premium but is 'capped' on the total cost by exercise at the strike. Would it not be better to pay the premium if the option is not exercised? This way a company pays the premium but gains from the better exchange rate or, if ITM, is able to exercise the option for free at the strike fixing cost at that level. For this reason, the pay-later option suits the speculator more than the hedger.

Digital options

The buyer of a standard European option has loss limited to the premium paid, but profit potential is unlimited as the underlying spot rate has no boundaries, either up or down. In other words, maximum loss is known but maximum profit is unknown. The digital, or binary, option changes this as the profit element is fixed to a predetermined amount. So, if the option is ITM on maturity, a fixed sum is paid irrespective of the apparent intrinsic value.

This type of digital option is also sometimes referred to as an 'all-or-nothing' option; the buyer receives either the fixed amount, or nothing depending on whether the option is ITM at expiry. Because of the constricted payout profile, digital options are cheaper than the ordinary European options.

The idea of paying out a fixed, predetermined sum if the option is ITM sounds a bit like the contingent (pay-later) option described in the previous section. There are two differences:

(1) The contingent option delivers the currencies at the strike rate like a regular European option (the digital does not).
(2) The digital has an initial premium similar to an ordinary European option (the contingent does not).

Given that the contingent option premium amount is predetermined, a digital option that pays out the same fixed amount can be bought if the option is ITM at expiry, and the same strike, amount and maturity date can be used. The following example demonstrates this:

Example:

(1) Buy contingent USD Call (DEM Put), strike 1.60 (DEM per USD), 6 months maturity, in USD 10 000 000. Premium USD 600 000 to be paid if spot above 1.60 on expiry.
(2) Buy digital USD Call (DEM Put), strike 1.60 (DEM per USD), 6 months maturity, in USD 10 000 000. Fixed payout USD 600 000 if spot above 1.60 on expiry. Premium USD 250 000.

Result on maturity:

Spot below 1.60	(1)	No exercise, no premium paid, cost = zero.
	(2)	No payout, premium already paid, cost = USD 250 000.
		Net result: initial payment of USD 250 000.
Spot above 1.60	(1)	Exercise of option, settlement of currencies, premium paid USD 600 000.
	(2)	Fixed receipt of USD 600 000, no settlement of currencies, premium already paid USD 250 000.
		Net result: Settlement of currencies, fixed payments zero, initial payment of USD 250 000.

By looking at the two net results, below and above 1.60 strike level, the reader will note exactly the same circumstances exist as if an ordinary European 1.60 USD Call (DEM Put) had been bought with 6 months maturity for premium of USD 250 000. Therefore, there is a direct relationship between the all-or-nothing digital and the pay-later contingent options which can be simply expressed as:

Pay-later option + all-or-nothing option = ordinary European

Note that the expression 'all-or-nothing' has been used rather than 'digital'; this is because there is another form of digital option that does not conform to the above relationship. This is a path dependent type called a 'one-touch' that pays out a predetermined amount if the spot FX rate reaches the strike at any time during the life of the option. The degree to which spot goes ITM is irrelevant, as the payout will always be all-or-nothing so the two digital, or binary options are all-or-nothing and one-touch (all-or-nothing).

Digital barriers

The strike of the one-touch (all-or-nothing) option is sometimes referred to as the barrier and, indeed, the option acts like a knock-in barrier, although the payout is a predetermined amount rather than the creation of an option. In the absence of option creation, there is no need for a strike rate hence the one-touch (all-or-nothing) is, in fact, a digital knock-in barrier. The Call would be a digital up-and-in, and the Put a digital down-and-in option.

The payout on a one-touch digital (digital knock-in barrier) is made at the time the strike (barrier) is hit. Another form of this option has the payout at expiry which then allows for the digital knock*out* barrier; payment is made, on expiry, if the barrier is not hit.

One final step to complete the digital family is to combine the one-touch digital barrier (at expiry) to the principle of having both barrier and strike (standard knockout and knock-ins). A knock-in option of this type would pay out if the barrier was hit and the option finished ITM relative to the strike. Similarly, the knockout would pay out if the barrier was not hit and the option expired ITM relative to spot.

Figure 15.1 shows a matrix of digital options.

Basket options

Multinational corporations tends to have FX risk in many currency denominations. Hedging this risk can be achieved by the purchase of options in each currency or by the purchase of a single option to cover the whole 'basket' of currencies.

Basket options work in the same way as ordinary European options except that the strike price is based on the weighted value of each currency in relation to a buyer's specified currency (usually, the accounting currency). For example, suppose a US dollar based company has currency balances currently valued at USD 10 000 000. An ATM (spot) basket Put option would have a strike of USD 10 000 000; an OTM Put would be USD 9 000 000, etc. On exercise, the buyer would have the option to sell (Put) the basket of currencies and buy (Call) the USD to the amount of the strike. Usually, the intrinsic value of maturity is cash settled, rather than the currencies exchanged. The main advantage is that a basket of currencies will carry less volatility than the individual components resulting in a lower premium for the basket option. The saving in premium cost will vary according to the composition of the basket and to the extent of any correlation between individual currencies, but savings of 25–35% are common.

The scenario is similar to that of the AVRO in the sense that premium reduction is achieved through grouping so that volatility is less. With AVROs, the daily, weekly, or monthly options are added together; in basket options, the currencies are added together. It is, however, possible to have an average rate basket option!

The basket option is a very efficient method of controlling multi-currency risk if the buyer views all the different currency values as one e.g. a currency fund manager who has invested in various currencies, but reports performance on the total.

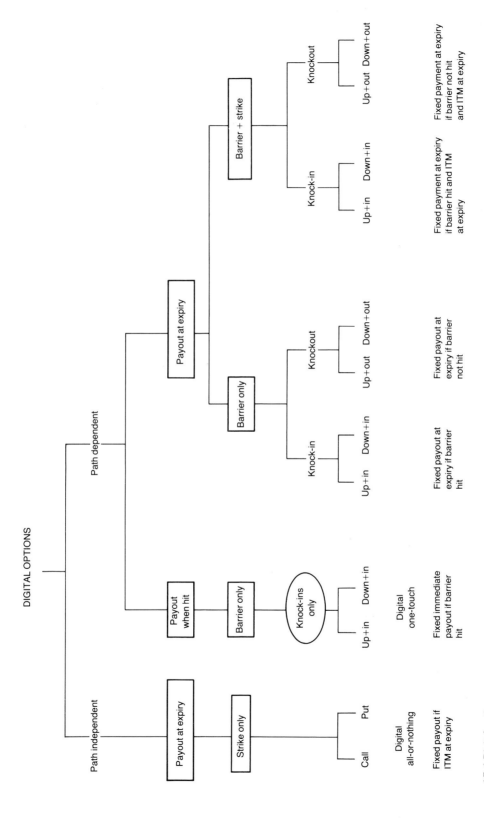

15.1 Digital options.

In other instances, basket options may not always provide the best solution. Imagine that a buyer bought ten individual options that resulted in six being OTM and four being ITM on expiry (assume also the basket option for the ten currencies was OTM on maturity). In the first case, the buyer could exercise the four ITM options and receive some value, whereas the basket option would yield zero.

The question is whether the value received from exercising is greater than the difference in premium paid between the total of the ten options and the one basket.

Basket options should be more popular than is currently the case, but given the premium cost savings, many corporate customers are expected to enter the market in the future. It is mainly a matter of education.

Forward start option

The forward start (or delayed, deferred or start) option is a standard Call or Put option that begins life after the elapse of a specified time. The buyer receives an option with strike set ATM at the time of the option creation rather than the transaction date. For example, a company may buy a six month DEM Call (USD Put) to start three months later. Premium is paid immediately but in three months, the buyer receives a six month option with strike set at whatever the ATM rate is at that time.

While those normally transacted are ATM options, it is possible to arrange for option strikes that are proportionally ITM or OTM on the forward creation date.

Forward start options can be useful where a buyer feels the current value of an ATM option is good but does not have need for such an option until a specific time in the future.

Other option derivatives

There are several other types of options, but many are specific to markets other than FX and therefore do not appear in this chapter. However, there follows a brief discussion of some that the reader may come across.

Dual factor options

The dual factor (or dual asset, or two colour rainbow) option is an option which pays out the better of two different investments against one base i.e. cash. For example, a speculator may feel the USD will weaken substantially, but is uncertain whether to invest in DEM or GBP. A dual currency DEM/GBP Call option (USD Put) would pay out on the better of the two (DEM/USD and GBP/USD exchange rates) i.e. whichever one moved the most. This option is cheaper than buying two standard options (one in DEM/USD and one in GBP/USD) but is more expensive than one.

Multi-factor options

The multi-factor (or multi-asset, or rainbow) option is similar to the dual asset option, except the pay-off is the best of more than two different assets, investments, etc.

Quanto options

The quanto is a variation of the multi-factor option which involves an option on an uncertain amount of an underlying.

Supershare options

The supershare option is a member of the digital family. The buyer of a super-share receives a predetermined payout if, at expiration, the strike equals the underlying i.e. is exactly ATM. For all other expiration values, the payout is zero.

The future

There are certain factors that will dominate the financial markets in the future; one is options. Another is the management of FX risk – not for much longer will it be sufficient to tell shareholders that profits are down because of 'adverse movement in the exchange rate'. The tools for managing FX risk already exist, and it is only the more widespread use of these tools, such as options and their derivatives, that is missing at the moment.

Options, especially applied to FX, are still in their infancy as is evident from the fact that OTC liquidity only exceeded that of the listed exchanges in 1987. The oldest listed currency option on an exchange is the GBP/USD from December 1982 (PHLX). The OTC market needs to develop into the more popular of the exotics, such as barriers, to create the liquidity needed to further expand the use of option products.

Young people entering the options markets in the 1990s will be more attuned to the product, and may ultimately replace some of the resistance presently embodied in the structure of many corporations. Even today, the most common resistance uttered about options is that they are 'too risky!' The philosophy that it is better to do nothing and blame the exchange rate is not likely to be relevant in the future.

Don't forget, if volatility is zero, then an option is free! The last few years of the twentieth century will carry no free lunches, but it will almost certainly be the decade of the derivatives!

APPENDIX

I

Exchange Market Specifications

The Philadelphia Stock Exchange (PHLX)

Contract specifications

Margin requirements

Settlement procedure

List of offices for further information and enquiries
(Reproduced with the permission of the Philadelphia Stock Exchange)

Chicago Mercantile Exchange (CME)

Contract specifications

Margin requirements (determined by the 'Standard Portfolio Analysis of Risk' (SPAN) margin system)

Notes on the CME trading process

List of offices for further information and enquiries
(Reproduced with the permission of the Chicago Mercantile Exchange)

PHLX Currency Option Contract Specifications

TICKER SYMBOLS* (*American/European*)	Australian Dollar	British Pound	Canadian Dollar	Deutsche Mark	European Currency Unit	French Franc
REGULAR OPTIONS	XAD/CAD	XBP/CBP	XCD/CCD	XDM/CDM	ECU/n.a.	XFF/CFF
Half-Point Strike (Three near-term months only)	n.a./n.a.	n.a/n.a.	n.a./n.a.	XDZ/CDZ	n.a./n.a.	n.a./n.a.
MONTH-END OPTIONS	ADW/n.a.	BPW/n.a.	CDW/n.a.	DMW/n.a.	ECW/n.a.	FFW/n.a.
Half-Point Strike	n.a./n.a.	n.a./n.a.	n.a./n.a.	DMZ/n.a.	n.a./n.a.	n.a./n.a.
LONG-TERM OPTIONS†‡						
13 to 24 Months	n.a./YAD	n.a./YPX	n.a./YCD	n.a./YDM	n.a./n.a.	n.a./YFF
25 to 36 Months	n.a./ZAD	n.a./ZPX	n.a./ZCD	n.a./ZDM	n.a./n.a.	n.a./ZFF
CONTRACT SIZE	50 000	31 250	50 000	62 500	62 500	250 000
BASE CURRENCY QUOTATION	US dollar	US dollar	US dollar	US dollar	US dollar	US dollar
EXERCISE PRICE INTERVALS						
Three Nearest Months	1¢	2.5¢	.5¢	.5¢	2¢	.25¢
6, 9 and 12 Months	1¢	2.5¢	.5¢	1¢	2¢	.25¢
Over 12 Months	2¢	5¢	1¢	2¢	n.a.	.50¢
PREMIUM QUOTATIONS	Cents per unit	Cents per unit	Cents per unit	Cents per unit	Cents per unit	Tenths of a cent per unit
MINIMUM PREMIUM CHANGE	$.(00)01 per unit = $5.00	$.(00)01 per unit = $3.125	$.(00)01 per unit = $5.00	$.(00)01 per unit = $6.25	$.(00)01 per unit = $6.25	$.(000)02 per unit = $5.00
MARGIN	US dollar	US dollar	US dollar	US dollar	US dollar	US dollar

*Fluctuations in the underlying may cause a "wrap around' situation whereby alternate symbols may be added. Contact the PHLX for information on alternate symbols that may be in use.

**Changes will occur due to holidays. Please contact the PHLX for more information.

†The PHLX may not have yet listed all Cross Rates and/or Long-Term Options. Contact the PHLX for information on which options are available for trading.

‡When a Long-Term Option has only 12 months remaining until expiration it becomes the one year European-style regular option. (Please note for symbol purposes: a 36 month option on the Deutsche mark will trade under the symbol ZDM. The symbol will change to YDM when the option has 24 months left to expiration and change to CDM when it has 12 months to expiration).

Expiration months	Regular Options: March, June, September and December + two near-term months
	Month-End Options: Three nearest months
	Long-Term Options: 18, 24, 30 and 36 months (June and December)
Expiration date**	Regular Options: Saturday before the third Wednesday of expiring month
	Month-End Options: Saturday following the last Friday of the month
	Long-Term Options: Saturday before the third Wednesday of expiring month
Expiration settlement date**	Regular Options: Third Wednesday of expiring month
	Month-End Options: Wednesday following the last Friday of the month
	Long-Term Options: Third Wednesday of expiring month
Last trading day**	*Providing it is a business day, otherwise the day immediately prior:*
	Regular Options: Friday before the third Wednesday of expiring month
	Month-End Options: Last Friday of the month
	Long-Term Options: Friday before the third Wednesday of expiring month

TICKER SYMBOLS* (*American/European*)	Japanese Yen	Swiss Franc	Deutsche Mark/ Japanese Yen	British Pound/ Deutsche Mark	British Pound/ Japanese Yen†
REGULAR OPTIONS	XJY/CJY	XSF/CSF	n.a./MYX	n.a./PMX	n.a./PYX
Half-Point Strike (Three near-term months only)	XJZ/CJZ	XSZ/CSZ	n.a./MYZ	n.a./n.a.	n.a./n.a.
MONTH-END OPTIONS	JYW/n.a.	SFW/n.a.	n.a./MYW	n.a./PMW	n.a./PYW
Half-Point Strike	JYZ/n.a.	SFZ/n.a.	n.a./MXZ	n.a./n.a.	n.a./n.a.
LONG-TERM OPTIONS†‡					
13 to 24 Months	n.a./YJY	n.a./YSF	n.a./YDY	n.a./YPM	n.a./YPY
25 to 36 Months	n.a./ZJY	n.a./ZSF	n.a./ZDY	n.a./ZPM	n.a./ZPY
CONTRACT SIZE	6 250 000	62 500	62 500 DM	31 250 BP	31 250 BP
BASE CURRENCY QUOTATION	US dollar	US dollar	Japanese yen	Deutsche mark	Japanese yen
EXERCISE PRICE INTERVALS					
Three Nearest Months	.005¢	.5¢	.5 JY	.02 DM	2 JY
6, 9 and 12 Months	.01¢	1¢	1 JY	.02 DM	2 JY
Over 12 Months	.02¢	2¢	2 JY	.04 DM	4 JY
PREMIUM QUOTATIONS	Hundredths of a cent per unit	Cents per unit	Japanese yen	Deutsche mark	Japanese yen
MINIMUM PREMIUM CHANGE	$.(0000)01 per unit = $6.25	$.(00)01 per unit = $6.25	.01 JY per unit = 625 JY	.0002 DM per unit = 6.25 DM	.02 JY per unit = 625 JY
MARGIN	US dollar	US dollar	US dollar or JY	US dollar or DM	US dollar or JY

Exercise style

Regular Options:
    Dollar Based: American and European (except ECU which is American-style only)
Cross Rates: European
Month-End Options: American in dollar based. European in cross rates
Long-Term Options: European
American-style: Exercise any time until expiration
European-style: Exercise at expiration only

Settlement of exercise

Exchange of Underlying Currencies

Issuer and guarantor

The Options Clearing Corporation

Position and exercise limits

100,000 contracts in aggregate for each currency

Trading hours

EST: 6:00 p.m.–10:00 p.m./11.30 p.m.–2:30 p.m.
EDT: 7:00 p.m.–11:00 p.m./12:30 a.m.–2:30 p.m.
Trading hours for CD, ECU and FF are 3:30 a.m.–2:30 p.m. EST/EDT.
The trading week commences on Sunday evening and ends on Friday afternoon.

.

CUSTOMER MARGIN REQUIREMENTS FOR US DOLLAR BASED FOREIGN CURRENCY OPTIONS

INTRODUCTION

This publication explains the Philadelphia Stock Exchange's foreign currency option requirements for customer transactions. The Options Clearing Corporation's margin requirements are not discussed: OCC clearing members should consult OCC directly for information on OCC margin requirements.

It should be noted that the PHLX rules set forth the minimum margin requirements. PHLX member organisations, as well as non-member organisations, are of course free to set more stringent requirements if they see a need to do so. Therefore the examples shown here refer only to the **minimum** margin required and, just as importantly, do **not** consider commissions, taxes, and other possible expenses.

PHLX rules are subject to change: all member firms should endeavour to be aware of current requirements. The Philadelphia Stock Exchange's European office in London is equipped to provide up-to-date information on PHLX rules and margining procedures.

I. MINIMUM MARGIN REQUIREMENTS FOR CURRENCY OPTION CUSTOMERS

FOR OPTION BUYER
AND COVERED OPTION
WRITER

: No margin required

FOR UNCOVERED
OPTION WRITER

: 100% of option premium plus 4% of contract spot value less any out of the money amount , down to a minimum of 100% of option premium plus 3/4% of contract spot value.

FOR A CALL SPREAD
OR A PUT SPREAD

: Where the long position expires before the short position, the spread is treated as two separate positions (i.e. in the case of a call spread: a long call and a short uncovered call).

Where the long position expires at the time of or after the expiration of the short position, the margin required is the lesser of:

* the margin required on the short position (as described above
  OR
* the amount by which the exercise price of the long call (or short put) exceeds the exercise price of the short call (or long put).

NOTE: If the exercise price of the long call (or short put) is less than the exercise price of the short call (or long put), **no margin is required.**

FOR A SHORT
UNCOVERED
STRADDLE OR
STRANGLE

: Combine the margin required on either the short call or short put (whichever is greater) and 100% of the current market value of the other option.

NOTES:

* Margins are calculated and paid in U.S. dollars

* The Philadelphia Stock Exchange lists both European and American currency options. Margin calculation is the same for both. An American style option can be exercised at any time until expiration. A European style option can be exercised on the expiration day only

* European and American style options on the same currency are treated as inter-changeable for margin purposes. For example, if an investor holds a short American style Japanese Yen call, he would be entitled to the same margins, whether the short call was hedged with the purchase of an American or European style Yen call.

* Uncovered Short option positions are marked to market **daily.**

* "Contract spot value" is calculated by PHLX for each of the currencies underlying PHLX options. The calculation, done at the 2:30 pm close of the PHLX currency option market involves averaging a number of current spot rates to determine a representative "contract spot value". These exchange rates are then disseminated and used for margin calculations. **Contract spot values are available by phone on the dedicated phone line of 215 (Philadelphia area code) 496-6707.**

  The initial margin required on a short, uncovered position is 100% of option premium received plus 4% of the contract spot value (as calculated by PHLX at 2.30pm less any out of the money amount, down to a minimum of 100% of the premium received plus 3/4% of contract spot value.

* On subsequent days margin for the uncovered option writer is calculated using the daily contract spot value and the closing price of the short option. This new premium is then used to calculate the margin required, thereby creating a marked-to-market position.

POSITION LIMITS   *   Position limits for PHLX currency options are 100,000 contracts on the same side of the market (ie long calls/short puts or short calls/long puts) per currency pair (eg $/DM, DM/JY)

The 100,000 limit refers to each currency pair. Positions held across various expiration months will be totalled.

Alternatives to cash margining for the uncovered writer :

*   Securities   See Section III, **"Meeting Margin Requirements"**

*   Letter of Credit   See Section III, **"Meeting Margin Requirements"**

In computing margins, individual currency option premiums must be translated into aggregate premiums. This is done by multiplying the quoted premium by the number of units of underlying currency. Listed below are the contract sizes and premium quotation methods:

CURRENCY OPTION	PREMIUMS		
British Pound	US cents/£	£	31,250
Australian Dollar	US cents/A$	A$	50,000
Canadian Dollar	US cents/C$	C$	50,000
Deutsche Mark	US cents/DM	DM	62,500
Swiss Franc	US cents/SF	SF	62,500
European Currency Unit	US cents/ECU	ECU	62,500
French Franc	1/10 US cent/FF	FF	250,000
Japanese Yen	1/100 US cent/Yen	JY	6,250,000

NOTE: All the above options except the ECU are available in both European and American exercise style. The ECU is available only in American exercise style.

To calculate the total premium the individual premium is multiplied by the contract size. For example:

A DM option premium is quoted at 2.53.

Aggregate premium = $.0253/DM x DM62,500 = $ 1,581.25

II. MARGIN CALCULATION EXAMPLES

NOTE: In the following examples the US $/£ spot rate of $1.3920/£ is used. The margin calculated in each example is the minimum margin required; often customers may be required by their broker to make larger margin payments.

UNCOVERED SHORT CALL OR UNCOVERED SHORT PUT:

In-the-money:

Postion:	Sell one XBP Dec 135 call at 7.90		
Calculation:	Premium = ($.0790 x £31,250)	=	$2468.75
	4% of contract spot value		
	= (.04 (31,250 x $1.3920/£))	=	1740.00
Margin Requirement:			**$4,208.75**

Just-out-of-the-money:

Position:	Sell one XBP Dec 140 call at 5.35		
Calculation:	Premium = ($.0535 x £31,250)	=	$1671.87
	4% of contract spot value		
	= (.04 (31,250 x $1.3920/£))	=	1740.00
	Out-of-the-money amount =		
	(($1.400 - $1.3920) x £31,250)	=	(250.00)
Margin Requirement			**$3,161,87**

Far-out-of-the-money

Position:	Sell one XBP Dec 130 put at 1.05		
Greater of:	1) Premium ($.0105 x £31,250)	=	$ 328.12
	4% of contract spot value		
	(.04 (31,250 x $1.3920))	=	1740.00
	Less out-of-the-money amount		
	(1.3920 - 1.3000) x £31,250	=	(2,875.00)
	Total		**$ (806.88)**
	2) Premium ($.0105 x £31,250)	=	$ 328.12
	¼% of contract spot value		
	(.0075 (31,250 x $1.3920))	=	326.25
	Total		$ 654.37
Margin Requirement			**$ 654.37**

CALL SPREAD OR PUT SPREAD

Position:	Buy one XBP Mar 140 call at 7.15		
	Sell one XBP Mar 135 call at 9.50		
Calculation:	Premium :		
	long call ($.0715 x £31,250)	=	$ 2,234.37
	short call ($.0950 x £31,250)	=	$ 2,968.75
Lesser of:	1) Short call margin (in-the-money):		
	Premium plus 4% contract spot value		
	= ($.0950 x £31,250) +		
	(.04 (31,250 x $1.3920/£))	=	$ 4,708.75
	or		
	2) Long exercise - short exercise		
	= ($1.400 - $1.3500) x £31,250	=	$ 1,562.50
Margin Requirement:			**$ 1,562.50**

SHORT CALL AND SHORT PUT (Strangle)

Position:	Sell one XBP Dec 135 call at 7.90
	Sell one XBP Dec 145 put at 8.10

Calculation: 1) The margin required for the short put
or the short call, whichever is the
greater

plus

2) 100% of the current market value of
the other option

1) Call margin:

£31,250 x $.0790	=	$ 2,468.75
4% of $1.3920/£	=	1,740.00
		$ 4,208.75

Put margin:

£31,250 x $.0810	=	$ 2,531.25
4% of $1.3920/£	=	1,740.00
		$ 4,271.25

(Put margin is selected as this is the
greater of the two)

2) Current market value of written call=

£31,250 x $.0790	$ 2,468.75

Margin on short put =	$ 4,271.25
Current market value of short call	2,468.75

Margin Requirement:	**$ 6,740.00**

SHORT CALL AND SHORT PUT (Straddle)

Position:	Sell one XBP Dec 135 call at 7.90		
	Sell one XBP Dec 135 put at 4.10		

Premium:
short call ($.0790 x £31,250)	=	$ 2,468.75
short put ($.0410 x £31,250)	=	$ 1,281.25

Calculation:

1) The margin required for the short put or the short call, whichever is the **greater**

    plus

2) 100% of the current market value of the other option

1) Call margin:
£31,250 x $.0790	=	$ 2,468.75
4% of $1.3920/£	=	1,740.00
		$ 4,208.75

Put margin:
£31,250 x $.0410	=	$ 1,281.25
4% of $1.3920/£	=	1,740.00
less out-of-the-money amount		
($1.3920 - $1.3500) £31,250	=	(1,312.50)
		$ 1,708.75

(Call margin is selected as this is the greater of the two)

2) Current market value of written put =
£31,250 x $.0410	$ 1,281.25

Margin on short put	$ 4,208.75
Current market value of short call	1,281.25

Margin Requirement:	**$ 5,490.00**

III. MEETING MARGIN REQUIREMENTS

Once the initial margin payment has been calculated, the option writer may choose one of two methods of margin payment: depositing cash (US dollars only) or securities or providing a letter of credit from an approved issuer.

A. Depositing Cash or Securities

The initial margin requirement on options written in the Margin Account may be met by depositing the appropriate amount of cash or by depositing fully-paid for securities whose loan value equals or exceeds the margin requirement. Additionally, any existing equity in the margin account may be applied to the margin due. When an option transaction creates or increases a margin deficiency, additional margin will normally be required.

In September 1988 the US Federal Reserve Board, amended Regulation T to make certain **non US sovereign debt securities** acceptable margin for broker dealers. This will permit brokers dealers to extend "good faith" loan value on long term debt securities issued or guaranteed by a sovereign foreign government so long as the securities are rated in one of the two highest rating categories by a recognised statistical rating organisation. It should be noted, however, that such acceptable foreign sovereign debt **cannot** currently be "passed through" to the OCC as a type of margin also acceptable to them. Instead, customers may prefer to use the foreign paper to secure a letter of credit which can them be pledged

B. Providing Letters of Credit

PHLX's Rule 722 allows customers to meet initial and maintenance margin requirements by presenting to their broker a letter of credit issued on the customer's behalf by an Exchange-approved bank or trust company.

A letter of credit is an irrevocable commitment by the issuer to pay - if required - a specified U.S. dollar amount to the member firm on behalf of the customer.

In order for a letter of credit to be used it must be issued by an approved bank or trust company and it be written in the form shown in Appendix A.

1. How to use Letters of Credit

When a letter of credit is used to meet a margin requirement, the full U.S. dollar value of the letter of credit is reflected in the Non-Securities Credit Account. Foreign currency option positions written in that account and the margins subsequently required are "debited" against the amount of the letter of credit. A letter of credit does not represent the aggregate exercise amount of the options written (the underlying currency in the case of short calls or the aggregate US dollar amount in the case of short puts), but rather only represents funds available to meet **margin** requirements. The broker may require submission of the letter of credit when the option is written; at the latest it must be deposited with the broker no later than seven business days after the option has been written.

Many customers will obviously have letters of credit in excess of the initial margin requirement of any single option position written. The customer may write options whose initial and maintenance margin requirements will be aggregated and allocated against the total amount of the letter of credit. A customer may **not** write options against available amounts of the letter of credit, nor may the aggregate margin requirements of all open options written and carried "short" against the letter of credit exceed the total amount of the letter of credit

2. Conditions of and Limitations on Letters of Credit

Letters of credit issued for foreign currency option margin are subject to the following conditions:

a) The letter of credit must be issued by an Exchange approved institution (see Appendix C). The qualifications and procedures necessary to receive Exchange approval are discussed in more detail under item 3 (below).

b) The letter of credit must contain the commitment of the approved issuer to pay on demand a specified U.S. dollar amount equal to or greater than the amount of margin required on the short option position(s).

c) The letter of credit must be irrevocable and must not expire prior to the expiration date of the short option position(s).

d) A letter of credit may not be issued for a period longer than eighteen months.

There are limitations on the total U.S. dollar amount of letters of credit written by an Exchange-approved issuer: a bank or trust company may not have outstanding for any one customer letters of credit in excess of 15% of the institution's unimpaired capital and surplus. Additionally, the aggregate amount of letters of credit naming the same Exchange member firm as beneficiary may not exceed 20% of the issuing institution's unimpaired capital and surplus.

Letters of credit from approved non-U.S. institutions must be issued and payable at a U.S. federal or state branch or agency of the non-U.S. institution. If the customer for whose account a letter of credit is issued is itself a bank or trust company, the letter of credit must be issued by another bank or trust company. A bank or trust company cannot issue a letter of credit on its own behalf.

3. Qualification and Approval of issuers of Letters of Credit

The commentary to Rule 722 defines the types of financial institutions which may issue letters of credit once they are approved by the Exchange. Both U.S. and non-U.S. institutions may be approved provided the following qualifications are met:

U.S. banks or trust companies must:

1) Be organised under the laws of the United States or a State thereof and be regulated and examined by federal or state authorities having regulatory authority over banks or trust companies:

2) Have, at the time of approval and continuously thereafter, unimpaired capital and surplus of U.S. $ 100,000,000 or more.

Non U.S. banks or trust companies must:

1) Be organised under the laws of a country other than the United States and have a U.S. Federal or State branch or agency (as defined in the International Banking Act of 1978) located in the United States;

2) Have, at the time, of approval and continuously thereafter unimpaired capital and surplus in excess of U.S. $200,000,000.

3) Have its principal executive office located in a country that

   a) Is rated "AAA" by Moody's Investor Services or Standard & Poor's, or

   b) Has been approved by the Business Conduct Committee of the Exchange as a "AAA" equivalent country based on consultations with at least two entities or persons satisfactory to the Business Conduct Committee as experienced in international banking and finance matters:

4) a) Have a "P-1" rating from Moody's Investor Service and/or an "A-1" rating from Standard & Poor's on its commercial paper or other short-term obligations, or)

   b) In the event that the non-U.S. banks or trust companies have no rating on their commercial paper or other short-term obligations:

      i) Any such commercial paper or short-term obligations issued by a parent or an affiliated entity has such a rating equivalent to 4)a) above;

      (ii) Any such commercial paper or short-term obligations issued by an entity not affiliated with the issuing institution and supported or guaranteed by the institution and supported or guaranteed by the institution which has a rating equivalent to 4)a) above;

      (iii) Have an "AAA" rating from Moody's Investor Service and/or an "AAA" rating from Standard & Poor's on the long-term obligations of the institution, its parent or affiliated entity: and

      (iv) Have been approved by the Business Conduct Committee as a "P-1" or "A-1" equivalent institution.

An institution meeting the above criteria and interested in becoming an approved issuer must submit to the Exchange an application for approval as an issuer of letters of credit. A sample letter of application is shown in Appendix B. The applications shall include the following items:

1) The institution's most recent financial annual report, and, in the event that this is more than 90 days prior to the date of the application, its most recent published quarterly statement, (preferably in the form of "Consolidated Reports of Condition and Income for Banks with Domestic Offices and Foreign Offices", if applicable).

2) The names of individuals authorized to sign letters of credit on the institution's behalf; and

3) Documentation as to the institution's legal authority to issue letters of credit.

If approved as an issuer of letters of credit, the institution shall provide the Exchange with annual reports and quarterly financial statements as issued ("Consolidated Reports") Additionally, the institution will notify the Exchange promptly but in no event later than thirty days, of any changes to the information filed with the institution's initial application for approval.

Following a PHLX rule change on April 5th 1991, banks approved by the Options Clearing Corporation (OCC) to issue letters of credit are now automatically approved to issue letters of credit to PHLX customers without having to make a separate application to the Exchange. This rule change increases the number of banks approved to issue letters of credit from 11 to 97. PHLX, however, continue to reserve the right in its sole discretion to refuse or revoke approval of any financial institution as an issuer of letters of credit at any time.

A list of financial institutions approved to issue letters of credit is included in Appendix C.

4. Reporting Requirements of Member Firms

Member firms named as beneficiaries of letter of credit must provide certain information to the Exchange. The following information must be maintained as part of the organisation's books and records and preserved by the member for at least three years, two years in an easily accessible place (in accordance with SEC rules).

For each letter of credit received the member firm must retain the following information:

1.   The name of the financial institution issuing the letter of credit

2.   The name of the customer for whose account the letter of credit is issued.

3.   The U.S. dollar amount specified in the letter of credit

4.   The expiration date of the letter of credit

5.   The class and series of each option position for which the letter of credit serves as margin

6.   The date the option position(s) was/were established

7.   The customer's net worth, net income, occupation, and experience in trading securities and/or commodities

8.   Notification of withdrawal of the letter of credit

9.   Notification of liquidation of any option position for which the letter of credit serves as initital margin

10.   Notification of exercise of any short option position for which a letter of credit serves as margin

Information concerning the letter of credit and the customer's background should be submitted promptly upon receipt of a letter of credit. Information concerning foreign currency option transactions for which the letter of credit serves as payment of margin required may be submitted monthly in the form of customer account statements. All information required should be directed to the Examination Department, Philadelphia Stock Exchange, Inc. 1900 Market Street, Philadelphia PA 19103, U.S.A.

IV. COVERED OPTION POSITIONS

No margin is required when a short position is "covered". The following items are approved under Regulation T (see Appendix D) as "cover" for foreign currency option positions:

In the case of short call options:

1. Deposit of the aggregate amount of foreign currency.

2. A "call option guarantee letter" issued by an approved custodian certifying that the custodian certifying that the custodian holds for the account of the customer foreign currency in an amount greater than or equal to the number of units of foreign currency underlying (or represented by) the short call option position(s).

-   In the case of short put options:

1. U.S. dollars in the amount greater than or equal to the aggregate exercise price of the put option positions(s), or the following instruments which may be considered substitutes for U.S. dollars ("cash equivalents") provided that the market value of these instruments equals or exceeds the aggregate exercise price of the short put option position(s) when written and the instrument matures in one year or less:

    -   securities issued and guaranteed by the United States or its agencies;

    -   negotiable bank certificates of deposit; or

    -   banker's acceptances issued by banking institutions in the United States and payable in the United States; or

2. A "put option guarantee letter" issued by an approved custodian certifying that the custodian holds for the account of the customer U.S. dollars or cash equivalents in an amount greater than or equal to the aggregate size of the put position(s).

An option guarantee letter received by a member firm on behalf of a customer is reflected in the Cash or Margin Account as cover for the option position depending upon the account in which the option is written. The option guarantee letter should be received by the member the same day the option position is written, but no later than seven business days after the option is written.

An option guarantee letter issued by an approved custodian is a guarantee to the member that the custodian is holding, on behalf of the member's customer, adequate funds - either foreign currency or US dollar cash equivalents. An escrowee or bailee of the funds, the custodian must segregate these funds from operating assets.

The option guarantee letter may not expire before the fourth full business day **after** the expiration of the option position (i.e. exercise settlement date).

There are two types of option guarantee letters, **single** transaction and **multiple** transaction.

The single transaction foreign currency option guarantee letter follows the format of an equity option guarantee letter. A custodian issues a letter on behalf of a customer for a specific short option position. Each time the customer opens a short position, the custodian must issue a guarantee letter to the member firm identifying the amount of foreign currency or U.S. dollars/cash equivalents covering the customer's position. The Options Clearing Corporation's list of custodian banks is approved by PHLX for purposes of issuing currency option guarantee letters.

The multiple transaction foreign currency option guarantee letter is designed to cover numerous uncovered short option positions in a single currency; these positions may be written at various times against a predefined amount of foreign currency or U.S. dollars/cash equivalents being held by the custodian on behalf of the customer. All positions covered by this type of guarantee letter must have the same expiration but not necessarily the same exercise price.

The number of units of underlying foreign currency (in the case of a call option), or U.S. dollars/U.S. dollar value of cash equivalents (in the case of a put option) identified in the multiple transaction option guarantee letter dictates the total number of option positions which the customer may write as "covered". For example, a custodian may hold on deposit C$50,000,000 on behalf of a customer. Upon presentation of a multiple transaction option guarantee letter, a customer may write up to 1,000 Canadian dollar call options of the same expiration, even though the transactions are effected at various times and with various exercise prices.

The determination of which type of option guarantee letter should be used is subject to mutual agreement among the parties involved. Sample option guarantee letters for both put and call writing are available from PHLX.

V. MAINTENANCE MARGIN REQUIREMENTS

Foreign currency option positions are **marked-to-market daily.** Maintenance margin is determined using the same formula as used for the initial margin, except, that the maintenance margin formula uses the current day's closing price for the option position and the "closing " spot foreign exchange rate as calculated by PHLX. Members may choose to use either the closing bid or ask price when determining the present value of the option premium. The most important aspect of deciding whether the bid or ask price is used is that the broker is consistent in his method of making margin determinations.

When additional margin is required for an uncovered short option position (i.e. , there are not sufficient funds or equity in the customer's margin account to meet the maintenance margin requirement), payment is due from the customer promptly to reduce any deficit in margin. The broker should collect this maintenance margin immediately, and in no event later than seven business days after the margin call.

Customer's using letters of credit to meet initial margin requirements will most likely use the same letter of credit to meet subsequent maintenance margin calls. The PHLX member must continually monitor the customer's total margin requirement to ensure that the face amount of the letter of credit is always greater than (or equal to) the total margin required on the option position(s). Otherwise, the customer must meet the maintenance margin requirement by a deposit of cash or securities (whose loan value is equal to or greater than the additional margin) or by the submission of an additional letter of credit

VI. BOOKEEPING

The Board of Governors of the Federal Reserve System, through various interpretations of Regulation T, have also determined in which accounts foreign currency and foreign currency options may be carried and in which accounts related transactions may be effected.

Foreign currency may be carried in the Cash or Non-Securities Credit Accounts - it may not be carried in the Margin Account. Foreign currency may only be received into the Margin Account if it is to be **immediately** converted into U.S. dollars. However, foreign currency carried in any of the permissible customer accounts will not be translated into a U.S. dollar value for debit or credit balance purposes since foreign currency has no loan value under Regulation T, nor does it contribute to the account's equity balance. Foreign currency will only be "priced" when it is sold or converted into U.S. dollars. A member may extend credit in the Non-Securities Credit Account using the foreign currency as collateral, however the loan must be a non-purpose loan (a loan not for buying, carrying or trading in securities).

Foreign currency options may be purchased or sold in the Cash or margin Account depending upon the type of transaction involved. Since foreign currency options, like all options, have no loan value, they must be paid for in full when purchased and may be carried in either of the above-mentioned accounts. Foreign currency options sold uncovered must be written and carried in the Margin Account except when a letter of credit is used to meet the margin required, in which case the option must be written in the Non-Securities Credit Account. Foreign currency options which are sold on a covered basis (covered by foreign currency in the case of calls, by cash or an acceptable equivalent in the case of puts or calls) may be written in either the Cash or margin Accounts.

However, since foreign currency may not be carried in the Margin Account unless it is to be immediately converted into U.S. dollars, a memorandum entry will be necessary to carry a "covered" position in a Margin Account if the cover is foreign currency. The memorandum entry would indicate that the foreign currency is being carried in some other account, such as the Cash or Non-Securities Credit Account.

1) CUSTOMER MARGIN PROCEDURE

For calculating margin on cross-rate currency options, both contract size and the base currency in which the premium of the contract is priced and settled need to be known. Broadly speaking, cross rate margin procedures are the same as for PHLX's existing currency options with the important difference that margin is calculated in the base currency for the relevant option rather than the U.S.$.

Cross Rate Option	Symbol	Underlying Currency	Contract Size	Base Currency
£/DM	PMX	British Pound	31,250 BP	Deutsche mark
DM/JY	MYX	Deutsche mark	62,500 BP	Japanese Yen
£/JY	PYX	British Pound	31,250 BP	Japanese Yen

NOTE: Sizes were revised on July 12th 1992. DM/JY was originally 1,000,000 DM.

As with PHLX's existing foreign currency options ($/DM, $/SF, $/JY, $/£, $/A$, $/C$, $/FF and $/ECU), initial margin requirements for cross-rate option positions must be satisfied within seven (7) full business days from trade date unless otherwise agreed. Margin requirements may be satisfied by the deposit of cash, securities or letter of credit. Acceptable securities include the list of foreign margin stocks published by the US Federal Reserve Board that meet the requirements of Regulation T. Also included are investment grade foreign denominated debt securities which at the time of receipt must be rated in one of the two highest rating categories by an internationally recognised statistical rating organisation and which are also acceptable to the Options Clearing Corporation (OCC).

Additionally, since the base currencies of the cross rate contracts are non US $ currencies, separate foreign currency (ie non US $) denominated sub accounts will have to be set up in the margin account.

MARGIN REQUIREMENTS FOR CROSS-RATE FOREIGN CURRENCY OPTION POSITIONS

NOTE: The current market value of the underlying contract is determined by multiplying the closing spot price of the cross rate currency by the number of units of currency per option contract.

POSITION	MARGIN REQUIREMENT
Long call or put	100% of premium in the base currency of the contract
Uncovered short call or put	100% of the option premium plus 4% of the underlying contract value less any out-of-the-money amount down to a minimum of 100% of the option premium plus 3/4% of the underlying contract value.
Call spread or put spread	The lesser of:- 1) margin required for the short position or 2) the amount by which the exercise price of the long call (or short put) exceeds the exercise price of the short call (or long put).

The cost of the long position must be paid in full and the premium received from the sale of the short position may be fully applied toward the spread margin requirement.

If the exercise price of the long call (or short put) does not exceed the exercise price of the short call (or long put), not additional margin is required other than payment in full for the long option position.

Long position must expire on or after the expiration of the short position. If the long position expires before the short position, the spread is margined as if it consisted of two unrelated positions (a long option and an uncovered short option).

Short call and short put (straddle):   The margin required on the short call or short put position whichever is greater, plus the option premium of the other position.

MARGIN CALCULATIONS:　WORKED EXAMPLES

Deutsche Mark/Japanese Yen Cross Rate (Symbol MYX)
Spot Rate = 86.50

Long call or long put

Position:	Buy one MYX June 89 put at 3.5
Computation:	Premium = (3.5 x 1,000,000)
Margin Requirement:	3,500,000 JY

Short call or short put

In-the-money

Position:	Buy one MYX June 85 put at 3.0	
Computation:	Premium = (3.0 x 1,000,000) =	3,000,000 JY
	4% of market value of underlying	
	contract = [.04(1,000,000 x 86.5)] =	3,460,000 JY
Margin Requirement:		6,460,000 JY

Just -out-of-the-money

Position:	Sell one MYX June 87 call at 1	
Computation:	Premium = (1.0 x 1,000,000) =	1,000,000 JY
	4% of market value of underlying	
	contract = [.04(1,000,000 x 86.5)] =	3,460,000 JY
	out-of-the-money amount	
	[(87 - 86.50)1,000,000] =	(500,000) JY
Margin Requirement:		3,960,000 JY

Deep-out-of-the-money

Position:	Sell one MYX June 91 call at .05	
Computation:	Premium = (.05 x 1,000,000) =	50,000 JY
	4% of market value of underlying	
	contract = [.04(1,000,000 x 86.5)] =	3,460,000 JY
	less out-of-the-money amount	
	[(91-86.5) 1,000,000] =	(4,500,000) JY
		(990,000 JY)
	Minimum Margin required:	
	Premium + 3/4% market value of	
	underlying contract =	
	50,000 + [.0075(1,000,000 x 86.5)]=	698,750 JY
Margin Requirement:		698,750 JY

Call spread or put spread

Position:	Buy one MYX June 86 call at 1.7	
	Sell one MYX June 85 call at 2.5	
Computation:	Premium of long call (1.7 x 1,000,000) =	1,700,000 JY
	Premium of short call (2.5 x 1,000,000) =	2,500,000 JY
Lesser of:	1) short call margin (in-the-money)	
	Premium ÷ 4% market value of	
	underlying contract	
	2,500,000 + [.04(1,000,000 x 86.5)] =	5,960,000 JY
	2) Long exercise > Short exercise	
	(86 - 85) x 1,000,000 =	1,000,000 JY
Margin Requirement:		**1,000,000 JY**

Straddle

Short call and short put:

Position:	Sell one MYX June 85 call at 2.5 Sell one MYX June 85 put at 0.7	
Computation:	Premium short call (2.5 x 1,000,000) = Premium short put (0.7 x 1,000,000) =	2,500,000 JY 700,000 JY
Lesser of:	1) Short call margin (in-the-money)	
	Premium ÷ 4% market value of underlying contract 2,500,000 ÷ [.04(1,000,000 x 86.5)] =	5,960,000 JY
	2) Short put margin (out-of-the-money)	
	Premium ÷ 4% market value of underlying less out-of-the-money amount 700,000 ÷ 3,460,000 - [(86.5-85) 1,000,000] =	2,660,000 JY
Margin Requirement:	Greater of call or put plus premium of other position 5,960,000 ÷ 700,000 =	**6,660,000 JY**

British Pound/Deutsche Mark Cross-Rate (Symbol PMX)
Spot rate = 2.9248

Long call or long put

Position:	Buy one PMX June 2.8 call at 14.5	
Computation:	Premium = (.145 x 500,000) =	72,500 DM
Margin Requirement:	=	72,500 DM

Short call or Short put

In-the-money:

Position:	Sell one PMX June 2.86 call at 7.2	
Computation:	Premium = (.072 x 500,000) =	36,000 DM
	4% market value of underlying	
	contract = [.04(500,000 x 2.9248)] =	58,496 DM
Margin Requirement:		94,496 DM

Just-out-of-the-money:

Position:	Sell one PMX June 2.94 call at 1.2	
Computation:	Premium = (.012 x 500,000) =	6,000 DM
	4% market value of underlying	
	contract = [.04(500,000 x 2.9248)] =	58,496 DM
	out-of-the-money-amount	
	[(2.94 - 2.9248) 500,000] =	(7,600) DM
Margin Requirement:		56,896 DM

Deep-out-of-the-money

Position:	Sell one PMX June 3.04 call at 0.2	
Computation:	Premium = (.002 x 500,000) =	1,000 DM
	4% market value of underlying	
	contract = [.04(500,000 x 2.9248)] =	58,496 DM
	less out-of-the-money-amount	
	[(3.04 - 2.9248) 500,000] =	(57,600) DM
		1,896 DM
	Minimum margin required =	
	Premium + 3/4% market value of	
	underlying contract = 1,000 DM +	
	[.0075(500,000 x 2.9248)] =	11,968 DM
Margin Requirement:		11,968 DM

Call spread or put spread

Position:	Buy one PMX June 2.90 at 2.9	
	Sell one PMX June 2.94 at 1.2	
Computation:	Premium of long call (.029 x 500,000) =	14,500 DM
	Premium of short call (.012 x 500,000) =	6,000 DM
Lesser of:	1) short call margin (out-of-the-money)	
	Premium + 4% market value of	
	underlying contract	
	6,000 DM + [.04(500,000 x 2.9248)] =	64,496 DM
	less out of money amount	
	[(2.94 - 2.9248) 500,000] =	(7,600) DM
	2) Long exercise>Short exercise	
	(2.9 - 2.94) x 500,000 =	0 DM
Margin Requirement:		0 DM

Straddle

Short call and short put

Position:	Sell one PMX June 2.90 call at 2.90
	Sell one PMX June 2.90 put at 0.8

Computation:	Premium of short call (.029 x 500,000) =	14,500 DM
	Premium of short put (.008 x 500,000) =	4,000 DM

Greater of:

1) short call margin (in-the-money)

Premium + 4% market value of underlying
14,500 DM + [.04(500,000 x 2.9248)] =   72,996 DM

2) short put margin (out-of-the-money)

Premium + 4% market value of underlying
less out-of-the-money amount
4,000 DM + 72,996 DM-[(2.9248-2.9)500,000]=   69,396 DM

Margin Requirement: 72,996 ÷ 4,000 DM   76,996 DM

2) SETTLEMENT PROCEDURE

1. CLEARING FIRM ELIGIBILITY

Clearing firms, including those firms currently qualified to trade currency options, must obtain separate approval to trade cross rate options. Firms must qualify for all cross rates and establish the necessary banking arrangements in each currency country. Please note that give-up transactions will require both the executing and the CMTA firm to be qualified. OCC will reject any trades received for ineligible clearing members.

II. TRADES AND POST TRADES

Cross rate options will trade on the PHLX with Japanese yen and Deutsche marks as base currencies. These trades will be processed alongside PHLX's existing currency options and sent to OCC for clearance. OCC clearing members can continue to use OCC's C/MACS systems for the entry of cross rate post trade activity to the ICS processing system. This input will be reflected with existing foreign currency options on standard ICS output reports.

III. DAILY SETTLEMENT

Premium settlement for cross rate options will take place at the first opportunity in the trading currency's country of origin. The settlement time in Japan and Germany is anticipated to be two hours after the opening of business. Clearing members must establish settlement accounts at OCC approved banks.

IV. MARGINS

Cross rate options will be margined with all other non-equity options during regular processing time frames. The OCC Daily Margin Report will show the margin requirement in the strike currency and a US dollar equivalent.

V. REVISED "REGULAR WAY" SETTLEMENT PROCEDURE FOR CROSS RATES

OCC has had to modify the "regular way" settlement process to accommodate the unique nature of DM/JY and BP/JY settlements which due to the difference in banking hours would require the settlement of the strike price currency (yen) prior to the delivery of the underlying British pounds or Deutsche marks. OCC presently drafts settlement dollars on T+2 and requires delivery of the underlying currency on T+4 for dollar denominated currency options.

The Revised "Regular Way" settlement procedures are as follows:

(days given are Tuesday after expiration etc)

1. For the **DM/JY** and **BP/JY** contracts, OCC will collect the underlying Deutsche marks or British pounds at the opening of business on T+3 in the U.K. and Germany (approx 3:00 am U.S. CT Tuesday). OCC obviously does not want to pay out the strike currency (yen) to the clearing member prior to receiving the delivery of the underlying currency.

2. OCC will collect and then pay out the Yen (strike currency) for DM/JY and BP/JY at the opening of business on T+4 in Japan (approx 7:00 pm U.S. CT Tuesday).

3. Assuming receipt of the Yen, OCC will deliver Deutsche marks and British pounds at the opening of business on T+4 in the U.K. and Germany (approx. 3:00 am U.S. CT Wednesday).

4. OCC is currently exploring the possibility of accepting Letters of Credit as collateral in lieu of the British pound or Deutsche mark drafts on T+3 described above.

5. In the case of the **BP/DM** contract, OCC will collect both the underlying (British pound) and strike currency (Deutsche mark) at a designated settlement time on T+4 in the country of origin. Assuming receipt of all currency at this time, OCC will then effect the appropriate currency payments approximately one hour later.

Philadelphia Stock Exchange

Philadelphia Stock Exchange
1900 Market Street
Philadelphia, PA 19103
Telephone: 1-800-THE-PHLX
or (215) 496-5000
Fax: (215) 496-5653

European Office

Philadelphia Stock Exchange
12th Floor, Moor House, 119 London Wall
London, EC2Y 5ET England
Telephone: (44-71) 606-2348
Fax: (44-71) 606-3548
Telex: 892735

Far Eastern Office

Philadelphia Stock Exchange
Kyobashi Tokiwa Building II, 4th Fl.
8-5, Kyobashi 2-chome
Chuo-ku Tokyo 104 Japan
Telephone: (81-3) 561-2851
Fax: (81-3) 561-2850

CME Contract Specifications: Currency Futures and Options

Commodity/ Size	Hours	Months	Codes CLR/Tick	Minimum fluctuation in price	Limit	Strike price intervals
Australian Dollar 100,000	7:20–2:00 (9:16) (RTH) 2:30 P.M.–4:00 P.M.@ 6:00 P.M.–6:00 A.M.@	Jan, Mar, Apr Jun, Jul, Sep Oct, Dec & Spot Month	AD AD	.0001 (1 pt) ($10.00/pt) ($10.00)	OPENING LIMIT BETWEEN 7:20 AM–7:35 AM [RTH] 200 POINTS Expanded Limits: Contact CME 6:00 P.M.–6:00 A.M. [GLBX] 200 POINTS	N/A
Australian Dollar Options	7:20–2:00 (2:00) [RTH] 2:37 P.M.–4:00 P.M.@ 6:11 P.M.–6:00 A.M.@	Quarterly and Serial Months Long-Dated (LD) and Short Dated (SD) Options +	LD: AD/KA Calls JA Puts ——— SD: QA/QAC Calls QAP Puts	.0001 (1 pt) ($10.00/pt) ($10.00) cab = $5.00	Option ceases trading when corresponding future locks limit	$/AD** $.01 intervals e.g. $.76, $77
British Pound 62,500	7:20–2:00 (9:16) (RTH) 2:30 P.M.–4:00 P.M.@ 6:00 P.M.–6:00 A.M.@	Jan, Mar, Apr Jun, Jul, Sep Oct, Dec & Spot Month	BP BP	.0002 (2 pt) ($6.25/pt) ($12.50)	OPENING LIMIT BETWEEN 7:20 AM–7:35 AM [RTH] 400 POINTS Expanded Limits: Contact CME 6:00 P.M.–6:00 A.M. [GLBX]	N/A
British Pound Options	7:20–2:00 (9:16) (RTH) 2:34 P.M.–4:00 P.M.@ 6:08 P.M.–6:00 A.M.@	Quarterly and Serial Months Long-Dated (LD) and Short Dated (SD) Options +	LD: BP/CP Calls PP Puts ——— SD: QB/QBC Calls QBP Puts	.0002 (2 pt) ($6.25/pt) ($12.50) cab = $6.25	Option ceases trading when corresponding future locks limit	$/BP $.025 intervals e.g. $1.600, $1.625

Times in parentheses indicate close on last day of trading (Central Time). RTH = REGULAR TRADING HOURS
@ GLOBEX = Electronic Trading Hours (ETH) begin at 2:30 p.m. to 4:00 p.m., and 6:00 p.m. to 6:00 a.m. (Central Time).
All currency spreads begin trading on GLOBEX at 2:38 P.M. to 4:00 P.M. and 6:00 P.M. to 6:00 A.M. (Central Time).
Revised April 26, 1993

Currency Futures and Options

Commodity/ Size	Hours*	Months	Codes CLR/Tick	Minimum fluctuation in price	Limit	Strike price intervals
Canadian Dollar 100,000	7:20–2:00 (9:16) (RTH) 2:30 P.M.–4:00 P.M.@ 6:00 P.M.–6:00 A.M.@	Jan, Mar, Apr Jun, Jul, Sep Oct, Dec & Spot Month	C1 CD	.0001 (1 pt) ($10.00/pt) ($10.00)	OPENING LIMIT BETWEEN 7:20 AM–7:35 AM [RTH] 200 POINTS Expanded Limits: Contact CME 6:00 P.M.–6:00 A.M. [GLBX] 200 POINTS	N/A
Canadian Dollar Options	7:20–2:00 (9:16) (RTH) 2:35 P.M.–4:00 P.M.@ 6:09 P.M.–6:00 A.M.@	Quarterly and Serial Month Long-Dated (LD) and Short Dated (SD) Options +	LD: C1/CV Calls PV Puts SD: QD/QDC Calls QDP Puts	.0001 (1 pt) ($10.00/pt) ($10.00) cab = $5.00	Option ceases trading when corresponding futures locks lim	$/CD $.025 $.005 intervals e.g. $.800, $.805
Deutsche Mark 125,000	7:20–2:00 (9:16) (RTH) 2:30 P.M.–4:00 P.M.@ 6:00 P.M.–6:00 A.M.@	Jan, Mar, Apr Jun, Jul, Sep Oct, Dec & Spot Month	D1 DM	.0001 (1 pt) ($12.50/pt) ($12.50)	OPENING LIMIT BETWEEN 7:20 AM–7:35 AM [RTH] 200 POINTS Expanded Limits: Contact CME 6:00 P.M.–6:00 A.M. [GLBX] 200 POINTS	N/A

Deutsche Mark Options	7:20–2:00 (9:16) (RTH) 2:32 P.M.–4:00 P.M.@ 6:06 P.M.–6:00 A.M.@	Quarterly and Serial Month Long-Dated (LD) and Short Dated (SD) Options +	LD: D1/CM Calls PM Puts — SD: QM/QMC Calls QMP Puts	.0001 (1 pt) ($12.50/pt) ($12.50) cab = $6.25	Option ceases trading when corresponding futures locks lim	$/DM** $.01 intervals e.g. $.63, $.64
Japanese Yen 12,500,000	7:20–2:00 (9:16) (RTH) 2:30 P.M.–4:00 P.M.@ 6:00 P.M.–6:00 A.M.@	Jan, Mar, Apr Jun, Jul, Sep Oct, Dec & Spot Month	J1 JY	.000001 (1 pt) ($12.50/pt) ($12.50)	OPENING LIMIT BETWEEN 7:20 AM–7:35 AM [RTH] 200 POINTS Expanded Limits: Contact CME 6:00 P.M.–6:00 A.M. [GLBX] 200 POINTS	N/A
Japanese Yen Options	7:20–2:00 (9:16) (RTH) 2:31 P.M.–4:00 P.M.@ 6:05 P.M.–6:00 A.M.@	Quarterly and Serial Month Long-Dated (LD) and Short Dated (SD) Options +	LD: J1/CJ Calls PJ Puts — SD: YQ/YQC Calls YQP Puts	.000001 (1 pt) ($12.50/pt) ($12.50) cab = $6.25	Option ceases trading when corresponding futures locks lim	$/JY** $.0001 intervals e.g. $.0072, $.0071

Times in parentheses indicate close on last day of trading (Central Time). RTH = REGULAR TRADING HOURS

@ GLOBEX = Electronic Trading Hours (ETH) begin at 2:30 p.m. to 4:00 p.m., and 6:00 p.m. to 6:00 a.m. (Central Time).

All currency spreads begin trading on GLOBEX at 2:38 P.M. to 4:00 P.M. and 6:00 P.M. to 6:00 A.M. (Central Time).

Revised April 26, 1993

Currency Futures and Options

Commodity/Size	Hours*	Months	Codes CLR/Tick	Minimum fluctuation in price	Limit	Strike price intervals
Swiss Franc 125,000	7:20–2:00 (9:16) (RTH) 2:30 P.M.–4:00 P.M.@ 6:00 P.M.–6:00 A.M.@	Jan, Mar, Apr Jun, Jul, Sep Oct, Dec & Spot Month	E1 SF	.0001 (1 pt) ($12.50/pt) ($12.50)	OPENING LIMIT BETWEEN 7:20 AM–7:35 AM [RTH] 200 POINTS Expanded Limits: Contact CME 6:00 P.M.–6:00 A.M. [GLBX] 200 POINTS	N/A
Swiss Franc Options	7:20–2:00 (9:16) (RTH) 2:33 P.M.–4:00 P.M.@ 6:07 P.M.–6:00 A.M.@	Quarterly and Serial Month Long-Dated (LD) and Short Dated (SD) Options +	LD: E1/CF Calls PF Puts SD: QF/QFC Calls QFP Puts	.0001 (1 pt) ($12.50/pt) ($12.50) cab = $6.25	Option ceases trading when corresponding futures locks lim	$/SF** e.g. $.72, $.73
Foreign Currency-Denominated Deutsche Mark/ Japanese Yen DM125,000 x DM/JY XRATE	7:20–2:00 (9:16) (RTH) 2:30 P.M.–4:00 P.M.@ 6:00 P.M.–6:00 A.M.@	Mar, Jun, Sep Dec	DJ DJ	.01 (1 pt) (¥1,250/pt) (¥1,250)	OPENING LIMIT BETWEEN 7:20 AM–7:35 AM 150 POINTS 6:00 P.M.–6:00 A.M. (GLOBEX) 150 POINTS	N/A
Foreign Currency-Denominated Deutsche Mark/ Japanese Yen Options	7:20–2:00 (2:00) (RTH) 2:36 P.M.–4:00 P.M.@ 6:10 P.M.–6:00 A.M.@	Quarterly and Serial Month Long-Dated (LD) and Short Dated (SD) Options +	LD: DJ/DJ Calls DJ Puts SD: QJ/QJC Calls QJP Puts	.01 (1 pt) (¥1,250/pt) (¥1,250) cab = ¥625	Option ceases trading when corresponding futures locks lim	¥/DM at intervals of 1.00** e.g. 77.00, 78.00

Times in parentheses indicate close on last day of trading (Central Time). RTH = REGULAR TRADING HOURS
@ GLOBEX = Electronic Trading Hours (ETH) begin at 2:30 p.m. to 4:00 p.m., and 6:00 p.m. to 6:00 a.m. (Central Time).
All currency spreads begin trading on GLOBEX at 2:38 P.M. to 4:00 P.M. and 6:00 P.M. to 6:00 A.M. (Central Time).
Revised April 26, 1993

Specifications common to all CME options on currency futures

Strike Prices

When a new quarterly contract month is listed for trading, there will be nine put and call strike prices: the nearest strike to the underlying futures price, the next four higher, and the next four lower.* For example, if the March DM futures price closes at $.5651 on the previous day, the strikes listed for March puts and calls will be: 53¢, 54¢, 55¢, 56¢, 57¢, 58¢, 59¢, 60¢, 61¢.

A new strike price will be listed for both puts and calls when the underlying futures sale, bid, or offer price touches within half a strike price interval of either the fourth highest or fourth lowest strike prices. As an example, if the March DM futures price touches $.5751 after the options are listed as in the above example, then a new strike price at 62¢ will be listed for puts and calls the next day. (No new options that expire in the quarterly cycle will be listed, however, with less than 10 calendar days until expiration. For options that expire in the serial months, new options may be listed for trading up to and including the termination of trading.)

When a new serial contract month is listed for trading, the Exchange will list put and call options at any exercise price listed for trading in the next March quarterly cycle futures option that is nearest the expiration of the option. Thereafter, whenever a strike price is listed for a quarterly option, it will also be listed for the serial month option.

Last Day of Trading

The second Friday prior to the third Wednesday of the contract month. If that Friday is an Exchange holiday, the last trading day will be the immediately preceding business day.

Minimum Margin

No margin required for put or call option buyers, but the premium must be paid in full; option sellers must meet additional margin requirements as determined by the Standard Portfolio Analysis of Risk™ (SPAN) margin system.

Exercise Procedure

Option buyers may exercise on any trading day. Check with your brokerage firm for its exercise procedure.

Exercise results in a long futures position for a call buyer or a put seller, and a short futures position for a put buyer or a call seller. The futures position is effective on the trading day immediately following exercise, and is marked-to-market to the settlement that day. Initial margin will be required before trading begins on the second day following the long option holder's notice of exercise. If the futures position is not offset prior to the expiration of trading in the futures contract, delivery of physical currency will result or be required.

Expiration

Options expire at 7:00 p.m. (Chicago Time) on the last trading day. However, your broker may set a considerably earlier cut-off time for exercising expiring options. Always check with your broker for exercise deadlines.

There is no automatic exercise of the expiring in-the-money currency options by the CME Clearing House.

*Half-Strikes may also be listed for the first 3 consecutive months. Consult listing procedures for specific requirements.

Currency Futures – SPAN Performance
Bond Requirement (Exchange Minimums)

Commodity	I / M	Outrights SPEC	Outrights H/MEM	Outrights-del. Month	Intra-commodity spreads	Intra-commodity spreads delivery Month	Allowable inter-commodity spreads	SPEC Initial	Maint.	H/MEM I & M
Australian Dollar	I	$1215	$900	Same as Non-Delivery Month	MARKET	Same as Non-Delivery Month	AD vs. BP	$3375	$2500	$2500
	M	$900	$900				AD vs. CD	$1080	$800	$800
							AD vs. DM	$2970	$2200	$2200
							AD vs. JY	$1620	$1200	$1200
							AD vs. SF	$3780	$2800	$2800
British Pound	I	$4050	$3000	Same as Non-Delivery Month	MARKET	Same as Non-Delivery Month	BP vs. AD	$3375	$2500	$2500
	M	$3000	$3000				BP vs. CD	$2835	$2100	$2100
							BP vs. DM	$1350	$1000	$1000
							BP vs. JY	$2430	$1800	$1800
							BP vs. SF	$1485	$1100	$1100
Canadian Dollar	I	$1080	$800	Same as Non-Delivery Month	MARKET	Same as Non-Delivery Month	CD vs. AD	$1080	$800	$800
	M	$800	$800				CD vs. BP	$2835	$2100	$2100
							CD vs. DM	$2430	$1800	$1800
							CD vs. JY	$1620	$1200	$1200
							CD vs. SF	$2700	$2000	$2000
Deutsche Mark	I	$2700	$2000	Same as Non-Delivery Month	MARKET	Same as Non-Delivery Month	DM vs. AD	$2970	$2200	$2200
	M	$2000	$2000				DM vs. BP	$1350	$1000	$1000
							DM vs. CD	$2430	$1800	$1800
							DM vs. JY	$1350	$1000	$1000
							DM vs. SF	$945	$700	$700
Japanese Yen	I	$1688	$1250	Same as Non-Delivery Month	MARKET	Same as Non-Delivery Month	JY vs. AD	$1620	$1200	$1200
	M	$1250	$1250				JY vs. BP	$2430	$1800	$1800
							JY vs. CD	$1620	$1200	$1200
							JY vs. DM	$1350	$1000	$1000
							JY vs. SF	$2025	$1500	$1500
Swiss Franc	I	$3105	$2300	Same as Non-Delivery Month	MARKET	Same as Non-Delivery Month	SF vs. AD	$3780	$2800	$2800
	M	$2300	$2300				SF vs. BP	$1485	$1100	$1100
							SF vs. CD	$2700	$2000	$2000
							SF vs. DM	$945	$700	$700
							SF vs. JY	$2025	$1500	$1500

Foreign Currency Cross–Rate Futures –
SPAN Performance Bond Requirements
(Exchange Minimums)

Commodity	Outrights SPEC		H/MEM	Outrights-del. Month	Intra-commodity spreads	Intra-commodity spreads delivery Month	Allowable inter-commodity spreads	SPEC Initial	Maint.	H/MEM I & M	Notes
Deutsche Mark/ Japanese Yen	I	189 000	140 000 Y=	Same as Non-Del. Month	MARKET	Same as Non-Delivery Month	DJ XRATE vs. JY	$1620	$1200	$1200	
							DJ XRATE vs. DM	$1485	$1100	$1100	
Foreign Currency Cross-Rate	M	140 000	140 000 Y=				DJ XRATE vs. JY-DM Spread #	$405	$300	$300	Ratio – 1:1:1
							DJ XRATE vs. JY-DM Spread #	$405	$300	$300	Ratio: See notes below

* Long vs. Long or Short vs. Short
\# 3-Legged Spreads

ADDITIONAL NOTES:
The Clearing House will recognize 3-legged intercommodity spreads in ratios designed to estimate the appropriate arbitrage relationships. They are based on current market conditions and will change as the value of the component contracts fluctuate. For currently recognized ratios and additional information contact the Clearing House at (312) 648–3888.

Options – SPAN Short Option Minimums

Option/size	SPAN	SPAN Short Option Minimum
Australian $ Options–One AD Futures Contract	Refer to Daily SPAN risk arrays generated by the CME.	$23
British Pound Options–One BP Futures Contract	Refer to Daily SPAN risk arrays generated by the CME.	$75
Canadian $ Option–One CD Futures Contract	Refer to Daily SPAN risk arrays generated by the CME.	$20
Deutsche Mark Options–One DM Futures Contract	Refer to Daily SPAN risk arrays generated by the CME.	$50
Japanese Yen Option–One JY Futures Contract	Refer to Daily SPAN risk arrays generated by the CME.	$32
Swiss Franc Options–One SF Futures Contract	Refer to Daily SPAN risk arrays generated by the CME.	$58
S&P Options One S&P 500 Futures Contract	Refer to Daily SPAN risk arrays generated by the CME.	$100
S&P 400 Options One S&P 400 Futures Contract	Refer to Daily SPAN risk arrays generated by the CME.	$50

See Clearing House Manual of Operations for additional information on performance bond requirements for options.

Notes on the exchange trading process

The CME is a classic example of the auction market process at work. All bids and offers on currency and other financial futures and options contracts are made by open outcry in a competitive arena – one of the largest and most modern trading facilities in the world.

Unlike some securities exchanges that utilize the specialist system, the CME confers no special responsibility on individual trading members and makes certain that all participants have equal access to the market. This philosophy has allowed competition among traders to flourish and has fostered an efficient market environment that consistently seeks the best price for a given currency futures or options contract and a constant flow of bids and offers.

The cornerstone of this trading system is the Chicago Mercantile Exchange's membership – more than 2500 independent traders, members of partnerships and representatives of brokerage firms. These members perform two important market functions: Floor Broker and Floor Trader.

A *Floor Broker* serves as a 'broker's broker,' responsible for executing orders for the accounts of one or more of the Exchange's member firms. These orders may be for member firms themselves or for customers of those firms.

A *Floor Trader* is analogous to a market-maker in the securities markets. As individuals trading for their own accounts or for those of organization that they represent, floor traders are an important factor in creating market interest and in assuring that bids and offers always are available.

Together, floor traders and floor brokers form the marketplace for trading currency and other futures and options. The trading tactics and strategies they employ, combined with their knowledge and expertise, contribute significantly to successful, liquid markets.

Exercise of a currency option

Options expire at 7:00 p.m. on the last trading day. *However*, your broker may set a considerably earlier cut-off time for exercising expiring options. Note that there is *no* automatic exercise of expiring in-the-money options.

An option buyer may exercise on any trading day, if the buyer's Clearing Member presents an exercise notice to the Clearing House by 7:00 p.m. on the day of exercise. The option buyer will receive a futures position (long for a call, short for a put) marked-to-the-market from the strike price the following trading day. Initial margin will be required before trading begins on the second day following exercise.

By a process of random selection, the Clearing House assigns exercise notices to Clearing Members, which will then assign them by an approved selection process to their clients. Notice of assignment will be given to the Clearing Member before trading begins on the day following an exercise notice. Call writers who are assigned will receive short futures positions; put writers who are assigned will receive long futures positions. The futures will be assigned at the strike price and will be marked-to-market at the end of trading on the day following the long option holder's notice of exercise. Initial margin will be required before trading begins on the second day following the tender of an exercise notice.

IMM currency delivery system

Though relatively few holders of currency futures contracts ever take actual delivery of a currency, the integrity of the contracts rests heavily on the Exchange's ability to provide accurate, timely delivery when called upon to do so.

The IMM delivery system is structured so that neither currency involved in the delivery-exchange need leave its home country. In the case of dollar-based currencies, the long futures position holder delivers U.S. dollars in the U.S., and receives the contract currency in its home country. The short futures position holder delivers the contract currency in its home country, and receives dollars in the U.S. When non-dollar cross-rates such as the DM/JY are involved, the buyer of the contract receives Deutsche marks and pays Japanese yen; the seller delivers Deutsche marks and receives Japanese yen. (See strategy paper titled 'The CME's Innovative Non-Dollar Processing System for its New DM/JY Contracts.')

Prior to the last day of trading, there is an exchange of bank-related information among the various participants: the contract-holder, the holder's Clearing Member, the Clearing House and the Clearing House's agent bank. Through a pre-arranged banking transfer system, each buyer will pay the settlement price for the currency and will receive the contract amount of currency, both on the Wednesday following the last day of trading. On that same day, the seller will deliver the contract amount of the currency, and will receive the settlement price.

Chicago Mercantile
Exchange

International Monetary Market
Index and Option Market

Chicago
Chicago Mercantile Exchange
30 South Wacker Drive
Chicago, Illinois 60606
312/930-1000
FAX: 312/466-4410

New York
Chicago Mercantile Exchange
67 Wall Street
New York, New York 10005
212/363-7000

London
Chicago Mercantile Exchange
27 Throgmorton Street
London, EC2N 2AN England
44 71 920-0722

Tokyo
Chicago Mercantile Exchange
3-3-1 Kasumigaseki Chiyoda-ku
Tokyo 100 Japan
813 3595-2251

APPENDIX

II

Bank of England Annex A/B

Bank of England's paper on Foreign Currency Options, of April 1984.

Foreign Currency Exposure reporting form (S3), of December 1991, including Annex A and Annex B.

General Notes and Completion Notes for S3 and Annex A and B.

(Reproduced with the permission of the Bank of England)

Foreign currency options

A number of banks have shown considerable interest in writing currency options for customers or for other banks, or in dealing in contracts on option exchanges. The Bank's paper 'Foreign Currency Exposure' published in April 1981 does not cover this topic. The purpose of this paper is to explain how the Bank of England will treat banks' option business, particularly in relation to the guidelines agreed individually with banks for monitoring their foreign exchange exposure.

The nature of the risk

An option contract allows the holder to exchange (or equally to choose not to exchange) a specific amount of one currency for another at a predetermined rate (the 'exercise price') during some period in the future. In exchange for this right, the holder pays a premium to the person granting the option. The premium is charged to cover the risk borne by the bank or other institution writing the contract; some of this is absorbed by the transaction costs of the bank in covering the risk.

The main risk, therefore, rests with the institution writing the option. Its exposure to movements in the exchange rate between the two currencies involved may be as great as having an open position of the same size as the value of contracts written; it may of course be less to the extent that options are not exercised. An institution which *holds* an option has no exposure to loss, only the possible opportunity for gain (unless it is treating its expenditure on the premium payment as an investment rather than writing it off. If it treats it as an investment it is exposed to the extent of the book value given to the asset).

A bank which writes currency options for its customers may protect its position to the extent that it is able to purchase a corresponding contract either on an exchange or from another bank; but its position is only fully protected if the terms of the contract purchased are at least as favourable as those of the option written. As the organised options exchanges work to specific delivery dates they can never be used as perfect cover against a contract which is exercisable over a period beyond the delivery date of the exchange contract.

As an alternative to taking cover on the option exchanges, a bank might hedge its position on the cash market. If the bank can find a suitable formula for doing this – see below –, it is then able to write options for customers for non-standard amounts, for non-standard periods, and in any freely traded currency, thereby offering a tailor-made product for its customer's needs. It should be noted that because the risk needs to be monitored continuously the use of cash markets to hedge option contracts is restricted for banks which lack the ability to deal in all time zones.

In assessing the risk which a bank bears in writing currency options it is necessary to assume that its counterparties behave in a rational manner. A customer would not exercise his option to buy a currency from the bank if he could purchase it more cheaply on the spot market; similarly he would not opt to sell a currency to a bank at a rate less favourable than that obtainable on the spot market.

At first sight it would appear that all a bank need do to protect its position is to cover fully those options which currently it would be in the customer's interests to exercise ('in the money' options), and leave uncovered those which it would not ('out of the money' options). This method however fails to account for a bank being at risk not only from the current spot rate in relation to the exercise rate, but also to future changes in the spot rate until the expiry of the option. Such changes might alter the bank's position from being exposed to loss – when the rate favoured the customer's exercising the option – to being exposed to no loss – when it would be to the customer's disadvantage to exercise the option. If the spot rate fluctuated around the exercise price the bank would be involved in considerable costs fully covering and then fully uncovering its position, whilst the option holder delayed exercising his option in the hope of the spot rate moving (further) into the money, so enabling him to make a (larger) profit.

Several banks have developed techniques based on mathematical formulae to determine the premium which should be charged for writing an option contract, and the position which should be taken in the cash market to hedge its option contracts.

The variables on which the formulae depend include: the current spot rate and its relation to the exercise rate; the remaining period of the contract; the volatility of the exchange rate; and interest rates in the two currencies concerned. Thus a contract which is a long way 'out of the money' and which has only a short time to run requires virtually no cash cover; one which still has some time to run, other things being equal, will require more cover, particularly if the exchange rate is volatile. Such formulae have become widely accepted as the basis for both hedging and pricing contracts, although individual banks are developing various refinements which they hope will enhance their hedging techniques.

For accounting purposes banks which are active in the market are proposing to value their option contracts by marking them to market (e.g. options written are revalued to the price which would have to be paid to buy back the rights which have been extended to the option holder).

Foreign exchange guidelines

For the purposes of monitoring a bank's risk the Bank will expect any exposures arising out of option business to be contained within existing guidelines rather than be additional to them.

The Bank will need to have reported to it the extent of banks' exposures; reporting will take one of two forms. Unless a bank is able to satisfy the Bank that its hedging techniques are sufficiently developed, the Bank will take a 'worst view' approach. The approach will take account of the potential effect of the exercise of option rights held by a bank's customers on its open position in individual currencies, including the possibility that the bank's position in a particular currency may be transformed from a long position to a short (or vice versa). It is recognised that this system fails to take any account of the exercise price relative to the current spot rate (and therefore the likelihood of the option being exercised), nor is any credit given for options taken – on the grounds that without knowing the full details of the period and exercise rates of options written and options held there is no way of knowing whether options held are of any value in hedging the risks on options which the bank has written. An example of the reporting form (an annex to the existing 53 form and instructions is given as Annex A).

Where a bank has considered the mathematics of options in some detail, the Bank will allow it to use its own formula for measuring the extent of its exposure on currency options, which will be assessed with that on cash markets to determine the overall open position for the purposes of monitoring a bank's foreign exchange exposure against the agreed guidelines.

Before a bank will be permitted to use its own formula for calculating its exposure for guideline purposes, the Bank will need to be satisfied not only with the mathematical basis of the formula and procedures for monitoring-its continued validity, but also that the operating systems for conducting the business and controlling the options book (including limits) are adequate. The operation of a bank's own formula will be kept under review and the Bank will expect to discuss options business with these banks on a frequent and regular basis. An example of the reporting form for these banks is given in Annex B.

The arrangements outlined in this note will form the basis on which the

Bank assesses banks' foreign currency options for prudential purposes. However the case for separate guidelines for options business will be reviewed by the Bank in the light of market developments and discussions with individual banks.

Bank of England
April 1984

Foreign Currency Exposure

as at _____

Reporting institution _____

_____

Name (block letters please) and signature of authorised official at reporting institution

In the event of a query, the Bank of England may contact (block letters please)

_____ Tel No _____ Ext _____

Notes on completion

If you have any difficulty in completing this form, please telephone 071-601 4218/4544/5574. Telephone enquiries relating to general reporting difficulties should be made to the Financial Statistics Division's 'Help Desk' on 071-601 5360.

1. Complete form monthly as at the last day of the calendar month.

2. For definition of items refer to the blue *Banking statistics definitions* folder.

3. Enter amounts in sterling to nearest thousand omitting £000s.

4. Ensure that the items in the shaded areas agree with related items on Form BS column 2 (other currencies).

5. Return form within **TEN WORKING DAYS** of reporting date clearly addressed to:

   Financial Statistics Division
   Group 1 (HO-5)
   Bank of England
   Threadneedle Street
   London
   EC2R 8AH

6. Forms may also be delivered to the reception desk at the Threadneedle Street entrace of the Bank of England between 9.00 am and 5.00 pm, Monday to Friday. Envelopes should be clearly addressed as above.

Bank of England use only

Logged	Data entered	Amendments input

SECTION 1 - FOREIGN CURRENCY EXPOSURE OF REPORTING INSTITUTION

Analysis by currency		Operations transacted by the United Kingdom offices					Net purchases (sales) of currency and gold futures contracts
		Gross spot claims	Gross spot liabilities including internal accounts	Net spot claims (liabilities), including internal accounts (= col 1 minus col 2)	Net forward purchases (sales)	Known net future income (expense) not included already in column 3(d)	
		1	2	3	4	5	6
US dollars	US USA						
Belgian francs	BE BELG						
Canadian dollars	CA CANA						
Danish kroner	DK DENM						
Deutschemarks	DE RGER						
French francs	FR FRAN						
Irish pounds	IE EIRE						
Italian lire	IT ITAL						
Japanese yen	JP JAPA						
Netherlands guilders	NL NETH						
Saudi riyals	SA SAUA						
Spanish pesetas	ES SPAI						
Swedish kroner	SE SWED						
Swiss francs	CH SWIT						
Gold (a)	GO GOLD						
European Currency Units	EU ECUS						
Special Drawing Rights	SS SDRS						
(b)							
Foreign currencies not separately specified above(c)	long short						
Translation/revaluation adjustment (d)							
TOTAL							

(BS col 2 item 21)   (BS col 2 item 6)

SECTION 2 - NET POSITION OF EACH OVERSEAS BRANCH OR DEALING CENTRE OF REPORTING INSTITUTION

Analysis by currency		Location of branch or dealing centre				
US dollars	US USA					
Belgian francs	BE BELG					
Canadian dollars	CA CANA					
Danish kroner	DK DENM					
Deutschemarks	DE RGER					
French francs	FR FRAN					
Irish pounds	IE EIRE					
Italian lire	IT ITAL					
Japanese yen	JP JAPA					
Netherlands guilders	NL NETH					
Saudi riyals	SA SAUA					
Spanish pesetas	ES SPAI					
Swedish kroner	SE SWED					
Swiss francs	CH SWIT					
Gold (a)	GO GOLD					
European Currency Units	EU ECUS					
Special Drawing Rights	SS SDRS					
(b)						
Foreign currencies not separately specified above (c)						

(a) Includes bullion and coin

(b) Enter here details for other individual foreign currencies with net spot claims or liabilities (including, for UK registered banks, the balances of overseas branches and dealing centres) equivalent to £1 million or more. Institutions asked to report positions in silver should do so here.

£000s

Adjustment for profit and loss and specific provision account (d)	Adjusted options position	Net long (short) position of over-seas branches listed in section 2	Disaggregation of net positions in CCUs	Net overall long (short) position (= cols 3+4+5+6+7+7 A+8+8A)	Adjustment for structural assets (liabilities) (d)	Net dealing long (short) position (= col 9 minus col 10)	
7	7A	8	8A	9	10	11	
							US USA
							BE BELG
							CA CANA
							DK DENM
							DE RGER
							FR FRAN
							IE EIRE
							IT ITAL
							JP JAPA
							NL NETH
							SA SAUA
							ES SPAI
							SE SWED
							CH SWIT
							GO GOLD
							EU ECUS
							SS SDRS
							long
					( )		( )	short

Sterling balancing item (d)	
TOTAL	ZERO	ZERO
Aggregate of net short open positions (d)	( )	( )

£000s

					Total long (short) position of all branches and dealing centres

(c) Enter here details for currencies with a net spot claims on liabilities equivalent to less that £1 million. The subdivision into long and short positions is required only in columns 9 and 11 (see notes).

(d) See the notes regarding the completion of these boxes.

SECTION 3 - EXCEPTION REPORT (e)

£000s

Analysis by currency		Net dealing long (short) positions (equivalent to column 11 in section 1)						
		Date:	Date:-	Date:	Date:	Date:	Date:	Date:
US dollars								US USA
Belgian francs								BE BELG
Canadian dollars								CA CANA
Danish kroner								DK DENM
Deutschemarks								DE RGER
French francs								FR FRAN
Irish pounds								IE EIRE
Italian lire								IT ITAL
Japanese yen								JP JAPA
Netherlands guilders								NL NETH
Saudi riyals								SA SAUA
Spanish pesetas								ES SPAI
Swedish kroner								SE SWED
Swiss francs								CH SWIT
Gold (a)								GO GOLD
European Currency Units								EU ECUS
Special Drawing Rights								SS SDRS
(b)								
Foreign currencies not	long							long
separately specified above (c)	short							short
Sterling balancing item (d)								
TOTAL		ZERO	ZERO	ZERO	ZERO	ZERO	ZERO	ZERO

Aggregate of net short open positions (d)	( )	( )	( )	( )	( )	( )	( )

(a), (b), (c), (d) - see footnotes to sections 1 and 2

(e) A column should be completed for any date since the previous end-month reporting date on which banks have exceeded the guidelines agreed with Banking Supervision Division, Bank of England.

ANNEX A   £000s

Analysis by currency		Net dealing long (short) spot & forward position	Potential purchases under option rights granted to others	Potential sales under option rights granted to others	Dealing exposure to depreciation	Dealing exposure to appreciation	Options held to purchase currencies	Options held to sell currencies
		11	12	13	14	15	16	17
US dollars	US USA							
Belgian francs	BE BELG							
Canadian dollars	CA CANA							
Danish kroner	DK DENM							
Deutschemarks	DE RGER							
French francs	FR FRAN							
Irish pounds	IE EIRE							
Italian lire	IT ITAL							
Japanese yen	JP JAPA							
Netherlands guilders	NL NETH							
Saudi riyals	SA SAUA							
Spanish pesetas	ES SPAI							
Swedish kroner	SE SWED							
Swiss francs	CH SWIT							
Gold (a)	GO GOLD							
European Currency Units	EU ECUS							
Special Drawing Rights	SS SDRS							
(b)								
Foreign currencies not separately specified above(c)	long							
	short	( )	( )	( )	( )	( )	( )	( )
UK								
TOTAL		ZERO						
Aggregate of net short open positions		( )						

ANNEX B   £000s

Analysis by currency		Gross value of potential purchases under option rights granted	Gross value of potential sales under option rights granted	Gross value of potential purchases under options rights held	Gross value of potential sales under options rights held	Adjusted options position
		12	13	14	15	16
US dollars	US USA					
Belgian francs	BE BELG					
Canadian dollars	CA CANA					
Danish kroner	DK DENM					
Deutschemarks	DE RGER					
French francs	FR FRAN					
Irish pounds	IE EIRE					
Italian lire	IT ITAL					
Japanese yen	JP JAPA					
Netherlands guilders	NL NETH					
Saudi riyals	SA SAUA					
Spanish pesetas	ES SPAI					
Swedish kroner	SE SWED					
Swiss francs	CH SWIT					
Gold (a)	GO GOLD					
European Currency Units	EU ECUS					
Special Drawing Rights	SS SDRS					
(b)						
Foreign currencies not separately specified above(c)	long					
	short	( )	( )	( )	( )	( )
UK						
TOTAL						ZERO

(a), (b), (c) - **see** footnotes to sections 1 and 2

Foreign currency exposure (Form S3)

A   General notes

Foreign Currency Exposure paper

These notes should be read in conjunction with the Bank's paper on Foreign Currency Exposure dated April 1981. Copies of the paper can be obtained from general policy group of Banking Supervision Division.

Application and frequency of returns

The return should be completed as at the end of each calendar month by those institutions specifically requested to do so by the Bank. Normally the Bank will require the return to be completed by any recognised UK bank which maintains a dealing room and operates in the foreign exchange markets.

Reporting and translation

See the General definitions, paragraphs 8 and 10, for the translation into sterling of liabilities, assets and forward positions, and for the treatment and valuation of gold.

The return should be completed to show the equivalent values in sterling (£000's) of all currency and gold assets and liabilities, and of the contracted foreign currency and gold amounts of all forward transactions and of all currency and gold futures transactions. Positive or (in brackets) negative entries should be made as indicated by the column headings, or by the following notes.

Silver, platinum and palladium

Banks which have been specifically requested to report their positions in these metals should include the details in one of the blank rows provided, translating their positions at the relevant closing spot price on the reporting date.

Composite currencies

[BSR change]

Banks which have assets or liabilities denominated in composite currencies except Special Drawing Rights or European Currency Units should report them disaggregated into their component national currencies (see the General definitions, paragraph 9). The sterling components should be entered **in columns 1 and 2 of Section 1 only.** In these columns they should be entered in the boxes provided, to facilitate reconciliation with total non-sterling liabilities and assets as reported on Form BS (column 2).

B   Notes for the completion of Section 1

Arithmetic relationships

Please ensure that the following relationships hold for the completed return, taking into account that figures in brackets are negative:

(i)   for each row, column 1 less column 2 equals column 3;

[BSR change] (ii)   for each row, the sum of columns 3 to 8A equals column 9;

(iii)   for each row, column 9 less column 10 equals column 11;

(iv)   the aggregate of the net short open positions, in columns 9 and 11, should equal the sum of all the bracketed (ie negative) figures in the column.

Currencies not printed on the form

Details for individual currencies in which the reporting institution (including, for UK incorporated banks, overseas branches and dealing centres) has balances equivalent to £1 million or more should be entered in the blank rows provided.

Business in currencies with smaller balances should be aggregated and reported in the row "Foreign currencies not separately specified". The entries under columns 9 and 11 in this row should, however, be subdivided to show separate figures for currencies with "long" and "short" positions (see the notes to those columns).

Business denominated in Luxembourg francs should **not** be included under "Belgian francs".

Gross spot claims (column 1)

Enter in column 1 all spot claims in foreign currencies, gold bullion and gold coin. The sum of the entries in the column, including the sterling component of assets denominated in composite currencies, should equal the entry at item 21 in column 2 of Form BS, if completed as at the reporting date. All the entries should be positive.

Gross spot liabilities, including internal accounts (column 2)

Enter in column 2 all spot liabilities, including internal accounts[1], in foreign currencies, gold bullion and gold coin. **Entries in the currency rows of this column should not be in brackets,** except where negative currency or gold liabilities arise because of the inclusion of internal accounts.

Enter under **translation/revaluation adjustment** any change in the sterling valuation of foreign currency assets and liabilities, as a result of exchange rate movements, that has been included, or, in principle, would be included, as part of item 5.3 in column 2 of Form BS. If the figure included within this Form BS entry is negative then the entry in the box should be in brackets.

The sum of the entries in column 2, including the sterling component of liabilities denominated in composite currencies and the translation/revaluation adjustment, should equal the entry at item 6 in column 2 of Form BS, if completed as at the reporting date.

Net spot claims (liabilities) including internal accounts (column 3)

The entries in this column should equal the entries in column 1 less those in column 2.

Net forward purchases (sales) (column 4)

Enter in this column net forward and unmatured spot purchases and sales of foreign currency, gold bullion and gold coin, including positions with overseas offices of the reporting institution. Where one side of such a transaction is denominated in sterling, the sterling amount will not appear in this column. Exclude purchase and sales of futures contracts in currency and gold, which should be entered in column 6.

Known net future income (expense) not included already in column 3 (column 5)

Enter in this column all net flows of interest payable and receivable on deposits and loans associated with swap transactions (commonly known as "deposit swaps") which have not already been included in column 3. All such flows should be reported in this column, irrespective of whether or not they have been covered by spot or forward market transactions.

Do **not** include other uncovered interest flows; but do also include in this column all covered net flows, both of interest and of other income and expense, apart from those which have been accrued onto the balance sheet and which have therefore already been included in column 3.

---

1 See Appendix, paragraph 1.

Net purchases (sales) of currency and gold futures contracts (column 6)

Enter the net positions (purchases less sales) of currency and gold futures contracts. Include contracts transacted on the London International Financial Futures Exchange, the London Gold Futures Market or on similar exchanges abroad. Contracts should be entered at their nominal values translated at the closing middle market **spot** exchange rates. Where one side of a contract is denominated in sterling, the sterling amount will not appear in the column. Purchases and sales of contracts in interest rate futures and other commodity futures should **not** be included. Where trading on LIFFE is conducted through a subsidiary company specifically established for that purpose, reference should be made to the general policy group of Banking Supervision Division of the Bank of England, regarding the appropriate reporting of the subsidiary's positions.

[BSR change]
Adjustments for profit and loss and specific provision account (column 7)

Enter in column 7 the net of any balance of income and expense accounts denominated in foreign currencies. Net income should be shown as a positive figure, net expense should be shown in brackets[2].

Include also in this column all specific provision accounts which are denominated in currencies other than those of the assets for which they have been created. Banks should enter a positive figure in the currency row in which the provision is denominated and a corresponding negative figure (shown in brackets) in the row in which the asset is denominated[3].

Adjusted options position (column 7A)

[BSR change]
Banks given approval by the Bank to report their options business on Annex B should report in column 7A their adjusted options positions (ie the delta values) as calculated in column 16 of the Annex B.

Net long (short) position of overseas branches (column 8)

Column 8 should be completed by UK incorporated banks which have overseas branches which deal in foreign exchange. Banks should enter in this column the total net position in each currency of all its overseas branches listed in Section 2 of the report.

[BSR change]
Disaggregation of net positions in CCUs (column 8A)

In the preceding columns, ECU and SDR are shown as separate currencies (see General Notes). However, to enable hedges in the underlying currencies to offset net positions in ECU or SDR, such positions may, at the discretion of the reporting bank, be disaggregated into the component currencies in this column.

Net overall long (short) position (column 9)

Banks should report in column 9 the net overall position in each currency which, for the individually specified currencies should be divided into those with net long positions and those with net short positions. The sum of the net long positions (positive) and the sum of the net positions (in brackets) in these currencies should be entered in the two boxes provided. The sum of these two figures should equal the sum of the entries in columns 3 to 8B inclusive.

The entry under **sterling balancing item** should be the figure that is necessary in order that the total of the overall net long and short positions, in all currencies taken together, equals zero. In other words, it should be equal and opposite to the sum of the entries in the boxes above it.

---

2 See Appendix, paragraph 1.

3 See Appendix, paragraphs 1 and 2.

If branches of overseas banks feel that the adoption of a sterling balancing item results in a mis-statement of their currency exposure, further reference should be made to the Bank of England.

The **aggregate of net short open positions** should be the sum of any net short (ie bracketed) entries in the rows for individually specified currencies, the entry for currencies not individually specified and with short positions, and the entry for the sterling balancing item if it is negative. For UK-incorporated banks this aggregate will be included in the risk assets ratio described in the Bank's Notice "Implementation in the United Kingdom of the Solvency Ratio Directive". An adjustment will be made to the aggregate short position to take account of items which have already been deducted from banks' capital bases.

[BSR change]   **Optional adjustments for structural positions (column 10)**

Banks may include in column 10 any currency item which the Bank has agreed may be regarded as structural where the effect of its inclusion therein is to reduce the net overall open position in that currency (column 9).

Banks should attach a separate schedule to their reporting form setting out the items which have been included in column 10 in both their currency amounts and equivalent values in sterling.

Prior reference to the Bank is required before any item may be regarded as structural other than the following:

Premises
Fixtures and fittings (including plant and equipment)
Investments in subsidiaries[4]
Investment in associates
Remittable profits held in the domestic currency of the home country (UK branches of overseas banks only)[5]

[BSR change]   **Net dealing long (short) position (column 11)**

Column 11 shows the dealing position in each currency, against which the guidelines agreed between the Bank of England and each bank apply. It should be calculated by **subtracting** column 10 from column 9.

Currencies not individually specified should be divided into those with net long dealing positions and those with net short dealing positions. The sum of the net long dealing positions (positive) and the sum of the net short dealing positions (in brackets) in these currencies should be entered in the two boxes provided. The sum of these two figures should equal the sum of the corresponding entries in column 9, less any entry in column 10.

The entries under **sterling balancing item** and the **aggregate of net short open positions** should be calculated in the same way as for column 9.

C   *Notes for completion of Section 2*

Section 2 should be completed by UK incorporated banks which have overseas branches which deal in foreign exchange to show the individual branch's or dealing centre's[6] net position in each currency on the same basis as columns 1-7B inclusive on Section 1 of the form, and with the same currency details. Positions held by branches in the local currency of the country in which the branch is located and positions arising from transactions with other branches or the headquarters of the bank should be included.

---

4 Including the provision of working capital to fund structural assets in an overseas operation.

5 Remittable profits should be understood as being profits which are available for repatriation after provision has been made for all UK liabilities including tax.

6 Banks with a number of branches in one country or area which are amalgamated for internal reporting purposes may amalgamate them for the purpose of this return.

Returns need not be made in respect of branches or dealing centres which have an aggregate position, taking all currencies together regardless of sign, of less than 1/2% of the adjusted capital base of the reporting banks, as defined in the Bank's Notice "Implementation in the UK of the Directive on Own Funds of Credit Institutions".

Reference should be made to the Bank of England, telephone number 071-601 5694 in the event of any difficulties with this treatment, or if any branch maintains a position which is regarded as structural.

D   *Notes for the completion of Section 3*

Banks should complete Section 3 of the return to show the dealing position on each day that the reporting bank has exceeded the guidelines previously agreed with the Bank of England. These exception reports should be submitted to the Bank with the regular monthly report.

APPENDIX

1   Currency income and expense accounts and currency specific provision accounts are both included as internal accounts in the currency spot positions (columns 2 and 3). In certain circumstances these accounts may, however, mask exposures which should be measured as part of banks' overall positions. For example, for a given currency the net balance on the currency income and expense account ought to be excluded from the reported position otherwise it will offset the actual (or accounted for) asset or liability in that

[BSR change] currency. This is to be achieved by making an entry in column 7A to compensate for the inclusion of the net balance on currency income and expense account as an internal account in columns 2 and 3. It is recognised that this treatment may not be wholly appropriate for UK branches of overseas banks. Provision has therefore been made for such branches to adjust their overall position in respect of remittable profits held in the domestic currency of their home country (see instructions to column 10).

2   The specific provision account if denominated in a currency which differs from that of the asset for which it has been created gives rise to an exposure which should in principle be measured. An exposure arises from the diminution in the value of the asset which is the subject of the provision, and also from the asset in which the provision itself is held. Without adjustment, however, neither exposure will be reported, as the asset against which the provision has been made will remain at its gross value, while the position created by the provision asset itself will be masked by being offset, in the same currency, by the provision account. In order, therefore, to capture banks' true exposures it is necessary to transfer the provision account from the currency in which it appears to the currency of the asset for which it is required. This will have the effect of both writing down the value of the asset against which the provision has been made and revealing the position created by holding the provision asset in different currency.

ANNEX A

1   Enter in Col 12 (Col 13) total amounts of each currency including sterling that a bank might purchase (sell) through the exercise of currency options it has given.

2   Enter in Col 14 the sum of the entries in Cols 11 and 12, except that if this sum is negative, a nil entry should be made.

3   Enter in Col 15 the sum of the entires in Cols 11 and 13, except that if this sum is positive, a nil entry should be made.

Note that the entries in the sterling rows of Columns 12 and 13 arise from options directly involving sterling and are not balancing items as in Columns 9 and 11.

For the purposes of monitoring a bank's foreign exchange exposure the entries in columns 14 and 15 will each (separately) be assessed against the guidelines agreed with the Bank of England, Banking Supervision Division.

4   Enter in Col 16 (Col 17) total amounts of each currency <u>including sterling</u> that the bank might purchase (sell) through exercise of currency options it holds. Note that these entries are required only for statistical information about the market and do not form part of a bank's exposure.

ANNEX B

1   This form may be used only by reporting institutions which have been given specific permission by the Banking Supervision Division of the Bank of England to use their own formulae for determining their exposure in accordance with the Bank's paper Foreign Currency Options, dated April 1984.

Reporting institutions which have not received specific permission to use this form should report on Annex A.

2   Enter in Col 12 (Col 13) total amounts of each currency <u>including sterling</u> that the bank might purchase (sell) through the exercise of currency options it has given.

3   Enter in Col 14 (Col 15) total amounts of each currency including sterling that the bank might purchase (sell) through the exercise of currency options it holds.

Note   (a)   the entries in the sterling rows of Columns 12 to 15 arise from options directly involving sterling and are not balancing items as in Columns 9 and 11;

(b)   the entries in Columns 12 to 15 do not cross cast to the adjusted options position in Column 16. This information is required for statistical purposes and is not directly used to assess a bank's foreign exchange exposure.

4   Enter in Column 16 the adjusted value of options given and taken; the formula used should be that previously agreed between the bank and the Banking Supervision Division of the Bank of England. Note that any positions hedged in the cash market should be included on the main part of the S3 return. The total items of column 16 should sum to zero by using the sterling row as a balancing item.

5   The entries in column 16 will be transposed into column 7b, and column 11 will then be used for monitoring a bank's foreign exchange exposure against the existing guidelines with the Bank of England.

APPENDIX

III

The London Code of Conduct

As issued by the Bank of England, May 1992.
(Reproduced with the permission of the Bank of England)

INTRODUCTION

1   The London financial markets have a long-established reputation for their high degree of professionalism and the maintenance of the highest standards of business conduct. All those operating in these markets share a common interest in their health and in maintaining the established exacting standards.

2   The Code is applicable to all wholesale market dealings which are not regulated by the rules of a recognised investment exchange. These typically form part of 'treasury' operations and are undertaken in large amounts. A full list of the products covered and the appropriate size criteria are shown in the box below.

3   The Bank of England (the Bank) wishes to sustain the efficient functioning of the London wholesale markets in which these products are traded and to avoid over-burdensome regulation; and believes that this Code is consistent with these objectives.

4   The Code sets out the principles which should govern the conduct of management and individuals at broking firms (including electronic broking firms) and '**core principals**' (banks, building societies plus financial institutions authorised under the Financial Services Act 1986) transacting business in the relevant financial products.   Furthermore, the Chartered Institute of Public Finance and Accountancy and the Association of Corporate Treasurers commend the Code to their members, which are also participants in these markets, as best practice, to which they, too, should adhere.

5   Compliance with the Code is necessary to ensure that the highest standards of integrity and fair dealing continue to be observed throughout these markets. Breaches by those institutions which they supervise will be viewed most seriously by the Bank and by the Building Societies Commission; any such breaches may be reflected in their assessment of the fitness and propriety of these institutions.   In addition, the Securities and Investments Board and the UK Self-Regulating Organisations expect those core principals which they supervise to abide by the Code when dealing in the wholesale markets.

6   The Code has been developed in close consultation with market participants and will continue to be kept under regular review. A fuller description of the Bank's regulatory arrangements covering the wholesale markets, of which this Code is an integral part, is set out in the 'Grey Paper' (The regulation of the wholesale markets in sterling, foreign exchange and bullion) issued in April 1988.

FINANCIAL PRODUCTS COVERED BY THE LONDON CODE OF CONDUCT

1   Sterling wholesale deposits.

2   Foreign currency wholesale deposits.

3   Spot and forward foreign exchange.

4   Spot and forward gold and silver bullion.

5   Commercial bills (including bankers' and other acceptances).

plus the following which are defined as investments in the Financial Services Act 1986:

6   Certificates of deposit (CDs), or other debt instruments, issued by institutions authorised under the Banking Act 1987 or by UK building societies, with an original maturity of not more than 5 years. (This class of instrument is included in the Financial Services Act under the generic term 'debenture').

7   Other debentures with an original maturity of not more than 1 year (including commercial paper and non-London CDs).

8   Medium-term notes issued under the Banking Act 1987 (Exempt Transactions) (Amendment) Regulations.

9   UK local authority debt (bills, bonds, loan stock or other instruments) with an original maturity of not more than 5 years.

10 Other public sector debt with an original maturity of not more than 1 year (eg Treasury bills, but not gilt-edged securities - for which a separate regulatory regime exists).

11 Any certificate (or other instrument) representing the securities covered in items 6-10; or rights to, and interests in, these instruments.

12 Off-recognised investment exchange options (including warrants) or futures contracts on these particular investments/instruments; on any currency (including sterling); or on gold or silver. These include interest rate options.

13 Forward rate agreements, or other 'contracts for differences' involving arrangements to profit (or avoid loss) by reference to movements in the value of any of these particular instruments; or the value of any currency; or in the interest on loans in any currency. These include interest rate and currency swaps, regardless of their original maturity.

14 Sale and repurchase agreements ('repos') and stock borrowing and lending involving debentures, loan stock or other debt instruments of whatever original maturity where the repurchase or repayment will take place within twelve months.

Note 1   Instruments denominated in foreign currencies as well as in sterling are covered; and transactions may come within the Code's scope even if one of the other parties to the transaction is operating abroad.

Note 2   The regulation of deposit-taking under the Banking Act 1987 is not affected in any way.

Note 3   Government made clear in January 1988 that ordinary forward foreign exchange (and bullion) transactions fall outside the Financial Services Act; these nevertheless fall within the scope of the Code.

Note 4   Wholesale transactions between core principals in items 1 and 5 are not usually less than £100,000. For items 2 and 3, the usual minimum is £500,000 (or currency equivalent).   For bullion, the relevant amounts are 2,000 ounces for gold and 50,000 ounces for silver.

Note 5   For debentures, bonds, loan stock and sale and repurchase agreements, the minimum size of wholesale transactions is £100,000 (or the equivalent in foreign currency). For options, futures, forward rate agreements (FRAs), swaps and other 'contracts for differences', the minimum underlying value is £500,000 (or the equivalent in foreign currency).

GENERAL STANDARDS

Principals and broking firms - and their employees - should at all times abide by the spirit as well as the letter of the Code when undertaking transactions in the wholesale markets.

Managers of principals and broking firms must ensure that the fiduciary and other obligations imposed on them and their staff by the general law are observed and, where relevant, that the rules and codes of practice of other regulatory bodies are observed.

Responsibilities

- **Of the principal/broker**

7   All firms (principals and brokers) should ensure to the best of their ability that all parties act in a manner consistent with the maintenance of the highest reputation for the wholesale markets in London. Brokers and core principals should therefore seek to establish whether their clients/counterparties **in the UK** have a copy of the Code; and, if they do not, should offer to send them one or advise them that copies are available, free of charge, from the Bank.

8   The Bank will seek to implement appropriate arrangements to make **overseas based** counterparties/clients which may undertake wholesale market deals in the London market aware that such deals are undertaken in accordance with the London Code. If broking firms or core principals receive any questions from overseas based firms about their wholesale market deals they should, where appropriate, make them aware of the Code's existence; and that copies can be obtained from the Bank. Other principals are encouraged to adopt similar procedures.

9   It is **not** intended, as a general rule, that the Code will apply to dealings between core principals and individuals. Core principals which conduct non-investment business (items 1-5 in the box on page 1) with private individuals should have internal procedures which set out whether these individuals will be treated as retail customers or as wholesale market participants under the arrangements set out in this Code.

10   It is essential that all relevant staff are familiar with the Code and conduct themselves at all times in a thoroughly professional manner.

11   All firms will be held responsible for the actions of their staff. They must:

- ensure that any individual who commits the firm to a transaction has the necessary authority to do so.

- ensure that employees are adequately trained in the practices of the markets in which they deal/broke; and are aware of their own, and their firm's, responsibilities. Inexperienced dealers should not rely on a broker, for instance, to fill gaps in their training or experience; to do so is clearly **not** the broker's responsibility.

- ensure staff are made aware of and comply with any other relevant guidance that may from time to time be issued by the Bank.

12   When establishing a relationship with a **new** counterparty or client, firms must take steps to make them aware of the precise nature of firms' liability for business to be conducted, including any limitations on that liability and the capacity in which they act. **In particular, broking firms should explain to a new client or counterparty the limited role of brokers (see paragraphs 20 and 21 below).**

13   It is good practice for **principals**, subject to their own legal advice, to alert counterparties to any legal or tax uncertainties which they know are relevant to a proposed transaction, in order that the counterparty may seek its own advice if it so wishes.

14   Management of **broking** firms should advise their employees of the need to ensure that their behaviour could not **at any time** be construed as having misled counterparties about the limited role of brokers (see paragraphs 20 and 21 below); failure to be vigilant in this area will adversely affect the reputation of the broking firm itself.

- **Of the employee**

15   When entering into or arranging individual deals, dealers and brokers must ensure that at all times great care is taken not to misrepresent in any way the nature of any transaction. Dealers and brokers must ensure that:

- the identity of the firm for which they are acting and its role is clear to their counterparties/clients to avoid any risk of counterparty confusion. This is particularly important, for instance, where an individual dealer acts for more than one company, or in more than one capacity. If so, he must make absolutely clear, at the outset of any deal, on behalf of which company or in which capacity he is acting.

- it is clearly understood in which products they are proposing to deal.

- any claims or acknowledgements about, or relevant to, a particular transaction being considered should, as far as the individual dealer or broker is aware, be accurate.

- facts believed to be material to completing a specific transaction are disclosed before the deal is done, except where such disclosure would reveal confidential information about the activities of another client/counterparty.

16   When a deal is being arranged through a broker, the broker should act in a way which does not unfairly favour one client, amongst those involved, over another, irrespective of what brokerage arrangements exist between the broking firm and the counterparties involved.

Clarity of role

- **Role of principals**

17 The role of firms acting as principal is to deal for their own account. **Principals have the responsibility for assessing the creditworthiness of a counterparty or potential counterparty whether dealing direct or through a broking firm. It is for the principal to decide whether or not to seek independent professional advice to assist in this process.**

18 **It is also for the principal to decide what credence, if any, is given to any information or comment provided by a broker to a dealer. Where such information or comment might be interpreted as being relevant to a particular counterparty or potential counterparty, this does not alter the fact that the responsibility for assessing the creditworthiness of a counterparty, whether or not it is supervised, rests with the principal alone.**

19 Some firms may act as agent for connected or other companies as well as, or instead of, dealing for their own account. If so, such agents should:

— always make absolutely clear to all concerned the capacity in which they are acting (eg if they also act as principal or broker).

— declare at an early stage of negotiations the party for whom they are acting. It may be considered desirable to set out this relationship formally in writing for future reference.

— ensure that **all** confirmations make clear when a deal is done on an agency basis.

— when acting as agent for an unregulated principal, make clear at an early stage this qualification to potential counterparties; and include this on confirmations.

- **Role of brokers**

20 Typically the role of the specialist wholesale market broking firms in London supervised as such by the Bank is to act as **arrangers** of deals*. They:

— bring together counterparties on mutually acceptable terms and pass names to facilitate the conclusion of a transaction.

— receive payment for this service in the form of brokerage (except where a prior explicit agreement between the management of all parties to a deal provides otherwise).

— are **not** permitted, even fleetingly, to act as principal in a deal (even on a 'matched principal' basis), or to act in any discretionary fund management capacity**.

21 It is accepted that, in providing the service specified in the previous paragraph, individual brokers may be called upon to give advice or express opinions, usually in response to requests from individual dealers. While brokers should be mindful of the need not to reveal confidential information about the market activities of individual clients, there is no restriction on brokers passing, or commenting, on general information which is in the public domain. Equally, there is no responsibility upon a broker to volunteer general information of this type. Where information is sought or volunteered individual brokers should exercise particular care. For instance, brokers do not have sufficient information to be qualified to advise principals on the creditworthiness of specific counterparties and to do so is not their role.

Complaints procedure

22 If any principal or broking firm believes that an institution supervised by the Bank has breached either the letter or the spirit of the Code in respect of any wholesale market transaction in which it is involved, it is encouraged - whether or not it is itself supervised by the Bank - to seek to settle this amicably with the other party. If this is not possible, the institution which is subject to the complaint should make the complainant aware that it can bring the matter to the attention of the Head of the Wholesale Markets Supervision Division of the Bank of England. All such complaints will be investigated by the Bank.

Money laundering

23 All principals dealing in the wholesale markets are reminded of the need to 'know their customer' (see also paragraphs 47-50 below) and as part of this process must take all necessary steps to prevent their dealings in the wholesale markets being used to facilitate money laundering. As well as being familiar with their responsibilities under UK law (which is expected to be extended shortly to implement the EC Directive on Money Laundering) **principals** should have in place systems which take account of two publications on this subject: 'Guidance Notes for Banks and Building Societies' issued in December 1990; and 'Guidance Notes for Investment Business' issued in September 1991***.

24 Broking firms also have responsibilities to help guard against wholesale market transactions being used for money laundering. Apart from complying with their responsibilities under UK law, they too should take account of the 'Guidance Notes for Investment Business' issued in September 1991. However, **principals** must **not** regard the identity checks brokers undertake as a substitute for having their own systems in place and making their own, independent, comprehensive enquiries.

---

*   There are two exceptions to this rule. The first covers the specialist inter-dealer brokers, involved primarily in US Treasury bills, notes and bonds, which act solely as matched principals; separate arrangements are in place to supervise inter-dealer brokers in the gilt-edged market. The other exception is when name-passing broking firms are investing their own money; in such transactions, brokers must make clear to the relevant counterparties that they are acting as principal.

** The relationship between an institution offering a discretionary or advisory management service and its clients in any of the financial products described in the box on page 1 falls outside the scope of this Code and, if it constitutes investment business within the terms of the Financial Services Act 1986, should be conducted in accordance with the requirements of the relevant Self-Regulating Organisation.

*** Available from the British Bankers' Association, 10 Lombard Street, London EC3V 9EL.

Confidentiality

25 Confidentiality is essential for the preservation of a reputable and efficient market place. Principals and brokers share equal responsibility for maintaining confidentiality. Principals or brokers should not, without explicit permission, disclose or discuss, or apply pressure on others to disclose or discuss, any information relating to specific deals which have been transacted, or are in the process of being arranged, except to or with the parties directly involved or where this is required by law or to comply with the rules of a supervisory body. It is a responsibility of management to ensure that all relevant personnel are aware of, and observe, this fundamental principle.

26 Care should be taken over the use of open loudspeakers in both brokers' offices and principals' dealing rooms to ensure that they do not lead to breaches of confidentiality.

27 Individual dealers or brokers should not visit each others' dealing rooms except with the express permission of the management of both parties. In particular a principal's dealer should at no time deal from within the offices of a broker or another principal. Brokers should never conduct business from outside their own offices.

28 A principal should not place an order with a broker with the intention of ascertaining the name of a counterparty in order to make direct contact to conclude the deal.

Taping

29 Experience has shown that recourse to tapes proves invaluable to the speedy resolution of differences. The use of recording equipment in the offices of brokers and principals is becoming increasingly common. **The Bank strongly recommends taping by principals and brokers of all conversations by dealers and brokers** together with back-office telephone lines used by those responsible for confirming deals or passing payment and other instructions. The Bank expects firms which it supervises and which do not tape all their front and back office conversations to review this management policy periodically and to satisfy the Bank that there are particular reasons for them to continue with such an approach. Failure to tape will normally count against a firm if it seeks to use the arbitration process described in paragraph 91 to settle a difference.

30 When initially installing tape equipment, or taking on new clients or counterparties, firms should take steps to inform their counterparties and clients that conversations will be recorded. **Tapes should be kept for at least two months, and preferably longer. Tapes which cover any transaction which is in question should be retained until the problem has been resolved.** Management should ensure that access to taping equipment and tapes, whether in use or in store, is strictly controlled so that they cannot be tampered with.

Deals at non-current rates

31 As a general rule, deals at non-market rates should not be undertaken. However, it is accepted that the application of off-market rates can be necessary, for example in the swaps market to create deal structures which satisfy investor or borrower requirements or to construct 'synthetic securities' (sometimes known as 'asset swaps'*). Management should nevertheless be satisfied that proper controls are in place to ensure that such arrangements do not conceal fraud, create unacceptable conflicts of interest, or involve other illegal activity. It should be possible to demonstrate that the combination of cashflows, coupons and foreign exchange rates used in such transactions produces a result that is consistent with the current market price of a straightforward swap of similar maturity. It is also important to ensure that there is no ambiguity in such transactions over the amounts which each counterparty is to pay and receive.

32 Deals involving off-market rates should be undertaken in other wholesale market instruments only in exceptional circumstances. **Such deals, which are most likely to involve rolling-over an existing contract at the original rate, should only be undertaken by principals after most careful consideration and approval, ideally on a deal by deal basis, by senior management.** Senior management should therefore ensure that proper controls are in place to identify all such deals when they are proposed so that they can be made fully aware of the details before reaching a decision on whether a particular trade should go ahead on this basis. Before reaching such a decision, senior management should seek confirmation from the counterparty, also at senior management level, of the reasons for the transaction. This is essential not only because of the potential credit risk implications of rolling-over deals at historical rates but also because failure to use current rates could result in the principal unknowingly participating in the concealment of a profit or loss, or in perpetration of a fraud. In order to provide a clear audit trail, there should be an exchange of letters between the senior managements of both parties to any such deals to demonstrate that the above procedures have been followed.

33 A specific area where there has been some evidence of an undesirable increase in pressure to construct deals at non-current rates has been in foreign exchange swaps. Some dealers undertaking a foreign exchange swap seek to avoid the immediate fixing of the spot price underlying the trade. **This practice is judged by practitioners in the London market to be unethical and is not appropriate practice for UK based institutions. Spot rates should be determined at the first possible opportunity after completion of the foreign exchange swap transaction.**

• **After-hours dealing**

34 Extended trading after normal local hours has become accepted in some markets, most notably foreign exchange. Dealing after-hours into other centres forms an integral part of the operations of many firms both in London and elsewhere. Such dealing involves additional hazards. For example, when

---

*   Institutions 'listed' under the Grey Paper arrangements, and others, should be aware that while a listed institution's actions with regard to the associated swap are subject to this Code, the sale of the relevant underlying security may be subject to the regulations of the Securities and Investments Board or, where relevant, the appropriate Self-Regulating Organisation.

dealing continues during the evening from premises other than the principals' dealing rooms, one of the counterparties involved might subsequently forget, or deny, having done a deal. Brokers too might be involved (though they should never arrange deals outside their own premises). Management should therefore issue clear guidelines to their staff, both on the kinds of deal which may be undertaken in those circumstances and on the permitted limits of any such dealing. All deals should be confirmed promptly - preferably by telex or similar electronic message direct to the counterparty's offices - and carefully controlled when arranged off-premises. Management should consider installing answerphone facilities in the dealing area which dealers should use to record full details of all off-premises trades. These should be processed promptly on the next working day.

- **Stop-loss orders**

35 Principals may receive requests from branches, customers and correspondents to execute transactions - for instance to buy or sell a currency - if prices or rates should reach a specified level. These orders, which include stop-loss and limit orders from counterparties desiring around-the-clock protection for their own positions, may be intended for execution during the day, overnight, or until executed or cancelled. Management should ensure that the terms of such orders are explicitly identified and agreed, and that there is a clear understanding with the counterparty about the obligation it has assumed in accepting such orders. Moreover, management needs to establish clear policies and procedures for its traders who accept and execute stop-loss and limit orders. Management should also ensure that any dealer handling such an instruction has adequate lines of communication with the counterparty so that the dealer can reach authorised personnel in case of an unusual situation or extreme price/rate movement.

- **Dealing for personal account**

36 Management should consider carefully whether their employees should be allowed to deal at all for own account in any of the instruments covered by this Code. Personal dealing is not recommended by the Bank but, where allowed by management, it is its responsibility to ensure that adequate safeguards are established to prevent abuse. These safeguards should reflect the need to maintain confidentiality with respect to non-public price-sensitive information and to ensure that no action is taken by employees which might adversely affect the interests of the firm's clients or counterparties.

Conflicts of interest

37 Brokers have a legal obligation to disclose the nature and extent of any material conflict between their own interests and their responsibilities to clients. In the past the need to ensure the independence of the broker was reinforced in the foreign exchange, currency deposit and bullion markets by a prohibition on brokers arranging deals involving counterparties which held a shareholding of 10% or more in the broker. This prohibition has now been replaced with a different form of safeguard. Brokers should give all their clients formal written notification of any principal(s) where a material connection exists (unless a client explicitly waives its rights to this information in writing); and notify any subsequent changes to this list of principals as they occur. For the purposes of this Code, a material connection

would include situations where the relationship between the parties could have a bearing on the transaction or its terms, as a result for example of common management responsibilities or material shareholding links, whether direct or indirect. The Bank regards a shareholding of 10% or more in a broker as material; but, depending on the circumstances, a smaller holding may also represent a material connection.

38 Any deals arranged by a broker involving a connected principal must be at arm's length (ie at mutually agreed rates which are the same as those prevailing for transactions between unconnected counterparties).

Marketing

39 When listed institutions are operating within the boundaries of the Section 43 exempt regime, they will not be subject to advertising or cold-calling rules since these would be inappropriate in such professional markets. Nevertheless listed firms should take care to ensure that any advertisements for their services within the exempt area are directed so far as possible towards professional rather than inexperienced investors.

Entertainment, gifts and gambling

40 Management or employees must neither offer inducements to conduct business, nor solicit them from the personnel of other institutions. However it is recognised that entertainment and gifts are offered in the normal course of business and do not necessarily constitute inducements.

41 Management must formulate appropriate policies in this area and ensure that they are properly observed. These policies should include guidance on the provision and receipt of entertainment and gifts by staff including what may or may not be offered or accepted; and include procedures for dealing with gifts judged to be excessive which cannot be declined without causing offence.

42 These procedures should be drawn up bearing in mind that the activities of dealers of some of the principals active in the markets may be governed by statute. For instance, offering hospitality or gifts to officers and members of local authorities and other public bodies is subject to the provisions of legislation that carries sanctions under criminal law. One of the most onerous requirements of this legislation is that any offer or receipt of hospitality is, prima facie, deemed to be a criminal offence, unless the contrary is proved.

43 Similar guidelines should also be established on gambling with other market participants. **All these activities carry obvious dangers and, where allowed at all, it is strongly recommended that they are tightly restricted.**

Abused substances (including drugs and alcohol)

44 Management should take all reasonable steps to educate themselves and their staff about possible signs and effects of the use of drugs and other abused substances. Any member of staff dependent on such substances is likely to be vulnerable to outside inducement to conduct business not necessarily in the best interests of the firm or the market generally.

DEALING PRINCIPLES AND PROCEDURES: A STATEMENT OF BEST PRACTICE

Scope

Deals in the London wholesale markets (defined by the products covered in the box on page 1) should be conducted on the basis of this Code of Conduct.

45 Whilst this Code is designed for the London markets, its provisions may extend beyond UK shores, for example where a listed UK broker arranges a deal involving an overseas counterparty. Where deals involving overseas counterparties are to be made on a different basis in any respect, for example because of distinct local rules or requirements, this should be clearly identified at the outset to avoid any possible confusion.

Overseas market conventions

The trading of currency assets in London should follow recognised trading conventions that have been established internationally or in specific overseas markets, provided they do not conflict with the principles of this Code.

46 Where foreign currency-denominated short-term securities issued overseas are traded in London, there may be important differences in dealing practice compared with the trading of London instruments, partly reflecting the way the instruments are traded in their domestic markets. The London Code is intended to be complementary to any generally accepted local standards and practices for such instruments traded in London. The Bank would expect firms trading these instruments in London to abide by any such local conventions.

Know your customer

As noted in paragraphs 23 and 24 above principals (and brokers) need to 'know their customer' in order to help combat the use of the wholesale markets for money laundering. It is also an essential part of the process for proper assessment of creditworthiness.

Knowing your customer is also important when entering into more complicated deals, such as transactions in some derivative products, or when dealing with inexperienced counterparties. Even among core principals, there may be a number which are not experienced in dealing in derivative products. This inexperience, together with the more complex nature of such deals, means that there is more scope for confusion or misunderstanding to arise. It is therefore in the interests of both parties - and brokers where used - that they seek to establish at the outset of any such deals whether either of them lacks experience in dealing in the product being discussed.

47 There has been a growing trend towards discretionary management companies dealing in wholesale market products on behalf of their clients. For understandable reasons, the fund manager may not wish to divulge the name of the client(s) when concluding such deals. However, this practice does raise considerations - both in terms of assessing their credit risk and in meeting their money laundering prevention obligations -

which principals need to address most carefully before being prepared to transact business on this basis. Senior management should decide, as a matter of policy, whether to undertake such business. In doing so, they should consider all the risks involved and fully document the decision which they reach.

48 When entering into more complicated transactions, such as swaps, or where a counterparty might, from the available information, reasonably be considered inexperienced, it is regarded as good practice for principals to send pre-deal telexes outlining the key terms to inexperienced counterparties when they judge this would be appropriate, taking into account their assessment of the potential counterparty and the complexity of the deal involved; this may help to avoid misunderstandings.

49 The Bank also strongly recommends that market participants draw up a checklist, along the lines shown in Schedule 1 (based on the swaps market), for use when negotiating and finalising the arrangements for a swap or similarly complicated transaction.

50 Because the marketability of off-exchange instruments may be severely limited, it is desirable for principals to draw to the attention of new inexperienced counterparties the additional risks which may be associated with off-exchange transactions in derivatives and other instruments.

Procedures

- **Preliminary negotiation of terms**

Firms should clearly state at the outset, prior to a transaction being executed, any qualifying conditions to which it will be subject.

51 Typical examples of qualifications include where a price is quoted subject to the necessary credit approval; finding a counterparty for matching deals; or the ability to execute an associated transaction. For instance principals may quote a rate which is 'firm subject to the execution of a hedge transaction'. If a principal's ability to conclude a transaction is constrained by other factors, for example opening hours in other centres, this should be made known to brokers and potential counterparties at an early stage and before names are exchanged.

52 In the Euronote and commercial paper markets, principals should notify investors, at the time of sale, of their willingness or otherwise to repurchase paper. Investors should also be notified, before the sale, of any significant variation from the standard terms or conditions of an issue.

- **Firmness of quotation**

All firms, whether acting as principal, agent or broker, have a duty to make absolutely clear whether the prices they are quoting are firm or merely indicative. Prices quoted by brokers should be taken to be firm in marketable amounts unless otherwise qualified.

53 A principal quoting a firm price (or rate) either through a broker or directly to a potential counterparty is committed to deal at that price (or rate) in a marketable amount provided the counterparty name is acceptable. In order to minimise the scope for confusion where there is no clear market convention, dealers quoting a firm price (rate) should indicate the length of time for which their quote is firm.

54   It is generally accepted that when dealing in fast moving markets (like spot forex or currency options) a principal has to assume that a price given to a broker is good only for a short length of time - typically a matter of seconds. However, this practice would be open to misunderstandings about how quickly a price is deemed to lapse if it were adopted when dealing in generally less hectic markets, for example the forward foreign exchange or deposit markets, or when market conditions are relatively quiet. Since dealers have prime responsibility for prices put to a broker, the onus in such circumstances is on dealers to satisfy themselves that their prices have been taken off, unless a time limit is placed by the principal on its interest at the outset (eg 'firm for one minute only'). Otherwise, the principal should feel bound to deal with an acceptable name at the quoted rate in a marketable amount.

55   For their part brokers should make every effort to assist dealers by checking from time to time with them whether their interest at particular prices (rates) is still current. They should also do so when a specific name and amount have been quoted.

56   What constitutes a marketable amount varies from market to market but will generally be familiar to practitioners. A broker, if quoting on the basis of small amounts or particular names, should qualify the quotation accordingly. Where principals are proposing to deal in unfamiliar markets through a broker, it is recommended that they first ask brokers what amounts are sufficient to validate normal market quotations. If their interest is in a smaller amount, this should be specified by the principal when initially requesting a price from or offering a price to the broker.

57   In the swap market, considerable use is made of 'indicative interest' quotations. When arranging a swap an unconditional firm rate will only be given where a principal deals directly with a client, or when such a principal has received the name of a client from a broker. A principal who quotes a rate or spread as 'firm subject to credit' is bound to deal at the quoted rate or spread if the name is consistent with a category of counterparty previously identified for this purpose (see also paragraph 61 below). The only exception is where the particular name cannot be accepted, for example if the principal has reached its credit limit for that name, in which case the principal will correctly reject the transaction. It is not an acceptable practice for a principal to revise a rate which was 'firm subject to credit' once the name of the counterparty has been disclosed. Brokers and principals should work together to establish a range of institutions for whom the principal's rate is firm subject to credit.

• **Concluding a deal**

Principals should regard themselves as bound to a deal once the price and any other key commercial terms have been agreed. However, holding brokers unreasonably to a price is viewed as unprofessional and should be discouraged by management.

58   Where quoted prices are qualified as being indicative or subject to negotiation of commercial terms, principals should normally treat themselves as bound to a deal at the point where the terms have been agreed without qualification. Oral agreements are considered binding; the subsequent confirmation is evidence of the deal but should not override terms agreed orally. The practice of making a transaction subject to documentation is not good practice. In order to minimise the likelihood of disputes arising once documentation is prepared, firms should make every effort to agree all material points quickly during the oral negotiation of terms; and should agree any remaining details as soon as possible thereafter.

59   Where brokers are involved, it is their responsibility to ensure that the principal providing the price (rate) is made aware immediately it has been dealt upon. As a general rule a deal should only be regarded as having been 'done' where the broker's contact is positively acknowledged by the dealer. A broker should never assume that a deal is done without some form of oral acknowledgment from the dealer. Where a broker puts a specific proposition to a dealer for a price (eg specifying an amount and a name for which a quote is required), the dealer can reasonably expect to be told almost immediately by the broker whether the price has been hit or not.

• **Passing of names by brokers**

Brokers should not divulge the names of principals prematurely, and certainly not until satisfied that both sides display a serious intention to transact. Principals and brokers should at all times treat the details of transactions as absolutely confidential to the parties involved (see paragraph 25 above).

60   To save time and minimise frustration, principals should wherever practicable give brokers prior indication of counterparties with whom, for whatever reason, they would be unwilling to do business (referring as necessary to particular markets or instruments). At the same time brokers should take full account of the best interests and any precise instructions of the client.

61   To save subsequent awkwardness, principals (including agents) have a particular obligation to give guidance to the brokers on any particular features (maturities etc) or types of counterparty (such as non-financial institutions) which might cause difficulties. In some instruments, principals may also wish to give brokers guidance on the extent of their price differentiation across broad categories of counterparties. Where a broker is acting for an unlisted (or unsupervised) name he should disclose this fact as soon as possible; the degree of disclosure required in such a case will usually be greater. For instance credit considerations may require that such names be disclosed to a listed principal first (as in the swap market), in order that the listed principal may quote a rate at which it is committed to deal. Equally, disclosure of difficult names may be necessary since this may influence the documentation.

62   In all their wholesale market business, brokers should aim to achieve a mutual and immediate exchange of names. However this will not always be possible. There will be times when one principal's name proves unacceptable to another and the broker will quite properly decline to divulge by whom it was refused. This may sometimes result in the principal whose name has been rejected feeling that the broker may in fact have quoted a price (rate) which it could not in fact substantiate. In such cases, the Bank will be prepared to establish with the reluctant principal that it did have business to do at the quoted price and the reasons why the name was turned down, so that the aggrieved party can be assured the original quote was valid without, of course, revealing the reluctant party's name.

63 In the sterling and currency deposit markets, it is accepted that principals dealing through a broker have the right to turn down a name wishing to take deposits; this could therefore require predisclosure of the name before closing the deal. Once a lender has asked the key question 'who pays', it is considered committed to do business at the price quoted with that name, or an alternative acceptable name if offered immediately. The name of a lender shall be disclosed only after the borrower's name has been accepted by the lender.

64 In the case of instruments like CDs, where the seller may not be the same entity as the issuer, the broker shall first disclose the issuer's name to the potential buyer. Once a buyer has asked 'whose paper is it', the buyer is considered committed to deal at the price quoted. Once the buyer asks 'who sells' it is considered committed to deal with the particular seller in question (or an alternative acceptable name, so long as this name is immediately shown to the buyer by the broker). The name of the buyer shall be disclosed only after the seller's name has been accepted by the buyer. The seller has the right to refuse the particular buyer, so long as it is prepared at that time to sell the same amount at the same price to an alternative acceptable name immediately shown to it by the broker.

65 In the CD markets a price quoted is generally accepted as good for any name 'on the run'.

• **Use of intermediaries**

Brokers must not interpose an intermediary in any deal which could take place without its introduction.

66 An intermediary should only be introduced by a broker where it is strictly necessary for the completion of a deal, most obviously where a name switch is required because one counterparty is full of another's name but is prepared to deal with a third party. Any fees involved in transactions involving intermediaries must be explicitly identified by the broker and shown on the relevant confirmation(s).

• **Payment/settlement instructions**

Instructions should be passed as quickly as possible to facilitate prompt settlement. The Bank strongly recommends the use of standardised settlement instructions; their use can make a significant contribution to reducing both the incidence and size of differences arising from the mistaken settlement of funds.

67 The Bank is encouraged that the use of standard settlement instructions (SSIs) continues to increase. In order to facilitate still further progress in this direction guidelines have now been drawn up in consultation with the Joint Standing Committees which set out a framework which it is hoped principals will aim to adopt when using SSIs for wholesale market transactions. These guidelines are set out in Schedule 4.

68 In the foreign exchange and currency deposit markets, brokers do not pass payment instructions where both counterparties are based in the UK; unless both parties use SSIs the counterparties themselves must exchange instructions direct and with minimum delay.

69 Whether dealing direct or through a broker, principals should ensure that alterations to original payment instructions, including the paying agent where this has been specifically requested, should be immediately notified to the counterparty and, where a broker has been used and at least one of the principals is outside the UK, to the broker also. This notification should be supported by written, telex or similar confirmation of the new instructions. Failure to inform the broker of a change in instructions will clearly place the liability for any ensuing difference with the principal.

• **Confirmation procedures**

Prompt passing, recording and careful checking of confirmations is vital to minimise the possibility of errors and misunderstanding whether dealing direct or through brokers. Details should be passed as soon as practicable after deals have been done and checked upon receipt. The passing of details in batches is not recommended particularly when dealing in instruments with short settlement periods. For markets where standard terms are applicable it is recommended that confirmations conform to the formats specified under the standard terms and conditions for the market or instrument concerned.

(a) **Oral deal checks**

An increasing number of practitioners find it helpful to undertake oral deal checks at least once a day, especially when using a broker.

70 Particularly when dealing in faster moving markets like foreign exchange, but also when dealing in other instruments which have very short settlement periods, many principals now request regular oral deal checks - whether dealing through brokers or direct - prior to the exchange and checking of a written or electronically dispatched confirmation. Their use can be an important means of helping to reduce the number and size of differences particularly when dealing through brokers or for deals involving non-London counterparties. It is for each firm to agree with their broker(s) whether or not it wishes to be provided with this service; and, if so, how many such checks a day it requires. When arbitrating in disputes, the Bank will take into account the extent to which principals have sought to safeguard their interests by undertaking oral checks.

71 If a single check is thought to be sufficient, the Bank sees merit in this being undertaken towards the end of the trading day as a useful complement, particularly where late deals are concerned, to the process of sending out and checking confirmations.

72 As a matter of common sense, the broker should always obtain acknowledgment from a dealer on completion of the check that all the deals have been agreed or, if not, that any identified discrepancies are resolved as a matter of urgency. Lack of response should not be construed as acknowledgment.

(b) Written/electronic confirmations

In all markets, the confirmation (whether posted, telexed, or sent by other electronic means) provides a necessary final safeguard against dealing errors. Confirmations should be dispatched and checked carefully and promptly, even when oral deal checks have been undertaken. The issue and checking of confirmations is a back-office responsibility which should be carried out independently from those who initiate deals.

73 A confirmation of each deal must be sent out without delay so that, whenever possible, it will be received before the close of business on the dealing date. This is essential if dealing for same day settlement. Other than in the most exceptional circumstances, confirmations should always be with the principal by no later than the morning of the business day following the trade date. The Bank recommends that principals should enquire about any confirmations which have not been received by the close of business on the business day after the deal was concluded.

74 All confirmations should include the trade date, the name of the other counterparty and all other details of the deal, including where appropriate the commission charged by the broker. Some principals include their own terms and conditions of trading on their written confirmations. To avoid misunderstandings, any subsequent changes should be brought specifically to the attention of their counterparties.

75 In many markets, it is accepted practice for counterparties to confirm directly all the details of transactions arranged through a broker; the broker should nevertheless also send a confirmation to each counterparty.

76 Principals are reminded that the prompt sending and checking of confirmations is also invaluable in deals not arranged through a broker, including those with corporates and other customers.

77 When dealing for spot settlement, it is possible that the practice in some markets of sending an initial confirmation (eg by telex or other acceptable electronic means) followed by a written confirmation, which if posted could easily not arrive until after the settlement date, could cause confusion and uncertainty. For this reason, for spot deals the Bank wishes to encourage the use of a single confirmation by each party, sent, wherever possible, by one of the generally accepted electronic means now available (notably the ACS system, SWIFT, or telex). The Bank does not believe that it is good practice to rely solely on an oral check.

78 It is vital that principals check confirmations carefully and immediately upon receipt so that discrepancies can be quickly revealed and corrected. Firms that check within a few hours of receipt, or by close of business on the day deals are done, would be complying with best practice.

79 As a general rule, confirmations should be issued by, sent to and checked by the back-office rather than by dealers, whose involvement — if any — in these procedures should be closely controlled. The most common instance where it may sometimes be thought helpful to mark a copy of the confirmation for the attention of the person who has arranged the deal, in addition to

the back office, is in markets requiring detailed negotiation of terms (notably those involving contracts for differences).

80 Particular attention needs to be taken by all parties when confirming deals in which at least one of the counterparties is based outside London, and to any consequential differences in confirmation procedure.

- **Fraud**

81 There is a need for great vigilance by all staff against attempted fraud. This is particularly so where calls are received on an ordinary telephone line (usually in principal to principal transactions). As a precautionary measure, it is strongly recommended that the details of all telephone deals which do not include pre-agreed standard settlement instructions should be confirmed by telex or similar means without delay by the recipient, seeking an answer-back to ensure the deal is genuine.

- **Terms and documentation**

Documentation should be completed and exchanged as soon as possible after a deal is 'done'. The Bank endorses the use, wherever possible, of standard terms and conditions to facilitate this process.

82 Wherever possible, the Bank encourages the use of standard terms or conditions for wholesale market transactions. Such terms have been issued by the BBA for CDs and commercial paper; for forward rate agreements (FRABBA terms); for synthetic agreements for forward exchange (SAFEBBA master terms); for over-the-counter foreign currency options (ICOM terms); and for swaps (BBAIRS terms - used for London interbank swaps up to two years). A commonly used alternative to the BBAIRS terms for swaps is the International Swap Dealers Association (ISDA) Interest Rate and Currency Exchange Agreement. The London Bullion Market Association has issued guidelines for trading bullion options.

83 When using the ISDA Interest Rate and Currency Exchange Agreement, all material options and/or modifications allowed for in its Schedule A, and/or choices offered via the Interest Rate and Currency Exchange Definitions, must be clearly stated before dealing. Firms should make clear at an early stage, when trading any of the above mentioned products, if they are not intending to use standard terms; where changes are proposed these should also be made clear. For other wholesale instruments, where standard terms do not exist, particular care and attention should be paid to the negotiation of terms and documentation.

84 In more complex transactions like swaps, institutions should treat themselves as bound to a deal at the point where the commercial terms of the transactions are agreed. Making swap transactions subject to agreement on documentation is not best practice. Principals must make every effort to progress the finalisation of documentation. The Bank believes it should be possible for this to be accomplished within two months of the deal being struck; and regards longer than three months as excessive.

• **Assignments or transfers**

Assignments should not generally be undertaken without the consent of the parties concerned.

85 Assignments are becoming increasingly common, especially in the swap markets. Principals who enter into any wholesale market transaction with the intention of shortly afterwards assigning or transferring the deal to a third party should make clear their intention to do so when initially negotiating the deal. It is recommended that the confirmation sent by the principal should specify any intent to assign and give details of the procedure that will be used. The subsequent documentation should also make provision for assignment.

86 When a principal is intending to execute such a transfer it must obtain the consent of the transferee before releasing its name. If the principal proposes to use a broker to arrange the transfer, consent from the transferee for this to happen must also be obtained. The transferee has an obligation to give the principal intending to transfer sufficient information to enable the transaction to be conducted in accordance with the principles of best practice set out elsewhere in the Code. Where the transaction is conducted through a broker, this information should likewise be made available to him. In particular, the information from the transferee should include details of the type of credit the transferee is prepared to accept, and whether he is seeking any sort of reimbursement for the administrative costs that might be incurred. Principals and brokers arranging a transfer or assignment should also agree the basis of pricing the transfer at an early stage of the negotiations. When arranging assignments, it is important for participants to observe the general principle set out elsewhere in the Code that there should be mutual disclosure of names. Finally it should be noted that proper, clear documentation is as important for transfers as for the origination of deals.

Settlement of differences

If all the procedures outlined above are adhered to, the incidence and size of differences should be reduced; and those mistakes which do occur should be identified and corrected promptly. Failure to observe these principles could leave those responsible bearing the cost, without limit on size or duration, of any differences which arise. Except in the foreign exchange market, all differences must be settled in cash.

87 The prompt despatch and checking of confirmations is of paramount importance. Accepted practice in the foreign exchange market is that brokers are normally held to be liable for differences arising from their errors for a maximum of two business days from receipt of the broker's confirmation by the principal. The Bank accepts that there are arguments for retaining this limit on forex brokers' immediate liability as a guideline, particularly where the difference arises because payment instructions have been incorrectly executed. But it must be stressed that there can be no substitute for following best practice and no hard and fast rules can be set on the duration of brokers' or principals' liability.

88 In the foreign exchange and currency deposit markets arrangements have been drawn up to facilitate the payment of differences via the Secretary of the Foreign Exchange Joint Standing Committee*; these supersede the previous arrangements for settling differences via the Honorary Treasurer of the Foreign Exchange and Currency Deposit Brokers' Association (FECDBA). **In the foreign exchange market only,** and only with the explicit consent of principals, brokers may make use of 'points' to settle differences. Even here their use will only be permitted if arrangements for management control, recording and reporting of points consistent with the requirements set out in the Bank's market notice of October 1989 (reproduced in Annex 2) have been established.

89 Listed broking firms must agree their own procedures with the Wholesale Markets Supervision Division of the Bank before using 'points'. The informal use of 'points' between individual dealers and brokers is no longer acceptable. Using 'points' in lieu of cash to settle differences is not permitted in any market other than foreign exchange. As a matter of prudent housekeeping, all differences should normally be settled within 30 days from the date the original deal was undertaken. Where difference payments involving a broker arise because of errors in the payment of funds, principals are reminded that it is the view of the Bank and the Joint Standing Committees that they should not benefit from undue enrichment by retaining the funds.

90 In all the wholesale markets (including foreign exchange) if a broker misses a price he is required by the Bank to offer to close the deal at the next best price if held to the deal. The broker must then offer to settle the difference arising by cheque (or points if it is a foreign exchange transcation); **principals should always be prepared to accept this cash settlement since to do otherwise would put the broker in breach of the Code.** If a dealer refuses to accept a difference cheque - and insists the deal is honoured - individual brokers should advise their senior management who, if necessary, should contact the senior management of the client and also advise the Bank of the situation.

Arbitration procedure

91 The Bank is prepared to arbitrate in disputes about the application of the Code, or current market practice, to specific transactions in wholesale market products involving an institution supervised by the Bank. As a condition for doing so the Bank will expect the parties to have exhausted their own efforts to resolve the matter directly. All parties must then first agree to the Bank taking such a role and to accept its decision in full and final settlement of the dispute. In doing so, the Bank will draw on the advice and expertise of members of the Joint Standing Committees in the sterling, foreign exchange and currency deposit markets or other market practitioners as it feels appropriate. Requests for arbitration should be addressed to the Bank's Wholesale Markets Supervision Division. The Bank will not normally arbitrate in any dispute which is subject to, or is likely to be subject to, legal proceedings. The onus is on firms supervised by the Bank to alert their counterparties/clients to this

---

* All requests for settlement via these arrangements should be marked for the attention of The Secretary, Foreign Exchange Joint Standing Committee, Bank of England Dealing Room (HO-G), Bank of England, Threadneedle Street, London EC2R 8AH. They should be accompanied by a written report of the circumstances resulting in the difference.

arbitration procedure. Paragraphs 29 and 30 of the Code, on taping, and paragraph 70, on oral deal checks, are especially relevant to firms considering recourse to these arrangements.

Commission/brokerage

Brokers' charges are freely negotiable.

92   Brokerage charges should be agreed only by directors or senior management on each side. Any variation from previously agreed brokerage arrangements should be expressly approved by both parties and clearly recorded on the subsequent documentation.

93   Brokers normally quote dealing prices excluding commission/brokerage charges. An exception is in the swaps market where brokers normally quote rates gross of commission and separately identify their brokerage charge. In certain circumstances, broker (or principal) and client may agree on an acceptable net rate and the broker (or principal) will subsequently inform the client how that rate is divided between payments to counterparties and upfront commission. In this case it is essential that all parties are quite clear that this division will be made no later than the time at which the deal is struck.

94   The Bank is aware that some principals fail to pay due brokerage bills promptly. This is not good practice and can significantly disadvantage brokers since overdue payments are treated by the Bank, for regulatory purposes, as a deduction from their capital base.

Taking of security and repos

Procedures should be established to ensure that securities held in custody are appropriately segregated and accounted for.

95   The Bank has established appropriate arrangements for the borrowing and lending of gilt-edged stocks by the gilt-edged market makers through the medium of the Stock Exchange money brokers, and for the financing of positions in gilt-edged stock. These arrangements also cover the Stock Exchange money brokers' equity and other borrowing and lending.

96   Where sale and repurchase (or stock borrowing and lending) transactions not covered by the above arrangements are entered into, proper documentation and prior agreement of key terms and conditions are essential. Documentation should be finalised as soon as possible (see also paragraph 84). The Bank will expect the institutions involved in such transactions to pursue prudent policies in securing physical control of the securities concerned. No security should be pledged more than once. For 'hold in custody' repos the written consent of non-listed counterparties should be obtained for the segregation arrangements that are to apply and such correspondence should be available for inspection by the Bank or other relevant regulator. Where the arrangements do not require strict physical segregation, firms should still ensure that the securities are separately accounted for. Those engaging in repos should insist that the other counterparty indicates whether it is acting as a principal or as agent in the transaction.

97   The Bank is aware that when secured deposits are taken, the related collateral may be held to a customer's order rather than be physically delivered. This practice is long established for example in the discount market. The Bank may check the arrangements established by institutions for which it has supervisory responsibility to ensure that security cannot be pledged more than once.

Market terminology and conventions

Management should ensure that individual brokers and dealers are aware of their responsibility to act professionally at all times and, as part of this, to use clear, unambiguous terminology.

98   The use of clear language is in the interests of all concerned. Management should establish internal procedures (including retraining if necessary) to alert individual dealers and brokers who act in different markets (or move from one market to another) both to any differences in terminology between markets and to the possibility that any particular term could be misinterpreted. The use of generally accepted concise terminology is undoubtedly helpful. In those markets where standard terms and conditions have been published (see also paragraph 82) individual dealers and brokers should familiarise themselves with the definitions they contain. Since no such terms currently exist for the foreign exchange, deposit or currency asset markets, Schedule 2 sets out, without purporting to be exhaustive, accepted market terminology and definitions which should be used when trading these instruments.

99   Standard conventions for calculating the interest and proceeds on certain sterling and currency instruments, together with market conventions regarding brokerage, are set out in Schedule 3. There have been instances of general disruption to the wholesale markets which have, in turn, resulted in interruptions to the sterling settlement systems and consequent delays in sterling payments. It has been agreed by the Joint Standing Committees that in such unexpected circumstances the Bank should determine and publish the interest rate(s) which parties to deals affected by such interruptions should use to calculate the appropriate interest adjustment (unless all the parties to the deal agree instead on some other arrangement - such as to continue to apply the existing rate of interest on the original transaction). The Bank of England shall have absolute discretion in its determination of any interest rate(s), and shall not be required to explain its method of determining the same and shall not be liable to any person in respect of such determination.

SUGGESTED PRE-DEAL CHECKLIST*   Schedule 1

Trade date
Customer name
           country of incorporation
           guarantee (if any)
Telex to
Telex number
Credit approved by

Customer pays: fixed/floating
Notional amount
Effective date
Maturity date
Currency
Trading desk
Firm
Counterparty

Fixed rate
Coupon rate
Coupon frequency
Day type
Non-business day roll convention
1st coupon payment date
1st coupon payment amount

Variable rate (1) customer pays/receives
Index
Spread
Coupon frequency
Reset frequency
Day type
Determination source
Rounding convention
Agent
Determination date convention
Non-business day roll convention
1st variable payment date
Gross initial/current variable rate

Variable rate (2) customer pays/receives
Index
Spread
Coupon frequency
Reset frequency
Day type
Determination source
Rounding convention
Agent
Determination date convention
Non-business day roll convention
1st reset date
1st variable/current payment date
Gross initial/current variable date

Fees and collateral
Payment basis - gross/net
Premium/discount - they pay/we pay
        upfront amount
        paid by
        paid to
        account number
Broker name
        broker fee
Intermediary fee
Collateral
        letter of credit
        decline amount/year
        mark to market
Defer option
        defer rate
        defer benchmark
        benchmark spread
Asset information

Additional information

Salesperson
Trader

* For interest rate swaps.

MARKET TERMINOLOGY AND DEFINITIONS

1 Sterling deposit market

- **Put on**

When a principal 'puts a broker on' the broker is given an order to arrange a deal on the principal's behalf. The broker may be put on either 'firm' or 'under reference', with or without a specified amount, or time limit.

- **Firm**

   When a principal puts a broker on 'firm' and no specific amount is mentioned, the principal is bound to deal in a marketable amount at the quoted price provided that the names are acceptable.

   When a broker quotes without qualification he is bound to deal firm in a marketable amount at the time he makes the quote, provided that the names are acceptable.

- **Under reference**

When a principal puts a broker 'under reference', or puts him 'under reference' having previously put him on 'firm', the broker should refer to the principal before he passes his name. If a broker quotes a price 'under reference' he must have the opportunity to check with one of his principals before being expected to deal in a marketable amount.

- **Take off**

When a principal 'takes a broker off' either a single order or several orders, he must, if he has put the broker on 'firm', check whether the broker is already committed to deal on his behalf.

- **Putting a price on**

When a broker approaches a principal to 'put a price on' a transaction, then that price is for immediate acceptance or acceptance within an agreed period in respect of the particular transaction only - it is not tantamount to 'putting the broker on firm' for other transactions in or near to the particular period.

- **Put through**

This is where a principal is prepared to take funds and on-lend them to a borrower to whom the original giver is, for whatever reason, not prepared to lend.

- **Bids and offers**

To avoid confusion arising between CDs and deposits, 'bid' and 'offer' should be restricted to bids and offers for money; paper should be referred to as 'buy' and 'sell' or 'issue'.

- **Clean**

A 'clean' or 'straight' deposit is one where there is no CD involved; for example 'I pay for clean (or straight) threes' or 'I lend clean (or straight) sixes'.

- **Straight**

The words 'straight dates' mean 'even dates', ie a CD or deposit maturing on the same date of the month (eg 16 January-16 July). Long sixes or short sixes are maturities either side of this date.

- **Roll overs**

A 'roll over' loan is a loan for a fixed period during which there are regular specified intervals at which the interest rate is re-established.

A 'roll over' or 'reissuable' CD is one on which the term but not always the rate of interest is fixed; a new CD is issued at specific intervals.

2 The foreign exchange and currency deposit markets

The markets in foreign exchange and currency deposits operate at considerable speed and the many possibilities for misunderstanding can be minimised by the use of generally accepted, concise terminology. This section sets out commonly used expressions and endeavours to clarify their accepted meaning. Adherence to them will do much to reduce misunderstanding and frustration; their use is therefore strongly recommended. Special care should always be taken to specify the particular currency referred to and to adopt what is now standard spot market terminology, both in currencies and in sterling, so that all discussions are couched in terms of:

(i) round amounts of sterling bid and offered, when dealing in US dollars/sterling;

(ii) round amounts of US dollars bid and offered, when dealing in other currencies.

In cases which will be obvious the terms listed below may be used in relation to lending and borrowing as well as to selling and buying:

Offered at ...
Comes at ...   Seller of sterling - as in (i) above
I give at ...   US dollars - as in (ii) above
I sell at ...
I offer at ...

I bid at ...
I pay at ...   Buyer of sterling - as in (i) above
I take at ...   US dollars - as in (ii) above
I buy at ...

- **Spot**

Cash settlement two working days from today.

- **Forward**

All deals over two working days from today for periods of one month onward fixed at the time of dealing. (All deals for a broken number of days up to the one month date are known as shorts or short dates.) Where the maturity falls on a non-trading day, it takes place on the following working day. Where the deal is arranged on a day for which spot delivery occurs on the last working day of the month, it matures on the last working day of the appropriate month in the future.

Where dealers are trading for, say, 3 months forward, the maturity date will be taken as 3 months from the spot settlement date. If this maturity date falls on either a weekend or a Bank Holiday the maturity date will be on the next business day unless that day is in the following month in which case it should be the day prior to the Bank Holiday or weekend.

• **End/end**

Forward swaps or currency deposits arranged for implementation before or at spot delivery on the last working day of the month should be described as 'end/end' if it is intended that they should mature on the last working day of the appropriate future month.

• **Forward/forward**

A forward sale against a forward purchase or forward purchase against a forward sale.

• **Swap**

A spot sale against a forward purchase or spot purchase against a forward sale.

When talking about 'forwards', dealers refer only to the forward date, for example if a dealer buys spot and sells three months forward, he will say to his counterparty, 'I offer threes' or 'I sell threes'.

• **Par**

Price is the same on both sides of the swap.

• **At a premium**

A currency which is more expensive to purchase forward than for spot delivery.

• **Long (over-bought)**

Excess of purchases over sales.

• **Short (over-sold)**

Excess of sales over purchases.

• **Open position**

The difference between total spot and forward purchases and sales in a currency on which an exchange risk is run.

• **Square**

Purchases and sales are equal.

• **Firm**

A dealer making an offer or bid on a 'firm' basis commits the principal but he would be advised to add some qualification (for example 'firm for one minute' or 'firm for one million only').

• **Under reference**

A deal cannot be finalised without reference to the principal which placed the order.

• **Choice**

A principal is a buyer or seller at one price.

• **Details**

Information a dealer requires after the completion of a transaction, ie name, rate and dates.

• **Mine**

The dealer takes the 'spot' or 'forward', whichever has been quoted from his counterparty. NB This is a very dangerous term and must be qualified by the amount involved.

• **Yours**

Opposite to mine.

3 The currency asset markets

• **Euronote**

A short-term fully negotiable bearer promissory note typically of up to six months maturity. Euronotes are commonly distributed by an auction between members of a tender panel.

• **Euro-commercial paper**

A generic term applied to the growing market for Euronotes issued on a non-underwritten basis. Euro-commercial paper is commonly issued on a continuous tap basis by one or more dealers.

• **Absolute rate**

A bid/offer made on Euronotes which is not expressed in relation to a particular funding base such as Libor or US domestic certificate of deposit rates, ie '9.125%' instead of 'Libor + 0.05%'.

• **Aggressor brokerage**

Where brokerage is charged to the party which acts on the broker's market (ie hits the bid or takes the offer).

• **Basis point**

1/100th of one percentage point.

• **Bid**

The price or yield on a security at which a purchaser will buy it.

• **Carry**

The (positive or negative) return on a trader's book net of his financing cost.

- **Earlies**

Up to and including the 15th of the month in respect of Euronotes (and CDs).

- **Lates**

Beyond the 15th of the month in respect of Euronotes (and CDs).

- **Hit the bid (price)**

Sell at a bid price.

- **Take the offer**

Buy at the offer price.

- **Give-up**

The loss of yield resulting from the sale of securities at one yield and purchase of securities at a lower yield (cf pick-up).

- **Locked**

Either way (same) price (or yield) from a broker or dealer at which he will buy or sell a security.

- **Margin**

The stated margin (or spread) is expressed as a percentage, added to or subtracted from a reference interest rate (for example six month Libor) to establish the coupon of a floating rate instrument.

- **Minimum rate**

In the context of floating rate paper, that interest rate below which the coupon may not be fixed.

- **Market going better (or up)**

Terminology used in bond markets when prices are rising and interest rates are falling.

- **Market going worse (or down)**

Terminology used in bond markets when prices are falling and interest rates are rising.

- **Offer**

The price or yield of a security at which a vendor is willing to sell.

- **On the run**

With respect to Treasury bills, the most recently issued 3, 6 or 12 month bills. Also refers to top banks' issues of CDs.

- **Par**

100% of the nominal value of a debt security.

- **Paper**

Generic term referring to securities.

- **Pay-up**

The additional cash outlay incurred on the sale of one block of securities and purchase of another (cf take-out).

- **Pick-up**

The gain in yield resulting from the sale of one block of securities and the purchase of another (cf give-up).

- **Pip**

1/100 of one percent of the nominal value of a security, for example $0.10 per $1000.

- **Plus (+)**

1/64.

- **Point**

One percent of the nominal value of a security; ie one hundred basis points.

- **Settlement**

Cash settlement: The delivery of securities against payment where the settlement date is the same as the trade date. The term is typically used in the US money markets. Known as same-day settlement in the UK.

Regular way settlement: Trades in which the settlement occurs the next business day after the trade date.

Skip day settlement: Settlement on the second business day following the trade date. Usage of this term is confined to the US domestic market; known as spot settlement in the UK forex markets.

Corporate settlement: Settlement five business days after trade in the US but after one week in Eurobond trading.

- **Subject**

There are two common usages of 'subject':

Subject bid (or offer): Price subject to purchaser's approval of names which would be dependent on credit limits.

Bid (or offer) subject: Indication of a price a purchaser is willing to pay but may not be firm.

- **Take-out**

The additional cash to be received on the sale of one block of securities and purchase of another (cf pay-up).

- **Tick**

Smallest fraction of price at which a security is typically traded.

- **When issued (WI)**

Trades before issuance, in which settlement occurs when and if the Treasury or Agency issues the certificate, reflecting the period between the announcement of a security's auction and its issuance, as possibly modified.

MARKET CONVENTIONS

Schedule 3

1 Calculation of interest and brokerage in the sterling deposit market

• Interest

On CDs and deposits or loans this is calculated on a daily basis on a 365-day year.

Interest on a deposit or loan is paid at maturity, or annually and at maturity, unless special arrangements are made at the time the deal is concluded.

On secured loans the discount houses and Stock Exchange money brokers do not pay interest at intervals of less than 28 days. The current general practice is to calculate at the close of business on the penultimate working day interest outstanding on secured loans to the last working day of each calendar month and to pay the interest thereon on the last working day of the month.

• Brokerage

All brokerage is calculated on a daily basis on a 365-day year and brokerage statements are submitted monthly.

2 Calculation of interest in a leap year

The calculation of interest in a leap year depends upon whether interest falls to be calculated on a daily or an annual basis. The position may differ as between temporary and longer-term loans.

• Temporary loans

Because temporary loans may be repaid in less than one year (but may, of course, be continued for more than a year) interest on temporary money is almost invariably calculated on a daily basis. Thus any period which includes 29 February automatically incorporates that day in the calculation; in calculating the appropriate amount of interest, the number of days in the period since the last payment of interest is expressed as a fraction of a normal 365-day year, not the 366 days of a leap year, which ensures that full value is given for the 'extra' day.

Examples:

Assume last previous interest payment 1 February (up to and including 31 January) and date of repayment 1 April (in a leap year). Duration of loan for final interest calculation = 29 days (February) + 31 days (March) = 60 days.

Calculation of interest would be

$$P \times \frac{r}{100} \times \frac{60}{365} =$$

Assume no intermediate interest payments. Loan placed 1 March and called for repayment 1 March the following year (leap year). Total period up to and including 29 February = 366 days. Calculation of interest would be

$$P \times \frac{r}{100} \times \frac{366}{365} =$$

This is in line with banking practice regarding interest on deposits which is calculated on a 'daily' basis and no conflict therefore arises.

• Longer-term loans

The following procedure for the calculation of interest on loans which cannot be repaid in less than one year (except under a TSB or building society stress clause) was agreed between the BBA and the Chartered Institute of Public Finance and Accountancy on 12 December 1978.

(a) Fixed interest

The total amount of interest to be paid on a longer-term loan at fixed interest should be calculated on the basis of the number of complete calendar years running from the first day of the loan, with each day of any remaining period bearing interest as for 1/365 of a year.

Normal practice for the calculation of interest in leap years is to disregard 29 February if it falls within one of the complete calendar years. Only when it falls within the remaining period is it counted as an additional day with the divisor remaining at 365.

Example: 3 1/2 year loan, maturing on 30 June of a leap year.

First 3 years' interest: $P \times \dfrac{r}{100} \times 3 =$

Final 6 months' interest: $P \times \dfrac{r}{100} \times \dfrac{182}{365} =$

Certain banks, however, require additional payment of interest for 29 February in all cases, and it was therefore agreed that:

both the original offer or bid, and the agent's confirmation, must state specifically if such payment is to be made; and

the documentation must incorporate the appropriate phraseology.

Interest on longer term loans should be paid half-yearly, on the half-yearly anniversary of the loan or on other prescribed dates and at maturity.

(b) Floating rate

Interest on variable rate loans, or roll-overs, which are taken for a fixed number of years with the rate of interest adjusted on specific dates, should be calculated in the same manner as for temporary loans.

3 Brokerage and other market conventions in the foreign exchange and currency deposit markets

- **Brokerage**

    (a) General (foreign exchange and currency deposits)

    Brokerage arrangements are freely negotiable.

    These arrangements should be agreed by directors and senior management in advance of any particular transaction.

    (b) Currency deposits

    Calculation of brokerage on all currency deposits should be worked out on a 360-day year.

    Brokers' confirmations and statements relating to currency deposits should express brokerage in the currency of the deal.

    In a simultaneous forward-forward deposit (for example one month against six months), the brokerage to be charged shall be on the actual intervening period (in the above example, five months).

- **Other Market Conventions**

    Currency deposits

    Length of the year

    For the purpose of calculating interest, one year is in general deemed to comprise 360 days; but practice is not uniform in all currencies or centres.

    Spreads and quotations

    Quotations will normally be made in fractions, except in short-dated foreign exchange dealings, where decimals are normally used.

    Call and notice money

    For US dollars (and sterling), notice in respect of call money must be given before noon in London. For other currencies, it should be given before such time as may be necessary to conform with local clearing practice in the country of the currency dealt in.

4 Calculations in the foreign currency asset markets

- **Euro-commercial paper (and other such instruments)**

    The net proceeds of short-term interest-bearing and discount Euro-commercial paper, on which interest is determined on a 360-day basis, are calculated in the same manner as those for short-term, interest-bearing and discount CDs.

    Formula for non-interest bearing Euronotes quoted on a 'discount to yield' basis:

$$\frac{N}{1 + \left(\frac{Y}{100} \times \frac{M}{360}\right)} = \text{Purchase consideration}$$

where

N = Nominal amount or face value
Y = Yield
M = Number of days to maturity

Example:

A Euronote with a face value of US $5 million and with 90 days to run is sold to yield 7.23% per annum.

$$\frac{5,000,000}{1 + \left(\frac{7.23 \times 90}{36,000}\right)} = \$4,911,229.53$$

- **US Treasury bills (and other US discount securities such as bankers' acceptances and commercial paper)**

    The quoted trading rates for such assets are discount rates. The price of the asset is calculated on the basis of a 360-day year.

    The market price (Pm) on a redemption value of $100 can be calculated as follows:

$$Pm = 100 - \frac{(M \times D)}{(360)}$$

where

M = days to maturity or days held
D = discount basis (per cent).

GUIDELINES FOR EXCHANGING STANDARD SETTLEMENT INSTRUCTIONS (SSIs)

<h2>Schedule 4</h2>

These guidelines have been drawn up by the Bank of England in consultation with practitioners. While the parties to SSIs are free to agree changes to the detail on a bilateral basis, it is hoped that this framework will be useful and as such followed as closely as possible.

When **establishing** SSIs with a counterparty for the first time these should be appropriately authorised internally before being issued. It is desirable that SSIs be established by post (and issued in duplicate, typically under two authorised signatories). However authenticated SWIFT message can also be used if necessary.

Cancellation or amendment of a standard instruction should ideally be undertaken by authenticated SWIFT; tested telex is also an acceptable means when cancelling or making amendments. SWIFT broadcast is **not** an acceptable means for establishing, cancelling or amending SSIs.

A mutually agreed **period of notice** for changing SSIs should be given; typically this will be between 10 working days and one month. Some parties may also wish to provide for changes to be made at shorter notice in certain circumstances.

Recipients have a responsibility to acknowledge acceptance (or otherwise) of the proposed/amended SSI within the timescale agreed (see above). Failure to do so could result in a liability to compensate for any losses which result. In the case of written notification this should be undertaken by the recipient signing and returning the duplicate letter.

Recipients should also confirm the precise date on which SSIs will be activated (via SWIFT or tested telex).

Instructions should be issued for each currency and wholesale market product. Each party will typically nominate only one correspondent per currency for foreign exchange deals and one per currency for other wholesale market deals. The same correspondent may be used for foreign exchange and other wholesale market deals.

As a general rule, all outstanding deals, including maturing forwards, should be settled in accordance with the SSI in force at their value date (unless otherwise and explicitly agreed by the parties at the time at which any change to an existing SSI is agreed).

The SSI agreement for each business category should contain the following:

- the nature of the deals covered (for example whether they include same day settlement or only spot/forward forex deals).

- confirmation that a single SSI will apply for all such deals with the counterparty.

- the effective date.

- confirmation that it will remain in force 'until advised'.

- recognition that no additional telephone confirmation of settlement details will be required.

- recognition that any deviation from the SSI will be subject to an agreed period of notice.

When operating SSIs on this basis, the general obligations on both parties are to ensure that:

- they apply the SSI which is current on the settlement date for relevant transactions.

- confirmations are issued in accordance with the London Code of Conduct; the aim should be to send them out on the day a deal is struck.

- confirmations are checked promptly upon receipt in accordance with the London Code. Any discrepancies should be advised by no later than 3.00 pm on the business day following trade date, if not sooner.

Annex 1

LONDON INSTRUMENTS

The London Code of Conduct defines best market practice for secondary transactions. The act of issuing debentures (including CDs, commercial paper and medium-term notes) is not an investment activity under the Financial Services Act 1986, but such primary issues are expected to comply with the Bank's market guidelines. The Bank believes that particularly in the short-term paper markets as great a degree of homogeneity as possible at the primary issuing stage assists good order in the market. It reduces the scope for investor confusion about the nature of the instrument being traded and facilitates market trading itself.

Such homogeneity is achieved in the CD market by the Bank's guidelines together with a booklet produced by the British Bankers' Association setting out in detail the requirements governing the issuance of CDs. These allow London CDs to be clearly identified and distinguished from non-London CDs.

It is hoped that a similar degree of homogeneity will be achieved in the commercial paper and medium-term note markets in London following publication by the Bank of its notice entitled Commercial Paper, Medium-Term Notes and Other Financial Instruments. This provides for a distinction to be drawn between paper issued under the terms of the notice and other paper. This notice, and the Bank's guidelines on CDs referred to above, are reproduced in this Annex.

The Bank is willing to co-operate with market participants in any of the other wholesale markets where similar standards and homogeneity would be desirable.

CERTIFICATES OF DEPOSIT AND OTHER SHORT-TERM PAPER ISSUES BY DEPOSIT-TAKING INSTITUTIONS

Notice issued by the Bank of England, 31 March 1989*

1   This notice sets out the Bank of England's guidance for issues of certificates of deposit (CDs) and other short-term paper issues by institutions authorised under the Banking Act 1987 and by building societies authorised under the Building Societies Act 1986. It replaces the Bank's Notice of 26 November 1986. Attention is also drawn to the existence of a publication by the British Bankers' Association which provides specific guidance on market practices (including recommended minimum standards of security) when issuing or trading CDs; and to the London Code of Conduct (copies of which are available from the Wholesale Markets Supervision Division, Bank of England) which sets out accepted best practice for secondary trading in the wholesale markets generally.

2   Until now institutions able to issue London CDs have been required not to issue instruments of other title in the sub-5 year maturity range. This restriction will no longer apply; such institutions may **also** issue paper of any title (including commercial paper), provided that the title is not liable to cause confusion with CDs**. Where they issue CDs, these will continue to be subject to standard terms and conditions. Where they issue instruments of other title, these may or may not be subject to standard terms and conditions.

London CDs

3   The Bank's policy is designed to ensure that London CDs are issued under standard terms and conditions. The Bank believes that as great a degree of homogeneity as possible at the primary issuing stage assists good order in the CD market. It reduces the scope for investor confusion about the nature of the instrument being traded, and facilitates market trading itself.

4   CDs issued and payable in the United Kingdom may **only** be issued by institutions authorised to accept deposits under the Banking Act 1987 or by building societies authorised under the Building Societies Act 1986, and are termed 'London CDs'. Any institution contemplating its first issue is asked to inform the Gilt-Edged & Money Markets Division of the Bank. The Bank expects London CDs to display the following characteristics:

(i)   Currency Denomination***

Approval has been given to date for London CDs denominated in Sterling, US$, Yen, Can$, Aus$, SDR and ECU. However the Bank is prepared to accept CDs issued in London in any other currency where satisfactory evidence is provided that the relevant central bank or other competent authority is content.

(ii)   Maturity****

The Bank regards CDs as short-term market instruments whose maximum life should not exceed five years (although, where necessary, a few days' grace would be acceptable when the natural maturity date does not fall on a business day). Negotiable instruments evidencing deposit liabilities which are issued with an original life beyond five years should not, in the Bank's view, be referred to as CDs at any stage of their life.

---

*   Updated where relevant.

**   Issues of commercial paper, medium-term notes and other financial instruments, should observe the relevant guidelines issued by the Bank, currently set out in the Bank's Notice of 11 January 1990.

***   Approval has also been given for London CDs denominated in NZ$, Lire, N.Kr and D.Kr.

****   There is no longer a minimum CD maturity.

(iii)   Minimum Denomination

CDs should be issued with a minimum denomination of not less than £50,000, or its equivalent in foreign currency.

(iv)   Interest Basis and Calculation

CDs may carry interest at a fixed rate or variable rate. Where there is no agreed market practice, the Bank would like it to be clear from the instrument when payments of interest or repayment will be effected in the event of the due date falling on a non-business day. Calculation of interest on CDs should be on an actual day basis in conformity with British practice.

Discount CDs

5   The Bank does not object to issues of London CDs which carry no coupon and are issued at a discount, provided that the instruments are so worded that the basis of issue is obvious to all interested parties and, in the case of certificates with an original maturity in excess of one year, some means of periodically verifying the authenticity of such instruments is incorporated in the terms of issue.

Early Repayment Option

6   The Bank will no longer object to issues of London CDs which incorporate put or call options, provided that:

(i)   the terms of the option are clear to the initial and any subsequent holder of the paper, and the means by which a holder will be informed if the issuer proposes to exercise a call option or the procedure to be used if the holder wishes to exercise a put option are in no doubt; and

(ii)   issues of these instruments by foreign institutions do not run counter to the wishes of parent supervisory authorities.

CDs Purchased by Issuers

7   Institutions must not make a false market in their own paper but may purchase it before maturity in particular circumstances where this would assist the maintenance of an orderly market. The Bank's prior approval is always required when own name paper is purchased as a matter of deliberate policy.

CDs Issued with a Guarantee

8   The Bank does not object to London CDs (as defined in paragraph 4) issued under a guarantee where, and only where, the guarantor is an institution authorised under the Banking Act 1987. The name of the guarantor must be clearly marked on the face of the certificate.

Non-London CDs

9   The Bank does not seek to restrict the trading in London of Non-London CDs (ie CDs issued by institutions which are not authorised under the Banking Act 1987 but which nevertheless are intended to trade in the United Kingdom) provided that:

(i)   they are clearly labelled 'Non-London' on the face of the certificates;

(ii)   the BBA's standards for London Good Delivery are satisfied;

(iii)   the provisions of the Banking Act are not infringed; and

(iv)   where a UK issuing and/or paying agent is employed, this is made clear in an appropriate manner to purchasers of the paper.

Bank of England Operations

10   The Bank of England does not purchase CDs in its money market operations, nor are CDs eligible at the Bank as security or margin for advances to the Discount Market or to the Gilt-Edged Market.

Statistical Reporting

11   CDs outstanding, both issued and held (together with other short-term paper issued by institutions authorised under the Banking Act), should be reported by monetary sector institutions to the Financial Statistics Division of the Bank on the appropriate forms. (If a reporting institution holds CDs which it has itself issued, these should be excluded from both sides of its balance sheet.) Building societies similarly provide data on their outstanding short-term paper to the Building Societies Commission.

Impact on Eligible Liabilities

12   Issues by monetary sector institutions of sterling paper with an original maturity (or a date to first put or call) in the sub-5 year maturity range, will be classified, irrespective of their title, as eligible liabilities and will, where relevant, be subject to Cash Ratio Deposits or to Special Deposits. Holdings of such securities issued by other monetary sector institutions will be regarded as an offset against eligible liabilities.

Enquiries

13   The Bank recognises that problems which fall outside its province may arise from time to time in relation to the issue of CDs, eg taxation. The Bank remains willing to act as a channel of communication on such problems, where it can usefully do so.

14   Enquiries on the content of this Notice and on related matters should be addressed to the Gilt-Edged and Money Markets Division of the Bank (telephone 071 601 3100).

COMMERCIAL PAPER, MEDIUM-TERM NOTES AND OTHER FINANCIAL INSTRUMENTS

Notice issued by the Bank of England, 11 January 1990

1   This notice, which replaces the Bank's Notice of 14 March 1989 on Sterling Issues, sets out the arrangements for issues in the United Kingdom of:

(a)   commercial paper and medium-term notes, either under, or on terms consistent with, the Banking Act (Exempt Transactions) Regulations, to apply from 1 February 1990; and

(b)   other types of financial instrument*.

2   The latest revisions include the following features:

(i)   an extension to five years in the maximum permissible maturity** of paper issued under the relevant framework;

(ii)   provision for paper issued under the terms of this Notice with an original maturity of up to and including one year to continue to take the form of 'commercial paper'; and for paper issued for over one year and up to and including five years to take the form of 'medium-term notes';

(iii)   the Regulations are made non-currency specific, so that issues of paper may be made in the UK in sterling or other approved currencies without infringing the deposit-taking provisions of the Banking Act 1987;

(iv)   commercial paper and medium-term notes issued under the Regulations must carry a statement in **bold** print on the face of the paper that it is issued in accordance with the Regulations made under Section 4 of the Banking Act 1987. For paper issued by institutions authorised under, or exempted by Section 4(1) from, the Banking Act 1987, a statement to this effect should appear on the face of the paper in **bold** print;

(v)   the framework previously set out in the Regulations for the issue of sterling debt securities of an original maturity in excess of one year ('short-term corporate bonds') is withdrawn.

3   Revised Regulations*** are being laid today, to come into force on 1 February, to bring these changes into effect.

COMMERCIAL PAPER AND MEDIUM-TERM NOTES

Banks, building societies, insurance companies and certain international organisations

4   There is no objection to issues of commercial paper or medium-term notes by institutions authorised under the Banking Act 1987, building societies authorised under the Building Societies Act 1986, insurance companies authorised under the Insurance Companies Act 1982, or international organisations which are exempted from the Banking Act 1987, provided that where their issues are made under the terms of this notice they meet the conditions set out in paragraph 7 below.

Other qualifying issuers

5   The Regulations allow issues of commercial paper or medium-term notes to be made, without contravening the deposit-taking provisions of the Banking Act 1987, by the following:

---

*   Except certificates of deposit, guidelines for which remain as in the Bank's notice of 31 March 1989.

**   Made possible by the 1989 Companies Act which allows issues of unlisted securities up to five years' original maturity to be made onshore to professionals without the need for a prospectus.

***   The Banking Act 1987 (Exempt Transactions) (Amendment) Regulations 1990.

(a) Companies

Companies, both United Kingdom and overseas, which:

(i) have net assets, as defined in Section 264(2) of the Companies Act 1985, of at least £25 million;

and

(ii) (a) have shares or debt securities listed on the International Stock Exchange (ISE) or dealt in on the Unlisted Securities Market;

or (b) have shares or debt listed on a stock exchange, or on the official exchange in a country, included on the list currently in force of 'Authorised stock exchanges, financial market places and associations' produced by the ISE for the purposes of Rule 535.4a (or any successor rule) (see Appendix); and have provided in good faith, to the ISE*, the information required in Schedule 3 of the Regulations, which is equivalent to that required by the ISE for a euro-currency security debt listing**;

or (c) are companies incorporated in the UK not falling under (ii)(a) above which have provided in good faith, to the ISE, the information required in Schedule 3 of the Regulations, which is equivalent to that required by the ISE for a euro-currency security debt listing**.

(b) Overseas public sector bodies

The government of all countries or territories, or overseas public authorities, whose debt securities are admitted to trading on a stock exchange or official exchange as described under (a)(ii)(a) or (a)(ii)(b) above.

(c) Issues under guarantee

Issuers not falling into any of the groups above may make issues of commercial paper or medium-term notes if they are unconditionally guaranteed either by a company meeting the net assets requirement under (a)(i) above and falling within the category under (a)(ii)(a) above, or by an institution authorised under the Banking Act 1987.

Local authorities

6 From 1 April 1990, certain local authorities in England and Wales will be permitted to issue commercial paper or medium-term notes denominated in sterling. The necessary regulations will be made under the Local Government and Housing Act 1989 and will be announced in due course.

Conditions for issuing

7 The conditions attached to issues of commercial paper or medium-term notes, which if denominated in sterling should be issued and payable in the UK, are as follows***:

(a) Description

The securities must carry a statement that they are commercial paper or medium-term notes, give the name of the issuer, and:

(i) if issued under paragraphs 4 or 6 of this notice by an institution authorised under, or exempted by Section 4(1) from, the Banking Act 1987, carry a statement to that effect; or

---

* Quotations Department, Primary Markets Division, The International Stock Exchange.

** On receipt of the information from companies qualifying under paragraph 5(a)(ii)(b) or 5(a)(ii)(c), the ISE will make an announcement on its news service. It will levy an appropriate fee for its role. It bears no responsibility for the completeness or accuracy of the information provided by the companies.

*** Additional conditions may be imposed by market convention outside the terms of this notice.

(ii) if issued under paragraph 5 of this notice by any other institution, carry a statement that the issuer is not authorised under the Banking Act 1987; and that the paper is commercial paper or medium-term notes issued in accordance with Regulations made under Section 4 of the Banking Act 1987.

If any issue of commercial paper or medium-term notes is guaranteed, it must carry a statement to that effect, giving the name of the guarantor and stating whether or not the guarantor is an institution authorised under the Banking Act 1987.

(b) Title

Paper conforming to accepted standard terms and conditions should be entitled respectively 'commercial paper' for issues up to and including one year and 'medium-term notes' for issues over one year. However where issues are made with non-standard terms or conditions, the Bank will expect any unusual feature(s) to be highlighted and reflected in the title (for example medium-term notes issued with principal or interest linked to the gold price might be termed GOLD-LINKED MEDIUM-TERM NOTES).

(c) Maturity

Commercial paper must have an original maturity of not less than 7 days, and not more than one year. Medium-term notes must have an original maturity of more than one year and not more than five years*.

(d) Disclosure

Issuers or guarantors of commercial paper or medium-term notes which fall within paragraph 5(a) above must make a representation to the purchaser, in a statement reproduced on the securities, to the effect that the issuer or guarantor:

(i) is in compliance with the relevant listing or disclosure obligations referred to in paragraph 5(a) above; and

(ii) since the information was last provided in compliance with these obligations, having made all reasonable enquiries, has not become aware of any change in circumstances which could reasonably be regarded as significantly and adversely affecting its ability to meet its obligations on the paper as they fall due.

(e) Currency denomination

Issues of commercial paper or medium-term notes will be permitted in sterling or ECU, or any other currency where the relevant overseas authority is content.

(f) Minimum amount

Commercial paper or medium-term notes must be issued and transferable in minimum amounts of £100,000 or currency equivalent (defined in terms of redemption value).

(g) Put or call options

Issues of commercial paper may carry put or call options at any time during their life; medium-term notes may also carry put or call options exercisable after one year from their date of issue.

(h) Repurchase of paper by issuers before maturity

Whilst paper issued under the terms of this notice may be repurchased before maturity by those responsible for issuing it, this should not be done in a manner which creates a misleading impression about the market in the paper. In particular any person contemplating repurchasing commercial paper or medium-term notes which it has been responsible for issuing must ensure that both the spirit and letter of Section 47(2) of the Financial Services Act 1986 are not contravened.

(i) Monitoring

Those making issues under the terms of this notice must notify the Bank:

(a) at the commencement or extension of any commercial paper or medium-term note programme, of the total amount of paper they propose to issue under the programme, distinguishing between commercial paper and medium-term notes, details if known of the maturity and currency denomination(s), the name of the guarantor if relevant, and as full as possible a description of the intended uses of the funds raised; and

---

*   Institutions falling within paragraph 4 of this notice are permitted to issue medium-term notes with maturities longer than five years.

(b) within one week after the end of each subsequent calendar month, of the amounts (by currency) of commercial paper and medium-term notes outstanding as at that end-calendar month and of the amounts (by currency) of paper issued and redeemed since the previous report, distinguishing between commercial paper and medium-term notes. In each case a distinction should be made between paper guaranteed by an institution authorised under the Banking Act 1987 and paper not so guaranteed.

This information should be submitted in writing to the Bank of England, Threadneedle Street, London EC2R 8AH, addressed to Group 7, Financial Statistics Division, BB-4.

This responsibility may be delegated by an issuer to an appointed agent.

Arrangement of commercial paper and medium-term note issues

8 Managers, arrangers or dealers of issues should be aware that their activity in the UK constitutes investment business under the Financial Services Act 1986. Intermediaries acting in this capacity should be either fully authorised under the Act or exempted from it by virtue of Section 43 of the Act; other firms are invited to discuss with the Bank the terms on which they might arrange issues in the UK.

Secondary market transactions

9 Schedule 5 of the Financial Services Act 1986 is to be amended so that, in addition to embracing issues of debt instruments by banks and building societies of up to five years' original maturity, it will in future also include issues of paper of this maturity made under the Banking Act 1987 (Exempt Transactions) (Amendment) Regulations. Consequently transactions by institutions listed under Section 43 of the Financial Services Act 1986 in commercial paper and medium-term notes in both of these categories will be exempt from the Act.

UK Taxation

10 The Inland Revenue has indicated that the tax treatment of *commercial paper* remains as follows:

(i)   interest on commercial paper can normally be paid without deduction of income tax;

(ii) interest/discount incurred by the issuer as a trading expense will normally be allowable for corporation tax purposes;

(iii) the arrangements for taxation of the return earned by holders of commercial paper are those applying to certificates of deposit; and

(iv) the issue and transfer of commercial paper will be free of stamp duty;

whilst the tax treatment of *medium-term notes* is as follows:

(i)   the normal rules concerning medium-term securities will apply, including the deep discount or deep gain legislation if relevant. Interest paid will rank as annual interest; accordingly

(ii) the UK payer of the interest on medium-term notes will normally have to deduct basic rate income tax at source, unless all the conditions of Section 124 ICTA 1988 are met and the note qualifies as a 'quoted eurobond';

(iii) interest/discount incurred by the issuer as a trading expense will normally be allowable for corporation tax purposes;

(iv) the return earned by holders of medium-term notes in the UK is liable to income or corporation tax in the hands of the recipient, unless he is exempted from tax; and

(v)   the issue or transfer of medium-term notes will be free of stamp duty.

Any further enquiries concerning tax or stamp duty should be directed to the Inland Revenue.

OTHER FINANCIAL INSTRUMENTS

11 Issues of other financial instruments, in sterling or other currencies, in the form of bonds, FRNs etc, may be made if the provisions of all relevant statutes, including the Banking Act 1987, the Companies Acts and the Financial Services Act 1986 are satisfied*. Issues may carry put or call options operative at any time during their life.

---

*   It remains the position that UK local authorities may not issue deep discount (including zero coupon) or index-linked stocks.

Lead management of sterling issues

12   In order to promote the orderly development of the sterling capital market, the Bank will continue to require all capital market issues denominated in sterling (whether in the form of debt or equity, including securities carrying a sterling option or a sterling-related element, except issues of commercial paper or medium-term notes under paragraphs 4 to 10 above) to be managed in the UK, under the lead management of a UK-based firm which has satisfied the Bank that it has the capacity in the UK to act as an issuing house. Foreign-owned firms with such a capacity will be eligible to lead manage sterling issues only if in the Bank's view there are reciprocal opportunities in their domestic capital markets for UK-owned firms to lead manage issues. Firms which do not meet the guidelines for lead management are able to participate in sterling issues in a co-management position (but not as a co-lead manager).

New issues calendar

13   The ISE and the British Merchant Banking and Securities Houses Association have established procedures, operated by the Bank, for an exchange of information about the timing proposed for new sterling capital market issues of £20 million or more. Advisers to a new issue should give prior notification to the Bank of the proposed timing and main features of the issue. The Bank will indicate whether there is likely to be a clash with a competing issue. The advisers will then be able to consider whether to proceed on the specified date, or to change the timing, notifying the Bank accordingly. If a clash is likely to remain, the Bank will inform the sponsors of the competing issues.

14   The Bank also requires to be notified for the record of the main details of any new capital market issue in sterling for an amount of £20 million or more at the time it is made.

15   These notifications should be made to the Bank's Gilt-Edged and Money Markets Division (telephone 071 601 3100), as should enquiries about all aspects of this notice and any related matters.

Appendix

AUTHORISED STOCK EXCHANGES*, FINANCIAL MARKET PLACES AND ASSOCIATIONS
(RULE 535.4a: PERMITTED DEALINGS IN FOREIGN SECURITIES)

American Stock Exchange
Amsterdam Stock Exchange
Australian Stock Exchange
Boston Stock Exchange
Brussels Stock Exchange
Cincinnati Stock Exchange
Copenhagen Stock Exchange
France
Fukuoka Stock Exchange
Germany
Greece
Helsinki Stock Exchange
Hiroshima Stock Exchange
Hong Kong Stock Exchange
Italy
Johannesburg Stock Exchange
Kyoto Stock Exchange
Luxembourg Stock Exchange
Malaysia
Mexico
Mid-West Stock Exchange
Montreal Stock Exchange
Nagoya Stock Exchange
NASD
New York Stock Exchange
New Zealand
Niigata Stock Exchange
Norway
Osaka Stock Exchange
Pacific Stock Exchange
Philadelphia Stock Exchange
Portugal
Sapporo Stock Exchange
Securities Exchange of Thailand
Singapore
Spain
Sweden
Switzerland
Tel Aviv Stock Exchange
Tokyo Stock Exchange
Toronto Stock Exchange
Turkey
Vienna Stock Exchange
Official OTC markets in the Netherlands, Germany and Japan

---

*   The Vancouver Stock Exchange was added to this list with effect from 24 April 1990.

Annex 2

OPERATING A DUAL BROKING SYSTEM IN THE LONDON FOREIGN EXCHANGE MARKET

Notice issued by the Bank of England, 24 October 1989

1   The Bank's enquiries of foreign exchange market participants in March 1989 established that opinion was divided on use of the 'points' system in London*. The Bank has considered with the FECDBA and the Joint Standing Committee the kind of steps necessary to allow those institutions wishing to retain the use of points to do so, whilst ensuring that points are not used in deals with banks which reject this system. It has been agreed that the following general arrangements will be established.

2   Management in all banks (and other active market participants) will be expected to have internal rules for their dealers to minimise the scope for differences and to discourage dealers from acting unprofessionally, for example by 'stuffing' brokers.

Participating banks

3   Each broking firm will approach all their clients (based in the UK or overseas) at the appropriate management level to establish whether, in order to be provided as far as possible by the broker with the current firm price service, they are prepared to sign a client letter accepting the broker's involvement in points arrangements. Those banks which do agree client letters are referred to here as 'participating banks'.

4   Banks which explicitly accept the use of points in this way will be assumed to have given their informed consent to the practice. The arrangements described here are deemed satisfactory in the foreign exchange market because it is a professional market in which best execution is not normally expected. Obviously in abnormal circumstances, where a broker agrees to provide best execution to a client or the client is not a market professional or the broker performs an advisory or discretionary function** to a client, there must be full disclosure to the client of the broker's interest and explicit informed prior consent.

5   Signing such a client letter will **not** of itself commit any bank to **lending** points to brokers or to the use of positive points in lieu of cash payment for any differences. Any such decision should be taken quite separately by management and would require appropriate record keeping and reporting arrangements to be established.

Non-participating banks

6   For 'non-participating banks' which decline to provide a client letter, a broking firm will need to consider on a case-by-case basis whether it is prepared to continue to provide a broking service, and if so on what terms. Where a service continues to be provided, the broking firm will be required to take the following steps to ensure that these banks are not unwittingly involved in deals where there is an undisclosed benefit to the broker:

(i)   The broker will advise the management of these non-participating banks that it may no longer provide as firm a price service; banks will be expected to take steps to inform their dealers that the broker cannot be held to a price. Any attempts to 'stuff' a broker should in the first instance be brought to the attention of management in the broking firm; they in turn should raise it at the appropriate level with the bank(s) concerned. Any bank dealers attempting to pressurise a broker should be subject to internal disciplinary procedures. Furthermore, if necessary, brokers will have recourse to the Bank of England to complain.

(ii) Each broking firm will establish to the Bank of England's satisfaction appropriate arrangements to enable it to distinguish non-participating from participating banks. The precise means by which this distinction is achieved are likely to vary between

---

*   Examples of typical situations generating 'negative' and 'positive' points are set out in the Appendix.

** See paragraphs 20 and 21 of the May 1992 Code regarding the Role of brokers.

broking firms depending, inter alia, on the number of non-participating clients each broker has; the manner in which they receive a service (whether over an open voice box system or over an ordinary telephone line); and the number and volume of deals involved.

(iii) Any differences payable by the broker resulting from mistakes will normally be settled by cheque; where London banks are concerned, it is recommended that cheques be paid through the established FECDBA mechanism*. As a matter of equity, banks should also accept that any differences resulting from mistakes on the part of their dealers should be payable to the broker through the same procedures.

(iv) An up-to-date list of names distinguishing participating from non-participating banks will be maintained by the broker, with copies provided to all appropriate members of staff. The Bank of England will also be provided with a copy of the current list.

(v) Any 'cross-overs' involving a non-participating bank will, subject to acceptability of names, be completed either at a mutually acceptable middle rate or by the introduction of an intermediary bank; if an intermediary is introduced, none of the benefit to it from such a deal will accrue to the broker.

(vi) In the event of a 'name switch' becoming necessary involving one or more non-participating banks, the broker will reserve the right to adjust the brokerage charges to compensate. Any such adjustment should be arranged between management in both the broking firm and the bank(s) concerned.

7   Management in broking firms active in forex have indicated to the Bank that this framework forms an acceptable basis for accommodating banks' differing requirements for broking services. Its operation will be kept under close review by the Bank and by the Joint Standing Committee, and the first six months of operation will be regarded as experimental.

8   The Bank will require brokers to maintain records of deals involving points, including any such deals arranged involving correspondent brokers. These must ensure that accurate and verifiable points' tallies are kept on a deal by deal basis, and must be backed by rigorous management systems and controls. These requirements have been discussed with the broking firms concerned and are set out in a separate paper which has been provided to all listed brokers for implementation to the Bank's satisfaction.

9   The Bank accepts that on rare occasions individuals will inevitably make mistakes, when (positive) points may wrongly be taken by a broker from a deal involving a non-participating bank. Systems will therefore need to be in place in each broking firm to identify any such errors promptly and to ensure that full rectification takes place immediately so that no positive points accrue to the benefit of the broker. Any such adjustment will leave the original deal undisturbed. The Bank will monitor closely the frequency of any such errors in each firm; if they reveal an inability to distinguish participating from non-participating banks, the Bank may require a broking firm to give up the use of points altogether.

Arrangements for monitoring participating banks

10 In parallel to these arrangements for brokers, the Banking Supervision Division of the Bank will wish to be notified by those UK authorised banks which decide that they may be prepared to accept positive points to settle differences arising with broking firms. They will wish to discuss with these banks from time to time how these arrangements will work, including importantly the record keeping arrangements in place to enable individual transactions involving points (both negative and positive) to be identified.

---

*   See paragraph 88 of the May 1992 Code for details of new arrangements which supersede the FECDBA mechanism.

Appendix

EXAMPLES OF SITUATIONS GIVING RISE TO POINTS IN FOREIGN EXCHANGE DEALING

'Negative Points'

1 Suppose a broker quotes sterling at $1.8030/1.8035. Bank A hits the $1.8030 bid for 5 mn. However, before the broker could let Bank A know, this price had been withdrawn by the market maker who had originally indicated to the broker a willingness to deal at the rate. The market for sterling has moved to $1.8025/1.8030.

2 When told that the bid price of $1.8030 was no longer available, the trader at Bank A insists on selling 5 mn at the original price.

3 Suppose the broker accepts responsibility for not withdrawing the price quickly enough, or values highly his relationship with Bank A, and therefore agrees to be held to the price. He searches the market and finds Bank B (a participating bank) who is willing to help the broker by agreeing to buy from Bank A at $1.8030 (and hopefully sell to the current bidder in the market at $1.8025); the broker is committed to make good the $2,500 loss which results from Bank B doing the two trades. This dealer has lent the broker 25 'points' (ie 5 'points' per 1 mn in a 5 mn deal).

'Positive Points'

4 The $2,500 (25 'points') obligation of the broker in the above example to Bank B could obviously be settled in cash if Bank B so wished. Or Bank B may be prepared to see it reduced by the broker's ability to put to Bank B other transactions that produce a profit to Bank B's dealing position of at least $2,500. This might be achieved in various ways, one of which is as follows.

5 Suppose at some later time the market for sterling stands at $1.8070/75. This might reflect prices put into the broker as follows: Bank A bidding at 1.8070; Bank C is offering at 1.8075. Suppose two unrelated Banks, X and Y, simultaneously have a respective need to sell/buy 5 mn. Bank X hits the 1.8070 bid; Bank Y the 1.8075 offer. The broker now has these latter two banks committed to deal in opposite directions at overlapping rates (in this example equal to the market spread). The broker may, at its discretion, offer both these deals to Bank B.

6 The consequences of this would be:

(i) Bank X has sold sterling at the (market) rate desired;

(ii) Bank Y has bought sterling at the (market) rate desired;

(iii) by being given both deals Bank B earns a profit of $2,500 equal to the spread; it may, or may not, decide to reward the broker for this 'service' in the form of offsetting these 'positive points' against the 25 negative points the broker owes.

APPENDIX

IV

International Currency Options Market (ICOM)

OTC Market Terms and Conditions

United States

Introductory letter by The Foreign Exchange Committee; New York legal Opinion by Stroock & Stroock & Lavan; ICOM Master Agreement and Guide, as issued by the Foreign Exchange Committee.

(Reproduced with the permission of the Foreign Exchange Committee)

United Kingdom

ICOM Terms and Guide, as issued by the British Bankers' Association, August 1992.

(Reproduced with the permission of the British Bankers' Association)

Japan

ICOM Master Agreement and Guide, as issued by the Tokyo Foreign Exchange Market Practices Committee.

(Reproduced with the permission of the Tokyo FX Market Practices Committee)

THE FOREIGN EXCHANGE COMMITTEE

NEW YORK, N.Y. 10045

April 27, 1992

Dear Foreign Exchange Colleague:

The Foreign Exchange Committee is pleased to sponsor a model agreement for foreign exchange options, the International Currency Options Market (ICOM) Master Agreement. This model agreement is intended for participants in the interbank market and reflects the Committee's views of good practice for that market. To that end, the ICOM agreement defines key terms and addresses formation, exercise, and settlement procedures for foreign exchange options as well as procedures for liquidation and close-out in case of default. The agreement, a guide to the agreement, and a legal opinion concerning enforceability under United States law are included in this package. A legal opinion concerning enforceability under United Kingdom law and a legal opinion raising issues under Japanese law can be obtained by telephoning the Committee's Executive Assistant, Martin Mair, at (212) 720-6651.

The documentation has been prepared by a group of attorneys working under the auspices of the Foreign Exchange Committee in New York in conjunction with the British Bankers' Association and represents an important first step in cooperation between financial centers. This model agreement will provide a basis upon which dealers operating in the United States and the United Kingdom can trade foreign currency options with a wide range of dealing counterparties on both sides of the Atlantic without the need to negotiate costly bilateral agreements. Where necessary the agreement can also be modified to allow the terms to be extended to dealers' customers.

The Foreign Exchange Committee is sponsoring two seminars on the ICOM agreement and guide and their possible ramifications, both from a legal and from a trading perspective. The first seminar will be held on Wednesday, May 20, 1992, and a second seminar with the same agenda will be held on Wednesday, May 27, 1992. Both seminars will be held at the Federal Reserve Bank of New York from three until five in the afternoon. A panel of those lawyers and practitioners involved in preparing the agreement will discuss their own views on the evolution of the document and will be available for questions from the audience. Up to three representatives from your institution are invited to attend one of these presentations. Areas of your organization that might be interested include foreign exchange trading, legal and compliance. Please RSVP by fax, using the enclosed invitation response sheet. We are looking forward to a stimulating discussion.

Very truly yours,

John T. Arnold
Chairman, Foreign Exchange Committee

Stroock & Stroock & Lavan

Seven Hanover Square
New York, New York 10004-2594

212 806 5400
Fax: 212 806 6006
Telex: 177693 STROOCK NY

Direct Dial:

April 23, 1992

The Members of the
Foreign Exchange Committee
(independent of but sponsored
by and advisory to the
Federal Reserve Bank of New York)

Ladies and Gentlemen:

You have requested our opinion as to whether the substantive
provisions of specified insolvency laws will affect the
enforceability of certain setoff, netting and default provisions
contained in the International Currency Options Market Master
Agreement, a copy of which is annexed hereto (the "Agreement").
Unless otherwise defined below, terms defined in the Agreement
shall have the same meaning when used herein.

In connection with the opinions hereinafter expressed, we have
examined the Agreement and have also examined the United States
Bankruptcy Code (the "Code"), the Federal Deposit Insurance Act
(the "FDIA"), the Federal Reserve Act and the Home Owners' Loan
Act. We have also made such other examinations of law as we have
deemed necessary to form the basis of the opinions hereinafter
expressed.

Attorneys involved in the preparation of this opinion are
admitted to practice law in the State of New York. The opinions
set forth below are limited to the effect of the statutes expressly

Stroock & Stroock & Lavan

The Members of the
Foreign Exchange Committee
April 23, 1992
Page 2

referred to in the preceding paragraph and we express no opinion
with respect to the effect of any state fraudulent conveyance or
other laws.

Discussion.

I.   Introduction.

     The Agreement contains the following pertinent provisions: (i)
Section 6 provides for the automatic termination and discharge, in
whole or part, of Options that are identical except for the status
of the Parties as Buyer and Seller and the quantity of Currency
subject thereto, (ii) Section 7 provides that if certain payments
are due from each Party on the same day, such payments will be
netted so that only the difference shall be due and (iii) Section 8
provides that following an Event of Default (which includes the
commencement of a Code Proceeding or an Insolvency Proceeding, as
defined below) the Non-Defaulting Party may close-out outstanding
Options, determine the damages to each Party resulting from such
close-out, net the aggregate amount of such damages due to each
Party and set off any net damage amount against any margin held by
the Parties so that a single net liquidated amount will be due from
one Party to the other Party.

     The Code and the FDIA limit the enforceability of setoff and
default provisions against a party that has become subject to a
proceeding under Chapter 7 or Chapter 11 of the Code (a "Code
Proceeding") or that has had a receiver or conservator appointed
with respect to it under the FDIA (an "Insolvency Proceeding").
Setoffs occurring within specified periods of time prior to the
commencement of such a Proceeding may be subject to attack as a
"preference," while default remedies predicated on the occurrence
of such a Proceeding may be deemed ineffective. As described
below, however, the Code and the FDIA also provide certain
exceptions to these general limitations.

II.   The Bankruptcy Code.

     1. General Provisions.

     Upon commencement of a Code Proceeding, the following Code
provisions generally apply: (i) under Section 362, all creditors
are automatically stayed from taking any action with respect to
property of the debtor's estate and claims against the debtor, (ii)

Stroock & Stroock & Lavan

The Members of the
Foreign Exchange Committee
April 23, 1992
Page 3

under Section 365(e)(1), an executory contract may not be
terminated at any time after the commencement of a Code Proceeding
solely because of a contractual provision (a so-called _ipso facto_
or bankruptcy clause) providing for such right in the event of
bankruptcy, (iii) under Section 553, certain setoffs against the
debtor effected during the 90 day period prior to the commencement
may be recovered from that creditor, (iv) under Section 547,
certain transfers of property to a creditor occurring within the 90
day (or, in some cases, one year) period prior to the commencement
may be recovered as preferences and (v) under Section 548, certain
transfers of property to a creditor occurring within the one year
period prior to the commencement of a Code Proceeding may be
recovered as a fraudulent transfer. Other Code Sections, such as
544 and 545, provide other bases on which the interests of a
creditor may be avoided.

   2. _Forward Contracts_.

   (a) _Relevant Provisions_. The Code contains several
provisions which specifically relate to "forward contracts." The
basic purpose of the Code's forward contract provisions is to
prevent the insolvency of one party to a forward contract from
threatening the solvency of the other party to that forward
contract and, in so doing, the solvency of some or all of the other
persons with which the second party does business. _See, e.g._, 124
Cong. Rec. S. 14724 (daily ed. Sept. 7, 1978) (remarks of Senator
Mathias). One of the principal means through which the Code
attempts to achieve this purpose is Section 556, which authorizes a
forward contract merchant to exercise its contractual rights, if
any, to liquidate outstanding forward contracts with a counterpart
that becomes the subject of a Code Proceeding. Although the Code,
in contrast to the prior Bankruptcy Act, generally invalidates _ipso
facto_ or bankruptcy clauses, Section 556 of the Code states that
the right to liquidate a forward contract "shall not be stayed,
avoided, or otherwise limited by operation of any provision of this
title or by the order of a court in any proceeding under this
title."

   Section 362(b)(6) of the Code provides that the commencement
of a Code Proceeding shall not stay a setoff by a forward contract
merchant of "any mutual debt and claim under or in connection
with...forward contracts...that constitutes the setoff of a claim
against the debtor for a margin payment...or settlement
payment...arising out of...forward contracts...against cash,

Stroock & Stroock & Lavan

The Members of the
Foreign Exchange Committee
April 23, 1992
Page 4

securities, or other property held by or due from such...forward contract merchant...to margin, guarantee, secure or settle...forward contracts...." Thus, for example, if as a result of the liquidation of two forward contracts pursuant to Section 556, a forward contract merchant owes an insolvent counterpart a settlement payment under one contract and is owed a settlement payment under the other contract, Section 362(b)(6) would permit the forward contract merchant to set off or net the two obligations. Other setoffs, including the setoff of margin payments (as defined in Section 101(34) of the Code), are also permitted by Section 362(b)(6).

The right set forth in Code Section 553(b) to recover for the debtor's estate setoffs that occur within the 90 day period prior to the commencement of a Code Proceeding does not apply to a setoff "of the kind described in section 362(b)(6)...."

Section 546(e) provides, among other things, that margin payments and settlement payments made by or to a forward contract merchant prior to the commencement of a Code Proceeding may not be avoided except if such payments were made for the reasons described in Section 548(a)(1).[1] Section 548(d) provides that a forward contract merchant will be deemed to have taken for value any margin payment or settlement payment it receives, thereby removing any such payment from the definition of a "constructive" fraudulent transfer as defined under Section 548(a)(2).

(b) <u>Applicability</u>. For the Code's forward contract provisions to apply, several conditions must be satisfied:

First, the transaction in question must satisfy the Code's definition of a forward contract which, in pertinent part, reads as follows:

---

[1] Section 548(a)(1) provides for avoiding transfers by the debtor if the debtor:

"made such transfer or incurred such obligation with actual intent to hinder, delay, or defraud any entity to which the debtor was or became, on or after the date that such transfer was made or such obligation was incurred, indebted..."

Stroock & Stroock & Lavan

The Members of the
Foreign Exchange Committee
April 23, 1992
Page 5

> "forward contract" means a contract. . . for
> the purchase, sale, or transfer of a commodity.
> . . or any similar good, article, service,
> right, or interest which is presently or in the
> future becomes the subject of dealing in the
> forward contract trade, or product or byproduct
> thereof, with a maturity date more than two
> days after the date the contract is entered
> into, including, but not limited to, a[n]. . .
> option. . . .

A forward contract must relate to a "commodity" as defined in
the Commodity Exchange Act ("CEA") or to "any similar good,
article, right or interest which is presently or in the future
becomes the subject of dealing in the forward contract trade, or
product or byproduct thereof."

The CEA's definition of a commodity generally includes all
"goods and articles" and all "services, rights and interests" that
are now, or in the future become, the subject of futures contracts.
7 U.S.C. § 2. When narrowly interpreted, this definition has been
construed to include all currencies which are subject to exchange-
traded futures contracts, See e.g., Commodity Future Trading
Commission ("CFTC"), Statutory Interpretation of Trading in foreign
currencies for future delivery, October 23, 1985, [1984-1986
Transfer Binder] Comm. Fut. L. Rep. (CCH) ¶ 22,750 (hereinafter the
"CFTC Statutory Interpretation") and CFTC Interpretative Letter No.
84-7 [1982-1984 Transfer Binder] Comm. Fut. L. Rep. (CCH) ¶ 22,025.
See also, CFTC and State of Georgia v. Sterling Capital Co. [1980-
1982 Transfer Binder] Comm. Fut. L. Rep. (CCH) ¶ 21,169. The scope
of the CEA's definition of commodity could be broader if currencies
are deemed to be goods or articles. This characterization seems
appropriate where foreign currencies are traded pursuant to forward
contracts, rather than used as media of exchange, because the
currencies are treated as goods by the parties to such contracts.
See Official Comment 1 (fourth paragraph) to Section 2-105 of the
New York Uniform Commercial Code ("NY-UCC"), which states that for
purposes of the NY-UCC the term "goods" is intended to cover sales
of foreign currency in which such currency is treated as a
commodity rather than as a medium of payment. See also, United
Equities Co. v. First National Bank, 374 N.Y.S.2d 937 (Sup. Ct.
1975).

Stroock & Stroock & Lavan

The Members of the
Foreign Exchange Committee
April 23, 1992
Page 6

As noted above, the Code's definition of "forward contract" covers more than just "commodities" as defined in the CEA. Any good, article, right or interest which is similar to a commodity as defined in the CEA and is the subject of forward trading is also covered. Under this language, assuming that all currencies are goods, articles, rights or interests which are similar to one another, any currency that is commonly traded in the forward markets should constitute the appropriate subject matter for a forward contract.

We note that the "Treasury Amendment" to the CEA does limit the applicability of the CEA to certain types of currency transactions.[2] However, to our knowledge, this limitation has not been interpreted by the CFTC to narrow the general meaning of the term "commodity." The CFTC's position, noted above, is that it has jurisdiction over at least all foreign currencies traded on exchanges. This position, by implication, supports the view that the scope of the CEA's commodity definition is unaffected by the Treasury Amendment. Furthermore, the CEA's definition of commodity, as incorporated into the Code, does not incorporate any such limitation.

The Code's forward contract definition also requires that such a contract provide for the "purchase, sale or transfer" of the commodity "more than two days after the contract is entered into[....]" It is our understanding that, in the wholesale or inter-dealer market, most currency options satisfy this requirement. (Options not meeting this requirement would not constitute forward contracts for purposes of the Code.)

Second, a party invoking the Code's forward contract provisions must be a "forward contract merchant" as defined in the Code. This definition contains two requirements:

---

[2]   The Treasury Amendment states that "[n]othing in this Act shall be deemed to govern or in any way be applicable to transactions in foreign currency . . . unless such transactions involve the sale thereof for future delivery on a board of trade."

Stroock & Stroock & Lavan

The Members of the
Foreign Exchange Committee
April 23, 1992
Page 7

(1) A forward contract merchant must be a person[3] whose "business consists in whole or in part" of entering into forward contracts. This requirement can be satisfied by a person whose sole business is forward contracting as well as by a person who enters into forward contracts as part of a broader business.

(2) In entering into forward contracts, a forward contract merchant must do so "as or with merchants in commodities." The most basic meaning of the term "merchant" is a person who buys and sells goods as part of its business or who holds himself out as having knowledge peculiar to the goods involved in the transaction. See, for example, the definition of "merchant" in Section 2-104 of the NY-UCC. Under these standards, any person, including a bank or other entity, which, as part of a business, buys and sells currency for actual delivery (so as to be a merchant in the physical commodity) should qualify as a commodity merchant for purposes of Section 101(25).

Further, a person who does not qualify as a commodity merchant should still be deemed a forward contract merchant for purposes of the Code if that person enters into forward contracts with a counterpart that does qualify as a commodity merchant and becomes the subject of a proceeding under the Code. As noted above, the second element of the forward contract merchant definition can be satisfied by a person who conducts forward transactions "with" a commodity merchant.

Third, a party invoking the Code's forward contract provisions must have a "contractual right" to cause the liquidation of the forward contracts it wishes to liquidate. For purposes of Section 556, a "contractual right" is broadly defined.

3. Swap Agreements.

(a) **Relevant Provisions**. The Code contains several provisions that relate specifically to "swap agreements." These provisions are similar, in purpose and scope, to the Code's forward contract provisions. Section 560 of the Code authorizes a "swap participant" to exercise its contractual right, if any, to

---

[3] As defined in the Code, "person" includes "individual, partnership, and corporation; but does not include governmental unit. . . ." See Section 101(38).

Stroock & Stroock & Lavan

The Members of the
Foreign Exchange Committee
April 23, 1992
Page 8

terminate a swap agreement with a counterpart that becomes subject
to a Code Proceeding. Again, contrary to the Code's general
provisions, Section 560 states that the right to terminate a swap
agreement and to offset or net out any termination values or
payment amounts arising under or in connection with any swap
agreement shall not be stayed, avoided or otherwise limited by
operation of any provision of this title or by order of a court or
administrative agency in any proceeding under this title. Section
362(b)(14) of the Code exempts from the automatic stay a setoff by
a swap participant of "any mutual debt and claim under or in
connection with any swap agreement that constitutes the setoff of a
claim against the debtor for payment due from the debtor under or
in connection with any swap agreement against any payment due to
the debtor from the swap participant under or in connection with
any swap agreement or against cash, securities or other property of
the debtor held by or due from such swap participant to guarantee,
secure or settle any swap agreement." A setoff of the kind
permitted by Section 362(b)(14) is excluded from the general effect
of Section 553(b) of the Code.

Section 546(g) provides that transfers made under a swap
agreement by or to a swap participant prior to commencement of a
Code Proceeding may not be avoided except if such transfers were
made for the reasons described in Section 548(a)(1). Section
548(d)(2)(D) provides that a swap participant will be deemed to
have taken for value any transfer it receives in connection with a
swap agreement, thereby removing any such transfer from the
definition of "constructive" fraudulent transfer under Section
548(a)(2).

(b) Applicability. The applicability of the Code's swap
provisions depends on the satisfaction of several conditions.

First, the transaction in question must constitute a "swap
agreement." A variety of transactions are encompassed by the
Code's definition of swap agreement, including "currency
option[s]." The definition also states that a swap agreement will
include a "master agreement" for any of these specified
transactions.

Second, the party invoking the Code's swap provisions must be
a "swap participant" which is defined as an entity that, at any
time before the filing of the petition, has an outstanding swap
agreement with the debtor[.]"

Stroock & Stroock & Lavan

The Members of the
Foreign Exchange Committee
April 23, 1992
Page 9

Third, a party invoking the Code's swap provisions must have a "contractual right" to cause the termination of those swap agreements it intends to terminate. As with Section 556, the term is broadly defined.

4. Treatment of Broker-Dealers Subject to Liquidation Under the Code or the Securities Investor Protection Act

Under Section 109 of the Code, a broker-dealer may become the subject of a Chapter 7 liquidation proceeding, but not the subject of a Chapter 11 reorganization proceeding.

Upon a broker-dealer's becoming subject to a Chapter 7 proceeding, Section 362(a) of the Code operates generally to stay all actions which may be taken by creditors of such broker-dealer. However, Section 742 of the Code provides that, notwithstanding Section 362 of the Code, the Securities Investor Protection Corporation (the "SIPC") may file an application for a protective decree under the Securities Investor Protection Act of 1970 (the "SIPA"), 15 U.S.C. § 78aaa et seq. The filing of such application stops all proceedings under the Code unless and until the application is dismissed, thereby affording the SIPC an opportunity to administer a proceeding for the liquidation of the broker-dealer. The SIPA, which was enacted in 1970, established the SIPC. 15 U.S.C. § 78ccc. The SIPC generally is responsible for providing customers of failed broker-dealers with insurance and other protections and for liquidating such broker-dealers in appropriate cases. Subject to certain limited exceptions, all persons registered as brokers or dealers under the Securities Exchange Act of 1934 are required to be members in the SIPC. See 15 U.S.C. § 78ccc(a)(2)(A).

If the SIPC determines that a member has failed or is in danger of failing to meet its financial obligations to customers, the SIPC may apply to an appropriate federal district court for a decree declaring that the member's customers are in need of protection under the SIPA. Id. § 78eee(a)(3). If the broker-dealer fails to contest the application successfully, the district court will issue a protective decree and thereafter order removal of the proceeding to the federal bankruptcy court in the same judicial district. Id. §§ 78eee(b)(1-4). All pending proceedings to reorganize, conserve or liquidate the broker-dealer or its

Stroock & Stroock & Lavan

The Members of the
Foreign Exchange Committee
April 23, 1992
Page 10

property and any other suit against a receiver, conservator or trustee of the broker-dealer or its property are stayed by the protective decree. Id. § 78eee(b)(2)(B)(i). In addition, other actions involving the broker-dealer or its property may be stayed. Id. §§ 78eee(b)(2)(B)(ii-iii).

This general power to stay actions involving the broker-dealer or its property should not, however, interfere with the ability of a person that qualifies as a forward contract merchant or a swap participant for purposes of the Code to exercise its contractual rights to liquidate its outstanding forward contracts or terminate its outstanding swap agreements with a broker-dealer that becomes the subject of a SIPA liquidation proceeding. The SIPA expressly requires that broker-dealer liquidations be conducted, to the extent consistent with the SIPA, in accordance with the requirements of specified chapters of the Code, including chapter 5. Id. § 78fff(b). Sections 556 and 560 of the Code are part of chapter 5 of the Code. Accordingly, the criteria for qualification as a forward contract merchant or swap participant in this context should be the same as those described above.

Moreover, the legislative history of Section 556 clearly indicates that a SIPA proceeding does not interfere with rights under Section 556. Congress understood that the exercise by a forward contract merchant of its contractual rights to liquidate outstanding forward contracts with an insolvent broker-dealer would be consistent with the SIPA. Section 556 was added to the Code as part of the 1982 amendments which also included Section 555 of the Code. See Pub. L. No. 97-222, 96 Stat. 235, 236-237 (1982). Section 555 generally authorizes stockbrokers, financial institutions, and securities clearing agencies to exercise their contractual rights, if any, to liquidate securities contracts. See 11 U.S.C. § 555. In contrast to Section 556, however, Section 555 also provides that the exercise of such rights may be stayed pursuant to an order issued under the provisions of the SIPA. Id. The legislative history of Section 556 notes this distinction and explains it in the following terms:

> For purposes of Section 556, a court order authorized under the provisions of the Securities Investor Protection Act of 1970, as referred to in new Section 555 and issued with respect to an entity that is both a stockbroker

Stroock & Stroock & Lavan

The Members of the
Foreign Exchange Committee
April 23, 1992
Page 11

> and a . . . forward contract merchant, would
> not affect the rights relating to . . . forward
> contracts described in Section 556. 128 Cong.
> Rec. S 8133 (daily ed. July 13, 1982) (remarks
> of Senator Dole).[4]

The "rights" referred to in the foregoing quotation are the
contractual rights of forward contract merchants to liquidate their
outstanding forward contracts with broker-dealers that become the
subject of liquidation proceedings under the SIPA. Section 560,
which was added to the Code in 1990, parallels Section 556 (rather
than Section 555) in that it does not make reference to an order
issued under the SIPA. This suggests that, as with Section 556,
the Congressional intent is that the contractual rights referred to
in Section 560 would not be affected by the issuance of such an
order. If such rights were to be subject to a SIPA order, then
Congress would have elected to follow the clear example of Section
555 by making express reference to such order in Section 560.

Therefore, if a securities broker-dealer is a party to a
"forward contract" or "swap agreement" and becomes subject to a
liquidation proceeding under the SIPA, the other party to the
contract should be able to liquidate the contract or agreement in
accordance with the respective provisions of Sections 556 and 560
of the Code, again so long as (1) there is a contractual right to
liquidate or terminate (as the case may be) if the broker-dealer
becomes insolvent and (2) the non-insolvent party qualifies as a
forward contract merchant or swap participant within the meaning of
the Code.

---

[4] The general applicability of this legislative history is not
limited by its reference to the liquidation of entities that
are both broker-dealers and forward contract merchants. As
discussed above, a broker-dealer that buys and sells currency
as a merchant, or that enters into forward currency contracts
with a commodity merchant, should be deemed a forward contract
merchant.

Stroock & Stroock & Lavan

The Members of the
Foreign Exchange Committee
April 23, 1992
Page 12

III. <u>FDIA Provisions</u>.

    1. <u>Relevant Provisions</u>. The FDIA generally empowers the FDIC
or RTC, as receiver or conservator of a depository institution, to
enforce contracts entered into by that depository institution prior
to commencement of an Insolvency Proceeding affecting that
depository institution, notwithstanding any provisions providing
for termination, default, acceleration or exercise of rights upon,
or solely by reason of, insolvency or the appointment of a
conservator or receiver. 12 U.S.C.A. §1821(e)(12). The FDIA,
however, limits this general authority in the case of "qualified
financial contracts" ("QFCs"). 12 U.S.C.A. §1821(e)(8).

    The definition of "QFC" includes the term "forward contract,"
which "has the meaning given to such term in section 101(24) of
[the Code]," and the term "swap agreement," which has a definition
in substance almost identical to that contained in the Code
(including a similar reference to master agreements). 12 U.S.C.A.
§1821(e)(8)(D)(iv) and (vi). As noted above, the current Code
definition of "forward contract" expressly includes "option" and
the FDIA definition of "swap agreement" expressly includes
"currency options purchased." We note, however, that the
definition of QFC was adopted prior to the latest amendment of the
Code's forward contract definition. Since the QFC definition does
not by its terms include subsequent amendments of the Code, it
could be argued that the FDIA incorporates only the pre-amendment
definition of forward contract, which did not expressly refer to
options. However, based on the legislative history of the pre-
amendment definition of forward contract, it would appear that
Congress intended to include option within that definition. For
example, in the Senate Report on a bill containing a definition of
forward contract identical to that originally adopted, it was
stated that the terms "purchase," "sale" and "transfer" were used
in the forward contract definition

            in their broadest sense to include, at least,
            consignments, leases, swaps, hedge transactions,
            commercial options, deposits, loans, allocated and
            unallocated transactions, or any combination thereof. S.
            Rep. No. 98-65, 98th Cong., 1st Sess. 74 (1983).

It is our belief that the foregoing reference to "commercial"
options was intended to refer to options involving commercial users
and merchants of the related commodity.

Stroock & Stroock & Lavan

The Members of the
Foreign Exchange Committee
April 23, 1992
Page 13

In connection with the latest amendment of the Code's forward
contract definition, the legislative history contains comments by
several Representatives and Senators noting that the amendment was
necessary to clarify ambiguities regarding the scope of the
definition. Accordingly, options would appear to be included
within the meaning of forward contract as used in the FDIA
regardless of whether the Code's 1990 amendments are incorporated.

2. Receivership. The FDIA provides that, except as described
below, a party to a QFC shall not be stayed or prohibited from
exercising (i) any termination or liquidation right provided for in
the QFC which arises upon an FDIC or RTC[5] receivership of the other
party, (ii) any right under a security arrangement relating to such
QFC, or (iii) any right to offset or net termination values or
other payments or transfers relating to such QFC (including under a
master agreement covering such QFCs). 12 U.S.C.A. §1821(e)(8)(A).

To facilitate the prompt resolution of a failed depository
institution, the FDIA permits the institution's receiver to
transfer to another non-defaulting depository institution, (i) all
QFCs between the failed institution and a party and its affiliates,
(ii) all unsubordinated claims of that party and its affiliates
against the failed institution under such QFCs, (iii) all claims of
the failed institution against that party and its affiliates under
such QFCs and (iv) all property securing claims under such QFCs.
12 U.S.C.A. §1812(e)(9). None of these items, nor any portion
thereof, may be transferred, unless all of such items are
transferred in their entirety. The transferee
depository institution may include bridge banks and other
institutions organized by the FDIC for purposes of effecting
purchase and assumption transactions. See FDIC and RTC Policy
Statement Regarding Qualified Financial Contracts, December 12,
1989 (the "Policy Statement"). If notice of such a transfer is
given by the receiver to such party by the close of business (New
York time) on the business day following the day on which the
receiver was appointed, then that party will be stayed from
exercising any termination, foreclosure, setoff and netting rights

---

[5] Existing legislation provides that the RTC will be appointed
as receiver for all failed depository institutions during the
3 year period beginning on August 9, 1989 and that thereafter
the FDIC will be appointed as receiver.

Stroock & Stroock & Lavan

The Members of the
Foreign Exchange Committee
April 23, 1992
Page 14

that arise upon or as a result of the receiver's appointment. <u>See</u>
12 U.S.C.A §1812(e)(10) and the Policy Statement. If a party to a
QFC acts before the notice period has lapsed and, before the end of
that period, receives a transfer notice from the receiver, then
apparently such party would be required to rescind any actions it
may have taken during that period. For this reason, a party to a
QFC is, as a practical matter, forced to wait until the close of
business on the business day following the appointment of a
receiver before it exercises any rights available as a result of
such appointment. Furthermore, according to the Policy Statement,
a receiver may satisfy this notice requirement if it has taken
steps "reasonably calculated" to provide notice to such party.

3. <u>Conservatorship</u>. Under the FDIA, a provision permitting
a party to liquidate or terminate a QFC based upon the commencement
of an FDIC or RTC conservatorship would not be enforceable against
the conservator. However, this prohibition does not affect a
party's right to terminate, foreclose and setoff if such rights are
not based on the appointment of a conservator. In this case, the
FDIA provides that a party to a QFC shall not be stayed or
prohibited from exercising (i) any termination or liquidation right
provided for in a QFC "based upon a default enforceable under
applicable noninsolvency law," (ii) any right under a security
arrangement relating to such QFC, and (iii) any right to offset or
net termination values or other payments or transfers relating to
such a QFC. §1821(e)(8)(E).

4. <u>Differences from the Code</u>. Certain differences exist
between the insolvency provisions of the FDIA and the corresponding
provisions of the Code:

First, the FDIA does not require that the party exercising its
termination, foreclosure or setoff rights be a "forward contract
merchant" or a "swap participant." Any party to a forward contract
or a swap **agreement** may avail itself of such contractual rights.

Second, unlike the Code, the FDIA contains a provision
describing the damages a party is entitled to claim if the receiver
or conservator of a depository institution repudiates a QFC. These
damages shall be measured as of the date of repudiation and
"include normal and reasonable costs of cover or other reasonable
measures of damages utilized in the industries for such contract
and agreement claims. . . ." 12 U.S.C.A. § 1821(e)(8)(E).

Stroock & Stroock & Lavan

The Members of the
Foreign Exchange Committee
April 23, 1992
Page 15

Third, the FDIA uses the term "transfer" (as defined in the
Code) with respect to all QFCs. Although the Code uses "transfer"
with respect to swap agreements, it uses other terms, such as
settlement payment and margin payment, with respect to forward
contracts.

Fourth, the FDIA imposes certain conditions to be satisfied if
an agreement is to be enforceable against a depository institution
that is in receivership. The conditions (set forth in Section
13(e) of the FDIA) have been modified in the case of QFCs.
Specifically, a QFC must be evidenced by a writing (including a
confirmation) sent by one party to the other reasonably
contemporaneously with the agreement of such parties to enter into
the QFC, the party seeking to enforce the QFC shall have relied, in
good faith, either on a resolution (or an extract thereof) provided
by the corporate secretary or assistant secretary of the depository
institution or a written representation (which may be in a master
agreement) from a vice president or other higher officer of the
depository institution and the party seeking to enforce the QFC is
able to establish by appropriate evidence the writing and such
authority.

Fifth, the definition of swap agreement under the Code
includes "currency option" while the definition of swap agreement
under the FDIA includes "currency option purchased." Accordingly,
if a Non-Defaulting Party were to rely exclusively on the
definition of swap agreement to categorize an Option as a QFC, it
would appear that only Options purchased by the Non-Defaulting
Party would be entitled to the benefits of the FDIA provisions
regarding QFCs. However, a Non-Defaulting Party may also rely on
the definition of forward contract to categorize an Option as a
QFC. The definition of forward contract in the FDIA has the same
meaning as in the Code. If the 1990 amendments to the Code are
given effect for purposes of the FDIA, then all currency options
(both purchased and sold) would be categorized as QFCs. If the
1990 amendments to the Code are not given effect, the legislative
history to the Code, as noted above, suggests that the general
wording of the original definition of forward contract was intended
to include options, with the result that options (both purchased
and sold) would be treated as QFCs for purposes of the FDIA. We
note that both the commentators and the case law support the
general proposition that "[an] independent act incorporating the
provisions of another act is not affected by amendments made to the

Stroock & Stroock & Lavan

The Members of the
Foreign Exchange Committee
April 23, 1992
Page 16

latter after the incorporation." <u>See</u> Sutherland Stat. Const.,
§ 22.35 (4th Ed).

<u>Assumptions</u>.

For purposes of the opinions hereinafter expressed, we have,
with your permission, assumed that:

1. Two Parties have entered into the Agreement and each Party
is (i) a "person" as defined under the Code who is eligible to be a
debtor under Chapter 7 or Chapter 11 of the Code or (ii) a "Federal
depository institution" or an "insured State depository
institution" as defined under the FDIA.

2. Neither Party to the Agreement will be an "insider" of the
other Party as defined under the Code or "affiliate" of the other
Party as defined under the Securities Act of 1933, as amended.

3. One of the Parties to the Agreement has become subject to
a Code Proceeding or an Insolvency Proceeding and such Party is the
Defaulting Party under the Agreement and the other Party is the
Non-Defaulting Party under the Agreement. The commencement of the
Code Proceeding or Insolvency Proceeding is the only Event of
Default that has occurred.

4. The Agreement and all Options have been duly authorized,
executed and delivered by each Party thereto (in compliance, if
such Party is a Federal depository institution or an insured State
depository institution, with Section 13(e) of the FDIA such that it
is valid obligation of the FDIC or RTC as such party's receiver),
each of the Agreement and such Options constitutes a legal, valid
and binding obligation of each such Party and, absent a Code
Proceeding or an Insolvency Proceeding having been commenced by or
against such Party, the provisions of the Agreement and the Options
would be enforceable against such Party in accordance with their
respective terms.

5. Any right or remedy that may be exercised, and any action
taken or determination made, by either Party under or in connection
with the Agreement or any Option will be exercised, taken or made
in a commercially reasonable manner and in good faith.

6. In accordance with market practice, the date on which an Option is entered into will occur at least three days prior to that Option's Settlement Date.

7. No conflicts of law statutes, rules or principles (whether of New York or any other jurisdiction) would require the application to the Agreement, the Options or any agreement referred to in Section 11.7 of the Agreement of any laws other than the law of New York State or the federal law of the United States of America.

8. Neither Party has entered into the Agreement or an Option, or has made or received or will make or receive any transfer (as defined in the Code) of an interest or has incurred or will incur any obligation in connection with such Agreement or Option, with the actual intent to hinder, delay, or defraud (i) any entity to which the Defaulting Party was or becomes indebted on or after the date that such transfer was made or received or such obligation was incurred or (ii) any conservator or receiver appointed for such Defaulting Party.

9. Any collateral securing either Party's obligations under the Agreement or with respect to any Option shall constitute a "margin payment" as defined in Section 101(34) of the Code and payment of a Premium shall constitute a "settlement payment" within the meaning of Section 101(39) of the Code.

10. Each Party is a commercial user of or a merchant handling the Currencies subject to each Option and was offered or entered into each Option solely for purposes related to its business as such.

11. With respect to each Currency subject to an Option, there is a contract of sale for future delivery traded or executed on a contract market designated pursuant to the CEA or such currency is "the subject of dealing in the forward contract trade" within the meaning of the Code's definition of "forward contract."

12. The references in Section 8 of the Agreement to a "deemed" liquidation are intended solely to indicate that the Non-Defaulting Party need not enter into an actual offsetting transaction and do not detract from the status of the provisions of Section 8 as contractual rights to "liquidate" or "terminate" within the meaning of Sections 556 and 560 of the Code.

Stroock & Stroock & Lavan

The Members of the
Foreign Exchange Committee
April 23, 1992
Page 18

Conclusions.

Based upon the foregoing discussion and assumptions, and subject to any further qualifications noted below, we are of the following opinion:

1. A discharge of two Options pursuant to Section 6 of the Agreement occurring prior to the commencement of a Code Proceeding or an Insolvency Proceeding may not be avoided by a trustee or debtor-in-possession in a Code Proceeding or by a conservator or receiver in an Insolvency Proceeding.

2. A netting of payments pursuant to Section 7 of the Agreement occurring prior to the commencement of a Code Proceeding or an Insolvency Proceeding may not be avoided by a trustee or debtor-in-possession in a Code Proceeding or by a conservator or receiver in an Insolvency Proceeding.

3. (a) Following the commencement of a Code Proceeding, the Non-Defaulting Party may exercise its rights under Section 8 in accordance with the terms thereof with respect to all Options entered into prior to such commencement.

(b) Following the close of business (New York time) on the business day following the commencement of an Insolvency Proceeding in which a receiver is appointed, the Non-Defaulting Party may exercise its rights under Section 8 in accordance with the terms thereof with respect to all Options entered into prior to such commencement, provided that the receiver has not given the Non-Defaulting Party a notice of transfer with respect to (i) all QFCs between the failed institution and a party and its affiliates, (ii) all unsubordinated claims of that party and its affiliates against the failed institution under such QFCs, (iii) all claims of the failed institution against that party and its affiliates under such QFCs and (iv) all property securing claims under such QFCs.

With respect to opinion paragraphs 3(a) and (b) above, we express no opinion regarding (1) whether the Non-Defaulting Party may enforce its rights under Section 8 of the Agreement with respect to the amounts due under clause (d) of paragraph 8.1(i) of the Agreement, (2) whether the Non-Defaulting Party may enforce its rights to convert amounts due to it in U.S. dollars into its Base Currency if that currency is not U.S. dollars, (3) whether the Non-

Stroock & Stroock & Lavan

The Members of the
Foreign Exchange Committee
April 23, 1992
Page 19

Defaulting Party may enforce its rights to collect interest
accruing on or after the commencement of a Code Proceeding or an
Insolvency Proceeding or interest accruing at a rate in excess of
then current market rates and (4) whether the Non-Defaulting Party
may enforce its rights to collect amounts due to it under paragraph
8.4 of the Agreement.

    This opinion is solely for the benefit of the addressees
hereof as of the date hereof and may not be relied upon in any
manner by any other person or entity.

            Very truly yours,

            Stroock & Stroock & Lavan

            STROOCK & STROOCK & LAVAN

THE BRITISH BANKERS' ASSOCIATION

AND

THE FOREIGN EXCHANGE COMMITTEE

INTERNATIONAL CURRENCY OPTIONS MARKET
(ICOM)
MASTER AGREEMENT AND GUIDE

April 1992

PREFACE

The International Currency Options Market (ICOM) Master Agreement is intended to serve as a model foreign exchange options contract in the United States and the United Kingdom. The agreement defines key terms and addresses formation, exercise, and settlement procedures for foreign exchange options as well as procedures for the event of default. This model agreement will provide a basis upon which dealers operating in the United States and the United Kingdom can trade foreign currency options with a wide range of dealing counterparties on both sides of the Atlantic without the need to negotiate costly bilateral agreements. Where necessary the agreement can also be modified to allow the terms to be extended to dealers' customers.

The agreement and the accompanying guide were prepared by a group of attorneys working under the auspices of the Foreign Exchange Committee in New York in conjunction with the British Bankers' Association and represents an important first step in cooperation between financial centers. Work in the United Kingdom was carried out by a working party of the British Bankers' Association. The Foreign Exchange Committee in New York sponsored the work of a group of attorneys in the United States, which included the following members:

> Ruth Ainslie (Bankers Trust)
> Michael Bannon (Chase Manhattan Bank)
> Marc Baum (Merrill Lynch)
> Rakesh Bhala (Federal Reserve Bank of New York)
> Joshua A. Cohn, Esq. (Dai-ichi Kangyo Bank)
> John Emert (Citibank)
> Laurie Ferber (Goldman, Sachs)
> Margaret Grieve (Chase Manhattan Bank)
> Marjorie Gross (Chemical Bank)
> Douglas Harris (Morgan Guaranty Trust)
> Jess Hungate (The Royal Bank of Canada)
> Philip Levy (Manufacturers Hanover Trust)
> Jeffrey Lillien (First National Bank of Chicago)
> Ernest T. Patrikis (Federal Reserve Bank of New York)
> Jim Roselle (First National Bank of Chicago)
> Garland D. Sims (Chase Manhattan Bank)

INTERNATIONAL CURRENCY OPTIONS MARKET

MASTER AGREEMENT

MASTER AGREEMENT dated as of _____, 19__, by and between _____, a _____, and _____, a _____.

1.   DEFINITIONS

In this Agreement, unless otherwise required by the context, the following terms shall have the following meanings:

"American Style Option"	An Option which may be exercised on any Business Day up to and including the Expiration Time;
"Base Currency"	The currency specified as such by a Party in Part IV of the Schedule hereto;
"Base Currency Rate"	For any day, the average rate at which overnight deposits in the Base Currency are offered by major banks in the London interbank market as of 11:00 a.m. (London time) on such day or such other rate as shall be agreed by the Parties, in either case as determined in good faith by the Non-Defaulting Party;
"Business Day"	For purposes of: (i) Section 4.2 hereof, a day which is a Local Banking Day for the applicable Designated Office of the Buyer; (ii) Section 5.1 hereof and the definition of American Style Option and Exercise Date, a day which is a Local Banking Day for the applicable Designated Office of the Seller; (iii) the definition of Event of Default, a day which is a Local Banking Day for the Non-Defaulting Party; and (iv) any other provision hereof, a day which is a Local Banking Day for the applicable Designated Office of both Parties; provided, however, that neither Saturday nor Sunday shall be considered a Business Day hereunder for any purpose;

"Buyer"	The owner of an Option;
"Call"	An option entitling, but not obligating, the Buyer to purchase from the Seller at the Strike Price a specified quantity of the Call Currency;
"Call Currency"	The currency agreed as such at the time an Option is entered into;
"Confirmation"	A confirmation of an Option substantially in the form of <u>Exhibit I</u> hereto, which confirmation shall be in writing (which shall include telex or other electronic means from which it is possible to produce a hard copy);
"Currency Pair"	The two currencies which may be potentially exchanged upon the exercise of an Option, one of which shall be the Put Currency and the other the Call Currency;
"Designated Office"	As to either Party, the office or offices specified on Part I of the Schedule hereto and any other office specified from time to time by one Party and agreed to by the other as an amendment hereto as a Designated Office on Part I of the Schedule hereto;
"European Style" Option"	An Option for which Notice of Exercise may be given only on the Option's Expiration Date up to and including the Expiration Time, unless otherwise agreed;
"Event of Default"	The occurrence of any of the following with respect to a Party (the "Defaulting Party"): (i) the Defaulting Party shall default in any payment hereunder (including, but not limited to, a Premium payment) to the other Party (the "Non-Defaulting Party") with respect to any Option and such failure shall continue for two (2) Business Days after written notice of non-payment by the Non-Defaulting Party; (ii) the Defaulting Party shall commence a voluntary case or other proceeding seeking liquidation, reorganization or other relief with respect to itself or to its debts under any bankruptcy, insolvency or similar law, or seeking the appointment of a trustee, receiver, liquidator, conservator, administrator, custodian or other similar official (each, a "Custodian") of it or any substantial part of its assets; or shall take

any corporate action to authorize any of the foregoing; (iii) an involuntary case or other proceeding shall be commenced against the Defaulting Party seeking liquidation, reorganization or other relief with respect to it or its debts under any bankruptcy, insolvency or other similar law or seeking the appointment of a Custodian of it or any substantial part of its assets; (iv) the Defaulting Party is bankrupt or insolvent; (v) the Defaulting Party shall otherwise be unable to pay its debts as they become due; (vi) the failure by the Defaulting Party to give adequate assurances of its ability to perform its obligations with respect to an Option within two (2) Business Days of a written request to do so when the Non-Defaulting Party has reasonable grounds for insecurity; (vii) the Defaulting Party or any Custodian acting on behalf of the Defaulting Party shall disaffirm or repudiate any Option; or (viii) any representation or warranty made or deemed made pursuant to Section 3 of this Agreement by the Defaulting Party shall prove to have been false or misleading in any material respect as at the time it was made or given or deemed made or given and the Non-Defaulting Party shall have given the Defaulting Party one (1) Business Day's prior written notice thereof;

"Exercise Date"   The Business Day on which a Notice of Exercise received by the applicable Designated Office of the Seller becomes effective pursuant to Section 5.1;

"Expiration Date"   The date specified as such in a Confirmation;

"Expiration Time"   The latest time on the Expiration Date on which the Seller must accept a Notice of Exercise as specified in a Confirmation;

"In-the-money   (i) In the case of a Call, the excess of
    Amount"   the Spot Price over the Strike Price, multiplied by the aggregate amount of the Call Currency to be purchased under the Call, where both prices are quoted in terms of the amount of the Put Currency to be paid for one unit of the Call Currency; and (ii) in the case of a Put, the excess of the Strike Price over the Spot Price, multiplied by the aggregate amount of the Put Currency to be

sold under the Put, where both prices are quoted in terms of the amount of the Call Currency to be paid for one unit of the Put Currency;

"Local Banking Day"
For any currency or Party, a day on which commercial banks in the principal banking center of the country of issuance of such currency or in the location of the applicable Designated Office of such Party, respectively, are not authorized or required by law to close;

"Notice of Exercise"
Telex, telephonic or other electronic notification (excluding facsimile transmission), providing assurance of receipt, given by the Buyer prior to or at the Expiration Time, of the exercise of an Option, which notification shall be irrevocable;

"Option"
A Put or a Call, as the case may be, including any unexpired Put or Call previously entered into by the Parties, which shall be or become subject to this Agreement unless otherwise agreed;

"Parties"
The parties to this Agreement; and the term "Party" shall mean whichever of the Parties is appropriate in the context in which such expression may be used;

"Premium"
The purchase price of the Option as agreed upon by the Parties, and payable by the Buyer to the Seller thereof;

"Premium Payment Date"
The date specified as such in the Confirmation;

"Put"
An option entitling, but not obligating, the Buyer to sell to the Seller at the Strike Price a specified quantity of the Put Currency;

"Put Currency"
The currency agreed as such at the time an Option is entered into;

"Seller"
The Party granting an Option;

"Settlement Date"   In respect of: (i) an American Style Option, the Spot Date of the Currency Pair on the Exercise Date of such Option; and (ii) a European Style Option, the Spot Date of the Currency Pair on the Expiration Date of such Option;

"Spot Date"   The spot delivery day for the relevant Currency Pair as generally used by the foreign exchange market;

"Spot Price"   The price at the time at which such price is to be determined for foreign exchange transactions in the relevant Currency Pair for value on the Spot Date, as determined in good faith: (i) by the Seller, for purposes of Section 5 hereof; and (ii) by the Non-Defaulting Party, for purposes of Section 8 hereof;

"Strike Price"   The price specified in a Confirmation at which the Currency Pair may be exchanged.

2.   GENERAL

2.1   The Parties (through their respective Designated Offices) may enter into Options (neither being obliged to do so) for such Premiums, with such Expiration Dates, at such Strike Prices and for the purchase or sale of such quantities of such currencies, as may be agreed subject to the terms hereof.

2.2   Each Option shall be governed by the terms and conditions set forth in this Master Agreement and in the Confirmation relating to such Option. Each Confirmation shall supplement and form a part of this Master Agreement and shall be read and construed as one with this Master Agreement and with each other Confirmation, so that this Master Agreement and all Confirmations, Schedules and amendments hereto constitute a single agreement between the Parties (collectively referred to as this "Agreement"). The Parties acknowledge that all Options are entered into in reliance upon such fact, it being understood that the Parties would not otherwise enter into any Option.

2.3   Options shall be promptly confirmed by the Parties by Confirmations exchanged by mail, telex, facsimile or other electronic means. Unless either Party objects to the terms contained in any Confirmation within the earlier of (i) the time period recognized by local market practice or (ii) three (3) Business Days of receipt thereof, the terms of such Confirmation shall be deemed correct absent manifest error, unless a corrected Confirmation is sent by a Party within such three day period, in which case the Party receiving such corrected Confirmation shall have three (3) Business Days after receipt thereof to object to the terms contained in such corrected Confirmation. Failure by either Party to issue a Confirmation shall not alter the rights and obligations of either Party under an Option to which the Parties have agreed. In the event of any conflict between the terms of a Confirmation and this Agreement, such Confirmation shall prevail, except for purposes of this Section 2.3 and Section 6 hereof.

2.4   Neither Party may assign its rights nor delegate its obligations under any Option to a third party without the prior written consent of the other Party.

3.   <u>REPRESENTATIONS AND WARRANTIES; CONTRACTUAL STATUS</u>

Each Party represents and warrants to the other Party as of the date hereof and as of the date of each Option that: (i) it has authority to enter into this Master Agreement and such Option; (ii) the persons executing this Master Agreement and entering into such Option on its behalf have been duly authorized to do so; (iii) this Master Agreement and such Option are binding upon it and enforceable against it in accordance with their respective terms and do not and will not violate the terms of any agreements to which such Party is bound; (iv) no Event of Default, or event which, with notice or lapse of time or both, would constitute an Event of Default has occurred and is continuing with respect to it; and (v) it acts as principal in entering into and exercising each and every Option.

4.   <u>THE PREMIUM</u>

4.1   Unless otherwise agreed in writing by the Parties, the Premium related to an Option shall be paid on its Premium Payment Date.

4.2   If any Premium is not received on the Premium Payment Date, the Seller may elect either: (i) to accept a late payment of such Premium; (ii) to give written notice of such non-payment and, if such payment shall not be received within two (2) Business Days of such notice, treat the related Option as void; or (iii) to give written notice of such non-payment and, if such payment shall not be received within two (2) Business Days of such notice, treat such non-payment as an Event of

Default under clause (i) of the definition of Event of Default. If the Seller elects to act under either clause (i) or (ii) of the preceding sentence, the Buyer shall pay all out-of-pocket costs and actual damages incurred in connection with such unpaid or late Premium or void Option, including, without limitation, interest on such Premium in the same currency as such Premium at the then prevailing market rate and any other costs or expenses incurred by the Seller in covering its obligations (including, without limitation, a delta hedge) with respect to such Option.

5.   <u>EXERCISE AND SETTLEMENT OF OPTIONS</u>

5.1   The Buyer may exercise an Option by delivery to the Seller of a Notice of Exercise. Subject to Section 5.4 hereof, if an Option has not been exercised prior to or at the Expiration Time, it shall expire and become void and of no effect. Any Notice of Exercise shall (unless otherwise agreed): (i) if received prior to 3:00 p.m. on a Business Day, be effective upon receipt thereof by the Seller; and (ii) if received after 3:00 p.m. on a Business Day, be effective only as of the opening of business of the Seller on the first Business Day subsequent to its receipt.

5.2   An exercised Option shall settle on its Settlement Date. Subject to Section 5.3 and 5.4 hereof, on the Settlement Date, the Buyer shall pay the Put Currency to the Seller for value on the Settlement Date and the Seller shall pay the Call Currency to the Buyer for value on the Settlement Date.

5.3   An Option shall be settled at its In-the-money Amount if so agreed by the Parties at the time such Option is entered into. In such case, the In-the-money Amount shall be determined based upon the Spot Price at the time of exercise or as soon thereafter as possible. The sole obligations of the Parties with respect to such Option shall be to deliver or receive the In-the-money Amount of such Option on the Settlement Date.

5.4   Unless the Seller is otherwise instructed by the Buyer, if an Option has an In-the-money Amount at its Expiration Time that equals or exceeds the product of (x) 1% of the Strike Price and (y) the amount of the Call or Put Currency, as appropriate, then the Option shall be deemed automatically exercised. In such case, the Seller may elect to settle such Option either in accordance with Section 5.2 of this Agreement or by payment to the Buyer on the Settlement Date for such Option of the In-the-money Amount, as determined at the

Expiration Time or as soon thereafter as possible. In the latter case, the sole obligations of the Parties with respect to such Option shall be to deliver or receive the In-the-money Amount of such Option on the Settlement Date. The Seller shall notify the Buyer of its election of the method of settlement of an automatically exercised Option as soon as practicable after the Expiration Time.

5.5 Unless otherwise agreed by the Parties, an Option may be exercised only in whole.

6. <u>DISCHARGE AND TERMINATION OF OPTIONS</u>

Unless otherwise agreed, any Call Option or any Put Option written by a Party will automatically be terminated and discharged, in whole or in part, as applicable, against a Call Option or a Put Option, respectively, written by the other Party, such termination and discharge to occur automatically upon the payment in full of the last Premium payable in respect of such Options; <u>provided</u> <u>that</u> such termination and discharge may only occur in respect of Options:

(a) each being with respect to the same Put Currency and the same Call Currency;

(b) each having the same Expiration Date and Expiration Time;

(c) each being of the same style, i.e. either both being American Style Options or both being European Style Options;

(d) each having the same Strike Price; and

(e) neither of which shall have been exercised by delivery of a Notice of Exercise;

and, upon the occurrence of such termination and discharge, neither Party shall have any further obligation to the other Party in respect of the relevant Options or, as the case may be, parts thereof so terminated and discharged. In the case of a partial termination and discharge (i.e., where the relevant Options are for different amounts of the Currency Pair), the remaining portion of the Option which is partially discharged and terminated shall continue to be an Option for all purposes of this Agreement, including this Section 6.

7.   <u>PAYMENT NETTING</u>

7.1   If, on any date, and unless otherwise mutually agreed
        by the Parties, Premiums would otherwise be payable
        hereunder in the same currency between respective
        Designated Offices of the Parties, then, on such date,
        each Party's obligation to make payment of any such
        Premium will be automatically satisfied and discharged
        and, if the aggregate Premium(s) that would otherwise
        have been payable by such Designated Office of one
        Party exceeds the aggregate Premium(s) that would
        otherwise have been payable by such Designated Office
        of the other Party, replaced by an obligation upon the
        Party by whom the larger aggregate Premium(s) would
        have been payable to pay the other Party the excess of
        the larger aggregate Premium(s) over the smaller
        aggregate Premium(s).

7.2   If, on any date, and unless otherwise mutually agreed
        by the Parties, amounts other than Premium payments
        would otherwise be payable hereunder in the same
        currency between respective Designated Offices of the
        Parties, then, on such date, each Party's obligation to
        make payment of any such amount will be automatically
        satisfied and discharged and, if the aggregate amount
        that would otherwise have been payable by such
        Designated Office of one Party exceeds the aggregate
        amount that would otherwise have been payable by such
        Designated Office of the other Party, replaced by an
        obligation upon the Party by whom the larger aggregate
        amount would have been payable to pay the other Party
        the excess of the larger aggregate amount over the
        smaller aggregate amount.

8.   <u>DEFAULT</u>

8.1   If an Event of Default has occurred and is continuing,
        then the Non-Defaulting Party shall have the right to
        liquidate and/or to deem to liquidate all, but not less
        than all (except to the extent that in the good faith
        opinion of the Non-Defaulting Party certain of such
        Options may not be liquidated under applicable law),
        outstanding Options by notice to the Defaulting Party.
        The previous sentence notwithstanding, in the case of
        an Event of Default specified in clauses (ii), (iii) or
        (iv) of the definition thereof, such liquidation and/or
        deemed liquidation shall be automatic as to all
        outstanding Options, except where the relevant
        voluntary or involuntary case or other proceeding or
        bankruptcy or insolvency giving rise to such Event of
        Default is governed by a system of law which contains
        express provisions enabling close-out in the manner

described in clauses (i) to (iv) below (or a manner equivalent thereto) to take place after the occurrence of the relevant Event of Default in the absence of automatic liquidation. Such liquidation and/or deemed liquidation shall be effected by:

(i)   closing out each such Option at the time of liquidation so that each such Option is cancelled and market damages for each Party are calculated equal to the aggregate of (a) with respect to each Option purchased by such Party, the current market premium for such Option, (b) with respect to each Option sold by such Party, any unpaid Premium and, to the extent permitted by applicable law, interest on any unpaid Premium in the same currency as such Premium at the then prevailing market rate, (c) with respect to any exercised Option, any unpaid amount due in settlement of such Option and, to the extent permitted by applicable law, interest thereon from the applicable Settlement Date to the day of close-out at the average rate at which overnight deposits in the currency in which such unpaid amount was due are offered by major banks in the London interbank market as of 11:00 a.m. (London time) on each such day plus 1% per annum, and (d) any costs or expenses incurred by the Non-Defaulting Party in covering its obligations (including a delta hedge) with respect to such Option, all as determined in good faith by the Non-Defaulting Party;

(ii)   converting any damages calculated in accordance with clause (i) above in a currency other than the Non-Defaulting Party's Base Currency into such Base Currency at the Spot Price at which, at the time of liquidation, the Non-Defaulting Party could enter into a contract in the foreign exchange market to buy the Base Currency in exchange for such currency;

(iii) netting such damage payments with respect to each Party so that all such amounts are netted to a single liquidated amount payable by one Party to the other Party as a settlement payment; and

(iv) setting off the net payment calculated in accordance with clause (iii) above which the Non-Defaulting Party owes to the Defaulting Party, if any, and, at the option of the Non-Defaulting Party, any margin or other collateral ("Margin") held by the Non-Defaulting Party (including the liquidated value of any non-cash Margin) in respect of the Defaulting Party's obligations hereunder against the net payment calculated in accordance with clause (iii) above which the Defaulting Party owes to the Non-Defaulting Party, if any, and, at the option of the Non-Defaulting Party, any Margin held by the Defaulting Party (including the liquidated value of any non-cash Margin) in respect of the Non-Defaulting Party's obligations hereunder; <u>provided</u>, that, for purposes of such set-off, any Margin denominated in a currency other the Non-Defaulting Party's Base Currency shall be converted into such currency at the rate specified in clause (ii) above.

8.2   The net amount payable by one Party to the other Party pursuant to the provisions of Section 8.1 above shall be paid by the close of business on the Business Day following such liquidation and/or deemed liquidation of all such Options (converted as required by applicable law into any other currency, any such costs of conversion to be borne by, and deducted from any payment to, the Defaulting Party). To the extent permitted by applicable law, any amounts owed but not paid when due under this Section 8 shall bear interest at the Base Currency Rate plus 1% per annum (or, if conversion is required by applicable law into some other currency, either (x) the average rate at which overnight deposits in such other currency are offered by major banks in the London interbank market as of 11:00 a.m. (London time) plus 1% per annum or (y) such other rate as may be prescribed by such applicable law) for each day for which such amount remains unpaid.

8.3   Without prejudice to the foregoing, so long as a Party shall be in default in payment or performance to the other Party hereunder or under any Option and the Non-Defaulting Party has not exercised its rights under this Section 8, or during the pendency of a reasonable request to a Party for adequate assurances of its ability to perform its obligations hereunder or under any Option, the other Party may, at its election and without penalty, suspend its obligation to perform hereunder or under any Option.

8.4   The Party required to make a payment to the other Party pursuant to Sections 8.1 and 8.2 above shall pay to the other Party all out-of-pocket expenses incurred by such other Party (including fees and disbursements of counsel and time charges of attorneys who may be employees of such other Party) in connection with any reasonable collection or other enforcement proceedings related to such required payment.

8.5   The Parties agree that the amounts recoverable under this Section 8 are a reasonable pre-estimate of loss and not a penalty. Such amounts are payable for the loss of bargain and the loss of protection against future risks and, except as otherwise provided in this Agreement, neither Party will be entitled to recover any additional damages as a consequence of such losses.

8.6   The Non-Defaulting Party's rights under this Section 8 shall be in addition to, and not in limitation or exclusion of, any other rights which the Non-Defaulting Party may have (whether by agreement, operation of law or otherwise), and the Non-Defaulting Party shall have a general right of set-off with respect to all amounts owed by each Party to the other Party, whether due or not due (provided that any amount not due at the time of such set-off shall be discounted to present value in a commercially reasonable manner by the Non-Defaulting Party).

9.   <u>PARTIES TO RELY ON THEIR OWN EXPERTISE</u>

Each Option shall be deemed to have been entered into by each Party in reliance only upon its judgment. Neither Party holds out itself as advising, or any of its employees or agents as having its authority to advise, the other Party as to whether or not it should enter into any such Option (whether as Seller or Buyer) or as to any subsequent actions relating thereto or on any other commercial matters concerned with any currency options or transactions, and neither Party shall have any responsibility or liability whatsoever in respect of any advice of this nature given, or views expressed, by it or any of such persons to the other Party, whether or not such advice is given or such views are expressed at the request of the other Party.

10.   <u>ILLEGALITY, IMPOSSIBILITY AND FORCE MAJEURE</u>

If either Party is prevented from or hindered or delayed by reason of force majeure or act of State in the delivery or payment of any currency in respect of an Option or if it becomes unlawful or impossible for either Party to make or receive any payment in respect of an Option, then the Party for whom such performance has been prevented, hindered or delayed or has become illegal or impossible shall promptly give notice thereof to the other Party and either Party may, by notice to the other Party, require the liquidation and close-out of each affected Option in accordance with the provisions of Section 8 hereof and, for such purposes, the Party unaffected by such force majeure, act of State, illegality or impossibility shall be considered the Non-Defaulting Party and, for purposes of this Section 10, such Non-Defaulting Party shall perform the calculation required under Section 8.

11.   <u>MISCELLANEOUS</u>

11.1   Unless otherwise specified, the times referred to herein shall in each case refer to the local time of the relevant Designated Office of the Seller of the relevant Option.

11.2   Unless otherwise specified, all notices, instructions and other communications to be given to a Party hereunder shall be given to the address, telex (if confirmed by the appropriate answerback), facsimile (confirmed if requested) or telephone number and to the individual or Department specified by such Party in Part II of the Schedule attached hereto. Unless otherwise specified, any notice, instruction or other communication, shall be effective upon receipt if given in accordance with this Section 11.2.

11.3   All payments to be made hereunder shall be made in same day (or immediately available) and freely transferable funds and, unless otherwise specified, shall be delivered to such office of such bank and in favor of such account as shall be specified by the Party entitled to receive such payment in Part III of the Schedule attached hereto or as specified by such Party by notice given in accordance with Section 11.2. Time shall be of the essence in this Agreement.

11.4   The receipt or recovery by either Party of any amount in respect of an obligation of the other Party in a currency other than the Base Currency (other than receipt by the Defaulting Party pursuant to Sections 8.1 and 8.2 of a payment in the Non-Defaulting Party's Base Currency), whether pursuant to a judgment of any court or pursuant to Section 8 hereof, shall discharge such obligation only to the extent that, on the first day on which such party is open for business immediately following such receipt, the recipient shall be able, in accordance with normal banking procedures, to purchase the Base Currency with the currency received. If the amount of the Base Currency so purchasable shall be less than the original Base Currency amount calculated pursuant to Section 8 hereof, the obligor shall, as a separate obligation and notwithstanding any judgment of any court, indemnify the recipient against any loss sustained by it. The obligor shall in any event indemnify the recipient against any costs incurred by it in making any such purchase of the Base Currency.

11.5 The Parties agree that each may electronically record all telephonic conversations between them and that any such recordings may be submitted in evidence to any court or in any proceeding for the purpose of establishing any matters pertinent to any Option.

11.6 This Agreement shall supersede any other agreement between the Parties with respect to the subject matter hereof and all outstanding Options between the Parties on the date hereof shall be subject hereto, unless otherwise expressly agreed by the Parties.

11.7 A margin agreement between the Parties may apply to obligations governed by this Agreement. If the Parties have executed a margin agreement, such margin agreement shall be subject to the terms hereof and is hereby incorporated by reference herein. In the event of any conflict between a margin agreement and this Agreement, this Agreement shall prevail, except for any provision in such margin agreement in respect of governing law.

11.8 In the event any one or more of the provisions contained in this Agreement should be held invalid, illegal or unenforceable in any respect, the validity, legality and enforceability of the remaining provisions contained herein shall not in any way be affected or impaired thereby. The Parties shall endeavor in good faith negotiations to replace the invalid, illegal or unenforceable provisions with valid provisions the economic effect of which comes as close as possible to that of the invalid, illegal or unenforceable provisions.

12.   LAW AND JURISDICTION

12.1 This Agreement shall be governed by, and construed in accordance with, the laws of [the State of New York] [England and Wales] without giving effect to conflicts of law principles.

12.2 With respect to any suit, action or proceedings ("Proceedings") relating to any Option or this Agreement, each Party irrevocably (i) [submits to the non-exclusive jurisdiction of the courts of the State of New York and the United States District Court located in the Borough of Manhattan in New York City,] [agrees for the benefit of the other Party that the courts of England shall have jurisdiction to determine any Proceeding and irrevocably submits to the jurisdiction of the English courts] and (ii) waives any objection which it may have at any time to the laying of venue of any Proceedings brought in any such court, waives any claim that such Proceedings have been brought in an inconvenient forum and further waives the right to object, with respect to such Proceedings, that such court does not have jurisdiction over such Party. Nothing in this Agreement precludes either Party from bringing Proceedings in any other jurisdiction nor will the bringing of Proceedings in any one or more jurisdictions preclude the bringing of Proceedings in any other jurisdiction.

12.3   Each Party hereby irrevocably waives any and all right to trial by jury in any legal proceeding arising out of or relating to this Agreement or any Option.

12.4   Each Party hereby irrevocably waives, to the fullest extent permitted by applicable law, with respect to itself and its revenues and assets (irrespective of their use or intended use), all immunity on the grounds of sovereignty or other similar grounds from (i) suit, (ii) jurisdiction of any court, (iii) relief by way of injunction, order for specific performance or for recovery of property, (iv) attachment of its assets (whether before or after judgment) and (v) execution or enforcement of any judgment to which it or its revenues or assets might otherwise be entitled in any Proceedings (as defined in Section 12.2 hereof) in the courts of any jurisdiction and irrevocably agrees, to the extent permitted by applicable law, that it will not claim any such immunity in any Proceedings.

IN WITNESS WHEREOF, the Parties have caused this Agreement to be duly executed by their respective authorized officers as of the date first written above.

                                    _____

By:_____

       Title:

                                      _____

By:_____

       Title:

EXHIBIT I

CURRENCY OPTION CONFIRMATION

To:_____

_____ hereby confirms the following
terms of a currency option:

Reference:

Trade Date (DD/MMM/YY):

Buyer:

Seller:

Option Style (European or American):

Option Type (Put or Call):

Put Currency and Amount:

Call Currency and Amount:

Strike Price:

Expiration Date (DD/MMM/YY):

Expiration Time:

Expiration Settlement Date (DD/MMM/YY):

Premium:

Price:

Premium Payment Date (DD/MMM/YY):

Premium Payment Instructions:

Other terms and conditions:

This Option is subject to the International Currency Options
Market Master Agreement between [us] [_____ and
_____, dated as of _____, 19__].

Please confirm to us by return telex, mail, facsimile or other
electronic transmission that the above details are correct.

SCHEDULE

Part I: Designated Offices

        Each of the following shall be a Designated Office:

Part II: Notices

        Address
        Telephone Number
        Telex Number
        Facsimile Number
        Name of Individual or Department to whom Notices are to be
sent

Part III: Payment Instructions

        Name of Bank and Office, Account Number and Reference with
        respect to relevant Currencies

Part IV: Base Currency

INTERNATIONAL CURRENCY OPTIONS MARKET
MASTER AGREEMENT GUIDE

I. INTRODUCTION

Following the publication of "LICOM Terms" in August, 1985, which were intended to reflect and to encourage good market practice and to reduce the need for specific legal documentation between participants in the London interbank over-the-counter currency options market, the market continued to evolve internationally. By 1989, it became apparent that the original terms did not adequately reflect market practice. In particular, the number and diversity of market participants had increased substantially, and new practices had been adopted, such as volatility quoting, which were not envisaged in 1985.

Accordingly, in May, 1989, the British Bankers' Association ("BBA") re-established, through its Foreign Exchange Committee, a Working Party to liaise with market interests, including the Foreign Exchange and Currency Deposits Brokers' Association, with a view to updating the 1985 terms and to provide guidance as to market practice. The Working Party was comprised of members representing a broad spectrum of international financial institutions. In addition, emphasis was placed on the international acceptance of the revised terms, and a new title was developed: International Currency Options Market Terms and Conditions - "ICOM Terms". The Bank of England was represented as an observer on the Working Party.

During this same period, a similar effort was underway in the United States. In early 1986, The (U.S.) Foreign Exchange Committee issued draft Recommended Terms and Conditions For Dealing in the United States Market - "NYICOM Terms". (The Foreign Exchange Committee is an advisory committee, independent of the Federal Reserve Bank of New York (the "FRBNY"), but sponsored by it, and its members are participants in the interdealer foreign exchange market.) The NYICOM Terms, which were based upon, and substantially similar to, the original LICOM Terms, were intended to reflect general market practice in the United States. Over a period of time, the NYICOM Terms were retitled "USICOM Terms", for United States Interbank Currency Options Market Terms.

Although the USICOM Terms generally reflected market practices in the U.S., they did not address the increasingly important issue of counterparty credit risk and, in particular, the substantive rights and obligations of the parties upon (i) the nonperformance of an option by one of the parties, (ii) the insolvency of one of the parties or (iii) the occurrence of force majeure or some other event which makes it illegal or impossible for one of the parties to perform. The USICOM Terms also did not provide a method for closing out and liquidating options upon the occurrence of one of these events. In 1990, the USICOM Terms were revised into a draft form of master agreement, which attempted to reflect market practice with respect to the formation, exercise and settlement of options (including such matters as net cash settlement and automatic exercise), as well as set forth the substantive legal rights and obligations of the parties.

In the summer of 1990, representatives of the Working Party and The Foreign Exchange Committee met to resolve the differences between the ICOM Terms and the USICOM Terms and to develop a single document for use in the international over-the-counter foreign currency options market. The result is the attached form of International Currency Options Market Master Agreement (the "Master Agreement"), which should be considered as reflective of normal market practice for international interdealer transactions and which could be adopted by market participants as the standard agreement for dealing in this market.

The Working Party and the Foreign Exchange Committee have confined themselves to practices in the interbank and professional markets, and have not been directly concerned with the terms and conditions upon which individual institutions may choose to deal with their clients (although the Master Agreement could be used in such circumstances). Banks and other professional market participants are, of course, free to deal with each other on the basis of other terms or agreements if they wish, but should consider themselves under an obligation to make clear to each other in what way their terms or agreements differ from the Master Agreement.

The following sections of this Guide to the Master Agreement are intended (i) to provide further clarification of normal market practice and (ii) to explain various provisions of the Master Agreement and the significance of their inclusion in the Master Agreement. Therefore, this Guide should be read carefully. Though the Master Agreement does, and is intended to, stand on its own as a legal document, the Guide provides important commentary on current market practice and the Master Agreement.

II.   MARKET PRACTICE

A.   Price Quotation

There are two generally accepted methods of price quotation - Premium and Volatility. In each case, the counterparties shall agree upon:

> Option Style (American or European),
> Call Currency,
> Put Currency and Amount,
> Expiration Date,
> Expiration Time,
> Premium Payment Date,
> Settlement Date, and
> Strike Price.

Counterparties should also agree upon whether they are entering into a contemporaneous foreign exchange transaction (commonly known as a Delta hedge), although such transaction would not be subject to the Master Agreement.

Price quotation should be in the form of either:

(a)   a <u>Premium</u>, where the counterparties agree upon the above terms and on how the premium price should be expressed, e.g. as a percentage of either currency or as one currency in terms of the other (it is also necessary to agree upon a spot rate in the case of a Premium quotation where a Delta hedge forms part of the trade); or

(b)   <u>Volatility</u>, where the counterparties agree upon the above terms and that the Volatility be expressed as a percentage per annum. It is the factor which, when combined with the Spot Rate, interest factors of the Currency Pair concerned, the days to expiry of the Option and the Strike Price, is used to compute the Premium.

An Option is not a legally binding contract until, among other things, the Premium has been agreed. Therefore, to ensure the ongoing viability of the Volatility method of dealing, it is incumbent on the counterparties to agree on the Premium Price as soon as possible, and it is imperative that the calculation of the Premium accurately reflect the agreed Volatility and market conditions at the time Volatility was agreed. In the event of a dispute that cannot be resolved between the counterparties through good faith negotiation (or, in the first instance, by reference to recordings of conversations between the parties during which pricing was discussed), prompt reference to mutually acceptable third-party arbitration is suggested. Market participants should note that, as Premium calculation differences are more likely to occur in transactions involving American Style Options, due care should be exercised in entering into such Options.

In addition, when trading Volatility, it is necessary that a spot rate be agreed upon by the counterparties immediately upon entering into the Option. This forms the basis of the underlying foreign exchange transaction (Delta hedge), if any.

B.   Quotation of Expiration Dates

Generally, there are two methods for quotation of Expiration Dates - quotation of straight Expiration Dates and quotation of Expiration Dates by calendar month.

Straight Expiration Dates

An Option quoted for straight periods (such as 1 month, 2 months etc.) has as its final Expiration Date the date preceding the equivalent forward date (as dealt in the interdealer foreign exchange market) that will result in settlement on the forward date, if it is exercised on the Expiration Date. If there is more than one solution, the furthest date from the Trade Date will be the Expiration Date.

Example:

Today's date: March 4   -   Spot date: March 6
1 month FX date   -   April 6

The Expiration Date for a one-month Option quoted on March 4 will be that date which will result in a Settlement Date of April 6, i.e., April 4, (assuming no weekends or holidays between). To avoid misunderstanding, in the case of periods under one month, it is recommended that the parties refer to an actual date.

Expiration Dates by Calendar Month

Currently, it is market practice to quote for expiration in a particular month without reference to the actual date. In these instances, it is generally understood that the Expiration Date of the Option is the Monday before the third Wednesday of that particular month.

Expiration on Non-Business Days

Although the Master Agreement does not provide that the Expiration Date must be a Business Day (i.e., a Local Banking Day for the office of the Seller that has written the Option), this will customarily be the case. However, some dealers regularly sell Options with Expiration Dates that are not Local Banking

Days for their applicable Designated Office. (Similarly, some
dealers will accept Notice of Exercise on a non-Business Day.)
If the Expiration Date is not a Local Banking Day for the
Seller's Designated Office (or if the Seller is willing to accept
Notice of Exercise on a non-Business Day), it is incumbent upon
the Seller to make other arrangements (such as designating a
different office or an agent for receipt) to enable the Buyer to
exercise its Option. In these circumstances, the Seller should
notify the Buyer of such arrangements as soon as possible and
reconfirm them to the Buyer prior to the Expiration Date.

C.   Confirmations

The significant terms of an Option should always be
established by the parties at the time the Option is entered
into. The agreement of the parties on those terms will be set
forth in the Confirmation. However, there may be matters
relating to an Option that are not required to be set forth in
the Confirmation. Market participants are encouraged to include
information as to such matters in the "Other terms and
conditions" section of the Confirmation. In addition, market
participants should indicate at the beginning of negotiations,
and prior to entering into an Option, in which way their dealings
and the formation, exercise or settlement of the relevant Option
will differ from established market practice. Similarly, brokers
should be mindful of, and adhere to, market practice with respect
to the formation of Options and their dealings with Option
counterparties (including the issuance of Confirmations in the
recommended form).

As in the cash spot and forward currency markets, the prompt
exchange of Confirmations (preferably electronically) and their
immediate and thorough checking upon receipt (and querying where
necessary) is vital to the orderly functioning of the market
place, as well as providing a principal defense against many
types of fraud. However, the Option markets are more complex
than the cash markets because of the greater number of parameters
that need to be specified for each transaction and the different
types of Options that may be transacted. This additional
complexity reinforces the requirement for Confirmations to be
issued promptly by each of the parties. If there has been a
misunderstanding between the parties as to the Option terms, this
will usually be discovered upon the review of the Confirmations.
The non-receipt of expected Confirmations or any inconsistencies
or inaccuracies should be queried or objected to within the time
period recognized by local market practice or, at most, within
three Business Days of the date of the trade. It is suggested
that brokers, as well as the parties to an Option, send
Confirmations of any Options which they arrange to the
counterparties.

A recommended form of Confirmation is included as <u>Exhibit I</u> to the Master Agreement. Market participants (including brokers) are encouraged to follow the format and terminology suggested in order to reduce the risk of misunderstandings.

Market participants frequently enter into a contemporaneous Delta hedge at the time they enter into an Option (either with the Option counterparty or a third party). It is market practice (and market participants are encouraged) to separately confirm such transactions. In addition, it is suggested that brokers send confirmations of any Delta hedges which they arrange to the parties involved.

III. MASTER AGREEMENT PROVISIONS

A. Definitions

For the most part, the definitions used in the Master Agreement are those commonly used by currency options market participants. However, because of the nature of the document (i.e. the form of a master agreement) and because an attempt has been made to define some common terms and phrases which have not heretofore been defined, some of these definitions deserve comment.

1. "Base Currency" is defined as the currency specified by a party on the Schedule to the Master Agreement. Upon an Event of Default, or some other event, which results in the liquidation of outstanding Options, the Base Currency of the Non-Defaulting Party is the currency in which the payment will be calculated and, probably, paid. (See Section III.H.4 and III.H.7 hereof.) It is expected that each party will have a single currency in which it prefers to receive settlement: For example, for U.S. market participants, this will likely be U.S. dollars. U.K. market participants should specify Pounds Sterling as their Base Currency as a U.K. liquidation of a company is conducted in Pounds Sterling (i.e., all claims must be made, and all debts and credits are determined, in Pounds Sterling). The Base Currency Rate plus 1% per annum will be the interest rate used for purposes of determining the default rate on such payments.

2. "Business Day" has alternate definitions depending upon the context in which it is used. The Working Party/Foreign Exchange Committee found that a single definition would have affected, rather than reflected, market practice.

3. The Buyer of an Option (sometimes referred to as the "purchaser" or "holder") is defined as the owner of the Option. The Buyer may be either the original buyer, an assignee thereof or a subsequent assignee. In any event, for Options between counterparties to be subject to the Master Agreement, the parties must have executed the Master Agreement. If an Option is assigned by a Buyer to a party who has not entered into the Master Agreement with the Seller, the assignee will not have the rights and obligations with respect to automatic exercise, net cash settlement, set-off and termination, and liquidation and close-out set out in the Master Agreement. (Section 2.4 of the Master Agreement provides that neither party may assign nor delegate its rights or obligations, respectively, to a third party without the prior written consent of the non-assigning party.)

4. Counterparties are expected to specify their Designated Offices on the Schedule attached to the Master Agreement. These are the respective offices of the parties that will deal Options and whose transactions will be subject to the provisions of the Master Agreement.

5. The definition of "European Style Option" provides that it is an Option which may be exercised only on its Expiration Date. After considerable discussion among the Working Party/Foreign Exchange Committee it was agreed that few European Style Options are exercised prior to this time and that operational problems could result from the earlier exercise of European Options (although this problem was not considered significant). However, the definition does provide that the parties may agree on the acceptability of earlier delivery of Notice of Exercise of these Options.

6. The Events of Default are generally credit-related events, including insolvency, non-payment and the disaffirmation or repudiation of an Option.

Another credit-related Event of Default is found in clause (vi) of the definition, i.e., the failure of a party to provide adequate assurances of its ability to perform an Option after a reasonable request from its counterparty to do so. Such a provision protects a party when it has genuine and valid concerns with respect to the ability of its counterparty to perform, even though no other Event of Default has occurred. The concern may be triggered by, for instance, unconfirmed information about the counterparty circulating in the market, the action of a rating agency or the acknowledged credit problems (such as the filing of a petition for bankruptcy or the occurrence some other insolvency proceeding) of a parent, affiliate or subsidiary of the counterparty.

Clause (vi) requires that the request for adequate assurances must be reasonable given all the facts and circumstances: If, for example, shortly before the Expiration Date of an Option, the Seller of an Option had defaulted on an obligation to the Buyer which arose out of a transaction not covered by the provisions of the Master Agreement (for example, a securities transaction), it might be reasonable for the Buyer to request adequate assurances of the Seller's ability to perform the Option should the Buyer exercise the Option. On the other hand, it would probably be unreasonable of the Seller to request adequate assurances of a Buyer's ability to perform an unexercised Option which is deep out-of-the-money and has an Expiration Date two months in the future. Similarly, what constitutes adequate assurances in any given situation will depend upon a number of factors, including the reason for the requesting party's concern and request, and whether the party from whom adequate assurances are requested is a Buyer or Seller (or both). For example, if the party which is requested to provide adequate assurances is a Seller of in-the-money Options who has already defaulted on other obligations, adequate assurances may be the delivery of a guarantee or letter of credit to support such party's obligations or the deposit into an escrow account of the currency (or currencies) required to be delivered by the Seller upon exercise of the Option(s). If, on the other hand, a party's concern is triggered by unconfirmed rumors about the financial position of its counterparty, it may be sufficient for the counterparty to provide information to the requesting party proving those rumors to be false. In all cases, the determination of both the reasonableness of the request and the adequacy of the assurances should be fact intensive.

In addition, market participants may want to limit the circumstances that may give rise to a reasonable request for adequate assurances. Some market participants may want to use a side letter for this purpose. Such a side letter is neither required nor encouraged, and clause (vi) of the definition of Event of Default should be considered the standard language.

The failure to provide adequate assurances becomes an Event of Default only after two Business Days following the written request therefor. (Pursuant to the provisions of Section 8.3 of the Master Agreement, the party requesting such adequate assurances is entitled to suspend performance of its obligations with respect to any Option during the pendency of such request.)

Clause (viii) of the definition of "Event of Default" provides that it is an Event of Default with respect to a party if the representations and warranties made by such party in Section 3 shall have been false or misleading at the time they were made, provided that the counterparty has given one Business Day's notice of such fact. The representations and warranties made by a party pursuant to Section 3 are considered crucial to the validity and enforceability of an Option and a party's obligations thereunder. Therefore, if the representations and warranties are incorrect, it is deemed a material breach of the Master Agreement thereby allowing the counterparty to effect the close-out and liquidation of all Options pursuant to Section 8.

7. "Expiration Date" (sometimes referred to as the "maturity date" or "expiry date") is defined as the date specified as such in the Confirmation. The two methods commonly used for determining the Expiration Date are explained in Section II.B above. Section II.B also contains a discussion of non-Business Day Expiration Dates.

8. "Expiration Time" (sometimes referred to as the "cut-off time") is defined as the time specified as such in the Confirmation. It is expected that, in keeping with current

market practice, the Expiration Time specified will generally be either 10:00 a.m. (New York time) or, for transactions entered into in the Pacific rim, 3:00 p.m. (Tokyo time).

9. Notice of Exercise of an Option may be given by either telex, telephonic or other electronic means. However, in keeping with market practice, facsimile transmission is specifically excluded as an acceptable method of delivering a Notice of Exercise because of difficulties in ascertaining receipt. In order to avoid confusion, a Notice of Exercise is defined as being irrevocable. Some Sellers will accept a Notice of Exercise on a non-Business Day. In this regard, see the discussion under "Expiration on Non-Business Days" in Section II.B. above.

10. "Premium Payment Date" is defined as the date specified as such in the Confirmation. Generally, the Premium Payment Date will be the Spot Date for the Currency Pair (i.e. the currencies which will be exchanged upon the exercise of an Option). However, for some Options, the Premium will be payable in a currency other that the Put Currency or the Call Currency. In addition, certain Options (such as those commonly referred to as "Boston Options") call for payment of the Premium at a later date (in the case of Boston Options, on the Exercise Date of the Option). In these situations, it is imperative that market participants specifically agree on the Premium Payment Date. Market practice is that the Premium Payment Date is always specified in the Confirmation.

11. The term "Seller" has been used to describe the Party that grants an Option. This is the term commonly used for such purpose, although the Seller is sometimes referred to as the "grantor" or the "writer".

12. Generally, the Spot Date will be the second Business Day after a transaction is entered into. However, this general rule is affected by domestic holidays and, at times, the respective principal financial centers of the currencies involved may be dealing for different Spot Dates. In addition, spot transactions in certain currencies, for example Canadian dollars and Mexican pesos, generally settle on the business day succeeding the date of the transaction. Therefore, the term "Spot Date" has been defined by reference to general usage by foreign exchange market participants.

13. "Spot Price" is used in two Sections of the Master Agreement: (i) Section 5, where it is used for purposes of determining the In-the-money Amount, or intrinsic value, of an Option for purposes of net cash settlement (Section 5.3) and automatic exercise (Section 5.4), and (ii) Section 8, where it is used for the purpose of converting the damages calculated upon the liquidation of an Option into the Non-Defaulting Party's Base Currency. In Section 5, the determination of Spot Price is made

by the Seller, and in Section 8 it is made by the Non-Defaulting
Party. In either case, the definition requires that such
determination be made in good faith.

14. The term "currency" is not defined in the Master
Agreement. However, in accordance with market practice, the term
currency means not only the currency of any country,
but also any composite currency, such as the European Currency
Unit or ECU, in which the parties choose to deal.

B.   General

1. Section 2.2 states the general intention of the parties
(i) that all Options be governed by the terms and conditions set
out in the Master Agreement and (ii) that the Master Agreement
and all Confirmations be considered a single agreement. It
further states that the parties enter into Options under the
Master Agreement in reliance upon these facts. The intent of
these provisions is to provide a legal basis for the close-out,
liquidation and netting of all Options (as provided by Section 8)
upon the occurrence of an Event of Default with respect to one of
the parties. These provisions are considered crucial to avoid
the possibility that a trustee, receiver or conservator of an
insolvent Party would be upheld by a court in affirming and
enforcing some Options (e.g. those which it holds as Buyer which
are In-the-money) and rejecting and repudiating others (e.g those
as to which it is Seller), the practice commonly known as
"cherrypicking".

2. An Option becomes a legally binding contract when the
essential terms of the Option (Buyer and Seller, Premium, style,
type, Strike Price, Put Currency and amount, Call Currency,
Expiration Date, Expiration Time and Premium Payment Date) are
agreed by the parties. The Option will usually be concluded
orally by the traders, in which case the Confirmation will be
evidence of the contract.

3. Section 2.3 provides that Confirmations shall be deemed
correct absent manifest error three days after receipt by a
party. Such manifest error may be evidenced by the tape
recording of the conversation of the traders who entered into a
disputed Option. (Section 11.5 specifically provides for the
tape recording of conversations and for the use of such
recordings as evidence in any court or in any proceeding.)

C.   Representations and Warranties; Contractual Status

1. The representations and warranties contained in Section
3 are made by each of the counterparties and are intended to
satisfy each of the parties that (i) the Master Agreement and
each of the Options entered into pursuant thereto are valid and
enforceable obligations of its counterparty, (ii) no event which

calls into question the credit of its counterparty (i.e. an Event of Default) has occurred, and (iii) the counterparty with which it is dealing is the party that is obligated to perform the Option and the terms of the Master Agreement.

2.   The (U.S.) Commodity Exchange Act (the "CEA"), which is administered by the Commodity Futures Trading Commission (the "CFTC"), governs the trading of futures contracts and options on futures contracts on U.S. commodity exchanges. The Act also applies to the off-exchange trading of certain products and instruments. Section 2(a)(1)(A) of the Act, the so-called "Treasury Amendment", was adopted in 1974 and provides an exclusion from the Act for certain products as follows: "Nothing in this Act shall be deemed to govern or in any way be applicable to transactions in foreign currency, . . . unless such transactions involve the sale thereof for future delivery conducted on a board of trade". In 1986, the U.S. Court of Appeals for the Second Circuit held that an option on a foreign currency did not fall within this exclusion because it was not a transaction "in" a foreign currency until it was exercised. Commodity Futures Trading Commission v. The American Board of Trade, Inc. et al., 803 F. 2d 1242 (2nd Cir. 1986). As such, currency options may only be offered in the U.S. pursuant to a regulatory exemption from the general ban on the trading of such options contained in Section 4c(b) of the Act. The exemption most commonly relied upon for currency options is the so-called "Trade Option Exemption" contained in CFTC regulation section 32.4. The Trade Option Exemption provides an exemption from the general ban for commodity options offered to a "producer, processor, or commercial user of, or a merchant handling, the commodity which is the subject of the commodity option transaction, or the products or byproducts thereof" where such party is offered or enters into the option transaction solely for purposes related to its business as such. As the Master Agreement has been drafted for use by the professional market, a representation addressing the status of the parties for purposes of assuring compliance with the Trade Option Exemption was believed to be unnecessary. However, in those cases in which the Master Agreement is made subject to the laws of the State of New York (or any other state in the United States) and either of the parties is not a professional market participant, the parties should consider the propriety of including a representation as to the commercial status of the parties.

D.   The Premium

Section 4.2 provides for alternative courses of action in the event that a Premium is not received on the Premium Payment Date. As Premiums are sometimes paid late (due primarily to operational problems or mistakes), under appropriate circumstances a Seller should generally be willing to accept a late payment, and it is common practice in the market for a

Seller to do so. However, where the failure to pay the Premium
has not been remedied after a short period of time or is credit-
related, the Seller may choose either to void the Option or to
take the more drastic step of declaring an Event of Default.
Regardless of the course of action chosen by the Seller, the
Seller is entitled to recover its out-of-pocket costs and actual
damages incurred, specifically including interest on the amount
of any Premium (which would be calculated in the same manner as
any other late payment in the interdealer foreign exchange
market) and any costs or expenses in covering its obligations
(including a Delta hedge). Section 4.2 provides for such
recovery in the case of either a late payment or the decision to
treat the related Option as void. Where the Seller chooses to
declare an Event of Default, such amounts are recoverable under
the provisions of Section 8(i).

E.   <u>Exercise and Settlement of Options</u>

        1.   Section 5.1 states that the Buyer may exercise an Option
by Delivery to the Seller of a timely Notice of Exercise and
that, subject to the automatic exercise provisions contained in
Section 5.4, an Option which has not been exercised by its
Expiration Time shall expire and become void. Accordingly,
market participants should exercise particular care when clocks
worldwide are changed seasonally. In addition, it is the Buyer's
responsibility to ensure that a Notice of Exercise is addressed
to, and received by, the department or area specified by the
Seller in Part II of the Schedule to the Master Agreement.

        2.   The last sentence of Section 5.1 reflects the general
market practice that the close of business occurs at 3:00 p.m.
(local time of the Seller) and that a Notice of Exercise received
after that time is deemed received on the next Business Day. In
accordance with the definition of "Notice of Exercise", such
Notice should be given by telephone or other electronic means,
but may not be given by facsimile transmission.

        3.   Options may be entered into on the understanding that
physical delivery of the Put Currency and the Call Currency will
<u>not</u> take place and that the Option will be net cash settled by a
payment to the Buyer of the Option's In-the-money Amount (or
intrinsic value) if the Option is exercised. The intrinsic value
of an Option will be equal to the difference between the Spot
Price and the Strike Price multiplied by the amount of the Put or
Call Currency, as appropriate, to be exchanged upon exercise of
the Option. An example of the calculation of the intrinsic value
of a United States Dollar/Deutsche Mark Call is as follows -

USD Call / DEM Put: Spot Price (1.6850) - Strike Price (1.60)
            (DEM per USD) =

1.6850 - 1.60 = .0850 x USD 10,000,000 = DEM 850,000.00

The level of the Spot Price at the time of exercise is, therefore, crucial to the ultimate value of the net cash settlement. As the Spot Price that is used for such purposes is determined in good faith by the Seller, the Buyer should ascertain at the outset how the Seller will determine the Spot Price.

4. Section 5.4 provides for automatic exercise of Options which are in-the-money at the Expiration Time and have not been exercised by delivery of a Notice of Exercise. This provision is not meant to be a substitute for the delivery of a Notice of Exercise by the Buyer, which is good market practice and is encouraged. For this reason, (a) an Option will be deemed exercised under this Section only if, at its Expiration Time, it has an In-the-money Amount that equals or exceeds the product of (x) 101% of the Strike Price and (y) the amount of the Call or Put Currency, as appropriate, (b) the Seller determines the Spot Price that is used to calculate the In-the-money Amount, and (c) the Seller may choose to settle an automatically exercised Option either by physical delivery (in accordance with Section 5.2) or net cash settlement (in accordance with Section 5.3).

5. Because an exercised Option settles on the Spot Date for the Currency Pair, it is common practice for market participants to process an Option which is to be settled by physical delivery as if it were a spot foreign exchange contract, including the exchange of settlement instructions and confirmations. (If confirmations are issued upon the exercise of an Option, it is desirable that such confirmations indicate that the spot foreign exchange transaction relates to an Option exercise.) Notwithstanding such treatment, an exercised Option remains an Option and the parties' rights and obligations with respect thereto will continue to be governed by the Master Agreement. For example, should an Event of Default occur with respect to a party between the Exercise Date and the Settlement Date for an Option, the counterparty's rights to close-out and liquidate such Option (and other Options entered into by the parties) are those set forth in Section 8.

6. Section 5.5 provides that, unless otherwise agreed by the parties, an Option may be exercised only in whole and not in part.

7. Options are settled by payment of the Put Currency amount by the Buyer to the Seller and by the payment of the Call Currency amount by the Seller to the Buyer. In each case, such payments shall be made in immediately available and freely transferable funds to the bank and account number specified by the recipient of the payment in Part III of the Schedule attached to the Master Agreement. See Section 11.3.

F.   <u>Discharge and Termination of Options</u>

Section 6 of the Master Agreement provides for the <u>automatic</u> discharge and termination of Call Options written by both parties and Put Options written by both parties, provided that (i) the material terms of such Options are the same, (ii) Premiums with respect to such Options have been paid, and (iii) such Options have not been exercised. The effect of this Section is to net Options in the limited circumstances in which Options can effectively be netted. The sole remaining rights and obligations of the parties, with respect to Options discharged and netted under Section 6, are to exercise that portion, if any, of the one of the Options that is not discharged and terminated and to settle such portion upon the exercise thereof, respectively. Section 6 effectively allows counterparties to close-out existing Options or to reduce their exposure to each other by entering into offsetting Options.

G.   <u>Payment Netting</u>

Section 7 contains two separate payment netting provisions. Section 7.1 provides for the <u>automatic</u> netting of any Premium payments that would otherwise be made by the parties in the same currency on the same date. Section 7.2 provides for the netting of any payments, other than Premium payments, to be made by the parties to each other in the same currency on the same date. These provisions do not alter the parties' legal rights and obligations with respect to the underlying Options (as Section 6 does). The intent of this Section is to reduce the number and size of payments required to be made by the parties in connection with their Options transactions. Many Option dealers do not currently net Premium payments, primarily because they do not have the operational capability to do so. Presumably, such parties will agree with their counterparties not to net such payments (either by way of a side agreement or by striking Section 7.1 from the Master Agreement). However, since Premium payment netting reduces settlement exposure and the cost of transacting Options (because of the reduction in the number of payments), Premium payment netting is encouraged.

H.   <u>Default</u>

1. The provisions of Section 8 should be read carefully and understood as they set forth the rights and obligations of counterparties upon the occurrence of an Event of Default with respect to either of them. (In addition, the close-out and liquidation procedures set forth in Section 8.1 will also be followed in the event that it becomes illegal or impossible for a party to perform its obligations under an Option under the provisions of Section 10 of the Master Agreement.)

2. Section 8.1 sets forth the steps that a Non-Defaulting Party must take in closing out and liquidating Options. It requires that the Non-Defaulting Party liquidate all outstanding Options, except to the extent that such party believes in good faith that applicable law prohibits the liquidation of certain Options. This requirement is intended to support that statement made in Section 2.2 that the Master Agreement and all Confirmations (and, therefore, the Options which they evidence), Schedules and amendments to the Master Agreement constitute a single agreement between the parties. The single agreement concept is intended to prevent cherrypicking by a trustee, receiver or conservator of an insolvent Defaulting Party. Section 8.1 further provides that, in the case of specified Events of Default relating to the insolvency of the Defaulting Party, such liquidation shall be automatic with respect to all outstanding Options, unless the law governing the insolvency proceedings of the Non-Defaulting Party expressly allows liquidation to take place after the occurrence of the Event of Default and in the manner set forth in clauses (i) through (iv) of Section 8.1. In the absence of such express provision, automatic liquidation is considered preferable as it is less likely to be challenged in the insolvency proceedings of the Defaulting Party.

3. Clause (i) of Section 8.1 provides for the calculation and aggregation of market damages for each party for each Option closed out. The Non-Defaulting Party should endeavor to liquidate all outstanding Options on a single day. However, if this is impossible, the liquidation should be completed as soon as practicable. With respect to Options purchased by a party, those damages will be the current market premium (or replacement cost) for such Options. With respect to Options sold by a party, the only market damages will be any unpaid premium and any interest on such unpaid premium. With respect to exercised, but unsettled, Options, damages will be the unpaid settlement amount plus interest thereon. In addition, the Non-Defaulting Party is entitled to include any costs or expenses incurred in covering its obligations related to such liquidated Options, such as the obligations on a Delta hedge. The determination of market damages for each party in each instance must be made in good faith.

4. After calculation of each party's market damages, Clause (ii) of Section 8.1 provides for the conversion of such damages into the Non-Defaulting Party's Base Currency. As such damages may be in different currencies (corresponding to the different currencies in which Premiums on the liquidated Options were paid or payable), it is necessary to convert all such damage amounts into a single currency if such damages are to be aggregated (and netted pursuant to the provisions of clause (iii) of Section 8.1). In addition, the Non-Defaulting Party is given the benefit of converting these damages into its Base Currency (rather than

the Defaulting Party's Base Currency). For purposes of this conversion, the Non-Defaulting Party should use the applicable Spot Rate.

5. Following the conversion and aggregation of each party's market damages, clause (iii) provides that such market damages will be netted, resulting in a single liquidated amount in the Non-Defaulting Party's Base Currency that will be due and payable as a settlement payment to the party having the larger aggregated damage amount.

6. If one or both of the parties are holding any cash or non-cash collateral as margin or security for their respective obligations under outstanding Options or the Master Agreement generally, clause (iv) allows the parties to set off the value thereof (following any necessary conversion into the Non-Defaulting Party's Base Currency) against the liquidated damage amount calculated under the preceding clauses.

7. Section 8.2 provides that the net amount calculated pursuant to Section 8.1 shall be paid by one party to the other by the close of business on the Business Day following the liquidation of the Options. In some countries, a judgment can only be rendered in the currency of that country. Therefore, Section 8.2 provides that, if required by applicable law, the net amount payable by one party to the other will be converted into a currency other than the Non-Defaulting Party's Base Currency. Any costs of such conversion will be borne by the Defaulting Party. If this amount is not paid when due, Section 8.2 provides for the payment of interest at the applicable interbank rate plus 1% per annum for each day for which the amount remains unpaid. Section 8.2 also provides that Section 8 is not intended to limit, but rather that the rights provided for therein shall be in addition to, any other rights which the Non-Defaulting Party may have under applicable law, by agreement or otherwise, and that the Non-Defaulting Party is granted a general right of set-off with respect to all amounts owed by either party to the other, whether due or not due.

8. Section 8.3 establishes the right of one party to suspend performance of its obligations under any Option or the Master Agreement (i) if the counterparty is currently in default in the payment or performance of any of its obligations under an Option or the Master Agreement or (ii) during the pendency of a reasonable request to the counterparty to provide adequate assurances of its ability to perform such obligations. The default need not constitute an Event of Default. Therefore, if a Buyer has not paid a Premium on the applicable Premium Payment Date, even though the Seller has not sent written notice of non-receipt (or, if such notice has been sent, but two Business Days have not elapsed), the Seller is, nonetheless, entitled to

suspend its performance with respect to other Options between the parties until receipt of such Premium.

I.   Parties to Rely on Their Own Expertise

Section 9 establishes that each of the parties has relied on its own expertise and judgement in entering into each Option and as to all other subsequent actions or matters related thereto or any other currency option or transaction. The intent of this provision is to protect each of the parties from a claim or action by the other party wherein it is alleged that one of the parties exercised influence or control over the decisions or actions of the other to the extent that it is, therefore, liable for losses, costs, expenses or damages suffered or incurred as a result of such decisions or actions.

J.   Illegality, Impossibility and Force Majeure

Section 10 provides that, if either party is unable to perform, or is hindered or delayed in performing, its obligations in respect of any Option due to force majeure, or if it otherwise becomes illegal or impossible for either party to perform its obligations in respect of any Option, then either party may, after notice of the occurrence of such event, liquidate and close-out all affected Options. Although such events do not constitute Events of Default, the liquidation and close-out procedures to be followed are those provided for in Section 8. Either of the parties may take such action promptly upon notice to the other. Due to the volatile nature of the Option markets, it is important that the parties have the ability to liquidate positions promptly in order to limit their exposure to transactions which one of the parties may be unable to perform. If Section 10 is applicable to the obligations of both parties, the parties should mutually agree upon the close-out and liquidation of Options.

K.   Miscellaneous

1.   The intent of Section 11.4 is to insure that any settlement payment to a party resulting from the termination and liquidation of Options arising either as a result of an Event of Default or an event of illegality, impossibility or force majeure, and whether pursuant to the operation of Section 8 or the judgement of a court, is made in such party's Base Currency (or the Non-Defaulting Party's Base Currency) and is paid in the full amount in such Base Currency. If payment is made in some other currency, such payment is deemed to discharge the obligation of the payor only to the extent that the payee could purchase the full amount of the Base Currency (or the Non-Defaulting Party's Base Currency) with the amount of the currency received on the business day following the date of receipt. If the amount of the currency received is insufficient to purchase

the full amount of the Base Currency, the payor indemnifies the payee against any loss and, in any event, the payor indemnifies the payee against any costs incurred in purchasing the Base Currency.

2.   Pursuant to Section 11.5, the parties agree to the tape recording of any telephone conversations between them and agree that such tape recordings can be submitted in evidence in any proceeding relating to any Option transaction. It is standard market practice that conversations between traders and between traders and brokers are recorded. This practice is encouraged, as such recordings can substantially reduce the number of disputes that arise between market participants and the time which it takes to resolve such disputes. Such recordings are usually the best evidence of the essential terms of an Option as agreed by the parties.

3.   Some parties may choose to deal Options with each other on a margined or secured basis. Section 11.7 provides that, if the parties have entered into an agreement providing for such dealings, then such agreement is incorporated into the Master Agreement and is subject to the terms thereof. The possibility of such an arrangement is also addressed in Section 8.1(iv), which provides for the set-off of any collateral held as margin or security against the settlement payment otherwise calculated pursuant to Section 8.1. If the margin or security agreement conflicts with the Master Agreement, the Master Agreement would govern.

L.   Law and Jurisdiction

1.   Counsel has opined that the form of Master Agreement is valid and enforceable under the laws of both the State of New York and the laws of England and Wales. Copies of such opinions are attached hereto. It is expected that counterparties, and especially those physically located in either the U.K. or the U.S.A., will choose one of these systems of law to govern the Master Agreement and all Options entered into by the parties. It is also expected that parties will submit to the jurisdiction of either the courts in the State of New York or England consistent with their choice of governing law. However, as such submission to jurisdiction is non-exclusive, parties will be free to bring actions, suits or proceedings in other jurisdictions.

2.   Pursuant to Section 12.4, each party explicitly waives any sovereign immunity it may be entitled to assert in any legal proceeding arising out of the Master Agreement.

M.   Currency Option Confirmation

1.   The recommended form of Confirmation, which is attached
to the Master Agreement as <u>Exhibit I</u>, is substantially the same
as the form of confirmation generally used by market participants
to evidence options. All of the material terms of an Option are
to be set forth in the Confirmation. Material terms which are
not otherwise required to be specified in the Confirmation should
be included in the "Other terms and conditions" section.

2.   There are three headings in the form of Confirmation
which are not used or defined in the Master Agreement - Trade
Date, Expiration Settlement Date and Price.

The Trade Date is the day on which the parties agree to
enter into an Option.

The Expiration Settlement Date is the last possible day on
which an exercised Option could settle. In keeping with market
practice, this will generally be the Spot Date for the Currency
Pair as determined on the Expiration Date.

Price is the currency exchange rate or the percentage (of
one of the Currency Pair) upon which the Premium of an Option is
determined. See Section II.A above for an explanation of market
practice with respect to price quotation.

3.   Where dates are to be specified in the Confirmation
(e.g. Trade Date), the market convention is to specify the day
first (using two numbers), the month second (using three letters)
and, finally, the year (using two numbers, being the last two
numbers of the applicable year). For example, the date March 1,
1991 would be specified as "01/MAR/91".

N.   Schedule

Each of the parties will complete a Schedule in the form
attached to the Master Agreement. The Schedule contains
particulars concerning each party, such as the address,
telephone, telex and facsimile number, and contact person for
notices and other communications, and each party's Base Currency.
In addition, in Part I of the Schedule, the parties should
designate their branches or offices whose transactions and
dealings are intended to be covered by the Master Agreement.
Either because of concerns with respect to applicable law or
operational capabilities (which, for instance, may make the
settlement, payment netting or set-off of Options between certain
offices of the counterparties difficult), counterparties may
choose to limit the number of Designated Offices covered by a
particular Master Agreement and may choose to put in place more
than one Master Agreement between them, each covering a different
set of Designated Offices.

THE INTERNATIONAL CURRENCY OPTIONS MARKET (ICOM)

Terms and Guide

British Bankers' Association

August 1992

NOTICE

As from 30 September, 1992 the International Currency Options Master Agreement (ICOM for short) represents customary market terms for trading in currency options on the London market. Banks are free to deal on other terms if they wish, but after 30 September 1992, and in the absence of a prior agreement, any bank entering into currency options on the London market which it is intended *should not* be covered by ICOM must make clear to their proposed counterparty at the start of negotiations in what way their terms differ from ICOM. In the absence of such clarification or prior agreement, banks will be expected to be following the normal market custom of quoting on the basis of ICOM.

London Interbank Currency Options Master (LICOM) terms, as published by the British Bankers' Association in August 1985, will no longer be available after that date and banks are advised to consider carefully with their counterparties whether they wish existing currency options entered into under those terms to remain subject to LICOM, or if they are content for their currency options to be brought under ICOM by virtue of Section 11.6 of the ICOM terms.

Whilst the Schedule to the ICOM terms enables certain of the details required for the Schedule to be assumed in the absence of specific notification, all banks should ensure that the requisite details are given to counterparties before dealing commences. It is envisaged that banks entering into currency options on the London market will normally wish the Base Currency to be Sterling and their agreement to be governed by English law and subject to the jurisdiction of the English courts. If a bank requires the Base Currency to be other than Sterling, or the governing law to be other than English law or the jurisdiction to be other than that of the English courts, this should be agreed before dealing commences.

1992 ICOM terms also represent best practice in relation to currency options as agreed by the New York Foreign Exchange Committee and the Tokyo Market Practices Committee. Accordingly, it is not envisaged that banks entering into currency options on the London market will wish to make material changes to the ICOM terms.

London, 28 August, 1992

INTERNATIONAL CURRENCY OPTIONS MARKET

Guide to Master Agreement

I. INTRODUCTION

Following the publication of 'LICOM Terms' in August, 1985, which were intended to reflect and to encourage good market practice and to reduce the need for specific legal documentation between participants in the London interbank over-the-counter currency options market, the market continued to evolve internationally. By 1989, it became apparent that the original terms did not adequately reflect market practice. In particular, the number and diversity of market participants had increased substantially, and new practices had been adopted, such as volatility quoting, which were not envisaged in 1985.

Accordingly, in May, 1989, the British Bankers' Association ('BBA') re-established, through its Foreign Exchange Committee, a Working Party to liaise with market interests, including the former Foreign Exchange and Currency Deposits Brokers' Association, with a view to updating the 1985 terms and to providing guidance as to market practice. The Working Party was comprised of members representing a broad spectrum of international financial institutions. In addition, emphasis was placed on the international acceptance of the revised terms, and a new title was developed: International Currency Options Market Terms and Conditions – 'ICOM Terms'. The Bank of England was represented as an observer on the Working Party.

During this same period, a similar effort was underway in the United States. In early 1986, the (US) Foreign Exchange Committee issued draft Recommended Terms and Conditions For Dealing in the United States Market – 'NYICOM Terms'. (The Foreign Exchange Committee is an advisory committee, independent of the Federal Reserve Bank of New York (the 'FRBNY'), but sponsored by it, and its members are participants in the interdealer foreign exchange market.) The NYICOM Terms, which were based upon, and substantially similar to, the original LICOM Terms, were intended to reflect general market practice in the United States. Over a period of time, the NYICOM Terms were retitled 'USICOM Terms', for United States Interbank Currency Options Market Terms.

Although the USICOM Terms generally reflected market practices in the US, they did not address the increasingly important issue of counterparty credit risk and, in particular, the substantive rights and obligations of the Parties upon (i) the nonperformance of an option by one of the Parties, (ii) the insolvency of one of the Parties or (iii) the occurrence of force majeure or some other event which makes it illegal or impossible for one of the Parties to perform. The USICOM Terms also did not provide a method for closing out and liquidating options upon the occurrence of one of these events. In 1990, the USICOM Terms were revised into a draft form of master agreement, which attempted to reflect market practice with respect to the formation, exercise and settlement of options (including such matters as net cash settlement and automatic exercise), as well as set forth the substantive legal rights and obligations of the Parties.

In the summer of 1990, representatives of the Working Party and the Foreign Exchange Committee met to resolve the differences between the ICOM Terms and the USICOM

G2

Terms and to develop a single document for use in the international over-the-counter foreign currency options market. The result is the attached form of International Currency Options Market Master Agreement (the 'Master Agreement'), which should be considered as reflective of normal market practice for international interdealer transactions and which could be adopted by market participants as the standard agreement for dealing in this market.

The Working Party and the Foreign Exchange Committee have confined themselves to practices in the interbank and professional markets, and have not been directly concerned with the terms and conditions upon which individual institutions may choose to deal with their clients (although the Master Agreement could be used in such circumstances). Banks and other professional market participants are, of course, free to deal with each other on the basis of other terms or agreements if they wish, but should consider themselves under an obligation to make clear to each other in what way their terms or agreements differ from the Master Agreement.

The following sections of this Guide to the Master Agreement are intended (i) to provide further clarification of normal market practice and (ii) to explain various provisions of the Master Agreement and the significance of their inclusion in the Master Agreement. Therefore, this Guide should be read carefully. Though the Master Agreement does, and is intended to, stand on its own as a legal document, the Guide provides important commentary on both current market practice and the Master Agreement.

II. MARKET PRACTICE

A   Price Quotation

There are two generally accepted methods of price quotation – Premium and Volatility. In each case, the counterparties shall agree upon:

> Option Style (American or European),
> Call Currency,
> Put Currency and Amount,
> Expiration Date,
> Expiration Time,
> Premium Payment Date,
> Settlement Date, and
> Strike Price.

Counterparties should also agree upon whether they are entering into a contemporaneous foreign exchange transaction (commonly known as a Delta hedge), although such a transaction would not be subject to the Master Agreement.

Price quotation should be in the form of either:

(a) a *Premium*, where the counterparties agree upon the above terms and on how the premium price should be expressed, e.g. as a percentage of either currency or as one currency in terms of the other (it is also necessary to agree upon a spot rate in the case of a Premium quotation where a Delta hedge forms part of the trade); or

(b) *Volatility*, where the counterparties agree upon the above terms and that the Volatility be expressed as a percentage per annum. It is this factor which, when combined with the Spot Rate, interest factors of the Currency Pair concerned, the days to expiry of the Option and the Strike Price, is used to compute the Premium.

An Option is not a legally binding contract until, among other things, the Premium has been agreed. Therefore, to ensure the ongoing viability of the Volatility method of dealing, it is incumbent on the counterparties to agree on the Premium Price as soon as possible, and it is imperative that the calculation of the Premium accurately reflect the agreed Volatility and market conditions at the time Volatility was agreed. In the event of a dispute that cannot be resolved between the counterparties through good faith negotiation (or, in the first instance, by reference to recordings of conversations between the Parties during which pricing was discussed), prompt reference to mutually acceptable third-party arbitration is suggested. Market participants should note that, as Premium calculation differences are more likely to occur in transactions involving American Style Options, due care should be exercised in entering into such Options.

In addition, when trading Volatility, it is necessary that a spot rate be agreed upon by the counterparties immediately upon entering into the Option. This forms the basis of the underlying foreign exchange transaction (Delta hedge), if any.

B   Quotation of Expiration Dates

Generally, there are two methods for quotation of Expiration Dates – quotation of straight Expiration Dates and quotation of Expiration Dates by calendar month.

Straight Expiration Dates

An Option quoted for straight periods (such as 1 month, 2 months etc.) has as its final Expiration Date the date preceding the equivalent forward date (as dealt in the interdealer foreign exchange market) that will result in settlement on the forward date, if it is exercised on the Expiration Date. If there is more than one solution, the furthest date from the Trade Date will be the Expiration Date.

Example:

Today's date: 4 March – Spot date: 6 March
1 month FX date   – 6 April

The Expiration Date for a one-month Option quoted on 4 March will be that date which will result in a Settlement Date of 6 April, i.e. 4 April, (assuming no weekends or holidays between). To avoid misunderstanding, in the case of periods under one month, it is recommended that the Parties refer to an actual date.

Expiration Dates by Calendar Month

Currently, it is market practice to quote for expiration in a particular month without reference to the actual date. In these instances, it is generally understood that the Expiration Date of the Option is the Monday before the third Wednesday of that particular month.

Expiration on non-Business Days

Although the Master Agreement does not provide that the Expiration Date must be a Business Day (i.e. a Local Banking Day for the office of the Seller that has written the Option), this will customarily be the case. However, some dealers regularly sell Options with Expiration Dates that are not Local Banking Days for their applicable Designated Office. (Similarly, some dealers will accept Notice of Exercise on a non-Business Day.) If the Expiration Date is not a Local Banking Day for the Seller's Designated Office (or if the Seller is not willing to accept Notice of Exercise at its Designated Office on a non-Business Day), it is incumbent upon the Seller to make other arrangements (such as designating a different office or an agent for receipt) to enable the Buyer to exercise its Option. In these

G4

circumstances, the Seller should notify the Buyer of such arrangements as soon as possible and reconfirm them to the Buyer prior to the Expiration Date.

C   Confirmations

The significant terms of an Option should always be established by the Parties at the time the Option is entered into. The agreement of the Parties on those terms will be set forth in the Confirmation. However, there may be matters relating to an Option that are not required to be set forth in the Confirmation. Market participants are encouraged to include information as to such matters in the 'Other terms and conditions' section of the Confirmation. In addition, market participants should indicate at the beginning of negotiations, and prior to entering into an Option, in which way their dealings and the formation, exercise or settlement of the relevant Option will differ from established market practice. Similarly, brokers should be mindful of, and adhere to, market practice with respect to the formation of Options and their dealings with Option counterparties (including the issuance of Confirmations in the recommended form).

As in the cash spot and forward currency markets, the prompt exchange of Confirmations (preferably electronically) and their immediate and thorough checking upon receipt (and querying where necessary) is vital to the orderly functioning of the market place, as well as providing a principal defence against many types of fraud. However, the Option markets are more complex than the cash markets because of the greater number of parameters that need to be specified for each transaction and the different types of Options that may be transacted. This additional complexity reinforces the requirement for Confirmations to be issued promptly by each of the Parties. If there has been a misunderstanding between the Parties as to the Option terms, this will usually be discovered upon review of the Confirmations. The non-receipt of expected Confirmations or any inconsistencies or inaccuracies should be queried or objected to within the time period recognised by local market practice or, at most, within three Business Days of the date of the trade. It is suggested that brokers, as well as the Parties to an Option, send Confirmations of any Options which they arrange to the counterparties.

A recommended form of Confirmation is included as *Exhibit I* to the Master Agreement. Market participants (including brokers) are encouraged to follow the format and terminology suggested in order to reduce the risk of misunderstandings.

Market participants frequently enter into a contemporaneous Delta hedge at the time they enter into an Option (either with the Option counterparty or a third party). It is market practice (and market participants are encouraged) to separately confirm such transactions. In addition, it is suggested that brokers send confirmations of any Delta hedges which they arrange to the Parties involved.

III.   MASTER AGREEMENT PROVISIONS

A   Definitions

For the most part, the definitions used in the Master Agreement are those commonly used by currency options market participants. However, because of the nature of the document (i.e. the form of a master agreement) and because an attempt has been made to define some common terms and phrases which have not heretofore been defined, some of these definitions deserve comment.

1. 'Base Currency' is defined as the currency specified by a Party for the purposes of the Schedule to the Master Agreement. Upon an Event of Default, or some other event, which results in the liquidation of outstanding Options, the Base Currency of the non-defaulting Party is the currency in which the payment will be calculated and, probably, paid. (See Section III.H.4 and III.H.7 hereof.) It is expected that each Party will have a single currency in which it prefers to receive settlement: for example, for participants on the London market this is assumed to be Pounds Sterling as a UK liquidation of a company is conducted in Pounds Sterling (i.e. all claims must be made, and all debts and credits are determined, in Pounds Sterling). However, market participants, may agree a different Base Currency, provided this is done before dealing commences. The Base Currency Rate plus 1% *per annum* will be the interest rate used for purposes of determining the default rate on such payments.

2. 'Business Day' has alternate definitions depending upon the context in which it is used. The Working Party/Foreign Exchange Committee found that a single definition would have affected, rather than reflected, market practice.

3. The Buyer of an Option (sometimes referred to as the 'purchaser' or 'holder') is defined as the owner of the Option. The Buyer may be either the original buyer, an assignee thereof or a subsequent assignee. In any event, for Options between counterparties to be subject to the Master Agreement, the Parties must have traded on the basis of the Master Agreement. If an Option is assigned by a Buyer to a Party who has not entered into Options on the basis of the Master Agreement with the Seller, the assignee will not have the rights and obligations with respect to automatic exercise, net cash settlement, set-off and termination, and liquidation and close-out set out in the Master Agreement with respect to other Options he may have entered into. (Section 2.4 of the Master Agreement provides that neither Party may assign nor delegate its rights or obligations, respectively, to a third Party without the prior written consent of the non-assigning Party.)

4. Counterparties are expected to specify their Designated Offices in accordance with the Schedule attached to the Master Agreement. These are the respective offices of the Parties that will deal in Options and whose transactions will be subject to the provisions of the Master Agreement.

5. The definition of 'European Style Option' provides that it is an Option which may be exercised only on its Expiration Date. After considerable discussion among the Working Party/Foreign Exchange Committee it was agreed that few European Style Options are exercised prior to this time and that operational problems could result from the earlier exercise of European Options (although this problem was not considered significant). However, the definition does provide that the Parties may agree on the acceptability of earlier delivery of Notice of Exercise of these Options.

6. The Events of Default are generally credit-related events, including insolvency, non-payment and the disaffirmation or repudiation of an Option.

Another credit-related Event of Default is found in clause (vi) of the definition, i.e. the failure of a Party to provide adequate assurances of its ability to perform an Option after a reasonable request from its counterparty to do so. Such a provision protects a Party when it has genuine and valid concerns with respect to the ability of its counterparty to perform, even though no other Event of Default has occurred. The concern may be triggered by, for instance, unconfirmed information about the counterparty circulating in the market, the action of a rating agency or the acknowledged credit problems (such as the filing of a petition for bankruptcy or the occurrence of some other insolvency proceeding) of a parent, affiliate or subsidiary of the counterparty.

G6

Clause (vi) requires that the request for adequate assurances must be *reasonable* given all the facts and circumstances: if, for example, shortly before the Expiration Date of an Option, the Seller of an Option had defaulted on an obligation to the Buyer which arose out of a transaction not covered by the provisions of the Master Agreement (for example, a securities transaction), it might be reasonable for the Buyer to request adequate assurances of the Seller's ability to perform the Option should the Buyer exercise the Option. On the other hand, it would probably be unreasonable of the Buyer to request adequate assurances of a Seller's ability to perform an unexercised Option which is deep out-of-the-money and has an Expiration Date two months in the future. Similarly, what constitutes adequate assurances in any given situation will depend upon a number of factors, including the reason for the requesting Party's concern and request, and whether the Party from whom adequate assurances are requested is a Buyer or Seller (or both). For example, if the Party which is requested to provide adequate assurances is a Seller of in-the-money Options who has already defaulted on other obligations, adequate assurances may be the delivery of a guarantee or letter of credit to support such Party's obligations or the deposit into an escrow account of the currency (or currencies) required to be delivered by the Seller upon exercise of the Option(s). If, on the other hand, a Party's concern is triggered by unconfirmed rumours about the financial position of its counterparty, it may be sufficient for the counterparty to provide information to the requesting Party proving those rumours to be false. In all cases, the determination of both the reasonableness of the request and the adequacy of the assurances should take into account the relevant facts and circumstances prevailing at the time.

In addition, market participants may want to limit the circumstances that may give rise to a reasonable request for adequate assurances. Some market participants may want to use a side letter for this purpose. Such a side letter is neither required nor encouraged, and clause (vi) of the definition of Event of Default should be considered the standard language.

The failure to provide adequate assurances becomes an Event of Default only after two Business Days following the written request therefor. (Pursuant to the provisions of Section 8.3 of the Master Agreement, the Party requesting such adequate assurances is entitled to suspend performance of its obligations with respect to any Option during the pendency of such request.)

Clause (viii) of the definition of 'Event of Default' provides that it is an Event of Default with respect to a Party if the representations and warranties made by such Party in Section 3 shall have been false or misleading at the time they were made, provided that the counterparty has given one Business Day's notice of such fact. The representations and warranties made by a Party pursuant to Section 3 are considered crucial to the validity and enforceability of an Option and a Party's obligations thereunder. Therefore, if the representations and warranties are incorrect, it is deemed a material breach of the Master Agreement thereby allowing the counterparty to effect the close-out and liquidation of all Options pursuant to Section 8.

7.   'Expiration Date' (sometimes referred to as the 'maturity date' or 'expiry date') is defined as the date specified as such in the Confirmation. The two methods commonly used for determining the Expiration Date are explained in Section II.B above. Section II.B also contains a discussion of non-Business Day Expiration Dates.

8.   'Expiration Time' (sometimes referred to as the 'cut-off time') is defined as the time specified as such in the Confirmation. It is expected that, in keeping with current market practice, the Expiration Time specified will generally be either 10:00 a.m. (New York time) or, for transactions entered into on the Pacific rim, 3:00 p.m. (Tokyo time).

9.   Notice of Exercise of an Option may be given by either telex, telephonic or other electronic means. However, in keeping with market practice, facsimile transmission is

specifically excluded as an acceptable method of delivering a Notice of Exercise because of difficulties in ascertaining receipt. In order to avoid confusion, a Notice of Exercise is defined as being irrevocable. Some Sellers will accept a Notice of Exercise on a non-Business Day. In this regard, see the discussion under 'Expiration on non-Business Days' in Section II.B above.

10.   'Premium Payment Date' is defined as the date specified as such in the Confirmation. Generally, the Premium Payment Date will be the Spot Date for the Currency Pair (i.e. the currencies which will be exchanged upon the exercise of an Option). However, for some Options, the Premium will be payable in a currency other that the Put Currency or the Call Currency. In addition, certain Options (such as those commonly referred to as 'Boston Options') call for payment of the Premium at a later date (in the case of Boston Options, on the Exercise Date of the Option). In these situations, it is imperative that market participants specifically agree on the Premium Payment Date. Market practice is that the Premium Payment Date is always specified in the Confirmation.

11.   The term 'Seller' has been used to describe the Party that grants an Option. This is the term commonly used for such purpose, although the Seller is sometimes referred to as the 'grantor' or the 'writer'.

12.   Generally, the Spot Date will be the second Business Day after a transaction is entered into. However, this general rule is affected by domestic holidays and, at times, the respective principal financial centres of the currencies involved may be dealing for different Spot Dates. In addition, spot transactions in certain currencies, for example Canadian dollars and Mexican pesos, generally settle on the Business Day succeeding the date of the transaction. Therefore, the term 'Spot Date' has been defined by reference to general usage by foreign exchange market participants.

13.   'Spot Price' is used in two sections of the Master Agreement: (i) Section 5, where it is used for purposes of determining the In-the-money Amount, or intrinsic value, of an Option for purposes of net cash settlement (Section 5.3) and automatic exercise (Section 5.4), and (ii) Section 8, where it is used for the purpose of converting the damages calculated upon the liquidation of an Option into the non-defaulting Party's Base Currency. In Section 5, the determination of the Spot Price is made by the Seller, and in Section 8 it is made by the non-defaulting Party. In either case, the definition requires that such determination be made in good faith.

14.   The term 'currency' is not defined in the Master Agreement. However, in accordance with market practice, the term currency means not only the currency of any country, but also any composite currency, such as the European Currency Unit or ECU, in which the Parties choose to deal.

B   General

1.   Section 2.2 states the general intention of the Parties (i) that all Options be governed by the terms and conditions set out in the Master Agreement and (ii) that the Master Agreement and all Confirmations be considered a single agreement. It further states that the Parties enter into Options under the Master Agreement in reliance upon these facts. The intent of these provisions is to provide a legal basis for the close-out, liquidation and netting of all Options (as provided by Section 8) upon the occurrence of an Event of Default with respect to one of the Parties. These provisions are considered crucial to avoid the possibility that a trustee, receiver or conservator of an insolvent Party would be upheld by a court in affirming and enforcing some Options (e.g. those which it holds as Buyer which are in-the-money) and rejecting and repudiating others (e.g. those as to which it is Seller), the practice commonly known as 'cherrypicking'.

G8

2.   An Option becomes a legally binding contract when the essential terms of the Option (Buyer and Seller, Premium, style, type, Strike Price, Put Currency and amount, Call Currency, Expiration Date, Expiration Time and Premium Payment Date) are agreed by the Parties. The Option will usually be concluded orally by the traders, in which case the Confirmation will be evidence of the contract.

3.   Section 2.3 provides that Confirmations shall be deemed correct absent manifest error three days after receipt by a Party. Such manifest error may be evidenced by the tape recording of the conversation of the traders who entered into a disputed Option. (Section 11.5 specifically provides for the tape recording of conversations and for the use of such recordings as evidence in any court or in any proceeding.)

C   Representations and Warranties; Contractual Status

1.   The representations and warranties contained in Section 3 are made by each of the counterparties and are intended to satisfy each of the Parties that (i) the Master Agreement and each of the Options entered into pursuant thereto are valid and enforceable obligations of its counterparty, (ii) no event which calls into question the credit of its counterparty (i.e. an Event of Default) has occurred, and (iii) the counterparty with which it is dealing is the Party that is obligated to perform the Option and the terms of the Master Agreement.

2.   The (US) Commodity Exchange Act (the 'CEA'), which is administered by the Commodity Futures Trading Commission (the 'CFTC'), governs the trading of futures contracts and options on futures contracts on US commodity exchanges. The Act also applies to the off-exchange trading of certain products and instruments. Section 2(a)(1)(A) of the Act, the so-called 'Treasury Amendment', was adopted in 1974 and provides an exclusion from the Act for certain products as follows: '. . . Nothing in this Act shall be deemed to govern or in any way be applicable to transactions in foreign currency, . . . unless such transactions involve the sale thereof for future delivery conducted on a board of trade . . .' In 1986, the US Court of Appeals for the Second Circuit held that an option on a foreign currency did not fall within this exclusion because it was not a transaction 'in' a foreign currency until it was exercised. (*Commodity Futures Trading Commission v. The American Board of Trade, Inc. et al.*, 803 F. 2d 1242 (2nd Cir. 1986)). As such, currency options may only be offered in the US pursuant to a regulatory exemption from the general ban on the trading of such options contained in Section 4c(b) of the Act. The exemption most commonly relied upon for currency options is the so-called 'Trade Option Exemption' contained in CFTC regulation section 32.4. The trade option exemption provides an exemption from the general ban for commodity options offered to a 'producer, processor, or commercial user of, or a merchant handling, the commodity which is the subject of the commodity option transaction, or the products or byproducts thereof' where such Party is offered or enters into the option transaction solely for purposes related to its business as such. As the Master Agreement has been drafted for use by the professional market, a representation addressing the status of the Parties for purposes of assuring compliance with the trade option exemption was believed to be unnecessary. However, in those cases in which the Master Agreement is made subject to the laws of the State of New York (or any other state in the United States) and either of the Parties is not a professional market participant, the Parties should consider the propriety of including a representation as to the commercial status of the Parties.

D   The Premium

Section 4.2 provides for alternative courses of action in the event that a Premium is not received on the Premium Payment Date. As Premiums are sometimes paid late (due primarily to operational problems or mistakes), under appropriate circumstances a Seller should generally be willing to accept a late payment, and it is common practice in the market for a Seller to do so. However, where the failure to pay the Premium has not been remedied after a short period of time or is credit-related, the Seller may choose either to void the Option or to take the more drastic step of declaring an Event of Default. Regardless of the course of action chosen by the Seller, the Seller is entitled to recover its out-of-pocket costs and actual damages incurred, specifically including interest on the amount of any Premium (which would be calculated in the same manner as any other late payment in the interdealer foreign exchange market) and any costs or expenses in covering its obligations (including a Delta hedge). Section 4.2 provides for such recovery in the case of either a late payment or the decision to treat the related Option as void. Where the Seller chooses to declare an Event of Default, such amounts are recoverable under the provisions of Section 8(i).

E   Exercise and Settlement of Options

1.   Section 5.1 states that the Buyer may exercise an Option by delivery to the Seller of a timely Notice of Exercise and that, subject to the automatic exercise provisions contained in Section 5.4, an Option which has not been exercised by its Expiration Time shall expire and become void. Accordingly, market participants should exercise particular care when clocks worldwide are changed seasonally. In addition, it is the Buyer's responsibility to ensure that a Notice of Exercise is addressed to, and received by, the department or area specified by the Seller in pursuance of Part II of the Schedule to the Master Agreement.

2.   The last sentence of Section 5.1 reflects the general market practice that the close of business occurs at 3:00 p.m. (local time of the Seller) and that a Notice of Exercise received after that time is deemed received on the next Business Day. In accordance with the definition of 'Notice of Exercise', such Notice should be given by telephone or other electronic means, but may not be given by facsimile transmission.

3.   Options may be entered into on the understanding that physical delivery of the Put Currency and the Call Currency will *not* take place and that the Option will be net cash settled by a payment to the Buyer of the Option's In-the-money Amount (or intrinsic value) if the Option is exercised. The intrinsic value of an Option will be equal to the difference between the Spot Price and the Strike Price multiplied by the amount of the Put or Call Currency, as appropriate, to be exchanged upon exercise of the Option. An example of the calculation of the intrinsic value of a United States Dollar/Deutschemark Call is as follows:

USD Call / DEM Put: Spot Price (1.6850) – Strike Price (1.60)
(DEM per USD) = 0.0850

0.0850 x USD 10,000,000 = DEM 850,000

The level of the Spot Price at the time of exercise is, therefore, crucial to the ultimate value of the net cash settlement. As the Spot Price that is used for such purposes is determined in good faith by the Seller, the Buyer should ascertain *at the outset* how the Seller will determine the Spot Price.

4.   Section 5.4 provides for automatic exercise of Options which are in-the-money at the Expiration Time and have not been exercised by delivery of a Notice of Exercise. This provision is *not* meant to be a substitute for the delivery of a Notice of Exercise by the

G10

Buyer, which is good market practice and is encouraged. For this reason, (a) an Option will be deemed exercised under this Section only if, at its Expiration Time, it has an In-the-money Amount that equals or exceeds the product of (x) 101% of the Strike Price and (y) the amount of the Call or Put Currency, as appropriate, (b) the Seller determines the Spot Price that is used to calculate the In-the-money Amount, and (c) the Seller may choose to settle an automatically exercised Option either by physical delivery (in accordance with Section 5.2) or net cash settlement (in accordance with Section 5.3).

5.   Because an exercised Option settles on the Spot Date for the Currency Pair, it is common practice for market participants to process an Option which is to be settled by physical delivery as if it were a spot foreign exchange contract, including the exchange of settlement instructions and confirmations. (If Confirmations are issued upon the exercise of an Option, it is desirable that such confirmations indicate that the spot foreign exchange transaction relates to an Option exercise.) Notwithstanding such treatment, an exercised Option remains an Option and the Parties' rights and obligations with respect thereto will continue to be governed by the Master Agreement. For example, should an Event of Default occur with respect to a Party between the Exercise Date and the Settlement Date for an Option, the counterparty's rights to close-out and liquidate such Option (and other Options entered into by the Parties) are those set forth in Section 8.

6.   Section 5.5 provides that, unless otherwise agreed by the Parties, an Option may be exercised only in whole and not in part.

7.   Options are settled by payment of the Put Currency amount by the Buyer to the Seller and by the payment of the Call Currency amount by the Seller to the Buyer. In each case, such payments shall be made in immediately available and freely transferable funds to the bank and account number specified by the recipient of the payment pursuant to Part III of the Schedule attached to the Master Agreement. See Section 11.3.

F   Discharge and Termination of Options

Section 6 of the Master Agreement provides for the *automatic* discharge and termination of Call Options written by both Parties and Put Options written by both Parties, provided that (i) the material terms of such Options are the same, (ii) Premiums with respect to such Options have been paid, and (iii) such Options have not been exercised. The effect of this Section is to net Options in the limited circumstances in which Options can effectively be netted. The sole remaining rights and obligations of the Parties, with respect to Options discharged and netted under Section 6, are to exercise that portion, if any, of the one of the Options that is not discharged and terminated and to settle such portion upon the exercise thereof, respectively. Section 6 effectively allows counterparties to close-out existing Options or to reduce their exposure to each other by entering into offsetting Options.

G   Payment Netting

Section 7 contains two separate payment netting provisions. Section 7.1 provides for the *automatic* netting of any Premium payments that would otherwise be made by the Parties in the same currency on the same date. Section 7.2 provides for the netting of any payments, other than Premium payments, to be made by the Parties to each other in the same currency on the same date. These provisions do not alter the Parties' legal rights and obligations with respect to the underlying Options (as Section 6 does). The intent of this Section is to reduce the number and size of payments required to be made by the Parties in connection with their Options transactions. Many Options dealers do not currently net Premium payments, primarily because they do not have the operational capability to do so.

Presumably, such Parties will agree with their counterparties not to net such payments (either by way of a side agreement or by agreeing to strike Section 7.1 from the Master Agreement before dealing commences). However, since Premium payment netting reduces settlement exposure and the cost of transacting Options (because of the reduction in the number of payments), Premium payment netting is encouraged.

H Default

1. The provisions of Section 8 should be read carefully and understood as they set forth the rights and obligations of counterparties upon the occurrence of an Event of Default with respect to either of them. (In addition, the close-out and liquidation procedures set forth in Section 8.1 will also be followed in the event that it becomes illegal or impossible for a Party to perform its obligations under an Option under the provisions of Section 10 of the Master Agreement.)

2. Section 8.1 sets forth the steps that a non-defaulting Party must take in closing out and liquidating Options. It requires that the non-defaulting Party liquidate all outstanding Options, except to the extent that such Party believes in good faith that applicable law prohibits the liquidation of certain Options. This requirement is intended to support the statement made in Section 2.2 that the Master Agreement and all Confirmations (and, therefore, the Options which they evidence), Schedules and amendments to the Master Agreement constitute a single agreement between the Parties. The single agreement concept is intended to prevent cherrypicking by a trustee, receiver or conservator of an insolvent defaulting Party. Section 8.1 further provides that, in the case of specified Events of Default relating to the insolvency of the defaulting Party, such liquidation shall be automatic with respect to all outstanding Options, unless the law governing the insolvency proceedings of the non-defaulting Party expressly allows liquidation to take place after the occurrence of the Event of Default and in the manner set forth in clauses (i) through (iv) of Section 8.1. In the absence of such express provision, automatic liquidation is considered preferable as it is less likely to be challenged in the insolvency proceedings of the defaulting Party.

3. Clause (i) of Section 8.1 provides for the calculation and aggregation of market damages for each Party for each Option closed out. The non-defaulting Party should endeavour to liquidate all outstanding Options on a single day. However, if this is impossible, the liquidation should be completed as soon as practicable. With respect to Options purchased by a Party, those damages will be the current market premium (or replacement cost) for such Options. With respect to Options sold by a Party, the only market damages will be any unpaid Premium and any interest on such unpaid Premium. With respect to exercised, but unsettled, Options, damages will be the unpaid settlement amount plus interest thereon. In addition, the non-defaulting Party is entitled to include any costs or expenses incurred in covering its obligations related to such liquidated Options, such as the obligations on a Delta hedge. The determination of market damages for each Party in each instance must be made in good faith.

4. After calculation of each Party's market damages, Clause (ii) of Section 8.1 provides for the conversion of such damages into the non-defaulting Party's Base Currency. As such damages may be in different currencies (corresponding to the different currencies in which Premiums on the liquidated Options were paid or payable), it is necessary to convert all such damage amounts into a single currency if such damages are to be aggregated (and netted pursuant to the provisions of Clause (iii) of Section 8.1). In addition, the non-defaulting Party is given the benefit of converting these damages into its Base Currency (rather than the defaulting Party's Base Currency). For purposes of this conversion, the non-defaulting Party should use the applicable spot rate.

G12

5.   Following the conversion and aggregation of each Party's market damages, Clause (iii) provides that such market damages will be netted, resulting in a single liquidated amount in the non-defaulting Party's Base Currency that will be due and payable as a settlement payment to the Party having the larger aggregated damage amount.

6.   If one or both of the Parties are holding any cash or non-cash collateral as margin or security for their respective obligations under outstanding Options or the Master Agreement generally, Clause (iv) allows the Parties to set off the value thereof (following any necessary conversion into the non-defaulting Party's Base Currency) against the liquidated damage amount calculated under the preceding clauses.

7.   Section 8.2 provides that the net amount calculated pursuant to Section 8.1 shall be paid by one Party to the other by the close of business on the Business Day following the liquidation of the Options. In some countries, a judgment can only be rendered in the currency of that country. Therefore, Section 8.2 provides that, if required by applicable law, the net amount payable by one Party to the other will be converted into a currency other than the non-defaulting Party's Base Currency. Any costs of such conversion will be borne by the defaulting Party. If this amount is not paid when due, Section 8.2 provides for the payment of interest at the applicable interbank rate plus 1% *per annum* for each day for which the amount remains unpaid. Section 8.2 also provides that Section 8 is not intended to limit, but rather that the rights provided for therein shall be in addition to, any other rights which the non-defaulting Party may have under applicable law, by agreement or otherwise, and that the non-defaulting Party is granted a general right of set off with respect to all amounts owed by either Party to the other, whether due or not due.

8.   Section 8.3 establishes the right of one Party to suspend performance of its obligations under any Option or the Master Agreement (i) if the counterparty is currently in default in the payment or performance of any of its obligations under an Option or the Master Agreement or (ii) during the pendency of a reasonable request to the counterparty to provide adequate assurances of its ability to perform such obligations. The default need not constitute an Event of Default. Therefore, if a Buyer has not paid a Premium on the applicable Premium Payment Date, even though the Seller has not sent written notice of non-receipt (or, if such notice has been sent, but two Business Days have not elapsed), the Seller is, nonetheless, entitled to suspend its performance with respect to other Options between the Parties until receipt of such Premium.

I   Parties to Rely on Their Own Expertise

Section 9 establishes that each of the Parties has relied on its own expertise and judgement in entering into each Option and as to all other subsequent actions or matters related thereto or any other currency Option or transaction. The intent of this provision is to protect each of the Parties from a claim or action by the other Party wherein it is alleged that one of the Parties exercised influence or control over the decisions or actions of the other to the extent that it is, therefore, liable for losses, costs, expenses or damages suffered or incurred as a result of such decisions or actions.

J   Illegality, Impossibility and Force Majeure

Section 10 provides that, if either Party is unable to perform, or is hindered or delayed in performing, its obligations in respect of any Option due to force majeure, or if it otherwise becomes illegal or impossible for either Party to perform its obligations in respect of any Option, then either Party may, after notice of the occurrence of such event, liquidate and close out all affected Options. Although such events do not constitute Events of Default, the liquidation and close out procedures to be followed are those provided for in Section 8. Either of the Parties may take such action promptly upon notice to the other. Due to the volatile nature of the Option markets, it is important that the Parties have the ability to liquidate positions promptly in order to limit their exposure to transactions which one of the Parties may be unable to perform. If Section 10 is applicable to the obligations of both Parties, the Parties should mutually agree upon the close out and liquidation of Options.

K   Miscellaneous

1.   The intent of Section 11.4 is to ensure that any settlement payment to a Party resulting from the termination and liquidation of Options arising either as a result of an Event of Default or an event of illegality, impossibility or force majeure, and whether pursuant to the operation of Section 8 or the judgement of a court, is made in such Party's Base Currency (or the non-defaulting Party's Base Currency) and is paid in the full amount in such Base Currency. If payment is made in some other currency, such payment is deemed to discharge the obligation of the payer only to the extent that the payee could purchase the full amount of the Base Currency (or the non-defaulting Party's Base Currency) with the amount of the currency received on the Business Day following the date of receipt. If the amount of the currency received is insufficient to purchase the full amount of the Base Currency, the payer indemnifies the payee against any loss and, in any event, the payer indemnifies the payee against any costs incurred in purchasing the Base Currency.

2.   Pursuant to Section 11.5, the Parties agree to the tape recording of any telephone conversations between them and agree that such tape recordings can be submitted in evidence in any proceeding relating to any Option transaction. It is standard market practice that conversations between traders and between traders and brokers are recorded. This practice is encouraged, as such recordings can substantially reduce the number of disputes that arise between market participants and the time which it takes to resolve such disputes. Such recordings are usually the best evidence of the essential terms of an Option as agreed by the Parties.

3.   Some Parties may choose to deal Options with each other on a margined or secured basis. Section 11.7 provides that, if the Parties have entered into an agreement providing for such dealings, then such agreement is incorporated into the Master Agreement and is subject to the terms thereof. The possibility of such an arrangement is also addressed in Section 8.1(iv), which provides for the set off of any collateral held as margin or security against the settlement payment otherwise calculated pursuant to Section 8.1. If the margin or security agreement conflicts with the Master Agreement, the Master Agreement would govern.

L   Law and Jurisdiction

1.   Legal opinions exist to the effect that the form of Master Agreement is valid and enforceable under the laws of both the State of New York and the laws of England and Wales. The legal opinion in respect of the laws of England obtained by the BBA is reproduced in the final section of this booklet. (Attention is drawn to the disclaimer printed on the inside front cover.) It is envisaged that banks entering into currency Options on the London market will normally wish their agreements to be governed by English law and to be subject to the jurisdiction of the English courts. If a bank requires the governing law to be other than English law, or the jurisdiction to be other than that of the English courts, this should be agreed before dealing commences. However, as such

G14

submission to jurisdiction is non-exclusive, Parties will be free to bring actions, suits or proceedings in other jurisdictions.

2.   Pursuant to Section 12.4, each Party explicitly waives any sovereign immunity it may be entitled to assert in any legal proceeding arising out of the Master Agreement.

M   Currency Option Confirmation

1.   The recommended form of Confirmation, which is attached to the Master Agreement as *Exhibit I*, is substantially the same as the form of Confirmation generally used by market participants to evidence Options. All of the material terms of an Option are to be set forth in the Confirmation. Material terms which are not otherwise required to be specified in the Confirmation should be included in the 'Other terms and conditions' section.

2.   There are three headings in the form of Confirmation which are not used or defined in the Master Agreement – trade date, expiration settlement date and price.

The 'trade date' is the day on which the Parties agree to enter into an Option.

The 'expiration settlement date' is the last possible day on which an exercised Option could settle. In keeping with market practice, this will generally be the Spot Date for the Currency Pair as determined on the Expiration Date.

'Price' is the currency exchange rate or the percentage (of one of the Currency Pair) upon which the Premium of an Option is determined. See Section II.A above for an explanation of market practice with respect to price quotation.

3.   Where dates are to be specified in the Confirmation (e.g. trade date), the market convention is to specify the day first (using two numbers), the month second (using three letters) and, finally, the year (using two numbers, being the last two numbers of the applicable year). For example, the date 1 March, 1991 would be specified as '01/MAR/91'.

N   Schedule

All banks should ensure that, before entering into currency Options with a counterparty, details specified in the schedule should be given to counterparties. The schedule lists particulars concerning each Party, such as the address, telephone, telex and facsimile numbers, and contact person for notices and other communications, and each Party's Base Currency. In addition, in pursuance of Part I of the schedule, the Parties should designate their branches or offices whose transactions and dealings are intended to be covered by the Master Agreement. Either because of concerns with respect to applicable law or operational capabilities (which, for instance, may make the settlement, payment netting or set off of Options between certain offices of the counterparties difficult), counterparties may choose to limit the number of Designated Offices covered.

INTERNATIONAL CURRENCY OPTIONS MARKET

Master Agreement

1. DEFINITIONS

In this Agreement, unless otherwise required by the context, the following terms shall have the following meanings:

'Agreement'   The agreement between the Parties which pursuant to Section 2.2 governs all Options and the terms of which are the terms and conditions set forth in this Master Agreement as supplemented by each Confirmation and the Schedule hereto, all as from time to time amended by agreement between the Parties; and the terms 'this Agreement', 'hereof', 'herein' and 'hereunder' shall be construed as references to such agreement;

'American Style Option' An Option which may be exercised on any Business Day up to and including the Expiration Time;

'Base Currency'   In relation to a Party the currency specified as such by it for the purpose of Part IV of the schedule hereto;

'Base Currency Rate'   For any day, the average rate at which overnight deposits in the Base Currency are offered by major banks in the London interbank market as of 11:00 a.m. (London time) on such day or such other rate as shall be agreed by the Parties, in either case as determined in good faith by the non-defaulting Party;

'Business Day'   For purposes of: (i) Section 4.2 hereof, a day which is a Local Banking Day for the applicable Designated Office of the Buyer; (ii) Section 5.1 hereof and the definition of American Style Option and Exercise Date, a day which is a Local Banking Day for the applicable Designated Office of the Seller; (iii) the definition of Event of Default, a day which is a Local Banking Day for the non-defaulting Party; and (iv) any other provision hereof, a day which is a Local Banking Day for the applicable Designated Office of both Parties; provided, however, that neither Saturday nor Sunday shall be considered a Business Day hereunder for any purpose;

'Buyer'   The owner of an Option;

'Call'   An Option entitling, but not obligating, the Buyer to purchase from the Seller at the Strike Price a specified quantity of the Call Currency;

'Call Currency'   The currency agreed as such at the time an Option is entered into;

'Confirmation'   A confirmation of an Option substantially in the form of *Exhibit I* appended hereto, which Confirmation shall be in writing (which shall include telex or other electronic means from which it is possible to produce a hard copy);

A2

'Currency Pair'	The two currencies which may be potentially exchanged upon the exercise of an Option, one of which shall be the Put Currency and the other the Call Currency;
'Designated Office'	As to either Party, the office or offices specified for the purposes of Part I of the schedule appended hereto and any other office specified from time to time by one Party and agreed to by the other as an amendment hereto as a Designated Office for the purposes of Part I of the schedule appended hereto;
'European Style Option'	An Option for which Notice of Exercise may be given only on the Option's Expiration Date up to and including the Expiration Time, unless otherwise agreed;
'Event of Default'	The occurrence of any of the following with respect to a Party (the 'defaulting Party'): (i) the defaulting Party shall default in any payment hereunder (including, but not limited to, a Premium payment) to the other Party (the 'non-defaulting Party') with respect to any Option and such failure shall continue for two (2) Business Days after written notice of non-payment by the non-defaulting Party; (ii) the defaulting Party shall commence a voluntary case or other proceeding seeking liquidation, reorganisation or other relief with respect to itself or to its debts under any bankruptcy, insolvency or similar law, or seeking the appointment of a trustee, receiver, liquidator, conservator, administrator, custodian or other similar official (each, a 'custodian') of it or any substantial part of its assets; or shall take any corporate action to authorise any of the foregoing; (iii) an involuntary case or other proceeding shall be commenced against the defaulting Party seeking liquidation, reorganization or other relief with respect to it or its debts under any bankruptcy, insolvency or other similar law or seeking the appointment of a custodian of it or any substantial part of its assets; (iv) the defaulting Party is bankrupt or insolvent; (v) the defaulting Party shall otherwise be unable to pay its debts as they become due; (vi) the failure by the defaulting Party to give adequate assurances of its ability to perform its obligations with respect to an Option within two (2) Business Days of a written request to do so when the non-defaulting Party has reasonable grounds for insecurity; (vii) the defaulting Party or any custodian acting on behalf of the defaulting Party shall disaffirm or repudiate any Option; or (viii) any representation or warranty made or deemed made pursuant to Section 3 of this Agreement by the defaulting Party shall prove to have been false or misleading in any material respect as at the time it was made or given or deemed made or given and the non-defaulting Party shall have given the defaulting Party one (1) Business Day's prior written notice thereof;
'Exercise Date'	The Business Day on which a Notice of Exercise received by the applicable Designated Office of the Seller becomes effective pursuant to Section 5.1;
'Expiration Date'	The date specified as such in a Confirmation;
'Expiration Time'	The latest time on the Expiration Date on which the Seller must accept a Notice of Exercise as specified in a Confirmation;
'In-the-money Amount'	(i) In the case of a Call, the excess of the Spot Price over the Strike Price, multiplied by the aggregate amount of the Call Currency to be purchased under the Call, where both prices are quoted in terms of the amount of the Put Currency to be paid for one unit of the Call Currency; and (ii) in the case of a Put, the excess of the Strike Price

over the Spot Price, multiplied by the aggregate amount of the Put Currency to be sold under the Put, where both prices are quoted in terms of the amount of the Call Currency to be paid for one unit of the Put Currency;

'Local Banking Day'   For any currency or Party, a day on which commercial banks in the principal banking centre of the country of issuance of such currency or in the location of the applicable Designated Office of such Party, respectively, are not authorised or required by law to close;

'Notice of Exercise'   Telex, telephonic or other electronic notification (excluding facsimile transmission), providing assurance of receipt, given by the Buyer prior to or at the Expiration Time, of the exercise of an Option, which notification shall be irrevocable;

'Option'   A Put or a Call, as the case may be, including any unexpired Put or Call previously entered into by the Parties, which shall be or become subject to this Agreement unless otherwise agreed;

'Parties'   The Parties to this Agreement; and the term 'Party' shall mean whichever of the Parties is appropriate in the context in which such expression may be used;

'Premium'   The purchase price of the Option as agreed upon by the Parties, and payable by the Buyer to the Seller thereof;

'Premium Payment Date'   The date specified as such in the Confirmation;

'Put'   An Option entitling, but not obligating, the Buyer to sell to the Seller at the Strike Price a specified quantity of the Put Currency;

'Put Currency'   The currency agreed as such at the time an Option is entered into;

'Seller'   The Party granting an Option;

'Settlement Date'   In respect of: (i) an American Style Option, the Spot Date of the Currency Pair on the Exercise Date of such Option; and (ii) a European Style Option, the Spot Date of the Currency Pair on the Expiration Date of such Option;

'Spot Date'   The spot delivery day for the relevant Currency Pair as generally used by the foreign exchange market;

'Spot Price'   The price at the time at which such price is to be determined for foreign exchange transactions in the relevant Currency Pair for value on the Spot Date, as determined in good faith: (i) by the Seller, for purposes of Section 5 hereof; and (ii) by the non-defaulting Party, for purposes of Section 8 hereof;

'Strike Price'   The price specified in a Confirmation at which the Currency Pair may be exchanged.

2. GENERAL

2.1 The Parties (through their respective Designated Offices) may enter into Options (neither being obliged to do so) for such Premiums, with such Expiration Dates, at such Strike Prices and for the purchase or sale of such quantities of such currencies, as may be agreed subject to the terms hereof.

A4

2.2 Each Option shall be governed by the terms and conditions set forth in this Master Agreement and in the Confirmation relating to such Option. Each Confirmation shall supplement and form a part of this Master Agreement and with each other Confirmation, so that this Master Agreement and all Confirmations, schedules and amendments hereto constitute a single agreement between the Parties. The Parties acknowledge that all Options are entered into in reliance upon such fact, it being understood that the Parties would not otherwise enter into any Option.

2.3 Options shall be promptly confirmed by the Parties by Confirmations exchanged by mail, telex, facsimile or other electronic means. Unless either Party objects to the terms contained in any Confirmation within the earlier of (i) the time period recognized by local market practice or (ii) three (3) Business Days of receipt thereof, the terms of such Confirmation shall be deemed correct absent manifest error, unless a corrected Confirmation is sent by a Party within such three day period, in which case the Party receiving such corrected Confirmation shall have three (3) Business Days after receipt thereof to object to the terms contained in such corrected Confirmation. Failure by either Party to issue a Confirmation shall not alter the rights and obligations of either Party under an Option to which the Parties have agreed. In the event of any conflict between the terms of a Confirmation and this Agreement, such Confirmation shall prevail, except for purposes of this Section 2.3 and Section 6 hereof.

2.4 Neither Party may assign its rights nor delegate its obligations under any Option to a third party without the prior written consent of the other Party.

3. REPRESENTATIONS AND WARRANTIES; CONTRACTUAL STATUS

Each Party represents and warrants to the other Party as of the date hereof and as of the date of each Option that: (i) it has authority to enter into this Agreement and such Option; (ii) the persons entering into this Agreement and entering into such Option on its behalf have been duly authorised to do so; (iii) this Agreement and such Option are binding upon it and enforceable against it in accordance with their respective terms and do not and will not violate the terms of any agreements to which such Party is bound; (iv) no Event of Default, or event which, with notice or lapse of time or both, would constitute an Event of Default has occurred and is continuing with respect to it; and (v) it acts as principal in entering into and exercising each and every Option.

4. THE PREMIUM

4.1 Unless otherwise agreed in writing by the Parties, the Premium related to an Option shall be paid on its Premium Payment Date.

4.2 If any Premium is not received on the Premium Payment Date, the Seller may elect either: (i) to accept a late payment of such Premium; (ii) to give written notice of such non-payment and, if such payment shall not be received within two (2) Business Days of such notice, treat the related Option as void; or (iii) to give written notice of such non-payment and, if such payment shall not be received within two (2) Business Days of such notice, treat such non-payment as an Event of Default under Clause (i) of the definition of Event of Default. If the Seller elects to act under either Clause (i) or (ii) of the preceding sentence, the Buyer shall pay all out-of-pocket costs and actual damages incurred in connection with such unpaid or late Premium or void Option, including, without limitation, interest on such Premium in the same currency as such Premium at the then prevailing market rate and any other costs or expenses incurred by the Seller in covering its obligations (including, without limitation, a delta hedge) with respect to such Option.

5. EXERCISE AND SETTLEMENT OF OPTIONS

5.1 The Buyer may exercise an Option by delivery to the Seller of a Notice of Exercise. Subject to Section 5.4 hereof, if an Option has not been exercised prior to or at the Expiration Time, it shall expire and become void and of no effect. Any Notice of Exercise shall (unless otherwise agreed): (i) if received prior to 3:00 p.m. on a Business Day, be effective upon receipt thereof by the Seller; and (ii) if received after 3:00 p.m. on a Business Day, be effective only as of the opening of business of the Seller on the first Business Day subsequent to its receipt.

5.2 An exercised Option shall settle on its Settlement Date. Subject to Section 5.3 and 5.4 hereof, on the Settlement Date, the Buyer shall pay the Put Currency to the Seller for value on the Settlement Date and the Seller shall pay the Call Currency to the Buyer for value on the Settlement Date.

5.3 An Option shall be settled at its In-the-money Amount if so agreed by the Parties at the time such Option is entered into. In such case, the In-the-money Amount shall be determined based upon the Spot Price at the time of exercise or as soon thereafter as possible. The sole obligations of the Parties with respect to such Option shall be to deliver or receive the In-the-money Amount of such Option on the Settlement Date.

5.4 Unless the Seller is otherwise instructed by the Buyer, if an Option has an In-the-money Amount at its Expiration Time that equals or exceeds the product of (x) 1% of the Strike Price and (y) the amount of the Call or Put Currency, as appropriate, then the Option shall be deemed automatically exercised. In such case, the Seller may elect to settle such Option either in accordance with Section 5.2 of this Agreement or by payment to the Buyer on the Settlement Date for such Option of the In-the-money Amount, as determined at the Expiration Time or as soon thereafter as possible. In the latter case, the sole obligations of the Parties with respect to such Option shall be to deliver or receive the In-the-money Amount of such Option on the Settlement Date. The Seller shall notify the Buyer of its election of the method of settlement of an automatically exercised Option as soon as practicable after the Expiration Time.

5.5 Unless otherwise agreed by the Parties, an Option may be exercised only in whole.

6. DISCHARGE AND TERMINATION OF OPTIONS

Unless otherwise agreed, any Call Option or any Put Option written by a Party will automatically be terminated and discharged, in whole or in part, as applicable, against a Call Option or a Put Option, respectively, written by the other Party, such termination and discharge to occur automatically upon the payment in full of the last Premium payable in respect of such Options; *provided that* such termination and discharge may only occur in respect of Options:

(a)   each being with respect to the same Put Currency and the same Call Currency;

(b)   each having the same Expiration Date and Expiration Time;

(c)   each being of the same style, i.e. either both being American Style Options or both being European Style Options;

(d)   each having the same Strike Price; and

(e)   neither of which shall have been exercised by delivery of a Notice of Exercise;

and, upon the occurrence of such termination and discharge, neither Party shall have any further obligation to the other Party in respect of the relevant Options or, as the case may be, parts thereof so terminated and discharged. In the case of a partial termination and discharge (i.e. where the relevant Options are for different amounts of the Currency Pair), the remaining portion of the Option which is partially discharged and terminated shall continue to be an Option for all purposes of this Agreement, including this Section 6.

A6

7. PAYMENT NETTING

7.1 If, on any date, and unless otherwise mutually agreed by the Parties, Premiums would otherwise be payable hereunder in the same currency between respective Designated Offices of the Parties, then, on such date, each Party's obligation to make payment of any such Premium will be automatically satisfied and discharged and, if the aggregate Premium(s) that would otherwise have been payable by such Designated Office of one Party exceeds the aggregate Premium(s) that would otherwise have been payable by such Designated Office of the other Party, replaced by an obligation upon the Party by whom the larger aggregate Premium(s) would have been payable to pay the other Party the excess of the larger aggregate Premium(s) over the smaller aggregate Premium(s).

7.2 If, on any date, and unless otherwise mutually agreed by the Parties, amounts other than Premium payments would otherwise be payable hereunder in the same currency between respective Designated Offices of the Parties, then, on such date, each Party's obligation to make payment of any such amount will be automatically satisfied and discharged and, if the aggregate amount that would otherwise have been payable by such Designated Office of one Party exceeds the aggregate amount that would otherwise have been payable by such Designated Office of the other Party, replaced by an obligation upon the Party by whom the larger aggregate amount would have been payable to pay the other Party the excess of the larger aggregate amount over the smaller aggregate amount.

8. DEFAULT

8.1 If an Event of Default has occurred and is continuing, then the non-defaulting Party shall have the right to liquidate and/or to deem to liquidate all, but not less than all (except to the extent that in the good faith opinion of the non-defaulting Party certain of such Options may not be liquidated under applicable law), outstanding Options by notice to the defaulting Party. The previous sentence notwithstanding, in the case of an Event of Default specified in Clauses (ii), (iii) or (iv) of the definition thereof, such liquidation and/or deemed liquidation shall be automatic as to all outstanding Options, except where the relevant voluntary or involuntary case or other proceeding or bankruptcy or insolvency giving rise to such Event of Default is governed by a system of law which contains express provisions enabling close out in the manner described in Clauses (i) to (iv) below (or a manner equivalent thereto) to take place after the occurrence of the relevant Event of Default in the absence of automatic liquidation. Such liquidation and/or deemed liquidation shall be effected by:

(i) closing out each such Option at the time of liquidation so that each such Option is cancelled and market damages for each Party are calculated equal to the aggregate of (a) with respect to each Option purchased by such Party, the current market premium for such Option, (b) with respect to each Option sold by such Party, any unpaid Premium and, to the extent permitted by applicable law, interest on any unpaid Premium in the same currency as such Premium at the then prevailing market rate, (c) with respect to any exercised Option, any unpaid amount due in settlement of such Option and, to the extent permitted by applicable law, interest thereon from the applicable Settlement Date to the day of close out at the average rate at which overnight deposits in the currency in which such unpaid amount was due are offered by major banks in the London interbank market as of 11:00 a.m. (London time) on each such day plus 1% per annum, and (d) any costs or expenses incurred by the non-defaulting Party in covering its obligations (including a delta hedge) with respect to such Option, all as determined in good faith by the non-defaulting Party;

(ii) converting any damages calculated in accordance with Clause (i) above in a currency other than the non-defaulting Party's Base Currency into such Base Currency at the Spot Price at which, at the time of liquidation, the non-defaulting Party could enter into a contract in the foreign exchange market to buy the Base Currency in exchange for such currency;

A7

(iii) netting such damage payments with respect to each Party so that all such amounts are netted to a single liquidated amount payable by one Party to the other Party as a settlement payment; and

(iv) setting off the net payment calculated in accordance with Clause (iii) above which the non-defaulting Party owes to the defaulting Party, if any, and, at the option of the non-defaulting Party, any margin or other collateral ('margin') held by the non-defaulting Party (including the liquidated value of any non-cash margin) in respect of the defaulting Party's obligations hereunder against the net payment calculated in accordance with Clause (iii) above which the defaulting Party owes to the non-defaulting Party, if any, and, at the option of the non-defaulting Party, any margin held by the defaulting Party (including the liquidated value of any non-cash margin) in respect of the non-defaulting Party's obligations hereunder; *provided*, that, for purposes of such set off, any margin denominated in a currency other the non-defaulting Party's Base Currency shall be converted into such currency at the rate specified in Clause (ii) above.

8.2 The net amount payable by one Party to the other Party pursuant to the provisions of Section 8.1 above shall be paid by the close of business on the Business Day following such liquidation and/or deemed liquidation of all such Options (converted as required by applicable law into any other currency, any such costs of conversion to be borne by, and deducted from any payment to, the defaulting Party). To the extent permitted by applicable law, any amounts owed but not paid when due under this Section 8 shall bear interest at the Base Currency Rate plus 1% per annum (or, if conversion is required by applicable law into some other currency, either (x) the average rate at which overnight deposits in such other currency are offered by major banks in the London interbank market as of 11:00 a.m. (London time) plus 1% per annum or (y) such other rate as may be prescribed by such applicable law) for each day for which such amount remains unpaid.

8.3 Without prejudice to the foregoing, so long as a Party shall be in default in payment or performance to the other Party hereunder or under any Option and the non-defaulting Party has not exercised its rights under this Section 8, or during the pendency of a reasonable request to a Party for adequate assurances of its ability to perform its obligations hereunder or under any Option, the other Party may, at its election and without penalty, suspend its obligation to perform hereunder or under any Option.

8.4 The Party required to make a payment to the other Party pursuant to Sections 8.1 and 8.2 above shall pay to the other Party all out-of-pocket expenses incurred by such other Party (including fees and disbursements of counsel and time charges of attorneys who may be employees of such other Party) in connection with any reasonable collection or other enforcement proceedings related to such required payment.

8.5 The Parties agree that the amounts recoverable under this Section 8 are a reasonable pre-estimate of loss and not a penalty. Such amounts are payable for the loss of bargain and the loss of protection against future risks and, except as otherwise provided in this Agreement, neither Party will be entitled to recover any additional damages as a consequence of such losses.

8.6 The non-defaulting Party's rights under this Section 8 shall be in addition to, and not in limitation or exclusion of, any other rights which the non-defaulting Party may have (whether by agreement, operation of law or otherwise), and the non-defaulting Party shall have a general right of set off with respect to all amounts owed by each Party to the other Party, whether due or not due (provided that any amount not due at the time of such set off shall be discounted to present value in a commercially reasonable manner by the non-defaulting Party).

A8

9. PARTIES TO RELY ON THEIR OWN EXPERTISE

Each Option shall be deemed to have been entered into by each Party in reliance only upon its judgement. Neither Party holds out itself as advising, or any of its employees or agents as having its authority to advise, the other Party as to whether or not it should enter into any such Option (whether as Seller or Buyer) or as to any subsequent actions relating thereto or on any other commercial matters concerned with any currency Options or transactions, and neither Party shall have any responsibility or liability whatsoever in respect of any advice of this nature given, or views expressed, by it or any of such persons to the other Party, whether or not such advice is given or such views are expressed at the request of the other Party.

10. ILLEGALITY, IMPOSSIBILITY AND FORCE MAJEURE

If either Party is prevented from or hindered or delayed by reason of force majeure or act of State in the delivery or payment of any currency in respect of an Option or if it becomes unlawful or impossible for either Party to make or receive any payment in respect of an Option, then the Party for whom such performance has been prevented, hindered or delayed or has become illegal or impossible shall promptly give notice thereof to the other Party and either Party may, by notice to the other Party, require the liquidation and close out of each affected Option in accordance with the provisions of Section 8 hereof and, for such purposes, the Party unaffected by such force majeure, act of State, illegality or impossibility shall be considered the non-defaulting Party and, for purposes of this Section 10, such non-defaulting Party shall perform the calculation required under Section 8.

11. MISCELLANEOUS

11.1 Unless otherwise specified, the times referred to herein shall in each case refer to the local time of the relevant Designated Office of the Seller of the relevant Option.

11.2 Unless otherwise specified, all notices, instructions and other communications to be given to a Party hereunder shall be given to the address, telex (if confirmed by the appropriate answerback), facsimile (confirmed if requested) or telephone number and to the individual or Department specified by such Party for the purposes of Part II of the schedule attached hereto. Unless otherwise specified, any notice, instruction or other communication, shall be effective upon receipt if given in accordance with this Section 11.2.

11.3 All payments to be made hereunder shall be made in same day (or immediately available) and freely transferable funds and, unless otherwise specified, shall be delivered to such office of such bank and in favor of such account as shall be specified by the Party entitled to receive such payment for the purposes of Part III of the Schedule attached hereto or as specified by such Party by notice given in accordance with Section 11.2. Time shall be of the essence in this Agreement.

11.4 The receipt or recovery by either Party of any amount in respect of an obligation of the other Party in a currency other than the Base Currency (other than receipt by the defaulting Party pursuant to Sections 8.1 and 8.2 of a payment in the non-defaulting Party's Base Currency), whether pursuant to a judgment of any court or pursuant to Section 8 hereof, shall discharge such obligation only to the extent that, on the first day on which such Party is open for business immediately following such receipt, the recipient shall be able, in accordance with normal banking procedures, to purchase the Base Currency with the currency received. If the amount of the Base Currency so purchasable shall be less than the original Base Currency amount calculated pursuant to Section 8 hereof, the obligor shall, as a separate obligation and notwithstanding any judgement of any court, indemnify the recipient against any loss sustained by it. The obligor shall in any event indemnify the recipient against any costs incurred by it in making any such purchase of the Base Currency.

A9

11.5 The Parties agree that each may electronically record all telephonic conversations between them and that any such recordings may be submitted in evidence to any court or in any proceeding for the purpose of establishing any matters pertinent to any Option.

11.6 This Agreement shall supersede any other agreement between the Parties with respect to the subject matter hereof and all outstanding Options between the Parties on the date hereof shall be subject hereto, unless otherwise expressly agreed by the Parties.

11.7 A margin agreement between the Parties may apply to obligations governed by this Agreement. If the Parties have executed a margin agreement, such margin agreement shall be subject to the terms hereof and is hereby incorporated by reference herein. In the event of any conflict between a margin agreement and this Agreement, this Agreement shall prevail, except for any provision in such margin agreement in respect of governing law.

11.8 In the event any one or more of the provisions contained in this Agreement should be held invalid, illegal or unenforceable in any respect, the validity, legality and enforceability of the remaining provisions contained herein shall not in any way be affected or impaired thereby. The Parties shall endeavor in good faith negotiations to replace the invalid, illegal or unenforceable provisions with valid provisions the economic effect of which comes as close as possible to that of the invalid, illegal or unenforceable provisions.

12. LAW AND JURISDICTION

12.1 This Agreement shall be governed by, and construed in accordance with, the laws of* England and Wales without giving effect to conflicts of law principles.

12.2 With respect to any suit, action or proceedings ('Proceedings') relating to any Option or this Agreement, each Party irrevocably (i) *agrees for the benefit of the other Party that the courts of England shall have jurisdiction to determine any Proceeding and irrevocably submits to the jurisdiction of the English courts and (ii) waives any objection which it may have at any time to the laying of venue of any Proceedings brought in any such court, waives any claim that such Proceedings have been brought in an inconvenient forum and further waives the right to object, with respect to such Proceedings, that such court does not have jurisdiction over such Party. Nothing in this Agreement precludes either Party from bringing Proceedings in any other jurisdiction nor will the bringing of Proceedings in any one or more jurisdictions preclude the bringing of Proceedings in any other jurisdiction.

> * *Unless otherwise agreed between the Parties, it shall be assumed that in Section 12.1 the governing laws chosen shall be those of England and Wales and in Section 12.2 the submission will be to the jurisdiction of the Courts of England.*

12.3 Each Party hereby irrevocably waives any and all right to trial by jury in any legal proceeding arising out of or relating to this Agreement or any Option.

12.4 Each Party hereby irrevocably waives, to the fullest extent permitted by applicable law, with respect to itself and its revenues and assets (irrespective of their use or intended use), all immunity on the grounds of sovereignty or other similar grounds from (i) suit, (ii) jurisdiction of any court, (iii) relief by way of injunction, order for specific performance or for recovery of property, (iv) attachment of its assets (whether before or after judgment) and (v) execution or enforcement of any judgment to which it or its revenues or assets might otherwise be entitled in any Proceedings (as defined in Section 12.2 hereof) in the courts of any jurisdiction and irrevocably agrees, to the extent permitted by applicable law, that it will not claim any such immunity in any Proceedings.

A10

EXHIBIT 1

Currency Option Confirmation

To: _____

_____ hereby confirms the following terms of a currency option:

Reference:

Trade Date (DD/MMM/YY):

Buyer:

Seller:

Option Style (European or American):

Option Type (Put or Call):

Put Currency and Amount:

Call Currency and Amount:

Strike Price:

Expiration Date (DD/MMM/YY):

Expiration Time:

Expiration Settlement Date (DD/MMM/YY):

Premium:

Price:

Premium Payment Date (DD/MMM/YY):

Premium Payment Instructions:

Other terms and conditions:

This Option is subject to the BBA International Currency Options Market Master Terms dated August 1992.

Please confirm to us by return telex, mail, facsimile or other electronic transmission that the above details are correct.

A11

Schedule

Part I: **Designated Offices**

Specifiy details of Designated Offices in relation to a Party for the purposes of this Schedule. In the absence of any specification each office of a Party through which it enters into an Option shall be a Designated Office.

Part II: **Notices**

Specify details in relation to each Party of address, telephone number, telex number, facsimile number and name of individual or department to whom or to which notices are to be sent to it for the purposes of this Schedule.

In the absence of any specification the relevant details of a Party shall be the address, telephone number, telex number and facsimile number of its office through which, and the individual or department through whom or through which the first Option entered into by such Party on or after 30 September 1992 is entered into.

Part III: **Payment Instructions**

Specify details in relation to each Party for the purposes of this Schedule of its bank and office, account number and reference with respect to relevant currencies.

Part IV: **Base Currency**

Specify in relation to each Party, the Base Currency in relation to it for the purposes of this Schedule. In the absence of any specification the relevant Base Currency shall be Sterling.

CLIFFORD CHANCE

ROYEX HOUSE ALDERMANBURY SQUARE LONDON EC2V 7LD TELEPHONE 071-600 0808

TELEX 8959991 COWARD G   FAX 071-726 8561   DX 209 LONDON

AMSTERDAM BRUSSELS FRANKFURT HONG KONG LONDON MADRID MOSCOW NEW YORK PARIS SINGAPORE TOKYO UNITED ARAB EMIRATES WARSAW
ASSOCIATED OFFICES BAHRAIN SAUDI ARABIA

YOUR REFERENCE	IN REPLY PLEASE QUOTE	DATE
	SJP/B1676/0029/HNM	20 May 1992

To: The British Bankers' Association
       10 Lombard Street
       London EC3V 9EL

Dear Sirs,

International Currency Option Master Agreement

1.   You have asked us to opine on the above form of Master Agreement ("the Agreement"). This opinion relates to the specimen of the Agreement attached hereto.

2.   This opinion relates solely to matters of English law (as in force at the date hereof) in circumstances where the Agreement is expressed to be governed by English law and the submission to jurisdiction in Section 12 is to the jurisdiction of the English courts. It does not consider the impact of insolvency laws, other than English insolvency laws, even in the case where the Agreement is expressed to be governed by English law.

3.   On the basis specified in paragraph 2 above we are of the opinion that, subject to the specific qualifications and assumptions set out below, the Agreement would, if duly entered into (and if all relevant Options were duly entered into), be valid and enforceable.

4.   By "duly entered into" we mean that there must be nothing specific to the particular transaction or to either of the parties thereto (such as, without limitation, lack of capacity, lack of due authorisation, failure to comply with any applicable regulatory requirements, illegality under any law applicable to either of the parties, wrongful preference or undervalue) which could render the Agreement invalid or unenforceable or which could result in that transaction being set aside or otherwise being declared void or voidable on the insolvency of either of the parties.

5.   In relation to Section 8 of the Agreement, while it is our opinion that its provisions would be effective if either or both of the parties were the subject of English insolvency proceedings (although, of course, if the net amount payable was due from such an insolvent party, in the absence of effective security that would be an unsecured claim which would rank for payment in the same manner as other unsecured claims), we are bound to point out that the Insolvency Rules, which apply to the liquidation of insolvent companies and, generally speaking, provide for set off of mutual credits and debts, do not specifically address the question of how mutual options are to be dealt with and we are not aware

CLIFFORD CHANCE

of any case law which provides direct assistance. The basis of our reasoning which has led us to the opinion that the provisions of Section 8 would be effective in an insolvency is that we have concluded that the effect of that Section is not materially different from what the position would be in the event that a party had become subject to English liquidation proceedings in the absence of such a provision. If that conclusion should prove to be incorrect then it may well follow that the provisions of Section 8 would be unenforceable against a party which became subject to English liquidation proceedings on the ground that the Section was an attempt to vary by contract the basis on which the insolvent's assets were to be divided between its creditors, a result which cannot effectively be achieved by a contract which does not create some form of effective security interest.

In addition, where one party is subject to English liquidation proceedings it may be necessary to take as the rate for converting any damages, rather than the rate specified in Section 8.1(ii), the "official exchange rate" prescribed by Rule 4.91 of the Insolvency Rules, which is based on spot market exchange rates on the date on which the Court makes its liquidation order or the company concerned resolves to go into liquidation.

6.   The provisions in the Insolvency Rules relating to set off of mutual credits and debts do not apply to sums due under transactions which were entered into at a time when the creditor had notice that a meeting of creditors of the other party had been summoned under Section 98 of the Insolvency Act (which requires a company which goes into creditors' voluntary winding up to cause a meeting of creditors to be summoned for a day not later than the fourteenth day after the day on which there is to be held a shareholders' meeting at which the resolution for voluntary winding up is to be proposed) or that a petition for the winding up of the other party was pending. Accordingly we express no opinion as to the effectiveness of Section 6 of the Agreement in relation to any Options which may be entered into by a party at a time when it had notice of such a meeting or such a petition or as to whether or not any such Options could validly be included in the close out procedures prescribed by Section 8.

7.   Where a Court makes an order putting a company into liquidation the liquidation is retrospectively deemed to have commenced on the date on which the petition on which that order was made was presented to the Court. A consequence of this is that, unless the Court otherwise orders, any dispositions of the company's property made between the presentation of the petition and the making of the order are void. Accordingly we express no opinion as to the effectiveness of Section 6 of the Agreement in relation to any Options which may be entered into during such a period or as to whether or not any such Options could validly be included in the close out procedures prescribed by Section 8. It is also possible that any payments made by a company during such period by way of settlement of transactions or, indeed pursuant to Section 8, could be recovered by the liquidator.

8.   Section 4.2 of the Agreement provides that where a Premium is not paid by the due date the Seller of the relevant Option has the right to elect, inter alia, either to accept a late payment of such Premium or to treat that Option as void. In such events the Section provides that the Buyer is to pay any actual costs and damages suffered by the Seller, and interest on the premium (presumably, although this is not absolutely clear, for the period from the due date for payment of the premium to the

CLIFFORD CHANCE

date on which either the Premium is paid or, as the case may be, the Option becomes void). This payment may result in the Seller receiving a sum in excess of its actual loss (determined on the basis of the principles of general law relating to the calculation of damages). Accordingly, there is a possibility that the final sentence of Section 4.2 would be held to be penal and unenforceable insofar as it applies to subparagraphs (i) and (ii) of the previous sentence, and we, therefore, express no opinion as to its validity or enforceability. If it were held to be penal and unenforceable the Seller would be entitled to recover such damages as it could prove under the general law.

Similarly, in the event that payment of interest in accordance with Sections 8.1(i)(b) or (c) or 8.2 or payment of expenses in accordance with Section 8.4 would result in a party recovering more than its actual loss (determined on the basis of the principles of general law relating to the calculation of damages), there is a possibility that the provision in the Agreement for such payment would be held to be penal and unenforceable, and we, therefore, express no opinion as to its validity or enforceability.

9.   There is some possibility that an English Court would hold that a judgment on the Agreement, whether given in an English Court or elsewhere, would supersede the Agreement to all intents and purposes so that the obligations set forth in Section 11.4 of the Agreement would be held not to survive such a judgment.

10.   With regard to Section 11.8 of the Agreement, the question whether or not any provisions of the Agreement which may be invalid on account of illegality may be severed from the other provisions thereof in order to save those other provisions would be determined by the English Courts in their discretion.

11.   The term "enforceable" as used in this opinion means that the obligations assumed are of a type which the English Courts enforce; it does not mean that these obligations will necessarily be enforced in the circumstances or in accordance with their terms. The power of the English Courts to order specific performance of an obligation or to order any other equitable remedy is discretionary and, accordingly, an English Court might make an award of damages where specific performance of an obligation or any other equitable remedy was sought. (In addition to qualifying our opinion in paragraph 3 above, this qualification will also qualify the validity and enforceability of the representation made by a party under Section 3(iii) of the Agreement.)

12.   Any provision purporting to require a party to indemnify another against, or reimburse the costs or expenses of, proceedings in the English Courts is subject to the discretion of the Court to decide whether and to what extent a party to such proceedings should be awarded the costs and expenses incurred by it in connection therewith.

13.   Where any obligations of any person are to be performed in jurisdictions outside England, such obligations may not be enforceable under English law to the extent that such performance thereof would be illegal or contrary to public policy under the laws of such jurisdiction.

14.   Where any party to the Agreement is vested with a discretion or may determine a matter, English law may require that such discretion is exercised or determination is made reasonably. Any provision in the

CLIFFORD CHANCE

Agreement providing that any calculation or certification is to be conclusive and binding will not be effective if such calculation or certification is fraudulent, incorrect, unreasonable, arbitrary or shown not to have been given or made in good faith and will not necessarily prevent judicial enquiry into the merits of any claim by any party thereto. An English Court may regard any calculation, determination or certification as no more than prima facie evidence of the matter calculated, determined or certified.

15. The Agreement provides for the terms of an Option to be confirmed by the parties by way of the exchange of confirmations and provides for certain matters relating to an Option to be determined by reference to such a confirmation. We express no opinion as to the validity or enforceability of the Agreement in circumstances where the terms agreed between the parties when entering into an Option and the record of such terms contained in the respective confirmations of the parties are not wholly consistent with each other or where a party does not issue a confirmation or its confirmation is inaccurate or incomplete.

16. Where in relation to Section 8 the Defaulting Party is the subject of English insolvency proceedings, we have assumed that the currency into which damages will be converted under Section 8.1(ii) (the "Non-Defaulting Party's Base Currency") will be sterling.

17. We have assumed for the purposes of this opinion that the period for which interest will be calculated pursuant to Section 8.1(i)(b) will be from the date the relevant unpaid premiums became due to the day of close-out and that, for the purposes of Sections 8.1(i)(b), 8.1(i)(c) and 8.2, established market practice makes it clear and unambiguous (i) what are the rates of interest to be applied and how they are to be determined and (ii) that such rates may, at least for the purposes of Section 8.1, be determined as at the time of close-out; and, for the purposes of Section 8.6, established market practice makes it clear and unambiguous what is the manner in which the discounting to present value is to be effected and how it is to be determined.

18. If in fact a party has relied on the other or has given advice to the other then, insofar as Section 9 seeks to deem otherwise, that Section may not be effective, and it is possible that an English Court will not allow one of the parties to exclude its liability as envisaged by that Section merely because of the inclusion of the provision for exclusion of liability contained in that Section.

19. Where the position of either party is affected by force majeure, act of state, illegality or impossibility, then the validity and enforceability of the provisions of Section 10 whereby the liquidation and close-out provisions of Section 8 may be invoked and applied may also be subject to such force majeure, act of state, illegality or impossibility.

20. As regards jurisdiction, an English Court may stay proceedings if concurrent proceedings are being brought elsewhere. With reference to Section 12.2 there is some uncertainty as to the effect of Section 12.2 under the Convention on Jurisdiction and Enforcement of Judgment in Civil and Commercial Matters. In particular it is possible that the English Courts may treat Section 12.2 as restricting jurisdiction to that of the English Courts or that they may hold that, in circumstances where the Convention applies, the provision that neither party is precluded from

CLIFFORD CHANCE

bringing proceedings in a jurisdiction other than that of the English courts negates the submission to the jurisdiction of the English courts.

21.   Under English law, an agreement may be varied or superseded by agreement (which may be oral or in writing) between the parties. The validity and enforceability of Section 12.2 is therefore subject to such Section or the Agreement being varied or superseded by virtue of any such agreement between the parties.

22.   We express no opinion as to the validity or enforceability of Section 12.3.

23.   As this opinion is given in relation to the terms of the Agreement, it does not consider the impact of the Restrictive Trade Practices Act 1976 and Articles 85 and 86 of the Treaty of Rome, particularly in the context of the issue by the British Bankers' Association of the Agreement and the Guide pertaining to the Agreement. We are advising you separately on this.

24.   As a matter of English law, claims may become barred under the Limitation Acts.

25.   It is our understanding that any margin to be taken by a party to the Agreement, whether in the form of cash or in any other form, would be the subject of a separate collateral agreement. We should make it clear, for the avoidance of doubt, that this opinion does not address any question relating to the validity or enforceability of any such collateral or of the availability of set off in respect of it in the manner provided for by Section 8.1(iv). We assume for the purposes of this opinion that no margin agreement is incorporated by reference in the Agreement pursuant to Section 11.7.

This opinion is addressed solely to the body known as the British Bankers' Association ("BBA") and is for the sole benefit of such body and may not be relied upon by any other body or any person, including, without limitation, by any individual member of the BBA or any other body or any person in relation to any specific agreement or option entered into or to be entered into by such member or other body or person.

Yours faithfully,

Clifford Chance.

SJP$07$2.21

THE
INTERNATIONAL
CURRENCY
OPTIONS
MARKET
(ICOM)

MASTER AGREEMENT AND GUIDE

THE BRITISH BANKERS' ASSOCIATION
&
THE FOREIGN EXCHANGE COMMITTEE of NEW YORK

THE TOKYO FOREIGN EXCHANGE MARKET PRACTICES COMMITTEE
東京外国為替市場慣行委員会

MARCH 1993

PREFACE

Currency options market in Tokyo has made a rapid progress in these several years. The progress raised the greatest need to establish a master agreement which is to apply for market practice as a standard.

Therefore, the Tokyo Foreign Exchange Market Practices Committee decided to adopt The International Currency Options Master Terms (ICOM Terms for short) as the standard agreement for Tokyo interbank over-the-counter currency options market.

The ICOM Terms have been drawn up under auspices of the British Bankers' Association and the Foreign Exchange Committee of New York as representing good market practices for dealings in currency options.

The ICOM Terms defines key terms and addresses regular formations, exercise, and settlement procedures for foreign exchange options as well as procedures for the event of default.

Prior to dealing, you might as well ensure that your counterparties are in possession of the details specified in the Schedule so that exercise and settlement can take place smoothly.

Where necessary, the ICOM Terms can also be extended to customers as well.

INTERNATIONAL CURRENCY OPTIONS MARKET MASTER AGREEMENT

MASTER AGREEMENT dated as of(a) .... **19** .... **by and between**

(b) .... ,**a**(c) ....

of(d) .... **and**

(e) .... ,**a**(c) ....

of(d) ....

Notes
(a) *insert date of month and year*   (b) *insert name of party*
(c) *insert type of body (e.g. company)*   (d) *insert place of establishment*   (e) *insert name of counterparty*

1.   DEFINITIONS

In this Agreement, unless otherwise required by the context, the following terms shall have the following meanings:

"Agreement"	The agreement between the Parties which pursuant to Section 2.2 governs all Options and the terms of which are the terms and conditions set forth in this Master Agreement as supplemented by each Confirmation and the Schedule hereto, ***all*** as from time to time amended by agreement between the Parties; and the terms "this Agreement", "hereof", "herein" and "hereunder" shall be construed as reference to such agreement;
"American Style Option"	An Option which may be exercised on any Business Day up to and including the Expiration Time;
"Base Currency"	The currency specified as such by a Party in Part IV of the Schedule hereto;
"Base Currency Rate"	For any day, the average rate at which overnight deposits in the Base Currency are offered by major banks in the London interbank market as of 11:00 a.m. (London time) on such day or such other rate as shall be agreed by the Parties, in either case as determined in good faith by the Non-Defaulting Party;
"Business Day"	For purposes of: (I) Section 4.2 hereof, a day which is a Local Banking Day for the applicable Designated Office of the Buyer; (II) Section 5.1 hereof and the definition of American Style Option and Exercise Date, a day which is a Local Banking Day for the applicable Designated Office of the Seller; (III) the definition of Event of Default, a day which is a Local Banking Day for the Non-Defaulting Party; and (IV) any other provision hereof, a day which is a Local Banking Day for the applicable Designated Office of both Parties; *provided, however*, that neither Saturday nor Sunday shall be considered a Business Day hereunder for any purpose;
"Buyer"	The owner of an Option;

"Call"	An option entitling, but not obligating, the Buyer to purchase from the Seller at the Strike Price a specified quantity of the Call Currency;
"Call Currency"	The currency agreed as such at the time an Option is entered into;
"Confirmation"	A confirmation of an Option substantially in the form of *Exhibit I* hereto, which confirmation shall be in writing (which shall include telex or other electronic means from which it is possible to produce a hard copy);
"Currency Pair"	The two currencies which may be potentially exchanged upon the exercise of an Option, one of which shall be the Put Currency and the other the Call Currency;
"Designated Office"	As to either Party, the office or offices specified on Part I of the Schedule hereto and any other office specified from time to time by one Party and agreed to by the other as an amendment hereto as a Designated Office on Part I of the Schedule hereto;
"European Style Option"	An Option for which Notice of Exercise may be given only on the Option's Expiration Date up to and including the Expiration Time, unless otherwise agreed;
"Event of Default"	The occurrence of any of the following with respect to a Party (the "Defaulting Party"): (I) the Defaulting Party shall default in any payment hereunder (including, but not limited to, a Premium payment) to the other Party (the "Non-Defaulting Party") with respect to any Option and such failure shall continue for two (2) Business Days after written notice of non-payment by the Non-Defaulting Party; (II) the Defaulting Party shall commence a voluntary case or other proceeding seeking liquidation, reorganization or other relief with respect to itself or to its debts under any bankruptcy, insolvency or similar law, or seeking the appointment of a trustee, receiver, liquidator, conservator, administrator, custodian or other similar official (each, a "Custodian") of it or any substantial part of its assets; or shall take any corporate action to authorize any of the foregoing; (III) an involuntary case or other proceeding shall be commenced against the Defaulting Party seeking liquidation, reorganization or other relief with respect to it or its debts under any bankruptcy, insolvency or other similar law or seeking the appointment of a Custodian of it or any substantial part of its assets; (IV) the Defaulting Party is bankrupt or insolvent; (V) the Defaulting Party shall otherwise be unable to pay its debts as they become due; (VI) the failure by the Defaulting Party to give adequate assurances of its ability to perform its obligations with respect to an Option within two (2) Business Days of a written request to do so when the Non-Defaulting Party has reasonable grounds for insecurity; (VII) the Defaulting Party or any Custodian acting on behalf of the Defaulting Party shall disaffirm or repudiate any Option; or (VIII) any representation or warranty made or deemed made pursuant to Section 3 of this Agreement by the Defaulting Party shall prove to have been false or misleading in any material respect as at the time it was made or given or deemed made or given and the Non-Defaulting Party shall have given the Defaulting Party one (1) Business Day's prior written notice thereof;
"Exercise Date"	The Business Day on which a Notice of Exercise received by the applicable Designated Office of the Seller becomes effective pursuant to section 5.1;

"Expiration Date"	The date specified as such in a Confirmation;
"Expiration Time"	The latest time on the Expiration Date on which the Seller must accept a Notice of Exercise as specified in a Confirmation;
"In-the-money Amount"	(I) In the case of a Call, the excess of the Spot Price over the Strike Price, multiplied by the aggregate amount of the Call Currency to be purchased under the Call, where both prices are quoted in terms of the amount of the Put Currency to be paid for one unit of the Call Currency; and (II) in the case of a Put, the excess of the Strike Price over the Spot Price, multiplied by the aggregate amount of the Put Currency to be sold under the Put, where both prices are quoted in terms of the amount of the Call Currency to be paid for one unit of the Put Currency;
"Local Banking Day"	For any currency or Party, a day on which commercial banks in the principal banking center of the country of issuance of such currency or in the location of the applicable Designated Office of such Party, respectively, are not authorized or required by law to close;
"Notice of Exercise"	Telex, telephonic or other electronic notification (excluding facsimile transmission), providing assurance of receipt, given by the Buyer prior to or at the Expiration Time, of the exercise of an Option, which notification shall be irrevocable;
"Option"	A Put or a Call, as the case may be, including any unexpired Put or Call previously entered into by the Parties, which shall be or become subject to this Agreement unless otherwise agreed;
"Parties"	The parties to this Agreement; and the term "Party" shall mean whichever of the Parties is appropriate in the context in which such expression may be used;
"Premium"	The purchase price of the Option as agreed upon by the Parties, and payable by the Buyer to the Seller thereof;
"Premium Payment Date"	The date specified as such in the Confirmation;
"Put"	An option entitling, but not obligating, the Buyer to sell to the Seller at the Strike Price a specified quantity of the Put Currency;
"Put Currency"	The currency agreed as such at the time an Option is entered into;
"Seller"	The Party granting an Option;
"Settlement Date"	In respect of: (I) an American Style Option, the Spot Date of the Currency Pair on the Exercise Date of such Option; and (II) a European Style Option, the Spot Date of the Currency Pair on the Expiration Date of such Option;
"Spot Date"	The spot delivery day for the relevant Currency Pair as generally used by the foreign exchange market;
"Spot Price"	The price at the time at which such price is to be determined for foreign exchange transactions in the relevant Currency Pair for value on the Spot Date, as determined in good faith: (I) by the Seller, for purposes of Section 5 hereof; and (II) by the Non-Defaulting Party, for purposes of Section 8 hereof;
"Strike Price"	The price specified in a Confirmation at which the Currency Pair may be exchanged.

2.   GENERAL

2.1   The Parties (through their respective Designated Offices) may enter into Options (neither being obliged to do so) for such Premiums, with such Expiration Dates, at such Strike Prices and for the purchase or sale of such quantities of such currencies, as may be agreed subject to the terms hereof.

2.2   Each Option shall be governed by the terms and conditions set forth in this Master Agreement and in the Confirmation relating to such Option. Each Confirmation shall supplement and form a part of this Master Agreement and shall be read and construed as one with this Master Agreement and with each other Confirmation, so that this Master Agreement and all Confirmations, Schedules and amendments hereto constitute a single agreement between the Parties (collectively referred to as this "Agreement"). The Parties acknowledge that all Options are entered into in reliance upon such fact, it being understood that the Parties would not otherwise enter into any Option.

2.3   Options shall be promptly confirmed by the Parties by Confirmations exchanged by mail, telex, facsimile or other electronic means. Unless either Party objects to the terms contained in any Confirmation within the earlier of (I) the time period recognized by local market practice or (II) three (3) Business Days of receipt thereof, the terms of such Confirmation shall be deemed correct absent manifest error, unless a corrected Confirmation is sent by a Party within such three day period, in which case the Party receiving such corrected Confirmation shall have three (3) Business Days after receipt thereof to object to the terms contained in such corrected Confirmation. Failure by either Party to issue a Confirmation shall not alter the rights and obligations of either Party under an Option to which the Parties have agreed. In the event of any conflict between the terms of a Confirmation and this Agreement, such Confirmation shall prevail, except for purposes of this Section 2.3 and Section 6 hereof.

2.4   Neither Party may assign its rights nor delegate its obligations under any Option to a third party without the prior written consent of the other Party.

3.   REPRESENTATIONS AND WARRANTIES; CONTRACTUAL STATUS

Each Party represents and warrants to the other Party as of the date hereof and as of the date of each Option that: (I) it has authority to enter into this Master Agreement and such Option; (II) the persons executing this Master Agreement and entering into such Option on its behalf have been duly authorized to do so; (III) this Master Agreement and such Option are binding upon it and enforceable against it in accordance with their respective terms and do not and will not violate the terms of any agreements to which such Party is bound; (IV) no Event of Default, or event which, with notice or lapse of time or both, would constitute an Event of Default has occurred and is continuing with respect to it; and (V) it acts as principal in entering into and exercising each and every Option.

4.   THE PREMIUM

4.1   Unless otherwise agreed in writing by the Parties, the Premium related to an Option shall be paid on its Premium Payment Date.

4.2   If any Premium is not received on the Premium Payment Date, the Seller may elect either: (I) to accept a late payment of such Premium; (II) to give written notice of such non-payment and, if such payment shall not be received within two (2) Business Days of such notice, treat the related Options as void; or (III) to give written notice of such non-payment and, if such payment shall not be received within two (2) Business

Days of such notice, treat such non-payment as an Event of Default under clause (I) of the definition of Event of Default. If the Seller elects to act under either clause (I) or (II) of the preceding sentence, the Buyer shall pay all out-of-pocket costs and actual damages incurred in connection with such unpaid or late Premium or void Option, including, without limitation, interest on such Premium in the same currency as such Premium at the then prevailing market rate and any other costs or expenses incurred by the Seller in covering its obligations (including, without limitation, a delta hedge) with respect to such Option.

5. EXERCISE AND SETTLEMENT OF OPTIONS

5.1   The Buyer may exercise an Option by delivery to the Seller of a Notice of Exercise. Subject to Section 5.4 hereof, if an Option has not been exercised prior to or at the Expiration Time, it shall expire and become void and of no effect. Any Notice of Exercise shall (unless otherwise agreed): (I) if received prior to 3:00 p.m. on a Business Day, be effective upon receipt thereof by the Seller; and (II) if received after 3:00 p.m. on a Business Day, be effective only as of the opening of business of the Seller on the first Business Day subsequent to its receipt.

5.2   An exercised Option shall settle on its Settlement Date. Subject to Sections 5.3 and 5.4 hereof, on the Settlement Date, the Buyer shall pay the Put Currency to the Seller for value on the Settlement Date and the Seller shall pay the Call Currency to the Buyer for value on the Settlement Date.

5.3   An Option shall be settled at its In-the money Amount if so agreed by the Parties at the time such Option is entered into. In such case, the In-the-money Amount shall be determined based upon the Spot Price at the time of exercise or as soon thereafter as possible. The sole obligations of the Parties with respect to such Option shall be to deliver or receive the In-the-money Amount of such Option on the Settlement Date.

5.4   Unless the Seller is otherwise instructed by the Buyer, if an Option has an In-the-money Amount at its Expiration Time that equals or exceeds the product of (x) 1% of the Strike Price and (y) the amount of the Call or Put Currency, as appropriate, then the Option shall be deemed automatically exercised. In such case, the Seller may elect to settle such Option either in accordance with Section 5.2 of this Agreement or by payment to the Buyer on the Settlement Date for such Option of the In-the-money Amount, as determined at the Expiration Time or as soon thereafter as possible. In the latter case, the sole obligations of the Parties with respect to such Option shall be to deliver or receive the In-the-money Amount of such Option on the Settlement Date. The Seller shall notify the Buyer of its election of the method of settlement of an automatically exercised Option as soon as practicable after the Expiration Time.

5.5   Unless otherwise agreed by the Parties, an Option may be exercised only in whole.

6. DISCHARGE AND TERMINATION OF OPTIONS

Unless otherwise agreed, any Call Option or any Put Option written by a Party will automatically be terminated and discharged, in whole or in part, as applicable, against a Call Option or a Put Option, respectively, written by the other Party, such termination and discharge to occur automatically upon the payment in full of the last Premium payable in respect of such Options; *provided that* such termination and discharge may only occur in respect of Options:

(a)   each being with respect to the same Put Currency ant the same Call Currency;

(b)   each having the same Expiration Date and Expiration Time;

(c)   each being of the same style, i.e. either both being **American Style Options** or both being **European Style Options**;

(d)   each having the same Strike Price; and

(e)   neither of which shall have been exercised by delivery of a Notice of Exercise;

and, upon the occurrence of such termination and discharge, neither Party shall have any further obligation to the other Party in respect of the relevant Options or, as the case may be, parts thereof so terminated and discharged. In the case of a partial termination and discharge (i.e., where the relevant Options are for different amounts of the Currency Pair), the remaining portion of the Option which is partially discharged and terminated shall continue to be an Option for all purposes of this Agreement, including this Section 6.

7.   PAYMENT NETTING

7.1   If, on any date, and unless otherwise mutually agreed by the Parties, Premiums would otherwise be payable hereunder in the same currency between respective Designated Offices of the Parties, then, on such date, each Party's obligation to make payment of any such Premium will be automatically satisfied and discharged and, if the aggregate Premium(s) that would otherwise have been payable by such Designated Office of one Party exceeds the aggregate Premium(s) that would otherwise have been payable by such Designated Office of the other Party, replaced by an obligation upon the Party by whom the larger aggregate Premium(s) would have been payable to pay the other Party the excess of the larger aggregate Premium(s) over the smaller aggregate Premium(s).

7.2   If, on any date, and unless otherwise mutually agreed by the Parties, amounts other than Premium payments would otherwise be payable hereunder in the same currency between respective Designated Offices of the Parties, then, on such date, each Party's obligation to make payment of any such amount will be automatically satisfied and discharged and, if the aggregate amount that would otherwise have been payable by such Designated Office of one Party exceeds the aggregate amount that would otherwise have been payable by such Designated Office of the other Party, replaced by an obligation upon the Party by whom the larger aggregate amount would have been payable to pay the other Party the excess of the larger aggregate amount over the smaller aggregate amount.

8.   DEFAULT

8.1   If an Event of Default has occurred and is continuing, then the Non-Defaulting Party shall have the right to liquidate and/or to deem to liquidate all, but not less than all (except to the extent that in the good faith opinion of the Non-Defaulting Party certain of such Options may not be liquidated under applicable law), outstanding Options by notice to the Defaulting Party. The previous sentence notwithstanding, in the case of an Event of Default specified in clauses (II), (III) or (IV) of the definition thereof, such liquidation and/or deemed liquidation shall be automatic as to all outstanding Options, except where the relevant voluntary or involuntary case or other proceeding or bankruptcy or insolvency giving rise to such Event of Default is governed by a system of law which contains express provisions enabling close-out in the manner described in clauses (I) to (IV) below (or a manner equivalent thereto) to take place after the occurrence of the relevant Event of Default in the absence of automatic liquidation. Such liquidation and/or deemed liquidation shall be effected by:

(I) closing out each such Option at the time of liquidation so that each such Option is cancelled and market damages for each Party are calculated equal to the aggregate of (a) with respect to each Option purchased by such Party, the current market premium for such Option, (b) with respect to each Option sold by such Party, any unpaid Premium and, to the extent permitted by applicable law, interest on any unpaid Premium in the same currency as such Premium at the then prevailing market rate, (c) with respect to any exercised Option, any unpaid amount due in settlement of such Option and, to the extent permitted by applicable law, interest thereon from the applicable Settlement Date to the day of close-out at the average rate at which overnight deposits in the currency in which such unpaid amount was due are offered by major banks in the London interbank market as of 11:00 a.m. (London time) on each such day plus 1% per annum, and (d) any costs or expenses incurred by the Non-Defaulting Party in covering its obligations (including a delta hedge) with respect to such Option, all as determined in good faith by the Non-Defaulting Party;

(II) converting any damages calculated in accordance with clause (I) above in a currency other than the Non-Defaulting Party's Base Currency into such Base Currency at the Spot Price at which, at the time of liquidation, the Non-Defaulting Party could enter into a contract in the foreign exchange market to buy the Base Currency in exchange for such currency;

(III) netting such damage payments with respect to each Party so that all such amounts are netted to a single liquidated amount payable by one Party to the other Party as a settlement payment; and

(IV) setting off the net payment calculated in accordance with clause (III) above which the Non-Defaulting Party owes to the Defaulting Party, if any, and, at the option of the Non-Defaulting Party, any margin or other collateral ("Margin") held by the Non-Defaulting Party (including the liquidated value of any non-cash Margin) in respect of the Defaulting Party's obligations hereunder against the net payment calculated in accordance with clause (III) above which the Defaulting Party owes to the Non-Defaulting Party, if any, and, at the option of the Non-Defaulting Party, any Margin held by the Defaulting Party (including the liquidated value of any non-cash Margin) in respect of the Non-Defaulting Party's obligations hereunder; *provided*, that, for purposes of such set-off, any Margin denominated in a currency other the Non-Defaulting Party's Base Currency shall be converted into such currency at the rate specified in clause (II) above.

8.2 The net amount payable by one Party to the other Party pursuant to the provisions of Section 8.1 above shall be paid by the close of business on the Business Day following such liquidation and/or deemed liquidation of all such Options (converted as required by applicable law into any other currency, any such costs of conversion to be borne by, and deducted from any payment to, the Defaulting Party). To the extent permitted by applicable law, any amounts owed but not paid when due under this Section 8 shall bear interest at the Base Currency Rate plus 1% per annum (or, if conversion is required by applicable law into some other currency, either (x) the average rate at which overnight deposits in such other currency are offered by major banks in the London interbank market as of 11:00 a.m. (London time) plus 1% per annum or (y) such other rate as may be prescribed by such applicable law) for each day for which such amount remains unpaid.

8.3 Without prejudice to the foregoing, so long as a Party shall be in default in payment or performance to the other Party hereunder or under any Option and the Non-Defaulting Party has not exercised its rights under this Section 8, or during the pendency of a reasonable request to a Party for adequate assurances of its ability to perform its obligations hereunder or under any Option, the other Party may, at its election and without penalty, suspend its obligation to perform hereunder or under any Option.

8.4 The Party required to make a payment to the other Party pursuant to Sections 8.1 and 8.2 above shall pay to the other Party all out-of-pocket expenses incurred by such other Party (including fees and disbursements of counsel and time charges of attorneys who may be employees of such other Party) in connection with any reasonable collection or other enforcement proceedings related to such required payment.

8.5 The Parties agree that the amounts recoverable under this Section 8 are a reasonable pre-estimate of loss and not a penalty. Such amounts are payable for the loss of bargain and the loss of protection against future risks and, except as otherwise provided in this Agreement, neither Party will be entitled to recover any additional damages as a consequence of such losses.

8.6 The Non-Defaulting Party's rights under this Section 8 shall be in addition to, and not in limitation or exclusion of, any other rights which the Non-Defaulting Party may have (whether by agreement, operation of law or otherwise), and the Non-Defaulting Party shall have a general right of set-off with respect to all amounts owed by each Party to the other Party, whether due or not due (provided that any amount not due at the time of such set-off shall be discounted to present value in a commercially reasonable manner by the Non-Defaulting Party).

9. PARTIES TO RELY ON THEIR OWN EXPERTISE

Each Option shall be deemed to have been entered into by each Party in reliance only upon its judgment. Neither Party holds out itself as advising, or any of its employees or agents as having its authority to advise, the other Party as to whether or not it should enter into any such Option (whether as Seller or Buyer) or as to any subsequent actions relating thereto or on any other commercial matters concerned with any currency options or transactions, and neither Party shall have any responsibility or liability whatsoever in respect of any advice of this nature given, or views expressed, by it or any of such persons to the other Party, whether or not such advice is given or such views are expressed at the request of the other Party.

10. ILLEGALITY, IMPOSSIBILITY AND FORCE MAJEURE

If either Party is prevented from or hindered or delayed by reason of force majeure or act of State in the delivery or payment of any currency in respect of an Option or if it becomes unlawful or impossible for either Party to make or receive any payment in respect of an Option, then the Party for whom such performance has been prevented, hindered or delayed or has become illegal or impossible shall promptly give notice thereof to the other Party and either Party may, by notice to the other Party, require the liquidation and close-out of each affected Option in accordance with the provisions of Section 8 hereof and, for such purposes, the Party unaffected by such force majeure, act of State, illegality or impossibility shall be considered the Non-Defaulting Party and, for purposes of this Section 10, such Non-Defaulting Party shall perform the calculation required under Section 8.

11. MISCELLANEOUS

11.1   Unless otherwise specified, the times referred to herein shall in each case refer to the local time of the relevant Designated Office of the Seller of the relevant Option.

11.2   Unless otherwise specified, all notices, instructions and other communications to be given to a Party hereunder shall be given to the address, telex (if confirmed by the appropriate answerback), facsimile (confirmed if requested) or telephone number and to the individual or Department specified by such Party in Part II of the Schedule attached hereto. Unless otherwise specified, any notice, instruction or other communication, shall be effective upon receipt if given in accordance with this Section 11.2.

11.3   All payments to be made hereunder shall be made in same day (or immediately available) and freely transferable funds and, unless otherwise specified, shall be delivered to such office of such bank and in favor of such account as shall be specified by the Party entitled to receive such payment in Part III of the Schedule attached hereto or as specified by such Party by notice given in accordance with Section 11.2. Time shall be of the essence in this Agreement.

11.4   The receipt or recovery by either Party of any amount in respect of an obligation of the other Party in a currency other than the Base Currency (other than receipt by the Defaulting Party pursuant to Sections 8.1 and 8.2 of a payment in the Non-Defaulting Party's Base Currency), whether pursuant to a judgment of any court of pursuant to Section 8 hereof, shall discharge such obligation only to the extent that, on the first day on which such party is open for business immediately following such receipt, the recipient shall be able, in accordance with normal banking procedures, to purchase the Base Currency with the currency received. If the amount of the Base Currency so purchasable shall be less than the original Base Currency amount calculated pursuant to Section 8 hereof, the obligor shall, as a separate obligation and notwithstanding any judgment of any court, indemnify the recipient against any loss sustained by it. The obligor shall in any event indemnify the recipient against any costs incurred by it in making any such purchase of the Base Currency.

11.5   The Parties agree that each may electronically record all telephonic conversations between them and that any such recordings may be submitted in evidence to any court or in any proceeding for the purpose of establishing any matters pertinent to any Option.

11.6   This Agreement shall supersede any other agreement between the Parties with respect to the subject matter hereof and all outstanding Options between the Parties on the date hereof shall be subject hereto, unless otherwise expressly agreed by the Parties.

11.7   A margin agreement between the Parties may apply to obligations governed by this Agreement. If the Parties have executed a margin agreement, such margin agreement shall be subject to the terms hereof and is hereby incorporated by reference herein. In the event of any conflict between a margin agreement and this Agreement, this Agreement shall prevail, except for any provision in such margin agreement in respect of governing law.

11.8   In the event any one or more of the provisions contained in this Agreement should be held invalid, illegal or unenforceable in any respect, the validity, legality and enforceability of the remaining provisions contained herein shall not in any way be affected or impaired thereby. The parties shall endeavor in good faith negotiations to replace the invalid, illegal or unenforceable provisions with valid provisions the economic effect of which comes as close as possible to that of the invalid, illegal or unenforceable provisions.

12. LAW AND JURISDICTION

12.1 This Agreement shall be governed by, and construed in accordance with, the laws of [the State of New York] [England and Wales] without giving effect to conflicts of law principles.

12.2 With respect to any suit, action or proceedings ("Proceedings") relating to any Option or this Agreement, each Party irrevocably (I) [submits to the non-exclusive jurisdiction of the courts of the State of New York and the United States District Court located in the Borough of Manhattan in New York City,] [agrees for the benefit of the other Party that the courts of England shall have jurisdiction to determine any Proceeding and irrevocably submits to the jurisdiction of the English courts] and (II) waives any objection which it may have at any time to the laying of venue of any Proceedings brought in any such court, waives any claim that such Proceedings have been brought in an inconvenient forum and further waives the right to object, with respect to such Proceedings, that such court does not have jurisdiction over such Party. Nothing in this Agreement precludes either Party from bringing Proceedings in any other jurisdiction nor will the bringing of Proceedings in any one or more jurisdictions preclude the bringing of Proceedings in any other jurisdiction.

12.3 Each Party hereby irrevocably waives any and all right to trial by jury in any legal proceeding arising out of or relating to this Agreement or any Option.

12.4 Each Party hereby irrevocably waives, to the fullest extent permitted by applicable law, with respect to itself and its revenues and assets (irrespective of their use or intended use), all immunity on the grounds of sovereignty or other similar grounds from (I) suit, (II) jurisdiction of any court, (III) relief by way of injunction, order for specific performance or for recovery of property, (IV) attachment of its assets (whether before or after judgment) and (V) execution or enforcement of any judgment to which it or its revenues or assets might otherwise be entitled in any Proceedings (as defined in Section 12.2 hereof) in the courts of any jurisdiction and irrevocably agrees, to the extent permitted by applicable law, that it will not claim any such immunity in any Proceedings.

SCHEDULE

Part I : **Designated Offices**

Specify details of Designated Offices in relation to a Party for the purposes of this Schedule.

Part II : **Notices**

Specify details in relation to each Party of address, telephone number, telex number, facsimile number and name of individual or department to whom or to which notices are to be sent to it for the purposes of this Schedule.

Part III : **Payment Instructions**

Specify details in relation to each Party for the purposes of this Schedule of its bank and office, account number and reference with respect to relevant currencies.

Part IV : **Base Currency**

Specify in relation to each Party, the Base Currency in relation to it for the purposes of this Schedule.

Part V : **Other Provisions**

- The entire provision of Section 12.1 shall be deleted and replaced by the following provision:

  "12.1 This Agreement shall be governed by, and construed in accordance with the laws of Japan."

- The entire provision of Section 12.2 shall be deleted and replaced by the following provision:

  "12.2 With respect to any suit, action or proceedings ("Proceedings") relating to any Option or this Agreement, each party irrevocably (I) submits to the non-exclusive jurisdiction of the Tokyo District Court and (II) waives any objection which it may have at any time to the laying venue of any Proceedings brought in any such court, waives any claim that such Proceedings have been brought in an inconvenient forum and further waives the right to object, with respect to such Proceedings, that such court does not have jurisdiction over such Party. Nothing in this Agreement precludes either Party from bringing Proceedings in any other jurisdiction nor will the bringing of Proceedings in any one or more jurisdictions preclude the bringing of Proceedings in any other jurisdiction."

- For the purpose of Section 5.3, "In-the-Money Amount Settlement" does not apply to this Agreement.

- For the purpose of Section 6, "Discharge and Termination of Options" does not apply to this Agreement.

- For the purpose of Section 7, "Payment Netting" does not apply to this Agreement.

- For the purpose of Section 8, "Default" does not apply to this Agreement.

INTERNATIONAL CURRENCY OPTIONS MARKET MASTER AGREEMENT GUIDE

I. INTRODUCTION

Following the publication of "LICOM Terms" in August, 1985, which were intended to reflect and to encourage good market practice and to reduce the need for specific legal documentation between participants in the London interbank over-the-counter currency options market, the market continued to evolve internationally. By 1989, it became apparent that the original terms did not adequately reflect market practice. In particular, the number and diversity of market participants had increased substantially, and new practices had been adopted, such as volatility quoting, which were not envisaged in 1985.

Accordingly, in May, 1989, the British Bankers' Association ("BBA") re-established, through its Foreign Exchange Committee, a Working Party to liaise with market interests, including the Foreign Exchange and Currency Deposits Brokers' Association, with a view to updating the 1985 terms and to provide guidance as to market practice. The Working Party was comprised of members representing a broad spectrum of international financial institutions. In addition, emphasis was placed on the international acceptance of the revised terms, and a new title was developed: International Currency Options Market Terms and Conditions - "ICOM Terms". The Bank of England was represented as an observer on the Working Party.

During this same period, a similar effort was underway in the United States. In early 1986, The (U.S.) Foreign Exchange Committee issued draft Recommended Terms and Conditions For Dealing in the United States Market - "NYICOM Terms". (The Foreign Exchange Committee is an advisory committee, independent of the Federal Reserve Bank of New York (the "FRBNY"), but sponsored by it, and its members are participants in the interdealer foreign exchange market.) The NYICOM Terms, which were based upon, and substantially similar to, the original LICOM Terms, were intended to reflect general market practice in the United States. Over a period of time, the NYICOM Terms were retitled "USICOM Terms", for United States Interbank Currency Options Market Terms.

Although the USICOM Terms generally reflected market practices in the U.S., they did not address the increasingly important issue of counterparty credit risk and, in particular, the substantive rights and obligations of the parties upon (I) the nonperformance of an option by one of the parties, (II) the insolvency of one of the parties or (III) the occurrence of force majeure or some other event which makes it illegal or impossible for one of the parties to perform. The USICOM Terms also did not provide a method for closing out and liquidating options upon the occurrence of one of these events. In 1990, the USICOM Terms were revised into a draft form of master agreement, which attempted to reflect market practice with respect to the formation, exercise and settlement of options (including such matters as net cash settlement and automatic exercise), as well as set forth the substantive legal rights and obligations of the parties.

In the summer of 1990, representatives of the Working Party and The Foreign Exchange Committee met to resolve the differences between the ICOM Terms and the USICOM Terms and to develop a single document for use in the international over-the-counter foreign currency options market. The result is the attached form of International Currency Options Market Master Agreement (the "Master Agreement"), which should be considered as reflective of normal market practice for international interdealer transactions and which could be adopted by market participants as the standard agreement for dealing in this market.

The Working Party and the Foreign Exchange Committee have confined themselves to practices in the interbank and professional markets, and have not been directly concerned with the terms and conditions upon which individual institutions may choose to deal with their clients (although the Master Agreement could be used in such circumstances). Banks and other professional market participants are, of course, free to deal with each other on the basis of other terms or agreements if they wish, but should consider themselves under an obligation to make clear to each other in what way their terms or agreements differ from the Master Agreement.

The following sections of this Guide to the Master Agreement are intended (I) to provide further clarification of normal market practice and (II) to explain various provisions of the Master Agreement and the significance of their inclusion in the Master Agreement. Therefore, this Guide should be read carefully. Though the Master Agreement does, and is intended to, stand on its own as a legal document, the Guide provides important commentary on current market practice and the Master Agreement.

II. MARKET PRACTICE

A. Price Quotation

There are two generally accepted methods of price quotation - Premium and Volatility. In each case, the counterparties shall agree upon:

> Option Style (American or European),
> Call Currency,
> Put Currency and Amount,
> Expiration Date,
> Expiration Time,
> Premium Payment Date,
> Settlement Date, and
> Strike Price.

Counterparties should also agree upon whether they are entering into a contemporaneous foreign exchange transaction (commonly known as a Delta hedge), although such transaction would not be subject to the Master Agreement.

Price quotation should be in the form of either:

(a) a *Premium*, where the counterparties agree upon the above terms and on how the premium price should be expressed, e.g. as a percentage of either currency or as one currency in terms of the other (it is also necessary to agree upon a spot rate in the case of a Premium quotation where a Delta hedge forms part of the trade); or

(b) *Volatility*, where the counterparties agree upon the above terms and that the Volatility be expressed as a percentage per annum. It is the factor which, when combined with the Spot Rate, interest factors of the Currency Pair concerned, the days to expiry of the Option and the Strike Price, is used to compute the Premium.

An Option is not a legally binding contract until, among other things, the Premium has been agreed. Therefore, to ensure the ongoing viability of the Volatility method of dealing, it is incumbent on the counterparties to agree on the Premium Price as soon as possible, and it is imperative that the calculation of the Premium accurately reflect the agreed Volatility and market conditions at the time Volatility was agreed. In the event of a dispute that cannot be resolved between the counterparties through good faith negotiation (or, in the first instance, by reference to recordings of conversations between the parties during which pricing was discussed), prompt reference to mutually acceptable third-party arbitration is suggested. Market participants should note that, as Premium calculation differences are more likely to occur in transactions involving American Style Options, due care should be exercised in entering into such Options.

In addition, when trading Volatility, it is necessary that a spot rate be agreed upon by the counterparties immediately upon entering into the Option. This forms the basis of the underlying foreign exchange transaction (Delta hedge), if any.

B. Quotation of Expiration Dates

Generally, there are two methods for quotation of Expiration Dates - quotation of straight Expiration Dates and quotation of Expiration Dates by calendar month.

Straight Expiration Dates

An Option quoted for straight periods (such as 1 month, 2 months etc.) has as its final Expiration Date the date preceding the equivalent forward date (as dealt in the interdealer foreign exchange market) that will result in settlement on the forward date, if it is exercised on the Expiration Date. If there is more than one solution, the furthest date from the Trade Date will be the Expiration Date.

Example:

Today's date: March 4 – Spot date: March 6
1 month FX date – April 6

The Expiration Date for a one-month Option quoted on March 4 will be that date which will result in a Settlement Date of April 6, i.e., April 4, (assuming no weekends or holidays between). To avoid misunderstanding, in the case of periods under one month, it is recommended that the parties refer to an actual date.

Expiration Dates by Calendar Month

Currently, it is market practice to quote for expiration in a particular month without reference to the actual date. In these instances, it is generally understood that the Expiration Date of the Option is the Monday before the third Wednesday of that particular month.

Expiration on Non-Business Days

Although the Master Agreement does not provide that the Expiration Date must be a Business Day (i.e., a Local Banking Day for the office of the Seller that has written the Option), this will customarily be the case. However, some dealers regularly sell Options with Expiration Dates that are not Local Banking Days for their applicable Designated Office. (Similarly, some dealers will accept Notice of Exercise on a non-Business Day.) If the Expiration Date is not a Local Banking Day for the Seller's Designated Office (or if the Seller is willing to accept Notice of Exercise on a non-Business Day), it is incumbent upon the Seller to make other arrangements (such as designating a different office or an agent for receipt) to enable the Buyer to exercise its Option. In these circumstances, the Seller should notify the Buyer of such arrangements as soon as possible and reconfirm to the Buyer prior to the Expiration Date.

C. Confirmations

The significant terms of an Option should always be established by the parties at the time the Option is entered into. The agreement of the parties on those terms will be set forth in the Confirmation. However, there may be matters relating to an Option that are not required to be set forth in the Confirmation. Market participants are encouraged to include information as to such matters in the "Other terms and conditions" section of the Confirmation. In addition, market participants should indicate at the beginning of negotiations, and prior to entering into an Option, in which way their dealings and the formation, exercise or settlement of the relevant Option will differ from established market practice. Similarly, brokers should be mindful of, and adhere to, market practice with respect to the formation of Options and their dealings with Option counterparties (including the issuance of Confirmations in the recommended form).

As in the cash spot and forward currency markets, the prompt exchange of Confirmations (preferably electronically) and their immediate and thorough checking upon receipt (and querying where necessary) is vital to the orderly functioning of the market place, as well as providing a principal defense against many types of fraud. However, the Option markets are more complex than the cash markets because of the greater number of parameters that need to be specified for each transaction and the different types of Options that may be transacted. This additional complexity reinforces the requirement for Confirmations to be issued promptly by each of the parties. If there has been a misunderstanding between the parties as to the Option terms, this will usually be discovered upon the review of the Confirmations. The non-receipt of expected Confirmations or any inconsistencies or inaccuracies should be queried or objected to within the time period recognized by local market practice or, at most, within three Business Days of the date of the trade. It is suggested that brokers, as well as the parties to an Option, send Confirmations of any Options which they arrange to the counterparties.

A recommended form of Confirmation is included as *Exhibit I* to the Master Agreement. Market participants (including brokers) are encouraged to follow the format and terminology suggested in order to reduce the risk of misunderstandings.

Market participants frequently enter into a contemporaneous Delta hedge at the time they enter into an Option (either with the Option counterparty or a third party). It is market practice (and market participants are encouraged) to separately confirm such transactions. In addition, it is suggested that brokers send confirmations of any Delta hedges which they arrange to the parties involved.

III. MASTER AGREEMENT PROVISIONS

A. Definitions

For the most part, the definitions used in the Master Agreement are those commonly used by currency options market participants. However, because of the nature of the document (i.e. the form of a master agreement) and because an attempt has been made to define some common terms and phrases which have not heretofore been defined, some of these definitions deserve comment.

1. "Base Currency" is defined as the currency specified by a party on the schedule to the Master Agreement. Upon an Event of Default, or some other event, which results in the liquidation of outstanding Options, the Base Currency of the Non-Defaulting Party is the currency in which the payment will be calculated and, probably, paid. (See Sections III.H.4 and III.H.7 hereof.) It is expected that each party will have a single currency in which it prefers to receive settlement: For example, for U.S. market participants, this will likely be U.S. dollars. U.K. market participants should specify Pounds Sterling as their Base Currency as a U.K. liquidation of a company is conducted in Pounds Sterling (i.e., all claims must be made, and all debts and credits are determined, in Pounds Sterling). The Base Currency Rate plus 1% *per annum* will be the interest rate used for purposes of determining the default rate on such payments.

2. "Business Day" has alternate definitions depending upon the context in which it is used. The Working Party/Foreign Exchange Committee found that a single definition would have affected, rather than reflected, market practice.

3. The Buyer of an Option (sometimes referred to as the "purchaser" or "holder") is defined as the owner of the Option. The Buyer may be either the original buyer, an assignee thereof or a subsequent assignee. In any event, for Options between counterparties to be subject to the Master Agreement, the parties must have executed the Master Agreement. If an Option is assigned by a Buyer to a party who has not entered into the Master Agreement with the Seller, the assignee will not have the rights and obligations with respect to automatic exercise, net cash settlement, set-off and termination, and liquidation and close-out set out in the Master Agreement. (Section 2.4 of the Master Agreement provides that neither party may assign nor delegate its rights or obligations, respectively, to a third party without the prior written consent of the non-assigning party.)

4. Counterparties are expected to specify their Designated Offices on the Schedule attached to the Master Agreement. These are the respective offices of the parties that will deal Options and whose transactions will be subject to the provisions of the Master Agreement.

5. The definition of "European Style Option" provides that it is an Option which may be exercised only on its Expiration Date. After considerable discussion among the Working Party/Foreign Exchange Committee it was agreed that few European Style Options are exercised prior to this time and that operational problems could result from the earlier exercise of European Options (although this problem was not considered significant). However, the definition does provide that the parties may agree on the acceptability of earlier delivery of Notice of Exercise of these Options.

6. The Events of Default are generally credit-related events, including insolvency, non-payment and the disaffirmation or repudiation of an Option.

Another credit-related Event of Default is found in clause (VI) of the definition, i.e., the failure of a party to provide adequate assurances of its ability to perform an Option after a reasonable request from its counterparty to do so. Such a provision protects a party when it has genuine and valid concerns with respect to the ability of its counterparty to perform, even though no other Event of Default has occurred. The concern may be triggered by, for instance, unconfirmed information about the counterparty circulating in the market, the action of a rating agency or the acknowledged credit problems (such as the filing of a petition for bankruptcy or the occurrence some other insolvency proceeding) of a parent, affiliate or subsidiary of the counterparty.

Clause (VI) requires that the request for adequate assurances must be *reasonable* given all the facts and circumstances: If, for example, shortly before the Expiration Date of an Option, the Seller of an Option had defaulted on an obligation to the Buyer which arose out of a transaction not covered by the provisions of the Master Agreement (for example, a securities transaction), it might be reasonable for the Buyer to request adequate assurances of the Seller's ability to perform the Option should the Buyer exercise the Option. On the other hand, it would probably be unreasonable of the Seller to request adequate assurances of a Buyer's ability to perform an unexercised Option which is deep out-of-the-money and has an Expiration Date two months in the future. Similarly, what constitutes adequate assurances in any given situation will depend upon a number of factors, including the reason for the requesting party's concern and request, and whether the party from whom adequate assurances are requested is a Buyer or Seller (or both). For example, if the party which is requested to provide adequate assurances is a Seller of in-the-money Options who has already defaulted on other obligations, adequate assurances may be the delivery of a guarantee or letter of credit to support such party's obligations or the deposit into an escrow account of the currency (or currencies) required to be delivered by the Seller upon exercise of the Option(s). If, on the other hand, a party's concern is triggered by unconfirmed rumors about the financial position of its counterparty, it may be sufficient for the counterparty to provide information to the requesting party proving those rumors to be false. In all cases, the determination of both the reasonableness of the request and the adequacy of the assurances should be fact intensive.

In addition, market participants may want to limit the circumstances that may give rise to a reasonable request for adequate assurances. Some market participants may want to use a side letter for this purpose. Such a side letter is neither required nor encouraged, and clause (VI) of the definition of Event of Default should be considered the standard language.

The failure to provide adequate assurances becomes an Event of Default only after two Business Days following the written request therefor. (Pursuant to the provisions of Section 8.3 of the Master Agreement, the party requesting such adequate assurances is entitled to suspend performance of its obligations with respect to any Option during the pendency of such request.)

Clause (VII) of the definition of "Event of Default" provides that it is an Event of Default with respect to a party if the representations and warranties made by such party in Section 3 shall have been false or misleading at the time they were made, provided that the counterparty has given one Business Day's notice of such fact. The representations and warranties made by a party pursuant to Section 3 are considered crucial to the validity and enforceability of an Option and a party's obligations thereunder. Therefore, if the representations and warranties are incorrect, it is deemed a material breach of the Master Agreement thereby allowing the counterparty to effect the close-out and liquidation of all Options pursuant to Section 8.

7.   "Expiration Date" (sometimes referred to as the "maturity date" or "expiry date") is defined as the date specified as such in the Confirmation. The two methods commonly used for determining the Expiration Date are explained in Section II.B above. Section II.B also contains a discussion of non-Business Day Expiration Dates.

8.   "Expiration Time" (sometimes referred to as the "cut-off time") is defined as the time specified as such in the Confirmation. It is expected that, in keeping with current market practice, the Expiration Time specified will generally be either 10:00 a.m. (New York time) or, for transactions entered into in the Pacific rim, 3:00 p.m. (Tokyo time).

9.   Notice of Exercise of an Option may be given by either telex, telephonic or other electronic means. However, in keeping with market practice, facsimile transmission is specifically excluded as an acceptable method of delivering a Notice of Exercise because of difficulties in ascertaining receipt. In order to avoid confusion, a Notice of Exercise is defined as being irrevocable. Some Sellers will accept a Notice of Exercise on a non-Business Day. In this regard, see the discussion under "Expiration on Non-Business Days" in Section II.B above.

10.   "Premium Payment Date" is defined as the date specified as such in the Confirmation. Generally, the Premium Payment Date will be the Spot Date for the Currency Pair (i.e. the currencies which will be exchanged upon the exercise of an Option). However, for some Options, the Premium will be payable in a currency other that the Put Currency or the Call Currency. In addition, certain Options (such as those commonly referred to as "Boston Options") call for payment of the Premium at a later date (in the case of Boston Options, on the Exercise Date of the Option). In these situations, it is imperative that market participants specifically agree on the Premium Payment Date. Market practice is that the Premium Payment Date is always specified in the Confirmation.

11.   The term "Seller" has been used to describe the Party that grants an Option. This is the term commonly used for such purpose, although the Seller is sometimes referred to as the "grantor" or the "writer".

12.   Generally, the Spot Date will be the second Business Day after a transaction is entered into. However, this general rule is affected by domestic holidays and, at times, the respective principal financial centers of the currencies involved may be dealing for different Spot Dates. In addition, spot transactions in certain currencies, for example Canadian dollars and Mexican pesos, generally settle on the business day succeeding the date of the transaction. Therefore, the term "Spot Date" has been defined by reference to general usage by foreign exchange market participants.

13. "Spot Price" is used in two Sections of the Master Agreement: (I) Section 5, where it is used for purposes of determining the In-the-money Amount, or intrinsic value, of an Option for purposes of net cash settlement (Section 5.3) and automatic exercise (Section 5.4), and (II) Section 8, where it is used for the purpose of converting the damages calculated upon the liquidation of an Option into the Non-Defaulting Party's Base Currency. In Section 5, the determination of Spot Price is made by the Seller, and in Section 8 it is made by the Non-Defaulting Party. In either case, the definition requires that such determination be made in good faith.

14. The term "currency" is not defined in the Master Agreement. However, in accordance with market practice, the term currency means not only the currency of any country, but also any composite currency, such as the European Currency Unit or ECU, in which the parties choose to deal.

B. General

1. Section 2.2 states the general intention of the parties (I) that all Options be governed by the terms and conditions set out in the Master Agreement and (II) that the Master Agreement and all Confirmations be considered a single agreement. It further states that the parties enter into Options under the Master Agreement in reliance upon these facts. The intent of these provisions is to provide a legal basis for the close-out, liquidation and netting of all Options (as provided by Section 8) upon the occurrence of an Event of Default with respect to one of the parties. These provisions are considered crucial to avoid the possibility that a trustee, receiver or conservator of an insolvent Party would be upheld by a court in affirming and enforcing some Options (e.g. those which it holds as Buyer which are In-the-money) and rejecting and repudiating others (e.g. those as to which it is Seller), the practice commonly known as "cherrypicking".

2. An Option becomes a legally binding contract when the essential terms of the Option (Buyer and Seller, Premium, style, type, Strike Price, Put Currency and amount, Call Currency, Expiration Date, Expiration Time and Premium Payment Date) are agreed by the parties. The Option will usually be concluded orally by the traders, in which case the Confirmation will be evidence of the contract.

3. Section 2.3 provides that Confirmations shall be deemed correct absent manifest error three days after receipt by a party. Such manifest error may be evidenced by the tape recording of the conversation of the traders who entered into a disputed Option. (Section 11.5 specifically provides for the tape recording of conversations and for the use of such recordings as evidence in any court or in any proceeding.)

C. Representations and Warranties; Contractual Status

1. The representations and warranties contained in Section 3 are made by each of the counterparties and are intended to satisfy each of the parties that (I) the Master Agreement and each of the Options entered into pursuant thereto are valid and enforceable obligations of its counterparty, (II) no event which calls into question the credit of its counterparty (i.e. an Event of Default) has occurred, and (III) the counterparty with which it is dealing is the party that is obligated to perform the Option and the terms of the Master Agreement.

2. The (U.S.) Commodity Exchange Act (the "CEA"), which is administered by the Commodity Futures Trading Commission (the "CFTC"), governs the trading of futures contracts and options on futures contracts on U.S. commodity exchanges. The Act also applies to the off-exchange trading of certain products and instruments. Section 2 (a) (1) (A) of the Act, the so-called "Treasury Amendment", was adopted in 1974 and provides an exclusion from the Act for certain products as follows: "Nothing in this Act shall be deemed to govern or in

any way be applicable to transactions in foreign currency, ... unless such transactions involve the sale thereof for future delivery conducted on a board of trade". In 1986, the U.S. Court of Appeals for the Second Circuit held that an option on a foreign currency did not fall within this exclusion because it was not a transaction "in" a foreign currency until it was exercised. ***Commodity Futures Trading Commission v. The American Board of Trade, Inc. et al.***, 803 F. 2d 1242 (2nd Cir. 1986). As such, currency options may only be offered in the U.S. pursuant to a regulatory exemption from the general ban on the trading of such options contained in Section 4c(b) of the Act. The exemption most commonly relied upon for currency options is the so-called "Trade Option Exemption" contained in CFTC regulation section 32.4. The Trade Option Exemption provides an exemption from the general ban for commodity options offered to a "producer, processor, or commercial user of, or a merchant handling, the commodity which is the subject of the commodity option transaction, or the products or byproducts thereof" where such party is offered or enters into the option transaction solely for purposes related to its business as such. As the Master Agreement has been drafted for use by the professional market, a representation addressing the status of the parties for purposes of assuring compliance with the Trade Option Exemption was believed to be unnecessary. However, in those cases in which the Master Agreement is made subject to the laws of the State of New York (or any other state in the United States) and either of the parties is not a professional market participant, the parties should consider the propriety of including a representation as to the commercial status of the parties.

D. The Premium

Section 4.2 provides for alternative courses of action in the event that a Premium is not received on the Premium Payment Date. As Premiums are sometimes paid late (due primarily to operational problems or mistakes), under appropriate circumstances a Seller should generally be willing to accept a late payment, and it is common practice in the market for a Seller to do so. However, where the failure to pay the Premium has not been remedied after a short period of time or is credit-related, the Seller may choose either to void the Option or to take the more drastic step of declaring an Event of Default. Regardless of the course of action chosen by the Seller, the Seller is entitled to recover its out-of-pocket costs and actual damages incurred, specifically including interest on the amount of any Premium (which would be calculated in the same manner as any other late payment in the interdealer foreign exchange market) and any costs of expenses in covering its obligations (including a Delta hedge). Section 4.2 provides for such recovery in the case of either a late payment or the decision to treat the related Option as void. Where the Seller chooses to declare an Event of Default, such amounts are recoverable under the provisions of Section 8 (I).

E. Exercise and Settlement of Options

1. Section 5.1 states that the Buyer may exercise an Option by Delivery to the Seller of a timely Notice of Exercise and that, subject to the automatic exercise provisions contained in Section 5.4, an Option which has not been exercised by its Expiration Time shall expire and become void. Accordingly, market participants should exercise particular care when clocks worldwide are changed seasonally. In addition, it is the Buyer's responsibility to ensure that a Notice of Exercise is addressed to, and received by, the department or area specified by the Seller in Part II of the Schedule to the Master Agreement.

2. The last sentence of Section 5.1 reflects the general market practice that the close of business occurs at 3:00 p.m. (local time of the Seller) and that a Notice of Exercise received after that time is deemed received on the next Business Day. In accordance with the definition of "Notice of Exercise", such Notice should be given by telephone or other electronic means, but may not be given by facsimile transmission.

3.   Options may be entered into on the understanding that physical delivery of the Put Currency and the Call Currency will *not* take place and that the Option will be net cash settled by a payment to the Buyer of the Option's In-the-money Amount (or intrinsic value) if the Option is exercised. The intrinsic value of an Option will be equal to the difference between the Spot Price and the Strike Price multiplied by the amount of the Put or Call Currency, as appropriate, to be exchanged upon exercise of the Option. An example of the calculation of the intrinsic value of a United States Dollar/Deutsche Mark Call is as follows -

USD Call / DEM Put : Spot Price (1.6850) − Strike Price (1.60)
(DEM per USD) = 0.0850

0.0850 × USD 10,000,000 = DEM 850,000

The level of the Spot Price at the time of exercise is, therefore, crucial to the ultimate value of the net cash settlement. As the Spot Price that is used for such purposes is determined in good faith by the Seller, the Buyer should ascertain *at the outset* how the Seller will determine the Spot Price.

4.   Section 5.4 provides for automatic exercise of Options which are in-the-money at the Expiration Time and have not been exercised by delivery of a Notice of Exercise. This provision is *not* meant to be a substitute for the delivery of a Notice of Exercise by the Buyer, which is good market practice and is encouraged. For this reason, (a) an Option will be deemed exercised under this Section only if, at its Expiration Time, it has an In-the-money Amount that equals or exceeds the product of (x) 101% of the Strike Price and (y) the amount of the Call or Put Currency, as appropriate, (b) the Seller determines the Spot Price that is used to calculate the In-the-money Amount, and (c) the Seller may choose to settle an automatically exercised Option either by physical delivery (in accordance with Section 5.2) or net cash settlement (in accordance with Section 5.3).

5.   Because an exercised Option settles on the Spot Date for the Currency Pair, it is common practice for market participants to process an Option which is to be settled by physical delivery as if it were a spot foreign exchange contract, including the exchange of settlement instructions and confirmations. (If confirmations are issued upon the exercise of an Option, it is desirable that such confirmations indicate that the spot foreign exchange transaction relates to an Option exercise.) Notwithstanding such treatment, an exercised Option remains an Option and the parties' rights and obligations with respect thereto will continue to be governed by the Master Agreement. For example, should an Event of Default occur with respect to a party between the Exercise Date and the Settlement Date for an Option, the counterparty's rights to close-out and liquidate such Option (and other Options entered into by the parties) are those set forth in Section 8.

6.   Section 5.5 provides that, unless otherwise agreed by the parties, an Option may be exercised only in whole and not in part.

7.   Options are settled by payment of the Put Currency amount by the Buyer to the Seller and by the payment of the Call Currency amount by the Seller to the Buyer. In each case, such payments shall be made in immediately available and freely transferable funds to the bank and account number specified by the recipient of the payment in Part III of the Schedule attached to the Master Agreement. See Section 11.3.

F.   Discharge and Termination of Options

Section 6 of the Master Agreement provides for the *automatic* discharge and termination of Call Options written by both parties and Put Options written by both parties, provided that (I) the material terms of such Options are the same, (II) Premiums with respect to such Options have been paid, and (III) such Options have not been exercised. The effect of this Section is to net Options in the limited circumstances in which Options can effectively be netted. The sole remaining rights and obligations of the parties, with respect to Options discharged and netted under Section 6, are to exercise that portion, if any, of the one of the Options that is not discharged and terminated and to settle such portion upon the exercise thereof, respectively. Section 6 effectively allows counterparties to close-out existing Options or to reduce their exposure to each other by entering into offsetting Options.

G. Payment Netting

Section 7 contains two separate payment netting provisions. Section 7.1 provides for the *automatic* netting of any Premium payments that would otherwise be made by the parties in the same currency on the same date. Section 7.2 provides for the netting of any payments, other than Premium payments, to be made by the parties to each other in the same currency on the same date. These provisions do not alter the parties' legal rights and obligations with respect to the underlying Options (as Section 6 does). The intent of this Section is to reduce the number and size of payments required to be made by the parties in connection with their Options transactions. Many Option dealers do not currently net Premium payments, primarily because they do not have the operational capability to do so. Presumably, such parties will agree with their counterparties not to net such payments (either by way of a side agreement or by striking Section 7.1 from the Master Agreement). However, since Premium payment netting reduces settlement exposure and the cost of transacting Options (because of the reduction in the number of payments), Premium payment netting is encouraged.

H. Default

1.   The provisions of Section 8 should be read carefully and understood as they set forth the rights and obligations of counterparties upon the occurrence of an Event of Default with respect to either of them. (In addition, the close-out and liquidation procedures set forth in Section 8.1 will also be followed in the event that it becomes illegal or impossible for a party to perform its obligations under an Option under the provisions of Section 10 of the Master Agreement.)

2.   Section 8.1 sets forth the steps that a Non-Defaulting Party must take in closing out and liquidating Options. It requires that the Non-Defaulting Party liquidate all outstanding Options, except to the extent that such party believes in good faith that applicable law prohibits the liquidation of certain Options. This requirement is intended to support that statement made in Section 2.2 that the Master Agreement and all Confirmations (and, therefore, the Options which they evidence), Schedules and amendments to the Master Agreement constitute a single agreement between the parties. The single agreement concept is intended to prevent cherrypicking by a trustee, receiver or conservator of an insolvent Defaulting Party. Section 8.1 further provides that, in the case of specified Events of Default relating to the insolvency of the Defaulting Party, such liquidation shall be automatic with respect to all outstanding Options, unless the law governing the insolvency proceedings of the Non-Defaulting Party expressly allows liquidation to take place after the occurrence of the Event of Default and in the manner set forth in clauses (I) through (IV) of Section 8.1. In the absence of such express provision, automatic liquidation is considered preferable as it is less likely to be challenged in the insolvency proceedings of the Defaulting Party.

3.   Clause (I) of Section 8.1 provides for the calculation and aggregation of market damages for each party for each Option closed out. The Non-Defaulting Party should endeavor to liquidate all outstanding Options on a single day. However, if this is impossible, the liquidation should be completed as soon as practicable. With respect to Options purchased by a party, those damages will be the current market premium (or replacement cost) for such Options. With respect to Options sold by a party, the only market damages will be any unpaid premium and any interest on such unpaid premium. With respect to exercised, but unsettled, Options, damages will be the unpaid settlement amount plus interest thereon. In addition, the Non-Defaulting Party is entitled to include any costs or expenses incurred in covering its

obligations related to such liquidated Options, such as the obligations on a Delta hedge. The determination of market damages for each party in each instance must be made in good faith.

4. After calculation of each party's market damages, Clause (Ⅱ) of Section 8.1 provides for the conversion of such damages into the Non-Defaulting Party's Base Currency. As such damages may be in different currencies (corresponding to the different currencies in which Premium on the liquidated Options were paid or payable), it is necessary to convert all such damage amounts into a single currency if such damages are to be aggregated (and netted pursuant to the provisions of clause (Ⅲ) of Section 8.1). In addition, the Non-Defaulting Party is given the benefit of converting these damages into its Base Currency (rather than the Defaulting Party's Base Currency). For purposes of this conversion, the Non-Defaulting Party should use the applicable Spot Rate.

5. Following the conversion and aggregation of each party's market damages, clause (Ⅲ) provides that such market damages will be netted, resulting in a single liquidated amount in the Non-Defaulting Party's Base Currency that will be due and payable as a settlement payment to the party having the larger aggregated damage amount.

6. If one or both of the parties are holding any cash or non-cash collateral as margin or security for their respective obligations under outstanding Options or the Master Agreement generally, clause (Ⅳ) allows the parties to set off the value thereof (following any necessary conversion into the Non-Defaulting Party's Base Currency) against the liquidated damage amount calculated under the preceding clauses.

7. Section 8.2 provides that the net amount calculated pursuant to Section 8.1 shall be paid by one party to the other by the close of business on the Business Day following the liquidation of the Options. In some countries, a judgment can only be rendered in the currency of that country. Therefore, Section 8.2 provides that, if required by applicable law, the net amount payable by one party to the other will be converted into a currency other than the Non-Defaulting Party's Base Currency. Any costs of such conversion will be borne by the Defaulting Party. If this amount is not paid when due, Section 8.2 provides for the payment of interest at the applicable interbank rate plus 1% *per annum* for each day for which the amount remains unpaid. Section 8.2 also provides that Section 8 is not intended to limit, but rather that the rights provided for therein shall be in addition to, any other rights which the Non-Defaulting Party may have under applicable law, by agreement or otherwise, and that the Non-Defaulting Party is granted a general right of set-off with respect to all amounts owed by either party to the other, whether due or not due.

8. Section 8.3 establishes the right of one party to suspend performance of its obligations under any Option or the Master Agreement (Ⅰ) if the counterparty is currently in default in the payment or performance of any of its obligations under an Option or the Master Agreement or (Ⅱ) during the pendency of a reasonable request to the counterparty to provide adequate assurances of its ability to perform such obligations. The default need not constitute an Event of Default. Therefore, if a Buyer has not paid a Premium on the applicable Premium Payment Date, even though the Seller has not sent written notice of non-receipt (or, if such notice has been sent, but two Business Days have not elapsed), the Seller is, nonetheless, entitled to suspend its performance with respect to other Options between the parties until receipt of such Premium.

I. Parties to Rely on Their Own Expertise

Section 9 establishes that each of the parties has relied on its own expertise and judgment in entering into each Option and as to all other subsequent actions or matters related thereto or any other currency option or transaction. The intent of this provision is to protect each of the parties from a claim or action by the other party wherein it is alleged that one of the parties exercised influence or control over the decisions or actions of the other to the extent that it is, therefore, liable for losses, costs, expenses or damages suffered or incurred as a result of such decisions or actions.

J. Illegality, Impossibility and Force Majeure

Section 10 provides that, if either party is unable to perform, or is hindered or delayed in performing, its obligations in respect of any Option due to force majeure, or if it otherwise becomes illegal or impossible for either party to perform its obligations in respect of any Option, then either party may, after notice of the occurrence of such event, liquidate and close-out all affected Options. Although such events do not constitute Events of Default, the liquidation and close-out procedures to be followed are those provided for in Section 8. Either of the parties may take such action promptly upon notice to the other. Due to the volatile nature of the Option markets, it is important that the parties have the ability to liquidate positions promptly in order to limit their exposure to transactions which one of the parties may be unable to perform. If Section 10 is applicable to the obligations of both parties, the parties should mutually agree upon the close-out and liquidation of Options.

K. Miscellaneous

1.   The intent of Section 11.4 is to insure that any settlement payment to a party resulting from the termination and liquidation of options arising either as a result of an Event of Default or an event of illegality, impossibility or force majeure, and whether pursuant to the operation of Section 8 or the judgment of a court, is made in such party's Base Currency (or the Non-Defaulting Party's Base Currency) and is paid in the full amount in such Base Currency. If payment is made in some other currency, such payment is deemed to discharge the obligation of the payer only to the extent that the payee could purchase the full amount of the Base Currency (or the Non-Defaulting Party's Base Currency) with the amount of the currency received on the business day following the date of receipt. If the amount of the currency received is insufficient to purchase the full amount of the Base Currency, the payer indemnifies the payee against any loss and, in any event, the payer indemnifies the payee against any costs incurred in purchasing the Base Currency.

2.   Pursuant to Section 11.5, the parties agree to the tape recording of any telephone conversations between them and agree that such tape recordings can be submitted in evidence in any proceeding relating to any Option transaction. It is standard market practice that conversations between traders and between traders and brokers are recorded. This practice is encouraged, as such recordings can substantially reduce the number of disputes that arise between market participants and the time which it takes to resolve such disputes. Such recordings are usually the best evidence of the essential terms of an Option as agreed by the parties.

3.   Some parties may choose to deal Options with each other on a margined or secured basis. Section 11.7 provides that, if the parties have entered into an agreement providing for such dealings, then such agreement is incorporated into the Master Agreement and is subject to the terms thereof. The possibility of such an arrangement is also addressed in Section 8.1 (IV), which provides for the set-off of any collateral held as margin or security against the settlement payment otherwise calculated pursuant to Section 8.1. If the margin or security agreement conflicts with the Master Agreement, the Master Agreement would govern.

L. Law and Jurisdiction

1.   Counsel has opined that the form of Master Agreement is valid and enforceable under the laws of both the State of New York and the laws of England and Wales. Copies of such opinions can be obtained by contacting the Tokyo Foreign Exchange Market Practices Committee. It is expected that counterparties, and especially those physically located in either the U.K. or the U.S.A., will choose one of these systems of law to govern the Master Agreement and all Options entered into by the parties. It is also expected that parties will submit to the jurisdiction of either the courts in the State of New York or England consistent with their choice

of governing law. However, as such submission to jurisdiction is non-exclusive, parties will be free to bring actions, suits or proceedings in other jurisdictions.

2. Pursuant to Section 12.4, each party explicitly waives any sovereign immunity it may be entitled to assert in any legal proceeding arising out of the Master Agreement.

3. The legal opinion in respect of the laws of Japan obtained by the Tokyo Foreign Exchange Market Practices Committee is reproduced in the final section of this booklet.

M. Currency Option Confirmation

1. The recommended form of Confirmation, which is attached to the Master Agreement as *Exhibit I*, is substantially the same as the form of confirmation generally used by market participants to evidence options. All of the material terms of an Option are to be set forth in the Confirmation. Material terms which are not otherwise required to be specified in the Confirmation should be included in the "Other terms and conditions" section.

2. There are three headings in the form of Confirmation which are not used or defined in the Master Agreement - Trade Date, Expiration Settlement Date and Price.

The Trade Date is the day on which the parties agree to enter into an Option.

The Expiration Settlement Date is the last possible day on which an exercised Option could settle. In keeping with market practice, this will generally be the Spot Date for the Currency Pair as determined on the Expiration Date.

Price is the currency exchange rate or the percentage (of one of the Currency Pair) upon which the Premium of an Option is determined. See Section II.A above for an explanation of market practice with respect to price quotation.

3. Where dates are to be specified in the Confirmation (e.g. Trade Date), the market convention is to specify the day first (using two numbers), the month second (using three letters) and, finally, the year (using two numbers, being the last two numbers of the applicable year). For example, the date March 1, 1991 would be specified as "01/MAR/91".

N. Schedule

Each of the parties will complete a Schedule in the form attached to the Master Agreement. The Schedule contains particulars concerning each party, such as the address, telephone, telex and facsimile number, and contact person for notices and other communications, and each party's Base Currency. In addition, in Part I of the Schedule, the parties should designate their branches or offices whose transactions and dealings are intended to be covered by the Master Agreement. Either because of concerns with respect to applicable law or operational capabilities (which, for instance, may make the settlement, payment netting or set-off of Options between certain offices of the counterparties difficult), counterparties may choose to limit the number of Designated Offices covered by a particular Master Agreement and may choose to put in place more than one Master Agreement between them, each covering a different set of Designated Offices.

MITSUI, YASUDA, WANI & MAEDA

Nissei Ichibancho Bldg.
23, Ichibancho, Chiyoda-ku
TOKYO 102, JAPAN

TELEPHONE (03)3221-7760
FACSIMILE : (03)3221-7344
CABLE MYWMTYO
TELEX J33276 MYWMTYO

July 20, 1992

Mr. Yoshinobu Onishi
Chairman
The Tokyo Foreign Exchange
Market Practices Committee

Dear Sir,

We have been asked to advise on the legal aspects of currency options as provided in the International Currency Options Market Master Agreement and Guide particularly in relation to the Japanese Bankruptcy Law (Law No.71 of 1922) and the Corporate Reorganization Law (Law No.172 of 1952).

Our opinion herein is limited to the laws of Japan as in force and as applied and interpreted on the date hereof.

1. <u>General Treatment of Currency Options under the Bankruptcy Law</u>

This opinion examines how Japanese Bankruptcy Law is applied to the obligations and claims of the Parties in the event of a declaration of bankruptcy or a commencement of reorganization proceedings with respect to the Seller.

If the Seller is declared bankrupt after the Option agreement becomes effective but before the Premium is paid by the Buyer, it is quite unlikely that the Exercise Date of the Options would be accelerated, particularly in the case of European Style Options. (See also Article 17 of the Bankruptcy Law). If both the Buyer's obligation to pay the Premium and the Seller's obligation to grant the Option are unperformed at the time of the declaration of bankruptcy, the agreement for the Option is likely to be construed as a bilaterally executory contract at the time of the declaration of bankruptcy. If so, pursuant to Article 59 of the Bankruptcy Law, the agreement may be assumed or rejected at the option of the trustee in bankruptcy.

If the Seller is declared bankrupt after the Premium is paid but before the Option is exercised by the Buyer, the argument can be made that Article 59 of Bankruptcy Law will not be applied because a bilaterally executory contract does not exist at this stage. However, there is a decision by a lower court which applied Article 59 of the Bankruptcy Law in a situation where there was a promise to enter into a contract for sale of real property (<u>baibaiyoyaku</u>). A contract did not exist before the promisee exercised its right (<u>yoyakukanketsuken</u>). However, despite the fact that an actual sale and purchase agreement did not exist at the time of the declaration of bankruptcy and that the promisee exercised the right to call for the execution after the declaration of bankruptcy, the court held that there was a bilaterally executory contract. In this case, the provisional registration of the promise to enter into the sale and purchase agreement for a parcel of real estate had been made for the purpose of preserving a claim to ownership. (Judgement by Osaka Higher Court dated June 19, 1957; Lower Court's Judicial Precedents of Civil Cases 8-6-1136. See also the judgement of the Tokyo Higher Court dated April 1, 1969; Lower Courts' Judicial Precedents of Civil Cases 20-3.4-189). There are opinions among scholars that the trustee's right to reject should be recognized even where the right to fulfillment of a promise (<u>yoyakukanketsuken</u>) is not yet exercised.

If the Seller is declared bankrupt after the Option is exercised by the Buyer but before the currencies are exchanged by the Parties, a bilaterally executory contract may exist to which Article 59 of the Bankruptcy Law may be applied.

2. <u>The Effects and Validity of the Relevant Sections of Master Agreement</u>

(1) The Objectives of the Master Agreement

The Master Agreement provides for "netting by novation" and "close-out" the objectives of which are (a) to cut down the settlement costs and operational errors by reducing the amount and number of settlements, (b) to curtail the credit risks and liquidity risks by cutting back outstanding claims and obligations and (c) to avoid the adverse effects that would be brought by the trustee's cherry-picking.

(2) The Effects and Validity of Section 6

Section 6 of the Master Agreement provides for "termination and discharge" of any Call Option or any Put Option written by a Party against a Call Option or a Put Option, respectively, written by the other Party which meet the following conditions:

(a) each being with respect to the same Currency Pair;
(b) each having the same Expiration Date and Expiration Time;
(c) each being of the same style, i.e either both being American Style Options or both being European Style Options;
(d) each having the same Strike Price; and
(e) neither shall have been exercised.

The clause provides that, "such termination and discharge to occur automatically upon the payment in full of the last Premium payable in respect of such Options", which can be said to be "netting by novation" whereby obligations and claims having the same due date of payment are netted out at a time before the due date and are replaced by a new obligation. The netting by novation provided for in this Section 6 is an agreement between the Parties to consolidate a certain number of currency Options into one. This Section does not aim to circumvent the trustee's option to reject the contract under Article 59 of the Bankruptcy Law. Thus, the netting by novation under Section 6 is valid. Also, we are of the opinion that the rules of <u>dankaikogokeisan</u>, a concept recognized in legal literature and a modified type of <u>kogokeisan</u> (current account agreement) stipulated in Article 529 of the Commercial Code, is applicable to this clause. The same applies to FXNET in respect of currency exchange transactions.

The netting procedure pursuant to Section 6 leaves behind only the netted-out portion of the Options, which itself is also an Option, and thus, as far as netted Options are concerned, the "potential bilaterally executory contracts" with respect to each of the original Options disappear. Therefore, the possibility of the trustee rejecting some of the original Options and assuming others pursuant to Article 59 of the Bankruptcy Law and Article 103 of the Corporate Reorganization Law upon bankruptcy would be eliminated.

However, the validity of Section 6 may be questioned in light of the limitation on set-off rights under Article 104, paragraphs 2 and 4 of the Bankruptcy Law and Article 163, paragraphs 2 and 4 of the Corporate Reorganization Law and the right of avoidance (<u>hininken</u>) under Article 72, paragraphs 2 and 4 of the Bankruptcy Law and Article 78, division 1, paragraphs 2 and 3 of the Corporate Reorganization Law if the Option transactions entered into after there has been a suspension of payment or after a filing of petition for bankruptcy (<u>kikijiki</u>) are included in the netting procedure.

(3) Effects and Validity of Section 7

Section 7 provides for netting of obligations to pay Premiums and other amounts in the same currency which become payable on the same date. After the netting, those obligations are replaced by an obligation to pay an amount equal to the excess of the larger aggregate amount over the smaller amount upon the Party which initially owed the larger amount. Netting provided for in this clause is distinguished from the netting provided for in Section 6 which takes effect automatically upon the payment in full of the last Premium payable and it may be interpreted as having an effect substantially similar to "payment netting".

(4) Effects and Validity of Section 8

Section 8 provides for the procedures for close-out and liquidation. It provides that, if any specified Event of Default (as defined in the Master Agreement), such as a petition for proceedings seeking liquidation, reorganization or any other relief under applicable law, a petition for appointment of a trustee or other similar official of it, or an occurrence of bankruptcy or insolvency has occurred, the outstanding Options shall be automatically closed out without notice from the Non-Defaulting Party. On the other hand, if any other Event of Default (such as default in payment to the other Party or inability to pay, or failure to give adequate assurances of the ability to perform the obligations) has occurred and is continuing, the Non-Defaulting Party has the right to close out by notice to the Defaulting Party.

(a) Trustee's Right to Reject Bilaterally Executory Contracts at Declaration of Bankruptcy

Article 59 of the Bankruptcy Law and Article 103 of the Corporate Reorganization Law provide the trustee in bankruptcy or corporate reorganization with an option to either reject or assume bilaterally executory contracts at the declaration of bankruptcy or at commencement of the corporate reorganization procedures. This leads to the question of the validity of the agreement between the Parties as set out in Section 8. It could be argued that Section 8 is invalid because such an agreement circumvents the right accorded to the trustee. As discussed in 1. above, if every Option is a "potential bilaterally executory contract" to which the trustee may exercise his option to reject such contract, it is necessary to consider whether or not the close-out clause as provided for in Section 8 of the Master Agreement would contradict the trustee's right to reject. The following paragraphs will inquire into this issue in four aspects.

First of all, it is possible to argue that under the structure of the Master Agreement, the Master Agreement is the one and only contract that exists between the Parties and that the payments which arise under each of the Options are merely a series of payments under "one single contract", that is, the Master Agreement. Therefore, the obligations and claims thereunder are not subject to the trustee's right to reject. However, since the agreement to bring all Options under one Master Agreement is only an agreement between the Parties, it is questionable whether it would be sustained in the context of bankruptcy or corporate reorganization.

Secondly, it is possible to argue that as an exception to Article 59 of the Bankruptcy Law, Article 61 of the Bankruptcy Law may be applied. Under this Article, a contract in respect of sale of merchandise having exchange quotations is deemed to be rejected upon bankruptcy. However, there remain questions as to whether Article 61 of the Bankruptcy Law may be applied to Options which have no exchange quotation or in the case of corporate reorganization as there is no explicit provision in the Corporate Reorganization Law similar to Article 61.

Thirdly, if the Options are netted out and replaced with a resultant Option ("netting by novation") prior to the occurrence of an Event of Default by a Party, then, since the "potential bilaterally executory contracts" in respect of each of the original Options are eliminated when they are netted out, it can be argued that the trustee's right to reject in respect of each Option ceases to exist. To the extent covered by Section 6 of the Master Agreement, this argument applies. However, since the netting by novation under Section 6 is limited to those Options which meet certain conditions, there will be cases where original Options remain. Also there will be resultant Options to which the trustee may exercise his option to reject.

Lastly, we are of the opinion that the right to set-off preempts the trustee's right to reject. The contractual agreement to close-out under the Master Agreement aims at terminating the contractual relationship of the Option transaction between the Parties, eliminating the outstanding obligations and claims and consolidating them into a new obligation and claim. In substance this has an effect similar to that of contractual set-off (<u>sosaiyoyaku</u>), under which the Non-Defaulting Party can exercise the right to set-off in the Event of Default. If the effect of the close-out meets the conditions for set-off stipulated by Article 98 of the Bankruptcy Law and Article 162 of the Corporate Reorganization Law, it can be argued that the contractual agreement on close-out preempts the right of the trustee to reject.

Although there remain questions as to whether the right of set-off may be exercised among different currencies or whether conditions to set-off (<u>sosaitekijo</u>) are met, in the light of the Supreme Court judgement of June 24, 1970 (Minshu 24-6-587), which held that contractual set-off (<u>sosaiyoyaku</u>) is effective against a creditor who had made garnishment, we are of the opinion that such set-off provisions arising upon the occurrence of events of default or similar contractual agreements will be upheld in respect of the bankruptcy law. Regarding the effectiveness of the set-off provisions arising upon the occurrence of events of default there are opinions which place emphasis on opinions that the validity depends on whether such contractual agreement or provision is publicly known.

(b) The Intent and Purpose of the Bankruptcy Law and the Corporate Reorganization Law

A Supreme Court judgement of March 30, 1982 (Minshu 36-3-484) determined that a contractual provision is void if it provided for a purchase and sale agreement to terminate upon the occurrence of an event which is a cause of petition for corporate reorganization proceedings. The reasoning was that such a covenant violates the intent and purpose of the corporate reorganization proceedings which are to support the rehabilitation of stock corporations (<u>kabushiki kaisha</u>) in distress. However, the argument can be made that close-out under Section 8 does not breach the intent or purpose of the Bankruptcy Law or the Corporate Reorganization Law. First, the aforesaid ruling was based on a specific situation where the seller, who retained title of ownership, tried to repossess a machine which was indispensable equipment in the production line of a corporation under reorganization. Second, the relevant Parties evaluate and estimate their net profit or loss at the present market value and the law should protect and should not ruin such expectation in light of that Supreme Court judgement which held that contractual set-off is valid on the basis of the doctrine of freedom of contract (Supreme Court judgement dated June 24, 1970; Minshu 24-6-587).

(c)   The Limitations on Set-Off

Close-out pursuant to the Master Agreement is in substance and effect similar to set-off regardless of how it is characterized. Where a Non-Defaulting Party continues to carry out an Option transaction with a Defaulting Party after there has been suspension of payment or a filing of petition for bankruptcy (kikijiki), any obligation and claim arising therefrom will also be included in the above close-out. Such close-out might, however, be held invalid due to violations of the underlying purposes of Article 104, paragraphs 2 and 4 of the Bankruptcy Law and Article 163, paragraphs 2 and 4 of the Corporate Reorganization Law. Such concern could be avoided if the obligation and claim in question are excluded from such close-out. (See Section 8 of the Master Agreement.)

(d) Difference between "Optional Close-out" and "Automatic Close-out"

Close-out pursuant to the Master Agreement shall be made either in the form of "optional close-out" to be instituted upon notice by the Non-Defaulting Party to the Defaulting Party or in the form of "automatic close-out" to be made automatically upon the occurrence of an Event of Default without such notice. As to the "optional close-out", it could be argued that the exercise of the right to close-out itself might be subject to avoidance (hinin). Accordingly, it would be worthwhile considering whether the Agreement could be structured in a way that some of the Events of Default for "optional close-out" automatically trigger close-out without any notice by the Non-Defaulting Party. This would also contribute to the resolution of any potential difficulties arising from Option transactions entered into subsequent to the suspension of payment or after the petition for bankruptcy has been filed being included in the close-out.

(e)   Set-off against Collateral and the Prohibition of Self-help under the Corporate Reorganization Law

According to Article 213, paragraph 3 (application mutatis mutandis of Article 112) of the Corporate Reorganization Law, self-help by secured creditors is prohibited within reorganization proceedings. If a Non-Defaulting Party having a liquidated claim sets off such claim against any security received from a Defaulting Party, such set-off might be determined to be self-help. As a result, such set-off may be held to be invalid.

(5)   Effects and Validity of Section 5

To the extent that the Master Agreement provides for in-the-money amount net settlement (Section 5.3), the question as to whether it is characterized as a wagering contract is a matter of concern. In other words, will the Master Agreement fall under the habitual gambling provisions of the Penal Code (Penal Code Article 186, paragraph 1) and/or the provisions in the Commercial Code with regard to the director's breach of its duties (a crime for wasting corporate property; Commercial Code Article 489, paragraph 4), or will the validity of this Section under private law (Civil Code Article 90) be questioned. In-the-money amount net settlement by a bank may be justified as "justified business" (See Penal Law Article 35) if such activities fall within the scope of banking business recognized under the Banking Law. Therefore, it will be necessary to characterize currency options in the context of the Banking Law.

3. Conclusions and Proposals

The legal validity of the Master Agreement is as follows:

1. The netting by novation is valid;
2. The close-out provisions are, in our judgement, valid. Despite the divided opinions in the legal community, the Japanese courts are likely to uphold them to be valid; and
3. The above statements are subject to the following qualifications. If any claim acquired or any obligation assumed after a petition for bankruptcy is filed or after payment is suspended, is included in the netting by novation or close-out, the netting or close-out is quite likely to be found invalid to that extent. Moreover, as a general matter, the possibility of the inclusion of any Option transaction entered into before the suspension of payment or the petition for bankruptcy being avoided by the trustee as a preferential transfer cannot be denied.

Considering the above points, the following measures are desirable in order to make certain that the objectives of the Master Agreement are achieved:

1. The Event of Default which trigger close-out should include garnishment or provisional garnishment by a third party against any claim relating to an Option transaction or any resultant Option after netting;
2. The close-out provision should be stipulated in a way that would enable the close-out procedure to be triggered at an earlier stage;
3. The operating systems should be constructed in a way that would allow the exclusion of one or more claims from the procedures of netting by novation or close-out in the event that such claims or a group of claims are legally disallowed from inclusion in the netting by novation or close-out due to garnishment or for some other reasons.

Yours faithfully,

Index